AF840795

ADVANCE PRAISE FOR

African Digital Cultures

An intellectually audacious volume. Reifying digital technologies as inexorably now part of the everyday in Africa, the book draws on examples from across the continent to demons trate how African users creatively instrumentalise digital media to reimagine politicality and Africa's socialities. Curious in approach and conceptually and methodologically ambitious, the book sets ground for a new locally inflected decolonial episteme with which to engage the digital, emerging youth cultures and communicative spaces in Africa.

Prof. George Ogola, University of Nottingham, UK.

Instead of equating the African continent with a 'technological desert' or 'digital poverty', this volume demonstrates the varied ways in which African digital users make creative use of digital technologies and platforms to express themselves, perform their identity, monetize online content, and raise their voice through protest. By situating user agency within the constraints imposed by both platform capitalism and state power, African Digital Cultures: Platforms, Perspectives and Performances provides a rich and nuanced account of how African digital users across the continent incorporate digital platforms in their lives on an everyday basis.

Prof. Wendy Willems, Department of Media and Communications, London School of Economics and Political Science

African Digital Cultures

Admire Mare and Oswelled Ureke (eds.)

African Digital Cultures

Platforms, Performances, and Perspectives

PETER LANG
New York - Berlin - Bruxelles - Chennai - Lausanne - Oxford

Library of Congress Cataloging-in-Publication Control Number
LCCN: 2025004152

Bibliographic information published by the Deutsche Nationalbibliothek.
The German National Library lists this publication in the German National Bibliography; detailed bibliographic data is available on the Internet at http://dnb.d-nb.de.

Cover Credit: Mykyta Dolmatov/iStock

ISBN 9781636678733 (Print)
ISBN 9781636678740 (E-PDF)
ISBN 9781636678757 (E-PUB)
DOI 10.3726/b21680

© 2026 Peter Lang Group AG, Lausanne (Switzerland)
Published by Peter Lang Publishing Inc., New York (USA)
info@peterlang.com - www.peterlang.com

All rights reserved.
All parts of this publication are protected by copyright.
Any utilization outside the strict limits of the copyright law, without the permission of the publisher, is forbidden and liable to prosecution.
This applies in particular to reproductions, translations, microfilming, and storage and processing in electronic retrieval systems.

This publication has been peer reviewed.

Contents

List of Figures

List of Tables

PREFACE

Africans Here and Now and the Digital Magical

NHAMO ANTHONY MHIRIPIRI

Content creation for all types of topics and themes on digital has taken the African continent by storm. The content creators are largely ordinary people who would not ordinarily fit into the classification of traditional journalists and mass communicators. These are ordinary people who are experimenting with genres for different platforms, while carving out discursive spaces and a market niche that suits Africa's contemporary demands for alternative content on information and entertainment separate from what is produced for 'mainstream media'. In a way, digital platforms are mainstreaming themselves in various digital platforms, repositioning and reforming their presumed alternativism. Hence, the edited book '*African Digital Cultures: Platforms, Performances and Perspectives*' is a timely and most welcome addition to the growing corpus of research literature on the surging phenomenon of Africans on the continent and in the diaspora's production of content for digital platforms.

Digital technologies are now an intricate part of the lived experiences of most peoples of the world. Africans are no exception. Statistics show that more and more Africans, especially the young, are showing remarkable preference for production, distribution and consumption on digital platforms for all types of content. According to the statistical portal for market data *Statistica*, social media penetration in Africa across all user platforms in 2024 stands as follows: 40.4% in North Africa, 41.6% in Southern Africa, 15.8% in West Africa, 10.1% in East Africa, and 9.6% in Central Africa. Digital spaces, also interchangeably referred to as the internet or social media, host digital cultures with different intentions and objectives. These spaces or platforms include but are not limited to WhatsApp, Facebook, Instagram, YouTube, X (formerly Twitter), Snapchat and TikTok. These have different communication and information potentialities, most dependent on the type or nature of digital technologies and their functions. Such technologies and functions often determine the different genres of content production, distribution, presentations, and consumption. For instance, WhatsApp generally allows smaller publics space for more intimate conversations, although leading news organizations also use the channel's broadcast tools to send text, photos, videos, stickers, and polls. Audiences pick up these posts and resend them to their friends and acquaintances as individual and group chats. Levels of user "intimacy" may vary on platforms, with more "public" news posted on sites regarded as appropriate for purpose.

The Chinese social media app – TikTok – is more attuned for short-form videos stretching from 15 to 60 seconds in length. Amateur and professional creators use the app and platform whose format is popular for entertainment and comedy, although it is frequently used for infotainment. Sometimes audio-visual art and activism are combined as artivism that presents for a mass audience appealing texts that are catchy, light and less serious.

Sociality is a vital part of digital media cultures, and there is a level at which both intimate communications and public communication of a political nature are underpinned with an inevitable publicness. The highly private issues around representations of the self using selfies (cellphilms), travelogues, food diaries, quirky stuff, dating, and other personal exertions are not far much different from communications that direct their focus on governance and questions of public political power. Both are being played out in the public domain with various pretentions about publicness or privateness. The expressions of issues traditionally reserved for the private sphere on the democratized media spaces has imploded the liminal spaces of public and private. The Habermasian public sphere that presupposes rationality and discussion or debate on issues of public interest is turned on its head and the body of its epistemic and ontological purpose contorted in a grotesque manner that however represents the logic and ambiguity of contemporary communication cultural systems. Ordinary people are now mass communicators and they have burst the seams of normative standards, communicative etiquettes' and conservative formalities of the old Fourth Estate of 'professional' journalism. This is a dilemma but also an inevitable reality that makes Mare and Ureke ruefully note that "private affairs and spaces find expression in public and constitute what we may term "*public privacy*". This is not said with a nostalgia for the past communication structures and strictures.

The main objective of the book is to foreground African digital cultures in order to understand how Africans at home on the continent and in the diaspora interact with digital technologies while making sense of their everyday lives. The book makes bold assertions about the innovations and agency of Africans in the production of content for digital platforms, whether these are the seemingly innocuous mediatized 'soft content' of publicized private issues, or the political content that imbues itself with the decorum of serious hard news and whose publicness is often not questioned. On either extreme of "soft" content and "hard content" African producers and consumer of content, use digital communication technologies for the signification of a repertoire of content and genres representational of the local or diasporic African conditions. The seemingly frivolous and trial contain ultimately a 'serious' import that responds to and is expressive of the serious and important especially when notions of commodification and democracy in the local and global content are counterpoised to explain politics and power dynamics. Nothing is as innocent as it appears on the surface. Whether it is engaging with "trivia" such as selfies, or the publicly discursive materials on democracy and human rights, the book locates all its content within a neo-liberal capitalist system, whose main objectives are the realization of profit and exploitation of socio-economic relations (Fuchs, 2014). The point here is that digital technologies are connected to already existing local traditions and are shaped and transformed by them.

There is also a plurality of African cultures that depend on spatial conditions where people have traits, values and sensibilities in common but with distinct differences, notwithstanding their Africannness. The book is clear that there is no homogenous African culture. That does not mean there is no such thing as a transcendental African condition or personality. The scholarship in the book is commendable in how it is confident and assertive in championing for a new ontology and epistemic tradition predicated on emancipatory decoloniality. Stories are now told from the perspective of the Africans. Nothing is "trashy", to use Kenneth Harrow's appreciation of African cultural productions that exist at the margins of the dominant elitist neoliberal capitalist cultural production processes. Again, such alternative narratives outside the dominance of African elitism as represented and controlled by the African state, civil society organizations or the market on the one hand, or the global socio-economic, political and cultural centers provide a new hope for democratic communicative spaces. For example, even if the online content producers were to construct texts on the so-called superstitious paranormal – which for too long is a stereotypical archtype of Africa – the truth is that such content is not easily dismissible as primordial fetishes seen as the antithesis of rationality and development – but a new understanding of Africans' existential realities. The acceptance of a diversity of content that signifies Africanness rejects such condescension but thinks out its reason. Kenneth Harrow (2007) and Achille Mbembe (2001) have celebrated such experiences and practices and explained their significance. The Euro-American-centric conceptualization of development tended to undervalue and belittle African imaginaries, condemning everything to superstition and backwardness. Now African cosmologies and imaginaries are showing their transiency and how transcendental they are.

The different chapters explore how digital technologies are (re)shaping African societies. They are analytic about how African content producers and their audiences perform mediated citizenship in the cocoons of formal and informal politics, how they (re)produce and consummate intimate and public sociality online, how they entertain themselves online, express their individual and group identities, and how they resist external constructions of the continent, on the continent and abroad. African digital spaces are accommodating for instance what is deemed ludicrous and incredible, especially in the expression of spirituality and religion. New wave pastors and imams are online performing miracles before the full gaze of local and foreign audiences, marketing their metaphysical skills. Whilst they can be dismissed as charlatans, they still have lots of followers and believers. Africans have long infused 'life' into that which was viewed in a Cartesian sense as inanimate and 'lifeless'. Symbolic significance was a long held perspective in African culture-rocks talk, birds and animals have a life and presence beyond their mere existence. This is a world of 'magic' that was reduced to fetish and blind unthinking ritual. Human and Nature were intricately bound together and there was no clear demarcation of one from the other. Dehumanization is in part a denial of naturalization, that is why the new post-human movement is trying to reconnect to the essence and simplicity of life especially now when Western development has led to the dangerous road of possible human extinction due to climate change and widespread pollution of the soils, air and water bodies.

As Africans immerse themselves in digital technologies in order to create digital cultures what is particularly important is that the immersion entails a merging of the African agent with what is supposed to be the consumed experience or technology. They become one. There is nearly a constant merging (blending), emerging and re-emerging of technologies, self and community in much more complex forms that simulate closely the acts of engagement and reformation of Being. What is important is to ascertain that the new forms of Being are not harmful to both the Human and his or her environment. Do they rehumanize the being or they are (re)creations of a complex cyber-ogre without norms or values? The ethics of embracing the new technologies thus remain critical to the preservation and continuation of the Human spirit.

The new popular mass communicators are no longer just the conventional professionals that produce content in regular news and entertainment organizational bureaucratic structures, but ordinary citizens. These content creators come in different guises using difference social media platforms for content production and dissemination. They are mass communicators due to their reach of mass audiences via digital platforms that are often outside the ownership and control of governments or the corporate sectors. Such online content producers are known as "Influencers" and they are a vital part of the global media ecosystem. Governments, civil society organizations and the corporate sector do interact with their content willy-nilly. Africans are consuming online content and information on a regular basis. They have an impact on the forming of audiences or users' personal views, behavior, social engagement and identity and psychosocial development. Individuals constantly discover online community with diverse influencers, thereby solidifying their own senses of belonging. It is not always the case that online content imbues a positive impact on their audience. There is always lingering the misuse and abuse of content and the online behavior of content creators and influencers. Major risks are cyberbullying, misinformation, disinformation and imitation of psychopathic or unruly influencers.

A common facet is the commodification of African digital cultures that are quickly sprouting on various platforms. The personalities and new celebrities appearing on platforms exhibit a performativity of self and content that is intricately conscious of how texts and genres are both materials and commodities open to both social and financial transactioning. Most texts are monetized and distributed in innovative ways that rely on downloads, shares, livestreaming and cumulative audience 'likes'. In short, digital cultures and the texts in which they are packaged are part of an aggressive and assertive market economy.

In modern African democracies influencers are now implicated in the commodification of political discourses to the detriment of the formation of informed public opinion. South Africa's investigative newspaper *Daily Maverick*, for instance, bemoans the "the buying and selling of influence on the social media platform X". Timse et al. (2024) note that trusting content users unknowingly consume political content that is "part of carefully crafted, paid campaigns". Political parties and interest groups secretly invest substantial amounts of money "to manipulate public discourse, distorting the democratic process and shaping voter perceptions with endorsements that are anything but authentic" (Timse et.al., 2024). A growing culture industry of the "commodification of influence" deliberately manipulates public opinion through paid endorsements by "anonymous mega influencers". Such anonymous influencers are difficult to track as compared to accounts held by celebrities, politicians and popular content creators. Bots that are a facet of artificial intelligence are also worthy of consideration as they carve their spaces in the production of both soft and hard news/information, again with varying degrees of facticity.

The book brings a cohort of leading scholars from across Africa, presenting a menu of counter-narratives to the methodological and theoretical approaches often adopted from the global North in describing and analyzing the African context, thereby over-turning some of the widely held notions and stereotypes about media and communication research in Africa. As Africans perform their identities and express their displeasures, entertainment and aspirations on social media, they prove that cultural production is both an experience and process where they assert themselves in contradistinction to other global cultures, including the dominant cultures from the Global North. The discourse of decoloniality thus threads through the narratives on different topics about how Africans are active contemporary members of modern society. They are here and now and not leapfrogging the technological divide as has been presented in paradigms that thrust them on a linearity of development processes manufactured in the epistemic traditions of the Global North.

On the whole, this is a book that is insightful and a must have for serious academics, researchers, policy makers, graduate and post graduate students, and ordinary readers who just want to understand the multifaceted presence and use of social media content.

REFERENCES

Fuchs, C. (2014). Digital prosumption labour on social media in the context of the capitalist regime of time. *Time & Society*, *23*(1), 97–123.

Harrow, K. (2007). *Postcolonial African cinema: From political engagement to postmodernism*. Indiana University Press.

Timse, T., Findlay, K., & Cornelissen, A. (2024, May 26). Influence-for-hire trend is distorting public discourse, poses threat to foundation of democracy. *Daily Maverick*. Retrieved May 27, 2024, from https://www.dailymaverick.co.za/article/2024-05-26-influence-for-hire-distorts-public-discourse-threatens-democracy/?utm_source=Sailthru&utm_medium=email&utm_campaign=first_thing

Mbembe, A. (2001). *On the poscolony*. University of California Press.

SECTION ONE

TIKTOK, VERNACULAR CREATIVITY AND EMERGENT CONTENT PRODUCTION

CHAPTER ONE

African Digital Cultures, (De)Platformization and Cultural Production

ADMIRE MARE AND OSWELLED UREKE

INTRODUCTION

Despite the widely acknowledged fact that the increasing mass permeation of digital technologies into Africans' everyday lives has disruptive, transformative, progressive and repressive potential, there are a few studies (cf. Wasserman, 2021; Mabweazara, 2015) that explicitly focuses on the nexus between the digital and culture in an African context. Even the mere mention of the concept of 'African digital cultures' is generally rare in mainstream literature. In cases when and where the concept is explicitly mentioned, little attempt is made to define, problematize, and theorize it. In a special issue titled "*Mainstreaming African Digital Cultures, practices and emerging forms of citizen engagement*", Mabweazara (2015, p. 1) foregrounds what he calls "emerging digital cultures and practices in Africa". However, a close reading of the special issue shows that the focus is mainly on digital journalistic cultures and practices. It foregrounds theoretical and empirical insights on the diverse appropriations of digital technologies in Africa. Zeroing on "*New Optics on Digital Media Cultures in Africa*", Wasserman (2021) suggests three alternative theoretical lenses suited for analyzing digital media cultures in Africa and the wider Global South. The 2nd Biennial Africa Regional Conference of the International Communication Association (ICAfrica) which was hosted by the University of Ghana ran under the theme of "*African Digital Cultures: Emerging Research, Practices and Innovations*". Although this was one of the first conferences to discuss African digital cultures, it only debated on the materiality and affordances of digital technologies in the continent. Cognizant of the narrow framing of 'African digital cultures' within academic conferences organized on the continent, Uzuegbunam (2018) has bemoaned the little attention paid to the theme of children and digital media. This is very disconcerting because African digital cultures are mostly dominated by children and the youth. Yet their engagements, entanglements and interactions with digital media are rarely given serious scholarly and policy making attention. This chapter should be seen as part and parcel of attempts to "decolonize and de-westernize media and platform studies" (Poell et al., 2024).

Notwithstanding the above publications and conference proceedings, there are no fully-fledged books or journal articles that specifically address the issue of African digital cultures. This is very unfortunate given the complex appropriations, domestication, deployment and use of digital technologies by Africans within and outside the continent. As a result, this edited volume endeavours to fill this yawning lacuna by foregrounding the materialization, metamorphosis, resilience and hybridization of African digital cultures. This is done within a context that takes into account "the complexity of digital cultures and practices in Africa" (Mabweazara, 2015 p. 6). Such an approach refrains from seeing African countries, "and their myriad array of cultures, religions and languages", as self-contained or closed "homogeneous sets of continent-wide social and cultural [practices]" (Obijiofor and Hanusch, 2011, p. 53). Rather, the countries "comprise multiple cultures, with diasporic and global trends making for a poor mapping of culture onto nation" (Clifford cited in Livingstone, 2003, p. 479). We foreground digital 'cultures' instead of 'culture' in order to highlight the multiplicities, diversities and complexities of these practices in an ever changing, *globalizing* and *digitizing* continent. This book is more about understanding what Africans do with digital technologies in their everyday life and how to understand the world from their perspective. For us, 'the digital' always makes sense when studied and analyzed in context. Whilst Africans are increasingly living most of their productive time online, it is also important to examine how their non-digital lives are intricately interwoven with their digital lives. Thus, in this edited volume, a diverse range of contributors focus their attention on understanding how Africans relate to the digital that has significant bearing upon their everyday lives. In agreement with Bollmer (2018), this volume underscores that there are plural 'digital cultures' instead of a singular digital culture.

It is axiomatic to argue that digital technologies have become part of everyday life. Thanks to globalization and information capitalism, digital technologies have recalibrated, reconfigured, and recast our daily lives. We are caught up in a world full of digital technologies ranging from smartphones, laptops, smart watches, apps, social media, blogs, podcasts, and so forth. These digital technologies have "transformed the ways we communicate, create, and relate to one another" (Bollmer, 2018). The advent of digital technologies has been hailed as transformative, revolutionary, disruptive, and progressive. These superlatives have been used to foreground the changes affecting society at political, social, cultural, and technological levels. One such important social axis is culture. The digital is now an integral part of everyday cultural practices in Africa (Mabweazara, 2015; Bernal, 2020; Mare, 2016). This ubiquity makes studying digital culture both more complex and divergent (Junck & Yeku, n.d). Like elsewhere, digital technologies are said to have transformed everyday life in Africa. Yet, these transformations and changes have not been sufficiently documented. It is not clear how these digital technologies have (re)shaped African societies. It is also not evident how these *gizmos* are transforming the ways in which Africans perform mediated citizenship, engage in formal and informal politics, meet and consummate relationships online, play video games online, self-represent their identities, and resist external constructions of Africa.

Extant research suggests that Africans on the continent and in the diaspora have been quick to embrace digital media (Bernal, 2014; 2020). These situated actors have adopted and adapted digital technologies for sociality, communication, community building, connection, identity (re)construction, economic transactions, cultural preservation and political communication (Tsarwe & Mare, 2021; Wasserman, 2011). In cases where migration has dislocated African people, digital media has been hailed for sustaining long distance networks of social ties (Bernal, 2020). Through phatic communication, social media platforms have afforded Africans an opportunity to expand personal networks. In politically repressive regimes, Africans have been able to use alternative political venues to speak truth to power, engage in performative activism and insurgent politics (Karekwaivenane & Mare, 2018; Mpofu & Mare, 2020).

UNPACKING THE DIGITAL

The digital is part of the landscape of everyday life. In fact, humans and technologies are inseparable. There is mutual interdependence, interconnectedness and dependency between humans and things. This interdependence between humans and things has been theorized by Nyamnjoh (2019) as rooted in 'incompleteness' and 'compositeness'. In his theorization of 'ICTs as juju', Nyamnjoh argues that digital technologies extend the capabilities of humans and contribute to the strength of our autonomy. Thus, humans are incomplete and insufficient in and by themselves, hence, they employ digital technologies to enhance themselves and extend their cognitive reach to make up for their inadequacies. Nyamnjoh's ideas resonate with Mbembe's (2016) argument that "… the technological devices that saturate our lives have become extensions of our humanity. The novelty is that in the process, they have instituted a relationship between humans and other living things, or vital things African traditions had long anticipated." This also dovetails with Marshall McLuhan's theorization of technology as an 'extension of man' (McLuhan, 1964). In his theorization, McLuhan (1964) postulates that "... rapidly, we approach the final phase of the extensions of man – the technological simulation of consciousness, when the creative process will be collectively and corporately extended to the whole of human society, much as we have already extended our senses and our nerves by the various media" (p. 19). McLuhan distinguishes two broad classes of extensions of the organism: *extensions of the body* and *extensions of cognitive functions*, which include functions of the senses, central nervous system, and 'consciousness'. In the era of artificial intelligence (AI) and algorithms, the idea of *extensions of the body and cognitive functions* has taken centre stage. The increasing centrality of digital media as an area of concern in media and communication scholarship globally is shaping the field in important ways (Wasserman, 2021). African societies were especially receptive to experiencing life through digital media because of enduring and fluid African cosmologies that allow for expansive imaginaries and tolerate ambiguity (Bernal, 2021, p 51). Thus, Africans have long had an outlook akin to posthumanism. Miller (2018/2023) pushes this idea of trans-humanity and posthumanity further when he argues that "we might want to define humanity as including a latency that is achieved by each new technology" (p. 12). The point is that social scientists should study what people are becoming as well as what technologies are becoming. In a nutshell, when researchers talk about the digital, a lot of things are being insinuated. In the words of Livingstone (2024), "references to digital technologies ... encompass many layers of meaning, including the device itself as an object and a brand, the apps installed on it and their various settings, the networks to which ... people are thereby connected technologically and socially, the genres of content that characterize their tastes and preferences, the commercial and data-driven business models to which they become subject, the soft and hard regulatory regimes that frame or limit their possibilities, and the cultural and moral norms according to which people make their digital decisions" (p. 2).

In this volume, we define the 'digital' as the use of digital technologies, such as computers, the internet, applications, and mobile devices. Our definition also takes Bollmer's (2018) conceptualization into account. He defines digital technologies as the many computational devices that exist around us – devices that operate through calculation and mathematical processing, be they smartphones, laptops, or even cars and refrigerators. As Manovich (2001) surmises, digital media is by nature a numerical representation because all information is represented in 0–1 digital code. This chimes with another definition proposed by Daniel Miller (2023). For him, the digital is defined as new or digital technologies that are ultimately reducible to binary code. These have made many cultural artefacts easier and quicker to both reproduce and to share. Because of its numerical representation, digital information unlike its analogue counterpart is programmable, alterable and subject to algorithmic manipulation (Manovich, 2001). This means that digital media can be manipulated in ways that are extremely difficult with traditional analogue media and is alterable in several ways (Manovich, 2001).

Drawing on seminal works from Lev Manovich, Roland Barthes, Gilles Deleuze and Jean Baudrillard, Bollmer (2018) conceptualizes digital media based on three themes which, in combination present digital media as innovative when compared to media of the past: *technical processes*, *cultural form* and *immersive experience*. At the level of technical process, Bollmer (2018) classifies digital media as digital on the basis of being networked, interactive, hypertextual, automated and databased. As far as *the cultural form* is concerned, Bollmer (2018) argues that digital media are characterised by variability, rhizomic character and continual process. Then finally, the immersive experience relates to the telepresence, virtuality and simulation features of digital media.

Foregrounding the notion *of a system of infrastructure*, Miller (2020) argues that digital technologies enable certain practices and social relations. As a result, social media platforms from this perspective can be viewed as "… enabling … economic relations and ways of life" (Miller, 2011: n.p). This infrastructure provides a framework under which new forms of organisation, relationships, and experience (culture, including digital cultures) can emerge. Digital technologies have made it possible to connect with people all over the world, access information instantly, and create new forms of art and entertainment. The digital has made it easier to work from home, shop online, and stream movies, date online, participate in town hall meetings, and consume music at a distance. The digital is also making it easier for us to stay informed about current events and to participate in political and social movements. Whilst the verdict on the transformative and revolutionary role of digital media in society is still debatable, there is an emerging view that these technologies are *double-edged* (i.e., have both empowering and disempowering effects). There is no sufficient space here to retrace this debate, but it suffices to note that the effects of technology on culture are *complex*, *unpredictable*, and *multifaceted*. This is partly because digital technologies are entangled in the structures of society in many *different*, *complex*, and even *contradictory* ways (Dufva & Dufva, 2019). This is partly because "the same technology [digital technologies] can take on different meanings across changes in cultural contexts and thus be used in radically different ways" (Leonardi et al., 2006: 222). This highlights the necessity of understanding various cultures of use. Three approaches have been proposed, which are useful for conceptualising "the digital": (i) how people use digital media or technologies—this is to focus on the digital as tools, devices, contents, and services; (ii) how people engage within digital spaces or environments, focusing on whether and how these extend or transform or reinvent the possibilities for action and interaction; (iii) how society itself is reshaped by the increasingly wholesale adoption of digital infrastructures for information, education, work, commerce, entertainment, communication, and more—health, politics, welfare and, arguably, all other domains (Third, Livingstone & Lansdown, 2019; Plantin, Lagoze, Edwards, & Sandvig, 2018). This book takes these approaches into account in its quest to conceptualize and theorize African digital cultures.

WHAT IS CULTURE? SOCIOLOGICAL, ANTHROPOLOGICAL AND CULTURAL STUDIES PERSPECTIVES

At the core of this book is the concept of 'cultures'. In order to frame this issue of culture more appropriately, there is a need to foreground conceptualization of the terms from a wide range of disciplines. In this section, we focus on sociological, anthropological and cultural studies' understanding of culture. The origin of the Latin word *cultura* is clear. It is a derivative of the verb *colo* (infinitive *colere*), meaning "to tend," "to cultivate," and "to till," among other things (Tucker, 1931). Definitions of culture abound and range from very complex to very simple. At a general level, culture is defined as a shared system of beliefs, values, and practices that shape the way people live and interact with each other. Brown (1991) describes culture as consisting "of the conventional patterns of thought, activity, and artefact that are passed on from generation to generation" (p. 40). Another definition of culture underscores the set of shared symbols, meanings, and interpretations that help people make sense of the world around them. Culture refers to "transmitted and created content and patterns of values, ideas, and other symbolic-meaningful systems as factors in the shaping of human behaviour" (Kroeber and Parsons, 1958: p. 583). Hofstede (2001) defines culture as shared mental software, "the collective programming of the mind that distinguishes the members of one group or category of people from another".

Despite this multiplicity of definitions, scholars agree that culture is not static and monolithic. The argument here is that cultures are constantly evolving as people interact with each other and with the world around them. There are many different cultures in the world, each with its own unique set of beliefs, values, and practices. Culture provides us with a framework for making sense of our experiences and for interacting with others. It also helps us to create a sense of belonging and identity. Sociological and anthropological perspectives have dominated scholarly theorization of culture. There are contending views on what constitutes culture based on theoretical orientation. Anthropologically, culture is framed as embracing all the forms and results of human activity which are characteristic of some community, and which result from tradition, imitation, learning, and realization of commonly accepted patterns (Kloskowska, 1981). In this vein, culture extends over all spheres of man's social activity and its results, as well as to all fields of aesthetic and intellectual creation (Kloskowska, 1970).

Structural functionalists such as Emile Durkheim conceptualized culture as 'social facts'. From a structural-functionalist theory, culture is presented as an interdependent network where all parts, and structures, like social norms, roles, and institutions, work together to ensure the function of a society. Cultural norms function to support the fluid operation of society, and cultural values guide people in making choices. Sociobiological theorists view culture as social structures that arose from the human instinct to survive. Because of their orientation, sociobiologists argue that it is possible to identify cultural universals in [digital] society. Symbolic interactionists view culture as being created and maintained by the ways people interact and in how individuals interpret each others' actions. Marx argues that the superstructure grows out of the base and reflects the ruling class' interests. From a Marxian standpoint, culture is part of the superstructure. It follows that it is the *ideology* and *false consciousness* peddled by the economic elites. Whilst these sociological explanations are useful for thinking about culture, we embrace cultural studies' conceptualization in this volume.

For the purposes of this book, we lean on the understanding of culture from cultural studies. In the cultural studies tradition, we draw our analytical toolkits of culture from the writings of Stuart Hall, and Raymond Williams. Cultural studies scholars are united in their argument that culture as a text cannot be understood outside of material conditions of production, consumption, regulation, identity, and representation. This speaks to the importance of the 'circuit of culture'. Culture is not genetically inherited, and cannot exist on its own, but is always shared by members of a society (Hall et. al., 1997 p. 16). Starting from the basic premise that culture is 'a whole way of life' and 'a mode of interpreting all our common experiences' (1960 p. 18), Williams argues that culture is therefore not the culture of an elite, but a culture that is embedded in everyday experience. He coined the term 'structures of feeling', which refers to the lived experience of a particular moment in society and in history (Williams, 1960). For him, culture is synonymous with 'structures of meaning'. In his conceptualization, culture is a social practice and productive process that is rooted in material and social relations. Unlike orthodox Marxism, Williams' approach to culture emphasizes its entanglement and enmeshment with (but not simply determined by) the economic and political structures and experiences of life. Thus, culture is a site of political contest, as groups express their incorporation within the dominant order and their resistance to it.

Williams distinguishes between *dominant*, *residual* and *emergent* cultures, where *dominant* forms and practices, at any given moment, co-exist with older forms and *emergent possibilities* which may be absorbed by or challenge the dominant trends. The dominant culture in a society refers to the established language, religion, values, rituals, and social customs which are often considered as the norm for the society as a whole. It often achieves "its dominance by controlling social institutions such as communication systems, educational institutions, artistic expressions, laws, political processes, and businesses" (Marshall, 1998 p. 250). The term 'residual' is used by Williams to denote something different from the 'archaic'. In his scheme of things, any culture includes available elements of its past. By 'archaic', he refers to that which is wholly recognised as an element of the past, to be observed, to be examined, or even on occasion to be consciously 'revived', "in a deliberately specialised way" (Williams, 1977, p. 122). By 'emergent', Williams refers to the new meanings and values, news practices, new relationships and kinds of relationships are continually being created (1977, p. 123). In the context of this volume, these three interlinked concepts help us to analyse the role that subversive and oppositional identities and movements play within the dominant culture. This is explored further in chapters by Mbongeni Msimanga and Constance Kasiyamhuru, as well as by Allan Job Wefwafwa and Wambui Wamunyu in this volume.

Building on Williams' seminal work, Deuze (2006) has propounded two schools of thought that can be used to analyze the metamorphosis of culture in the digital age. The first school of thought argues that *existing cultures might find themselves essentially recreated in digital form* as more and more life experiences, from the exciting to the mundane, play out in digital spaces (Deuze, 2006). The second school of thought posits that the dominant digital culture emerging now is a *separate culture* unto itself. In light of the complex linkages between the old and new cultures, we propose the third school of thought. This school of thought acknowledges the remnants of the old which persists when new cultures are born. This approach talks about *hybrid digital cultures* (a mix of the new and the old). The concept of *hybridity* can be used to explain the complex coexistence between offline and online cultures.

DEFINING AND CONCEPTUALIZING DIGITAL CULTURES

The concept of digital culture has been conceptualized by mostly scholars from the global North (Deuze, 2006; Uzelac and Cvjeticanin, 2008; Gere, 2012; Hjorth, 2018; Miller, 2011; 2020; Bollmer, 2018; Punathambekar & Mohan, 2019). Synonyms of digital culture such as virtual culture, cyberculture, e-culture, internet culture, techno-culture, convergence culture, and new media culture have surfaced in the last three decades (Bell, 2002; Penley & Ross, 1991). These concepts are generally used to describe how the internet and its ancillary digital technologies are (re)shaping the way that people interact with each other. At the core of some of these concepts are utopian, even theological framing of technology's potential (Miller, 2011; Bollmer, 2018; Mbembe, 2016). These theoretical conceptions of digital culture view it as a metaphysical perfection of the human. This kind of metaphysical understanding of technology has been critiqued for promoting the discourse of technological determinism and solutionism. For instance, Vincent Miller in his book, *Understanding Digital Culture*, sheds light on diverse forms of digital culture, including mobile technologies, surveillance, algorithms, ambient intelligence, gaming, big data and technological bodies. The main thrust of this book is to examine how digital technologies are used within the wider contexts of our everyday lives (Miller, 2011). According to Miller, to understand digital culture, it is important not only to examine the economic and social impacts of an 'information society' but to examine these alongside the shifting and emerging cultural forms that are already playing an increasing part in mainstream consumer and media cultures (Miller, 2011). In this "information superhighway," there are many byways, intersections, routes and detours, which influence ways in which digital Africans engage with the digital. There are also invisible toll fees and gates that digital Africans have to engage with and navigate as they participate in the digital agora. As Benyera (2021) puts it, these emerging forms of digitalities are characterized by the "coloniality of data" whereby end users are dispossessed of their sovereignty as they tick the Terms and Conditions (T & Cs) in order to be accepted onto the online digital platforms and the resultant digital geographies.

As Bollmer (2018) observes, when we are talking about digital cultures we are essentially dealing with the relationship between digital media and culture. In other words, "it explains how digital media – in providing a material, infrastructural basis for practices and interactions – affect identities, bodies, social relations, the arts, and the environment" (Bollmer, 2018, n.p). These effects are neither neutral, nor are they inevitable. In many ways, the relationship between digital media and culture is *political*. It is also complex, ambiguous and unpredictable. For him, digital culture is made up of three elements, *narratives about technology*, *material infrastructures* that shape communication, and the *physical capacities* of bodies, human or otherwise, in their ability to move and perform specific acts (Bollmer, 2018). Digital media involve power relations that shape what human bodies are and do and legitimate these relations as neutral or natural. In mainstream literature, the concept of digital culture is often used as shorthand for the use of social media and smartphones in everyday life (Dobson, 2015). A lot of focus has been expended on how ordinary people deploy digital media for self-representation online. Such an approach dovetails with Couldry's (2012) clarion call that media researchers should focus on investigating *what people are doing with media*. The previous trend has been a heavy focus on *what the media are doing to people* (media effects studies). In the words of Gere (2008, 15), "To speak of the digital is to call up, metonymically, the whole panoply of virtual simulacra, instantaneous communication, ubiquitous media and global connectivity that constitutes much of our contemporary experience." In view of the going, digital culture can be defined as the knowledge, beliefs, and practices of people interacting on digital networks that may recreate tangible-world cultures or create new strains of cultural thought and practice native to digital networks (Gere, 2012).

The concept of digital cultures has similarities with Jenkins' (2006) convergence culture, and Axel Bruns' (2006) notion of 'produsage'. Due to the creation of converged media industries, a new form of media experience comes to the fore. This forms the convergence of media culture, which blurs the distinction between producer and consumer. For instance, the term 'produsage' captures the idea that the product is 'prodused' in a networked communal environment and where such product is not finished product owned and controlled by an author, but communally owned, unfinished 'processes.' In fact, building on Jenkins' idea of participatory media practices, digital cultures can be conceptualized as collaborative, interactive and co-creative cultural productions.

AFRICAN DIGITAL CULTURES: CONCEPT AND ITS BOUNDARIES

This book foregrounds the concept of African digital cultures to make sense of the complex ways in which Africans within and outside are interacting with digital technologies in their everyday life. The concept is also meant to foreground what Africans are doing to and with digital technologies in their everyday lives. It is also meant to highlight what digital technologies are doing to African cultures and vice versa. This dovetails with Ataguba (2020, p. 1) who argues that "African societies appropriate digital communication technologies into African cultural repertoire and assign meanings that are significant in the African context". The point here is that digital technologies are connected to already existing local traditions and are shaped and transformed by them. In mobilising the concept of African digital cultures, we are aware of the need to go beyond what Nyamnjoh (2021) has called "... dichotomies and binary oppositions, nor on zero-sum games of conquest and superiority" (p. 279) when discussing the relationship between humans and digital technologies. Indeed, this book contributes towards "... resist[ing] the uncritical adoption of scholarly agendas and frameworks from elsewhere" by "... engaging in more critical reflections that extend beyond the mechanic, while avoiding a lapse into 'a nativist romanticism'" (Wasserman, 2021, p. 19).

In our quest to shed light on the dominant, emergent and residual African digital cultures, we shy away from viewing this phenomenon as an attempt "to 'catch up' with the North or 'leapfrog' stages on a presumed universal technology trajectory" (Wasserman, 2021, p. 19). Rather, we call upon researchers to study African digital cultures on their own terms without necessarily imposing cultural standards and universals from the global North. This point is eloquently made by Mabweazara (2015) when he argues that "by exclusively using Western yardsticks to assess developments in Africa, we inadvertently run the risk of glossing over issues of vital concern to local contexts and experiences" (p. 4). In line with the decolonial turn, we acknowledge that there is a 'pluriverse' of technological possibilities, digitalities, and trajectories (Mignolo & Walsh, 2018). There is no one universal technological trajectory. It varies from continent to continent, from country to country and from community to community. Instead of being caught up or engrossed in strawman arguments about the goodness or badness of technological consequences, Miller & Wang (2021) chide us to situate new technologies within a much wider cultural and social context so that we can appreciate the inherent contradictions and complexities that emerge from the larger study of their use and consequence. This chimes with Wasserman's (2018) argument that we should "… avoid treating Africa as a monolith but allow for differences within and across African … societies and countries" (n.p). Further, he urges researchers to "… avoid treating Africa as an exception or a case to illustrate theories developed in the Global North but allow for theory-building from the ground up" (Wasserman, 2018: n.p).

Overall, in this book, we are heavily influenced by Nyamnjoh's (2005, p. 2) insightful observation that "… ordinary Africans are busy Africanizing their modernity and modernizing their Africanity in ways too often complex for simple dichotomies to capture ". Thus, besides bringing their own cultures to bear on digital platforms, African communities have been busy creolizing borrowed cultural forms and enriching them by infusing in them their own local cultures and traditions. In some cases, this has given rise to 'cultural hybridization'. This recognises "the creative ways in which Africans merge their traditions with exogenous influences to create realities that are not reducible to either but enriched by both" (Nyamnjoh, 2005: 5). The concept of African digital cultures is used in this book to reflect the creative adoption, adaptation and integration of digital technologies into people's lives. This allows us to de-essentialize users and audiences of digital platforms. As Miller (2011) observes, digital technologies are (re)produced and reconstituted in particular contexts where individuals draw upon their own cultural resources as they develop genres, registers, languages and practices of use in line with their needs and expectations.

Such a focus is very urgent in a context where Africans have been called 'invisible users' (Burrell, 2012) because their circumstances, habits, and desires have not figured into the thinking of digital developers (Bernal, 2020). This invisibilization of African agency and creativity has led to stereotypical framing of Africa as a 'technological desert' characterized by structural and endemic '*digital poverty*' (Mabweazara, 2015). The danger of this single narrative about Africa is that it presents the continent "passively awaiting external salvation" (Berger, 2005, p. 1). Whilst digital inequalities and divides are persistent challenges in Africa, there is creativity and ingenuity at the margins that cannot be ignored. Thus, in spite of Africa's current marginalization in the globalisation process, Africans manage to appropriate digital technologies, to use them in particular modes, and thereby, even to encounter their marginal status (Nyamnjoh, 2004, p. 53). The argument here is that "African journalists should hardly be viewed as second class Netizens. They have moulded internet [digital] tools to suit their specific needs, devised ingenious technical solutions to overcome the idiosyncrasies of their situations" (Accone, 2000, p. 69). Given the long history of stereotyping African viewers, listeners and users as "primitive", "ignorant", "gullible", or even "criminal" (Poell et al., 2024; Willems and Mano, 2016: 20), this book endeavours to shine the light on creative ways in which digital Africans are forging new and innovative ways of engaging with digitalities.

Extant studies show that Africans on the continent and in diaspora have not only used digital media, but they have also innovated and adapted it for their own diverse purposes (Mare, 2016; Mabweazara, 2012; Pype, 2016; Bernal, 2020). Rich and lucid accounts of 'technological adjustment' (Pfaffenberger, 1992) and 'cultural appropriation' (Hahn & Kibora, 2008) are coming to the centre as individuals and communities harness and adapt digital technologies to their lived realities in hitherto unimagined ways (De Bruijn, Nyamnjoh & Brinkman & 2009; Nyamnjoh, 2005). This further buttresses the observation that "because Africa is part of the world, and because its backwardness is less the result of choice than of circumstance, ordinary Africans are determined to be part of the technological revolutions of the modem world, even if this means accessing the information superhighway on foot, horseback, bicycles, bush taxis and second-hand cars, or relying on lifts and the generosity of the super-endowed in the latest sports and fancy cars" (Nyamnjoh, 2005, p. 4). Digital media offer African diasporas an immediacy of connection to people and institutions in the homeland as well as to communities and compatriots in the diaspora (Bernal, 2020). As infrastructures, digital media have made possible the creation of new public spheres, forms of protest, social groupings, and spaces of imagination (Bernal, 2020). In this book, several chapters take this argument further by examining the materialization of group dynamics on WhatsApp, use of YouTube for activism and hosting of political campaigns on X (formerly Twitter) and Facebook.

THE STATE OF DIGITAL AND SOCIAL MEDIA LANDSCAPE IN AFRICA

Digital cultures are formed at the intersections of infrastructures, platforms, and publics (Punathambekar & Mohan, 2019: 12). Digital infrastructures and platforms evolve in complex interaction with other media ecologies, and this is also shaped by regulatory and economic policies at play. To make sense of the emerging, emergent, resilient and enduring digital cultures in Africa, it is advisable to briefly look at the state of the digital and social media landscape in Africa. The internet and its ancillary digital technologies only became a major societal organizing force in Africa towards the mid-1990s and early 2000s (Mare, 2023). At that time, the internet was seen as an enabler for commerce and business operations. The industry was predominantly run and monopolized by state-owned telecommunication operators and other public agencies (Alemu, 2018; Mare, 2023). The telecommunications sector in Sub-Saharan Africa "was still characterised by poorly developed infrastructure, primarily concentrated in urban areas, and poor service provision with less than 1% of the population accessing telecommunications services" (Alemu, 2018, p. 1). Because of the inefficiencies associated with state-owned service providers, the cost of accessing the internet was extremely high throughout Africa. The situation changed significantly with the liberalization of the telecommunications industry in the late 1990s (Alemu, 2018). As Jobodwana (2009, p. 73) argues, "competition within the industry stimulated heavy economic investment in other sectors of the economy". Thus, the telecommunications reforms that facilitated the transition from monopoly to competition have enabled a great portion of the population to access telecommunications services (Alemu, 2018). It has facilitated the mass permeation of the Internet and mobile telephony into Africans' everyday lives. Unlike in the early 2000s, "where most telephone line subscribers on the African continent were located in South Africa as well as North Africa, the current data reveals increased access to telecommunications services in Sub-Saharan Africa countries" (Alemu, 2018, p. 1). Lethargic state-owned telecommunications providers found it difficult to compete with agile and innovative private companies. Slowly but surely, the telecommunications industry was significantly reconfigured.

Instead of relying on letters, telegrams, faxes and fixed telephone lines, new and better channels of communication began to take shape. These new channels of communication such as emails, blogs, and websites allowed previously passive consumers of information and news to speak back to the sender. Thus, 'people formerly known as audience' (Rosen, 2006) were presented with an opportunity for expressing their voice. In this case, voice is conceptualized in line with Couldry's (2010) definition which foregrounds the effective opportunity for people to speak and be heard on what affects their lives. Although this kind of effective and influential voice has not yet been realized in most postcolonial African countries, there is a general feeling that 'horizontal', and 'vertical' voice is being realized (Couldry, 2010). Horizontal voice is the utterance and exchange of opinion, concern, and criticism among citizens.[3] Vertical voice manifests itself through protest action, disengagement and making demands on rulers. Mare (2016) foregrounds the realization of oblique voice in politically repressive contexts. This concept of voice is discussed at length by Job Wefwafwa and Dercio Tsandzana in this volume.

Like elsewhere, the coming of the mobile phone in Africa was celebrated as 'revolutionary' and 'transformative' (Hahn & Kibora, 2008; Bernal, 2020; Moyo, 2009; Wasserman, 2011). In many ways, the mobile phone was framed as having the potential to help the continent to leapfrog into higher stages of development in line with the unilinear modernization theory (Mare, 2023). In this regard, Hahn & Kibora (2008) assert that mobile phones have played a much greater role in the change of the communications landscape in Africa than in Europe. This is because the mobile phone can provide previously unavailable opportunities for communication over long distances. Besides allowing voice calls, the mobile phone came with short service messaging applications. This opened what has been termed the 'parallel market of information' (Moyo, 2009) in some authoritarian and monarchical regimes in Africa. In these regimes, repressive and ideological state apparatuses are deployed to repress and suppress voice.

The coming of web 2.0 applications in the mid-2000s led to the mushrooming of various digital platforms. These included platforms like Myspace, Facebook, X (formerly Twitter), and YouTube. Prior to these platforms, older versions of social media such as Six Degrees, and Friendster existed. These rudimentary platforms attracted millions of users and enabled email address registration and basic online networking. In Africa, weblogs (also known as blogs), signify another early form of social media platforms that gained traction with the launch of the LiveJournal publishing site in 1999. This coincided with the launch of the Blogger publishing platform by Pyra Labs, which was later sold to Google in 2003. In Southern Africa, MXit, 2go and Viber made significant inroads into the lives of mostly young people. Blackberry messenger also had its fair share of popularity amongst the youth. This was followed by platforms such as Google+, Instagram, WhatsApp, and Pinterest. Besides the role played by web 2.0 technologies, it is important to acknowledge that third generation (3G) of wireless mobile telecommunications technology also facilitated the adoption of faster internet in Southern Africa.

Recent internet penetration statistics suggest that Africa has approximately 43.1% (Internetworldstats, 2023). Based on available data, Libya has an internet penetration rate of 94.8 %, making it the country with the highest internet penetration in Africa. It is followed by Kenya with 85.2 %, and then Algeria with

83.2% (Internetworldstats, 2023). Ekine (2010: x) reminds us of how misleading statistics may be, especially in developing contexts such as Africa where media usage may occur in patterns that differ quite radically from those in Western societies. Scholars (cf. Hahn & Kibora, 2008; Nyamnjoh, 2005) talk about sharing practices amongst Africans. Most people in Africa access the internet and social media through smartphones (Galal, 2024). This is in part because mobile connections are much cheaper and do not require the infrastructure that is needed for traditional desktop PCs with fixed-line internet connections (Johnson, 2022). Urban areas are more connected when compared to rural areas owing to the skewed infrastructural development in Africa. Mobile internet access has contributed significantly to this upsurge.

This is attributable to the influx of low-cost smartphones like Huawei and ZTE from China and other Asian markets as well as locally produced smartphones. Despite the mass adoption of the mobile phone in Africa, the costs of accessing mobile and broadband internet remain extremely high. The variations in internet and social media usage levels across the continent underscores the deep-seated digital divide between rural and urban areas (Mare, 2016). As a result, digital technologies are predominantly an urban phenomenon although people in rural areas are increasingly joining the bandwagon.

Platforms like Facebook, X, TikTok, Instagram, YouTube, and WhatsApp are extremely popular amongst Africans largely due to social media bundles[6] and zero-rated services associated with them (Mare, 2016). Because of these social bundles, more and more Africans are able to access social media for political news, engagement with elected officials and speaking truth to power (Mare, 2020). They are also enabling citizens, politicians, spin-doctors, and

Table 1.1. Top 10 African countries with highest internet penetration rates

Country	Internet penetration rate (%)	Facebook subscribers %
1 Libya	94.8%	94.8%
2. Kenya	84.1%	22.3%
3. Algeria	83.8%	63.3%
4. Mauritius	80.6%	80.6%
5. Morocco	79.4%	66.3%
6. Seychelles	78.6%	78.6%
7. Reunion	71.1%	71.1%
8. Tunisia	69.4%	71.6%
9. Nigeria	67.5%	16.1%
10. South Africa	63.1%	48.5%

(Source: Internet World Stats, 2023).

other stakeholders to create, disseminate and consume political content. This has created important convivial debating spaces (Ogola, 2022; Omanga, 2019). Omanga (2019) has shown how WhatsApp groups in Kenya compliment constitutional requirements of participation in county governance in Kenya. In particular, the more conversational platforms such as WhatsApp and Telegram amplify the centrality of voice in also understanding 'digital publics' in Africa (Srinivasan et. al 2018). In this volume, Job Wefwafwa focuses on this pertinent issue of actualization of voice within the context of Kenyan WhatsApp groups.

Despite the commendable growth in internet, social media and mobile phones penetration in Africa, there are concerns that some national governments are encroaching into this space through digital platforms regulation, surveillance and implementation of draconian laws (Munoriyarwa and Mare, 2022; Mare, 2020). In response to protests organised mostly via social media, several African governments have devised tactics and strategies to *technologically reconstitute* or *infrastructuring* the potential of digital technologies (Omanga, Mare and Mainye, 2023). These include introducing draconian laws, enforcing social media taxes, implementing state-ordered internet shutdowns, disinformation campaigns, and arresting ring leaders. These attempts to regulate the internet and digital platforms have been described as nascent strategies to ensure 'digital sovereignty' in the global South. Digital sovereignty refers to the power to erect borders around incoming information; trade protectionism in the digital sector, and enhanced state power over the online accounts, data and PII of its residents (Mueller, 2020).

Laws on fake news, cyber-crimes, data protection and protection of personal information have been implemented with deleterious impact on the enjoyment of digital rights. In Nigeria, President Muhammadu Buhari resorted to banning X (Twitter). In Uganda, President Yoweri Museveni banned Facebook. Countries like Ethiopia, Uganda, Madagascar, and Tanzania have placed some controls that regulate social media. Internet shutdowns have also been implemented in Burundi, Chad, Cameroon, Democratic Republic of Congo, Ethiopia, Sudan, and Zimbabwe (Mare, 2020). Realizing that the internet worked against the government's supreme authority over its information environment, African governments have started to copy the Chinese model with regards to limiting access to the internet and social media platforms. Through surveillance and legislation, some governments are in the process of asserting territorial control over digitized data and platform services, instituting severe data localization, restricting access to external cloud service providers, cutting off platforms' access. This has led to deplatformization of content production, which has negatively affected the creative economy in some African countries.

CULTURAL PRODUCTION IN THE DIGITAL AGE

We are living in an 'App age' where life revolves around internet-driven applications. The proliferation of internet-driven applications for self-expression is in tandem with the millennial zeitgeist. It has become almost obligatory for one to have presence(s) on social media, to the extent that our lives are equally divided between offline and online activities. There is space for virtually anything and everything on the internet. Everything is content, and content is everything. In Africa and other parts of the developing world, digital platforms are the new stage on which everyday culture plays out. What was considered trivial or silly in the past today constitutes the most popular social media content. Diversity and difference are major characteristics of this post-modern culture. To say culture is dynamic and ever changing has almost become a cliché. Yet it acquires a new meaning when said in the context of the digital age. Indeed, culture is always on the move, but in this digital age it is actually 'moving' in the sense that it is not confined to physical or geographical spaces but has become deterritorialized (Bischoff, 2017) and can be experienced while one is on the move physically and also moving (scrolling) within and across digital platforms.

Visual digital platforms allow users to capture ephemeral moments of their lives such as performances and (non) artistic presentations of everyday life, including those previously regarded as banal. The ubiquity of digital technology has ushered in numerous possibilities as well as questions around the mediation of previously undocumented practices and spaces, such as traditional rituals, indigenous diets, private events and domestic settings. The visual characteristics of social networking sites (SNSs) such as Instagram, TikTok, Snapchat and Facebook, among others, allow users to not only experience other worlds but also showcase diverse elements of their culture. As a result, the private is fast becoming public and the public more publicized, sometimes with worrying consequences for conservative societies which characterize most of Africa. Digital media platforms have also revolutionized the value chains of cultural productions. By cultural production, we mean "… the creation of symbolic goods that contribute to a shared sense of culture" (Poell et al., 2024: n.p). Creative arts such as fashion, dance, music and drama are increasingly finding expression on digital platforms and attracting the attention of interconnected users. Cultural productions that in the past depended on formal distribution, exhibition and live audiences are finding more avenues of expression and becoming accessible to all and sundry. Digital platforms and their attendant downloading and sharing practices that used to be treated as piracy are becoming an acceptable and commonplace architecture of the globalization of culture. For example, at the height of the Covid-19 pandemic when human movement and gathering was restricted, digital platforms such as YouTube and Facebook became the only avenues of enjoying live musical concerts. As a result of these platform-dependent cultural production, unknowns have become overnight celebrities.

Historically popular cultural forms originating in the global North, particularly the USA, have been the most influential to global popular culture. With the proliferation of digital platforms, although the global North continues to be prominent, increasingly popular culture and actors traditionally on the periphery are getting their space and niche too. For example, South Africa's *Indlamu* dances, Eswathini's *umhlanga* ceremonies, Nigeria's Afrobeat, and Malawi, Zambia and Zimbabwe's *Nyau* dances, formerly romanticized through ethnographic filmmaking, are increasingly becoming public spectacles on TikTok and YouTube, created and shared by those at the centre of the performances. In many cases, these representations use vernacular language and other localized registers of communication. Cultural productions are no longer exclusive to monolithic industries but have become more demotic, placing individual creatives and ordinary people at the centre. Dancing partygoers, imbibers in a pub or someone imitating a prominent person or re-enacting some newsworthy occurrences are all new forms of content that many find of interest. These often feature in Instagram and YouTube reels or as TikTok hashtag challenges. The online performances and self-exhibitions by individuals on this app economy are examples of vernacular creativity or domesticity, which draws from the familiar. As Ibrahim (2018, p. 20), argues "The banal offers codes of communication that are instantly recognizable and resonant with distant strangers but also anchoring imaging technologies as 'tamed' through its domestication with the everyday". Because of the local uniqueness of vernacular creativity, there is a need for thorough understanding of context to interpret it. Focusing on TikTok, Oswelled Ureke, John Ndavula, Johannes Tukondjeni, Gifty Appiah-Adjei, Elizabeth Owusu Asiamah, Rainbow Sackey and Belinda Osei-Mensah discuss the appropriation of this Chinese app by African creatives.

PLATFORMIZATION OF CREATIVE WORK

Platformization refers to the "penetration of digital platforms, economic, infrastructural and governmental extensions into the cultural industries, as well as the organization of cultural practices of labour, creativity and democracy around these platforms" (Poell, Nieborg & Duffy, 2022, p. 5). It does not follow that any organization that runs content online is a platform company. A platform is open to third party users, not just the owners of the channel of communication. Digital platforms share three common characteristics that "they are technologically mediated, enable interaction between user groups and allow those user groups to do particular things" (Koskinen, Bonina & Eaton, 2019: 320). Due to platformization, creative works or cultural productions such as film, humour, comedic skits, and music are commercialized on and via digital media applications. Through platforms like YouTube, TikTok, Facebook, X, Spotify, iTunes and so forth creative artists have direct access to markets and, in some cases, get instant feedback from consumers in ways that shape the direction of their future works. As far as creative works are concerned, platforms are simultaneously channels of distribution as well as the market where content is curated and immediately consumed.

While the ubiquity of SNSs opens numerous possibilities and routes to market for creatives, it is also indicative of a techno-capitalism where everything is a click away, but at a cost not comprehended by many. The commodification of cultural activities means their creation is unpaid labor. For example, TikTok and Instagram content creators have to invest in make-up, wardrobe and performance rehearsals which would normally be rewarded in most cultural industries. The reward for many content creators is mainly endorsement in the form of likes, shares and followings, which in many cases do not translate to direct revenue. The flood of content on platforms feeds into a frantic desire for users to consume more, sometimes with the chaotic effect that everyone is seeking everyone's attention, and no one is giving it. The net effect is that the proverbial public sphere, which these platforms ought to enrich, may actually be trivialized. At the same time, certain ideas and personalities are excluded or marginalized in this frenzy.

Platform governance is based on codes, community standards, and rules that users must live by. These include codes on nudity, profanity, hate language, political and religious extremism as well as use of intellectual property, among others. Because digital platforms accommodate diverse users, many may be constrained or marginalized by such codes and rules. Thus, there are users who are on the platforms simply to consume and comment, those who "make a living from readings comments" or are happy to be in the "terraces". Content moderation practices by internet intermediaries and platforms companies also significantly affect cultural production and the sustainability of the creative economy in Africa. Content moderation is the process of reviewing and monitoring user-generated content on online platforms to ensure that it meets certain standards and guidelines. Apart from platform governance, a plethora of other reasons affect inclusivity and monetization on platforms. As Poell et al. (2024) observe, "… global power imbalances and material inequalities … structure how [digital] platforms connect people and institutions around the world" (n.p). *Creatives at the periphery* are often marginalized in this emerging platform economy. This includes rural communities where telecommunication infrastructure is poor and often inaccessible or female content creators, whose content invariably attracts toxic sexist remarks in the comment sections. While influencers and celebrities harvest likes, followers and subscriptions, and grow famous for being famous, ideas and performances by subalterns are ignored even if they may be equally remarkable.

Digital media platforms for creative work rely on user generated content for their sustenance. Their algorithms are designed such that sometimes they deliberately promote particular creative works such as music, often rescuing and catapulting to stardom personalities and acts that were languishing in obscurity. Thus, platforms create their own star system akin to the Hollywood golden era. Before the advent of TikTok, Senegalese-born social media influencer Khabane 'Khaby' Lame was virtually unknown. TikTok catapulted him to fame, making him the most popular and one of the highest earning social media influencers. Initially platforms such as YouTube were seen as avenues of piracy but are increasingly seen by artists as important avenues of marketing and monetizing their work. Debates on the popularity of musicians often refer to platform metrics such as numbers of views and likes as a measure of success. Thus, platforms also serve as tools of endorsement for those working in cultural industries. Once shared online, cultural productions reach audiences beyond the geo-political borders of their origin. This has led to a *culture without borders* or *deterritolialisation of culture* characterised by transnational rather than national cultural industries. For instance, *Amapiano*, a South African music genre has grown into a global phenomenon, with international hits being created using its rhythm. The same is true of Nigeria's Naija music, Congolese Rhumba, Zimbabwe's Sungura and Tanzania's Bongo Flava. *Jerusalema*, a song composed and performed by South African artists, Master KG and Nomcebo, took the world by storm at the height of the COVID-19 pandemic, thanks to TikTok. Artists like Uncle Waffles (South Africa), Diamond Platinumz (Tanzania), Burna Boy and Wizkid (Nigeria), Jah Prayzah (Zimbabwe), Fille (Uganda) have become global household names in a manner never experienced by yesteryear artists, largely due to the reach and interconnectivity of digital media platforms. Thus, Africa has become a major player in global creative culture by contributing its own flavours such that it is no longer just a recipient periphery.

There is complementarity in the manner that a variety of actors are organized on platforms. Platforms act as "matchmakers" connecting a variety of actors, including advertisers, customers, content creators and content consumers (Poell et al., 2022). In some cases, online connections develop into physical interactions and relationships. For example, in 2022, Kenyan comedian Meshack Kiprop (Arap Uria), who rose to fame by imitating British football commentator Peter Drury on TikTok, ended up meeting his idol at the FIFA World Cup in Qatar after Drury was made aware of the comedian's acts.

SOCIAL MEDIA INFLUENCERS, MONETIZATION AND PROTEST CULTURES

The names Khabane Lame, Michael Blackson, Boity, Sisy Yemmie, Robert Alai, Shadaya, Mai TT, Madam Boss, Miss Abacar and Wode Maya have one thing in common. They are all social media influencers (SMIs). They grew to fame on social media and have gone on to use that fame to influence social and political behaviour. Social media influencers generate celebrity capital by attracting attention (Khamis et al., 2017). Once they reach a certain level of fame, SMIs can earn revenue through strategies such as endorsement deals, brand ambassadorship, selling their own products online, native advertising and virtual currency. Apart from monetary gains, internet celebrities enjoy general goodwill associated with their fame. As such, internet celebrities are able to influence ideas, which is the reason why corporations may want to associate with them. Senegalese born Italian SMI Lame started using TikTok seriously when he lost his job as a factory worker in 2020. Since then, he has become the world's most followed creator on TikTok and has landed massive commercial deals with companies like Hugo Boss and Binance. Operating within the confines of "platform capitalisms" (Steinberg, Mukherjee and Zhang, 2024), these celebrities generate more revenue because of higher 'CPM' (or cost per 1000 advertising impressions).

Social media influencers are mostly ordinary people, and without the resources that showbiz celebrities boast, can only achieve transient fame. Thus, they are attracted online by social media's promise of fame and (sometimes) money in what Ibrahim (2018, p. 37) calls a 'profile economy'. Apart from popularizing creative works, social media have also provided platforms for SMIs such as activists and other pressure groups to pursue their agendas. Examples include Zimbabwean born Netherlands based LGBTIQ+ activist Tatelicious, Zimbabwean journalist cum political activist Hopewell Chin'ono, South Africa's anti-immigrant campaigners Dudula Movement, South African podcaster Macgyver 'MacG' Mukwevho and South African opposition leader Julius Malema. Online celebrities depend on self-branding to popularize their content i.e. they associate themselves with particular ideas, thematic subjects and bodily adornments. Thus, the self is packaged into a commodity, a hyper-personalized advertisement whose value is measured at each instance, by the numbers of likes and following. Many of the case studies presented in this book are examples of SMIs hailing from various countries on the African continent.

IDENTITY POLITICS AND DIGITAL PLATFORMS

The concept of identity is important in the discussion of SNSs. Users utilize social media to communicate to networked others what they are thinking, what they feel about themselves or what they want others to think about them. For example, the Facebook application prompts one into a confession by posing the question "What's on your mind?" which is an equivalent to 'what are you doing?' or 'what's up?' This means posts on the platform are based on the innermost reflection of the meaning of life and the essence of being. Social media profiles represent users' online identities or, at least, their performance of who they think they are. The user profile is a constellation of key attributes that a user associates with themselves, much like a corporate logo. As Matt Hills (2002) argues about Facebook, the profile picture is a shorthand for constantly changing, up-to-the minute performances of self. Going through a user's profile and posts reveals the identity of that person in the same way a logo represents a corporate brand. Sometimes online identities are enmeshed with those offline, although it is equally common for users to portray personalities that are at variance with their actual selves.

Most SNS users derive a sense of self-worth from the volumes of likes and followings they get online. As Francis Fukuyama (2018) argues, human beings want positive judgements about their worth, particularly those made by other people around them. This compels users to post content about what they deem likeable, in the same manner a broadcasting station would react to audience ratings. Thus, other users' endorsements act as a commissioning device for creation of content (Ureke, 2021). After posting, users often audit the impact of their posts by checking who and how many have viewed and liked or commented on their content. Most of the content posted on SNSs revolves around depiction of the self, such as selfies, travelogues, food diaries and personal achievements. Thus, the user packages a best version of themselves and presents that to his/her audience, who are followers and friends. This represents production and commodification of the self. Questions arise on the extent to which one can 'reveal' themselves and their circumstances to others in the quest for attention. Sometimes there is a tendency to overshare, such that what are supposed to be private affairs and spaces find expression in public and constitute what we may term *public privacy*. In this volume, Maud Blose, Sihle Nyathi, Chikezie Uzuegbunam, Job Mwaura, and Richard Ononiwu zero in on Facebook and Instagram to unpack the complex processes of identity constructions online.

The 'who am I?' question is one that social media users continuously grapple with. Their identity is fluid and momentary often in response to external endorsements and criticism. Equally for connected users, the question 'who are you?' is important. It is, for example, a determining factor when users decide whom to connect with. The Facebook platform, for example, has an 'about' section, which is supposed to profile a user's identity with information such as where they reside, which school they attended, when they were born and their marital status among other issues. Decisions to connect can be based on how much information users divulge about themselves. In some cases, users choose to hide information such as pictures of themselves, their marital status and dates of birth or any other information they may consider to be ultra-revealing. Many of the users that are anonymous on Twitter and YouTube do so because they intend to troll other users or feel that their posts may lead to reprisals. As Fukuyama (2018) argues, individual self-esteem is related to the self-esteem conferred on a larger group to which one belongs such that the political affects the personal. This identity politics is quite apparent on SNSs where people choose to belong to groups, spaces or communities based on what they think about such associations. One is likely to join a LGBTIQ+ Facebook group or Twitter hashtag if their identity conforms to it. In those online communities, like-minded users interconnect and often become echo chambers in which unitary views of the world bounce and circulate.

HOW THE REST OF THE BOOK IS ORGANIZED

Cognizant of the diverse ways in which digital technologies are transforming how Africans (based on the continent and those domiciled in the diaspora) are engaging in mediated citizenship, resisting, and reconfiguring received identities, performing vernacular creativity, engaging in online dating, playful engagement with video games, partaking in online gambling and forging alternative forms of politics, this edited volume provides a platform for emerging and established African scholars to interrogate, conceptualize and theorize emergent digital cultures in the age of platformization, datafication and digitization. As Nieborg & Poell (2018, p. 4275) aptly put it, "the [ever increasing] penetration of economic and infrastructural extensions of digital platforms [into everyday life is significantly] affecting the production, distribution, and circulation of cultural content" (own emphasis). Building on widely acknowledged fact, this edited volume starts from the premise that material and immaterial digital cultures cannot be separated from digital technologies. The mutual (re)shaping of emergent cultures and 'the digital' invites scholars from the South to systematically examine the nuance between specific cultural performances and the affordances, infrastructure and architecture that constitute it in contemporary society. These global digital platforms are implicated in the various ways in which ordinary Africans are (re) producing, reimagining, recycling, and redistributing cultural products and practices. There is no denying that the rapid permeation of digital and mobile media technologies, the ongoing platformization of cultural production, and emergent forms of digital media practices are transforming cultural practices and performances in ways never imagined before.

Situated within the 'circuit of culture' as theorized by Cultural Studies scholars (du Gay et al., 1997), this volume acknowledges that digital cultural performances and articulations are produced through the articulation of a series of processes, stages, or moments in the biography of a given cultural artefact. These include production, consumption, identity, regulation, and representation (du Guy et al., 1992). Foregrounding the decolonial turn, the book endeavours to critique the taken for granted assumptions of data colonialism and surveillance capitalism that 'playbour', 'influencer culture' and 'free labor' promoted by digital platforms such as TikTok, Instagram, X, and Facebook contribute towards 'decent work'. The book argues that digital platforms are socially and economically embedded in the neo-liberal capitalist system, whose major objective is profit maximization, alienation of labor, exploitation and mystification of the real nature of social relations (Fuchs, 2014). Whilst the affordances of digital platforms like WhatsApp, Facebook, X, and TikTok allow Africans to (re)construct and resist certain political, cultural, sexual, and religious identities, they also constrain the realization of alternative mediated forms of citizenship. Our argument is that digital platforms as infrastructures have both an enabling and constraining logic inbuilt in their operations. Notwithstanding their repressive and limiting logics, digital platforms are contributing immensely to the emergence of new [creolized] languages (*emojis*), insurgent and dissident political cultures, creation of new digital subjectivities, sustaining virtual communities, and forging vibrant dating cultures.

Instead of normalizing the mainstream discourse that constructs Africa as a continent of '*digital poverty*' (Mabweazara, 2015), our volume highlights how Africans situated at the *centre, in-between, and margins* are negotiating and strategically harnessing the potential of the digital in *preserving, showcasing, performing, monetizing* and *platformizing* their everyday lives. It highlights the innovative and creative ways, albeit under structural constraints, in which the young and old Africans are culturally appropriating digital technologies for a wide range of political, cultural, economic and social purposes. It focuses on how Africans are navigating these structural impediments such as limited access to the internet, lack of digital devices, draconian cyber laws, social media taxes, and dilapidated infrastructure in their quest to produce and distribute their cultural artefacts and products in the digital agora. It looks at how ordinary people are deploying the 'digital' to speak truth to power whilst the powerful are using the same technology to prevent the truth from being spoken. This tug of war between the powerless and powerful–characterizes the creative use of the digital in the global South–where mainstream communicative platforms are already captured and censored by the elite. It reflects critically on the implications of the (de)platformization of cultural production in a continent historically dealing with enduring legacies of "coloniality of power, knowledge and being" (Quijano, 2007). This form of censoring alternative discourses, voices and epistemologies happen in a context where permissible forms of online speech are imposed on the users by dominant platform companies. Added to these stubborn legacies are emerging issues of coloniality of data, and digital colonialism (Kwet, 2018; Couldry & Mejias, 2019). Furthermore, this is happening in a context of pervasive digital surveillance, disinformation campaigns and state-ordered internet shutdowns (Munoriyarwa & Mare, 2023; Mare, 2020). The volume brings together some of the emerging researchers and scholars who are engaging in cutting edge research on African digital cultures. What is unique about their contributions is that they are centering African perspectives, which are often ignored and muted in mainstream literature.

As far as digital platforms are concerned, most chapters in this book are based on ethnographic studies of Facebook, TikTok, WhatsApp, YouTube, X, and Instagram. These platforms are generally popular among Africans as evidenced by social media penetration rates (InternetWorldStats, 2023). For instance, in the *State of Social Media for Africa 2023* published by Meltwater, it was revealed that five social media platforms are dominating the apps market on the continent. The report shows that Facebook (88%), Instagram (76%), LinkedIn (74%), X (67%) and WhatsApp (58%) are leading the pack (Meltwater, 2023). Although audio-visual platforms are still lagging behind, the report also reveals that TikTok is rapidly increasing (28%) (Meltwater, 2023). YouTube is also experiencing steady growth. This could be attributed to the high cost of data, which constrains downloading heavy data consuming apps. Furthermore, the popularity of traditional social media platforms can be explained by their indirect promotion through the introduction of social media bundles by most African telecommunication operators. Although there are emerging local digital platforms such as Ayoba, Abeg, MoyaApp, Nairaland, Superprof, Jiji, Softalk, Sasai in various African countries, their traction and magnetic appeal is not as great as that of global digital platforms coming from the United States of America and China. More research is needed on the social media ecosystem in Africa.

Methodologically, the chapters are largely informed by qualitative research methodology. The chapters rely on a diverse range of qualitative data collection instruments. These include in-depth interviews, focus groups discussions, virtual (digital) ethnography, qualitative content analysis, textual analysis, and critical discourse analysis. It is interesting to note that most of the chapters in this volume are based on virtual ethnography (Hine, 2005). This method has become more important in the post-pandemic world, where people are increasingly living most of their lives online. In its various manifestations, virtual ethnography "includes a broad range of methodological approaches aimed at answering the complexities of the object of research and the different ways in which this object has been constructed" (Domínguez, Beaulieu, Estalella, Gómez, Schnettler & Read, 2007, n.p). When studying diverse digital technologies with different architectures, algorithms and application programming interfaces (APIs), virtual ethnographers are "faced with the need to answer very pressing questions such as how to use heterogeneous data (text, audiovisual data, etc.) in their analysis, or how to combine research in front of the screen and in the virtual field"

(Domínguez et al., 2007: n.p). Lack of access to platforms' APIs and datasets also hinder meaningful data collection amongst researchers in the global South. These are some of the methodological nuggets that are foregrounded by contributors in this edited volume.

At a theoretical level, chapters in this volume makes use of a whole gamut of humanities and social science theories. These include theories from sociology, political science, psychology, cultural studies, marketing, journalism, media studies, public relations and crisis communication. This unique book provides valuable and much-needed perspectives and narratives on African digital cultures in an environment where *hysteria* and *moral panics* have defined the ways in which the digital is framed in mainstream media and policy making circles. In this eclectic and multidisciplinary volume, contributors focus on various issues including deliberative political cultures, representation, identity, social media influencers, performative activism, participatory dynamics in groups, digital labour, monetisation of content, humour and cultural production.

The book is made up of fourteen chapters which are sub-divided into three sections. The first section focuses on *TikTok, Vernacular Creativity and Emergent Cultural Productions*. The section comprises three chapters, which unpack novel forms of cultural productions taking place on TikTok, Metaverse and Facebook. The second section is titled *Identity Constructions, Performances and Perceptions*. It spotlights the complex nature of identity (re)constructions and the unfinished nature of such a quest in the age of platforms. Focusing on social media influencers and ordinary users of TikTok, Facebook and Instagram, the four chapters in this section examine how Africans construct and perform their identities in platform fields and habitus designed and moderated by huge global conglomerates. Section three of this volume explores the *Platformed Voices, Protests and Resistance Cultures* on specific digital platforms. Unpacking the role of humour, satire, and political influencers on digital platforms, the six chapters in this section, which include the conclusion, highlight the need to go beyond politics with capital letter 'P' and begin to embrace politics with a small letter 'p' in order to make sense how young people are engaging with politics in contemporary Africa.

In Chapter One, Admire Mare and Oswelled Ureke define key terms such as the digital, culture, and African digital cultures. They also look at the state of the digital and social media landscape in Africa. They offer theoretical toolkits that can be used to analyze African digital cultures. Building on the concepts of vernacular creativity, platformization and precarious agency, Mare and Ureke problematize the nexus between emerging digital cultures and cultural production occurring in a context of data and digital colonialism. The chapter further demonstrates that despite the well-documented cases of digital divide and inequalities, digital Africans are *digitizing their cultural practices* whilst at the same time *platformizing their cultural productions* in ways that defy stereotypical representations of the continent as the epitome of the 'periphery' in the context of digital societies. Mare and Ureke also highlight the concurrent process of (de) platformization of previously peripheralized and silenced cultures, stories, performances, representations, protest repertoires and informal modes of politics.

In Chapter Two, John Ndavula critically engages with the contextual understanding of production and monetization of cultural productions in Kenya. In this chapter, Ndavula investigates processes and implications of production of the culture of the Maragoli community in Kenya through TikTok. Drawing on interview data along with an analysis of TikTok videos, Ndavula demonstrates how creators adapt and negotiate their identities and activities, developing sets of tools for content creation and different styles of portrayal of their culture.

Chapter Three puts the spotlight on Namibian TikTok influencers. Authored by Johannes Tukondjeni, the chapter maps the identities of these influencers, thematic areas of their content, the reach and engagement of their short videos and their monetization strategies. Tukondjeni shows that some content creators have become motivational speakers, relationship coaches, comics, storytellers, dancers, composers and performers. He also reflects on the implications of the emergence of these various influencers on content creation and vernacular creativity in a multicultural environment.

Chapter Four focuses on the monetization strategies adopted by popular TikTok influencers in Ghana. Written by Gifty Appiah-Adjei, Elizabeth Owusu Asiamah, Rainbow Sackey and Belinda Osei-Mensah, this chapter investigates the different monetization strategies deployed by mega influencers such as @erkuahofficial, @wesleykessegh, @asantewaaaaa and @say.logan. The authors found that most TikTok influencers in Ghana relied on advertising and the TikTok live feature to gain both monetary and non-monetary benefits from their followers. They also argue that the affordances of the TikTok platform make it easy for ordinary people to gain popularity as well as monetize their digital labour.

In Chapter Five, Oswelled Ureke examines how Zimbabwean TikTokers curate themselves within the context of the country's well-documented multipronged socio-economic crisis. Building on a deep-dive qualitative approach, Ureke's chapter relies on a sample of 30 videos created by top-ranked influencers. He argues that when considered collectively, videos ascribed to a particular region, for example #zimtiktok, construct a cultural mural that reveals the 'bigger picture' or group identity of the concerned society. Thus, online identities interlink with and reveal something about Zimbabwean circumstances. Therefore, it is possible to discern what it means to 'be Zimbabwean' by assessing content disseminated by those creatives identified as 'being Zimbabwean'.

Chapter Six, written by Chikezie Uzuegbunam, Job Mwaura and Richard Ononiwu explores the ways in which young people in African contexts use digital and social media for self-presentation and self-performance, and the ways that the notion of authenticity is defined or redefined in such digital practices. They argue that youths are particularly susceptible to the influences of globalization, given their extensive exposure to diverse media, a wide range of cultural artefacts, and particularly given the dominating influence of digital technology. The authors observe that all self-representation is a conduit through which young people convey specific aspects of their identity. The chapter offers an exploration into the cultural, social, and political ramifications of digital self-representation within African contexts with the aim to understand how social media self-representations offer insights into concurrent online and offline societal dynamics.

Chapter Seven qualitatively explores the phenomenon of self-representation of identities through shared content and engagement on published posts by South African black women on the Ladies House Facebook group. Through autoethnography, Maud Blose studies members' engagement with other group members and how women represent themselves through text, visuals, and symbols during a period of three months from January to March 2023. Using discourse analysis and Gloria Anzaldua's notion of autohistoria, Blose finds that autohistoria is evident in the personal posts of experiences that women shared on the Ladies House. She argues that black women communicated eventful, traumatic, tragic, and beautiful stranger-than-fiction stories and the Ladies House platform enabled members to own their narratives, negotiate, and self-represent.

In Chapter Eight, Sihle Nyathi analyzes influencing as a discursive act that constitutes women as neoliberal subjects. Nyathi argues that through tools such as hashtags and platform affordances, young women are drawn to participate in content creation on Facebook, Tik Tok, and Instagram. She analyzes Pusheka Girl, a community of businesswomen in Bulawayo, Zimbabwe that produces content on Facebook, Instagram, and TikTok for the purpose of creating a network of female businesswomen in the city. She focuses on the discourses peddled by Pusheka Girl and their members through hashtags. Nyathi shows that social media influencers have changed the socialization of women in Zimbabwe as they play the role of 'aunties' by shaping their ideas on womanhood. From this, she argues that neoliberalism as a global politico-economic framework leads to the homogenization of culture and notions of womanhood.

Chapter Nine shifts its attention to the politically polarised nation of Kenya. Written by Job Allen Wefwafwa, this chapter asks the following questions: Why are there tensions and confrontations during WhatsApp group political engagements? Who initiates the engagements, why do they initiate them? In answering these questions, Wefwafwa draws data from participant observation within WhatsApp groups and face-to-face interviews. Wefwafwa argues that unlike the Western world, most African people have dual "citizenship", whereby they simultaneously belong to their ethnic associations and work as civil servants. In the Kenyan context, citizens are concurrently situated in primordial publics and civic publics during electoral engagements. The dual 'citizenship' leads to unique dialectical tensions and confrontations within themselves, which spill over into WhatsApp groups.

Mbongeni Msimanga and Constance Kasiyamhuru in Chapter Ten focus on the appropriation of YouTube by *Bus Stop* and *Magamba T.V.* to speak truth to power. Msimanga and Kasiyamhuru's chapter borrows theoretical concepts from Amber Day's seminal study of Satire and Dissent. Using a multi-modal approach to analysis, they trace how political satire has been appropriated during Zimbabwe's "New Dispensation" era. They argue that performative activism has been creatively used by citizens and comedians to raise socio-economic and socio-political injustice issues from government's excessive use of power and corruption that has turned citizens into paupers.

Chapter Eleven focuses on the nexus between humour and social media in Mozambique, Dércio Tsandzana uses the case studies of @guyzelh.ramos @txiobullet_madlipz @mana_dos_manos and @alcy_caluamba, to discuss the humorous content produced as well as the socio-political and economic issues addressed through these productions. Rooted in virtual ethnography, Tsandzana argues that although the Internet is relatively low in Mozambique, digital humor on TikTok has transformed political communication and engagement amongst the youth. Thus, social media constitutes a new context in which political and non-political content intermingle in complex ways.

In Chapter Twelve, Wambui Wamunyu argues that citizen participation and engagement are essential aspects of democracy, widely perceived as a model form of national governance. But in many parts of the world, Africa included, this is often rhetorically espoused by a powerful political elite rather than experienced or participated in by the average citizen, notwithstanding civic education programs. The chapter conceptualizes the term active digital citizen and qualitatively interrogates the nature of digital engagement from three individuals who exhibit 'active citizenship' on various digital platforms. The chapter illustrates how the deployment of social media platforms and tools of discourse contributes to a betterment of the lives of digital activists' compatriots, and also disrupts presumptions about the nature and enactment of democratic governance.

Chapter Thirteen scrutinizes Ethiopia's national dialogue initiative, launched in December 2021, focusing exclusively on the impact of digital repression on the process. In the chapter, Henok Kremte probes deeper into whether and how digital repression– the government's systematic use of repressive measures against dissenting voices online – corrodes the dialogue's credibility and transformative potential. Through an in-depth analysis of documented instances of digital repression post-launch, it contends that such actions expose the insincerity and pretense underlying the dialogue efforts, erode confidence-building measures, and betray core dialogue principles like inclusiveness, public participation and transparency, and public buy-in.

Chapter Fourteen concludes the volume with nuggets from the thirteen preceding chapters. In this chapter, Admire Mare and Oswelled Ureke show how the digital cultures captured in the volume can be rendered 'African' but are at the same time part and parcel of a global cultural tapestry enabled by the deterritorial nature of digital communication.

REFERENCES

Accone, T. (2000). Digital dividends for journalism in Africa. *Nieman Reports*, *54*(4), 67–69.

Alemu, R. (2018). Introduction. In R. Alemu (Ed.), *The liberalisation of the telecommunications sector in Sub-Saharan Africa and fostering competition in telecommunications services markets* (Vol. 6, pp. 33–35). *Munich Studies on Innovation and Competition*. Springer.

Ataguba, O. (2020). ICTs and Juju are Two Sides of the Same Magical Coin, Says Nyamnjoh: How True? Global Media Journal, 18(34): 1-2.

Bell, D. (2002), An Introduction to Cybercultures, London: Routledge

Benyera, E. (2021). *The fourth industrial revolution and the recolonization of Africa: The coloniality of data*. Routledge.

Berger G (ed.) (2005). Doing Digital Journalism: How Southern African Newsgatherers are using ICTs. Grahamstown: High Way Africa, 1–14.

Bernal, Victoria 2014 Nation as Network: Diaspora, Cyberspace, and Citizenship. Chicago: University of Chicago Press

Bernal, V. (2020). African digital diasporas: Technologies, tactics, and trends. *Introduction African Diaspora*, *12*(1–2), 1–10.

Bischoff, L. (2017), 'The future is digital: An introduction to African digital arts', Critical African Studies, 9;3, pp261-267

Bollmer, G (2018). Theorizing Digital Cultures. London: Sage

Bruns, A. (2006) Towards Produsage: Futures for User-Led Content Production. In C. Ess, F. Sudweeks & H. Hrachovec (Eds.) Proceeding of the 5th International Conference on Cultural Attitudes towards Technology and Communication. School of Information Technology, Australia, pp. 275-284.

Burrell, J. (2012). Invisible Users: Youth in the Internet Cafes of Urban Ghana, MA: MIT Press.

Couldry, N. (2010). *Why voice matters: Culture and politics after neoliberalism*. Sage Publications.

Couldry, N. (2012). Media, Society, World: Social Theory and Digital Media Practice. London: Wiley & Sons

Couldry, N. and Mejias, U.A. (2019). The costs of connection: how data is colonizing human life and appropriating it for capitalism, Stanford: Stanford University Press.

Deuze, M. (2006). Participation, Remediation, Bricolage: Considering Principal Components of a Digital Culture. The Information Society, 22:2, pp63–75. https://doi.org/10.1080/01972240600567170

de Bruijn, M., Nyamnjoh, F. B. and Brinkman, I. (2009). Mobile Phones: The New Talking Drums of Everyday Africa, Barmenda: Langaa RPCIG

Domínguez, F. D., Beaulieu, A., Estalella, A., Cruz, E., Schnettler, B., & Read, R. (2007). Virtual ethnography. *Forum: Qualitative Social Research*, *8*(3), 1–5.

du Gay, P., Hall, S., Janes, L., Mackay, H. and Negus, K. (1997) Doing Cultural Studies: The Story of the Sony Walkman. Sage Publications (in association with the Open University).

Dufva, T and Dufva M, (2019) Grasping the Future of the Digital Society, Futures,)107, pp17-28

Fuchs, C. (2014). Social Media: A Critical Introduction. London: SAGE Publications

Fukuyama, F. (2018), *Identity, the Demand for Dignity and the Politics of Resentment,* New York: Farrar, Straus and Giroux.

Galal, S. (2024). Internet usage in Africa - statistics & facts. Retrieved from https://www.statista.com/topics/9813/internet-usage-in-africa/#topicOverview. 7 April 2025.

Gere, C. (2008). Digital culture. London : Reaktion Books

Gere, C. (2012). Community without Community in Digital Culture, Cham: Palgrave Macmillan.

Hahn, H. P., & Kibora, L. (2008). The domestication of the mobile phone: Oral society and new ICT in Burkina Faso. *The Journal of Modern African Studies, 46*(1), 87–109.

Hills, M. (2002), Fan Cultures, Routledge

Hine, C. (2005). Virtual Ethnography, London: SAGE Publications Ltd;

Hjorth, L. (2018), 'Ambient and Soft Play: Play, Labour and the Digital in Everyday Life', European Journal of Cultural Studies, 21:1, pp3-12

Hofstede, G. (2001), Culture's Consequences: Comparing Values, Behaviors, Institutions, and Organizations Across Nations, 2nd ed. Sage, Thousand Oaks, CA.

Ibrahim, Y. (2018), *Production of the 'Self' in the digital age,* Cham: Palgrave Macmillan

Internet Word Stats (2023). Internet World Statistics. https://www.internetworldstats.com/stats.htm. Accessed 12 January 2025

Jenkins, H. (2006). Convergence Culture: Where Old and New Media Collide. New York: New York University Press.

Jobodwana, Z. N. (2009). Telecommunications liberalisation in Africa: Proposed regulatory model for the SADC region. *Journal of Digital Forensics, Security and Law, 4*(4), 73–94.

Khamis, S., Ang, L and Welling, R. (2017), 'Self-branding, 'micro-celebrity and the rise of Social Media influencers', *Celebrity Studies,* 8:2, pp191-208

Kloskowska, A. (1981): Socjologia kultury [Sociology of Culture]. Polish Scientific Publishers, Warsaw.

Koskinen, K., Bonina, C., Eaton, B. (2019). Digital Platforms in the Global South: Foundations and Research Agenda. In: Nielsen, P., Kimaro, H.C. (eds) Information and Communication Technologies for Development. Strengthening Southern-Driven Cooperation as a Catalyst for ICT4D. ICT4D 2019. IFIP Advances in Information and Communication Technology, vol 551. Springer, Cham. https://doi.org/10.1007/978-3-030-18400-1_26, pp319-330

Kroeber, A.L and Parsons, T. (1958). "The Concepts of Culture and of Social System," *American Sociological Review,* 23 pp. 582-583.

Kwet, M. (2018). Break the hold of digital colonialism. Mail & Guardian 29, pp1-9

Leonardi, P., Leonardi, M. E., & Hudson, E. (2006). Culture, organization, and contradiction in the social construction of technology: Adoption and use of the cell phone across three cultures. In A. Kavoori & N. Arceneaux (Eds.), *The cell phone reader: Essays in social transformation* (pp. 205–226). Peter Lang.

Livingstone, S. (2003). On the challenges of cross-national comparative media research. *European Journal of Communication, 18*(4), 477–500.

Livingstone, S. (2024). Reflections on the meaning of "digital" in research on adolescents' digital lives. Journal of Adolescence, 96:4, pp886-891.

Mabweazara, H. M. (2012). Normative Dilemmas and Issues for Zimbabwean Print Journalism in the Information Society Era. Digital Journalism, 1:1, pp135–151. https://doi.org/10.1080/21670811.2012.740272

Mabweazara, H. M. (2015). Mainstreaming African digital cultures, practices and emerging forms of citizen engagement. *African Journalism Studies*, *36*(4), 1–11.

Mare A (2016) Facebook, Youth and Political Action: A Comparative Study of Zimbabwe and South Africa. PhD dissertation, Rhodes University.

Mare, A. (2020). State-Ordered Internet Shutdowns and Digital Authoritarianism in Zimbabwe. International Journal of Communication 14:2020, pp4244–4263

Mare, A. (2023). Digital Spaces, Rights and Responsibilities: Towards a duty of care model in Southern Africa. Perspectives: FESMedia, January, 2023, Retrieved from https://library.fes.de/pdf-

Marshall, G. (1998). A Dictionary of Sociology. London: Oxford University Press.

Manovich, L. (2001). The Language of New Media. MIT Press

Mbembe, A. (2016). Decolonizing Knowledge and the Question of the Archive. Retrieved from https://wiser.wits.ac.za/system/files/Achille%20Mbembe%20-%20Decolonizing%20Knowledge%20and%20the%20Question%20of%20the%20Archive.pdf. Accessed 20 January 2025

McLuhan, M. (1964). *Understanding Media: The Extensions of Man,* McGraw Hill

Meltwater. (2023, January 17). Meltwater releases report on brands' social media usage in Africa. *Bizcommunity*. Retrieved June 10, 2023, from https://www.bizcommunity.com/Article/196/669/235086.html

Mignolo, W. D. & Walsh, C. E. (2018). On Decoloniality: Concepts, Analytics, Praxis. Duke University Press

Miller, D. (2011). *Tales from Facebook*. Polity Press.

Miller, D. (2018). Digital anthropology. In F. Stein (Ed.), *The Cambridge Encyclopedia of Anthropology*. http://doi.org/10.29164/18digital

Miller, V. (2020). *Understanding digital culture* (2nd ed.). Sage Publications.

Miller, D. and Wang, X. (2021). Smartphone-based visual normativity: Approaches from digital anthropology and communication studies. Global Media and China, 6:3, pp251–258

Moyo, D. (2009). Citizen journalism and the parallel market of information in Zimbabwe's 2008 election. *Journalism Studies*, *10*(4), 551–567.

Mpofu, S and Mare, A. (2020), '#ThisFlag: Social Media and Cyber-Protests in Zimbabwe. In Ndlela, M. and Mano, W. (eds). Social Media and Elections in Africa: Challenges and Opportunities, Volume 2. Palgrave and MacMillan, pp153-173

Mueller, M. (2020). Against sovereignty in cyberspace. International Studies Review, 22:4, pp779–801

Munoriyarwa, A. and Mare, A. (2022). Digital Surveillance in Southern Africa Policies, Politics and Practices, Cham: Springer.

Nieborg, D.B and Poell, T. (2018), The platformization of cultural production: Theorizing the contingent cultural commodity, *New Media and Society,* 20:11, pp4275-4292

Nyamnjoh, F. B. (2004). Globalisation, boundaries and livelihoods: Perspectives on Africa. *Identity Culture and Politics* *5*(1–2), 37–59.

Nyamnjoh, F. B. (2005). *Africa's media: Democracy and the politics of belonging*. Zed Books.

Nyamnjoh, F. B. (2019). ICTs as Juju: African Inspiration for Understanding the Compositeness of Being Human through Digital Technologies. Keynote Address at the 2019 Digital Humanities Conference, Utrecht University, The Netherlands, 9th – 12th July, 2019. https://

staticweb.hum.uu.nl/dh2019/dh2019.adho.org/wp-content/uploads/2019/07/Nyamnjoh_Digital-Humanities-Keynote_2019.pdf

Nyamnjoh, F. B. (2021). Being and becoming African as a permanent work in progress: inspiration from Chinua Achebe's proverbs. African Literature Association (ALA) Lecture, Cape Town, January 23,

Obijiofor, L., & Hanusch, F. (2011). *Journalism across cultures: An introduction*. Palgrave Macmillan.

Ogola, G. (2022). Social media is being misused in Kenya's political arena. Why it's hard to stop it. The Conversation. Retrieved from https://theconversation.com/social-media-is-being-misused-in-kenyas-political-arena-why-its-hard-to-stop-it-177586. Accessed 2 Jan

Omanga, D. (2019). WhatsApp as 'digital publics': The Nakuru Analysts and the evolution of participation in county governance in Kenya. Journal of Eastern African Studies, 13:1, pp175–191.

Omanga, D., Mare, A., and Mainye, P. (2023). Digital Technologies, Elections and Campaigns in Africa. London: Routledge

Pfaffenberger, B. (1992). Technological dramas. Science, Technology, & Human Values,17:3, pp282–312.

Plantin, J.-C., Lagoze, C., Edwards, P. N., & Sandvig, C. (2018). Infrastructure studies meet platform studies in the age of Google and Facebook. New Media & Society, 20:1, pp293-310. https://doi.org/10.1177/1461444816661553

Poell, T., Nieborg, D and Duffy, B.E. (2022), *Platforms and Cultural Production,* Cambridge: Polity Books

Poell, T., Duffy, B. E., Nieborg, D. B., Mutsvairo, B., Tse, T., Arriagada, A., de Kloet, J., & Sun, P. (2024). Global perspectives on platforms and cultural production. *International Journal of Cultural Studies*. https://doi.org/10.1177/13678779241292736

Punathambekar, A. and Mohan, S. (2019). Global Digital Cultures: Perspectives from South Asia. Michigan: University of Michigan Press

Pype, K. (2016). (Not) Talking like a Motorola: Practices of masking and unmasking in Kinshasa's mobile phone culture. *Journal of the Royal Anthropological Institute*, *22*(3), 633–653.

R. Williams. (1960). Culture and Society 1780-1950. New York: Anchor Books

Rosen, Jay. 2006. 'The people formerly known as the audience. Accessed 6 June, 2020 http://archive.pressthink.org/2006/06/27/ppl_frmr.html(open in a new window).

Quijano, A. 2007. "Coloniality and Modernity/Rationality," Cultural Studies 21:2-3, pp168 – 178.

S. Ekine (Ed.) (2010), SMS uprising: mobile phone activism in Africa (pp 86-104). Cape Town, Dakar: Pambazuka.

Srinivasan, S., Diepeveen, S., & Karekwaivanane, G. (2018). Rethinking publics in Africa in a digital age. Journal of Eastern African Studies, 13(1), 2–17. https://doi.org/10.1080/17531055.2018.1547259

Steinberg, M., Zhang, L., & Mukherjee, R. (2024). Platform capitalisms and platform cultures. *International Journal of Cultural Studies*, 28:1, pp21-29. https://doi.org/10.1177/13678779231223544

Stuart Hall, Lynne Segal and Peter Osborne, 'Stuart Hall: Culture and Power', Radical Philosophy 086, Nov/Dec 1997, pp. 24–41.

Third, A., Livingstone, S. and Lansdown, G. (2019). Recognizing children's rights in relation to digital technologies: challenges of voice and evidence, principle and practice. In Wagner, B., Kettemann, C. M., & Vieth, K. (eds), "Research Handbook on Human Rights and Digital Technology. (Edward Elgar Publishing) pp376-390. DOI:10.4337/9781785367724.0002

Tsarwe, S. and Mare, A. (2021). Mobile phones, informal markets and young urban entrepreneurs in Zimbabwe: An Exploratory Study. Area Development and Policy. 6:26, pp1-16. DOI:10.1 080/23792949.2020.1790021

Tucker, T. G. (1931). A Concise Etymological Dictionary of Latin. Halle: Niemeyer.

Ureke, O. (2021), 'Aesthetic norms and motivations of subaltern video-filmmaking: Comic skits and mobile journalism of the everyday in Zimbabwe', in A. Vailati and G.Z Villareal (ed), Ethnographies of *'On Demand' films: Anthropological explorations of commissioned audio-visual productions,* Cham: Palgrave Macmillan, pp219-241

Uzuegbunam, C. E. (2018). Research on African digital cultures: Are children's voices missing? *The Journalist (27 November 2018), pp1-4.*

Wasserman, H. (2011). Mobile phones, popular media, and everyday African democracy: Transmissions and transgressions. *Popular Communication*, *9*(2), 146–158

Wasserman, H. (2018). Where the social is political. Africa As a Country. Retrieved 7 April 2015 from https://africasacountry.com/2018/04/where-the-social-is-political

Wasserman, H. (2021). New optics on digital media cultures in Africa. In H. S. Dunn, D. Moyo, W. O. Lesitaokana, & S. B. Barnabas (Eds.), *Re-imagining communication in Africa and the Caribbean* (pp. 19–32). Palgrave Macmillan.

Willems, W., & Mano, W. (2016). Decolonizing and provincializing audience and internet studies: Contextual approaches from African vantage. In W. Willems & M. Winston (Eds.), *Everyday media culture in Africa: Audiences and users* (pp. 1–25). Routledge.

CHAPTER TWO

TikTok and the Platformization of the Maragoli Culture in Kenya

JOHN NDAVULA

INTRODUCTION

The growing popularity and increasing dependence of ordinary people on short video apps like TikTok are impacting culture and society. More than ever before, social media platforms have been expanded to become an integral space for holding social, cultural and political conversations (Ndaka, 2022). The emergence of Internet celebrities has tremendously diversified culture (Abdin, 2018). The short video app, TikTok, and its impact on culture remains an under-researched area of study in Kenya. Therefore, this chapter aims to examine the influence of the TikTok platform on Maragoli cultural production. The research questions under investigation are: Why do Maragoli content creators prefer TikTok compared to other platforms?? What thematic frames are covered in their online content? How do they perform their identities online? Which communication styles do they engage in? and What monetization strategies do they employ?

Compared with other social media platforms, TikTok is characterized by short videos with simple-to-use editing and music-inclusion functions (Zhu et al., 2019). These functions provide a non-complicated user interface for creating videos, allowing users to embed their preferred music choices and special effects into their recorded videos. According to Yang et al. (2019), short videos are characterized by a low threshold for creation, produced from the perspective of the audience, and easily accepted by the grassroots. TikTok pushes content according to users' needs, preferences, and perspectives, greatly contributing to its wide usage and increasing popularity. The app uses an algorithm that determines which videos to show to users based on factors such as user engagement, video information, user preferences, time and location, and trending topics. It also considers various aspects of the video, such as its caption, sound, hashtags, and visual content. Additionally, the algorithm learns from users' behaviour and preferences to personalize their content. By showing users content that they are likely to enjoy, the algorithm influences the circulation of viral content (Qin, Omar & Musetti, 2022).

Most research on the use of TikTok in Kenya has focused on short video content based on politics. However, there have been few studies on the production of cultural video content in Kenya and none among the Maragoli, one of Kenya's ethnic groups. Yet, Kenya is among the leading countries in the usage of social media platforms for social commentary and political engagement in Africa (Ndavula, 2018; Mukhongo, 2020). According to Statista (2022) TikTok is the fourth most popular social media platform in Kenya, with its popularity standing at 63 percent. Since the completion of the fibre-optic network in 2009, the number of Kenyans using the Internet has risen steadily amid increased access and popularity (Osiakwan, 2017; Bing, 2015; Ndavula & Mueni, 2014). At the start of 2023, there were 17.86 million internet users in Kenya, with an internet penetration rate of 32.7 percent (Datareportal, 2023). Through increased access to the Internet and with the proliferation of mobile devices, audiences are now able to take part as content creators (Willems and Mano, 2016). The term "content creator" describes digitally enabled cultural producers who create and circulate content on social media platforms, driven by an entrepreneurial spirit and desire to generate their online brands (Craig, 2019).

SOCIAL MEDIA AND IDENTITY PERFORMANCES

Social media has become a platform where individuals can perform and display their identities to others (boyd, 2014). Users engage in various identity performances such as self-presentation, impression management, and identity experimentation (Hogan, 2010). Firstly, self-presentation is controlling or guiding the impression others could make by altering the posters' settings, appearance and manner (Goffman, 1959). Goffman's work was extended to digital fora (Hogan, 2010; boyd, Chang & Goodman, 2004). Self-presentation refers to the way individuals present themselves to others on social media, often through carefully curated content such as photos, videos, and status updates (Hall & Caton, 2017). In the view of Goffman and Hogan self-representation is the display of the scenario-based ideal self, rather than a pattern of deception. This view was extended by Van Dijck (2013), who found that self-representation online could be for expressive, communicative, or promotional purposes.

Secondly, impression management involves controlling the information presented to others, to shape how others perceive and evaluate them. Users can employ social media for impression management by creating and curating their online identity to present specific images of themselves (Herring & Kapidzic, 2015). Impression management involves carefully selecting and filtering content, such as images, videos and posts, to create a particular impression (Van Dijck, 2013). The desire to create a positive online persona has been linked to factors such as self-esteem, social comparison and enhancement of social and professional aspects of life (Vogel, Rose, Roberts, & Eckles, 2014). However, the use of social media for impression management can also have negative consequences, such as the potential for exposure and scrutiny, and creation of a distorted online identity that does not reflect reality (Marwick & Boyd, 2011).

Thirdly, identity experimentation enables individuals to explore different aspects of their identity or try on different personas without the same social consequences as in face-to-face interactions. Through social media, users can explore different interests, adopt new personas, and interact with new communities while having control over their level of participation and the information they disclose about themselves (Marwick, 2013). These identity performances can be influenced by factors such as the intended audience, platform features, and cultural norms and can have implications for individuals' self-esteem, relationships, and social capital. TikTok's short-form video format, user-friendly editing tools, and algorithmic recommendation system have created an environment that enables users to showcase different facets of their personality, experiment with new personas, and engage with a global community of like-minded individuals (Bucher, 2021; Manovich, 2020). TikTok's emphasis on creativity and authenticity has also enabled users to challenge traditional social norms and stereotypes and to express themselves in ways that may not be possible in their offline lives. In essence, TikTok is transforming platform cultures and the dynamics of broader creative industries.

THE STATE OF SOCIAL MEDIA AND INTERNET IN KENYA

One of the earliest forms of digital content created by Internet users in Kenya was the blog, which can be traced back to 2003 – when the Kenya Bloggers Webring (KBW) was launched (Bloggers Association of Kenya [BAKE], 2015). These alternative media spaces challenged the government's effort to influence social, political and cultural thought in Kenya. Because of this stranglehold that the Kenyan state exercised over the Kenyan population, scholars (Ligaga, 2012: Ogola,

2017) agree that popular cultural forms became one of the few platforms Kenyans could use to challenge power and create expressive spaces.

Kenya has been witnessing a gradual shift to digital and social media platforms. These shifts have seen a mushrooming of online platforms that not only provide commentary on a wide range of social, political and economic issues but also curate different forms of artistic expression, personal experiences and journeys (Ndaka, 2022). At the time of writing, the TikTok application was the most downloaded in Kenya (Similarweb, 2022). The variety of video content on TikTok and a 15-second time limit are beneficial to the quick spread of information, as well as the spread of cultural content in a short period (Leffer, 2022).

Kenyan content creators have found creative ways to highlight and celebrate Kenya's rich cultural heritage on TikTok. Of the numerous video content produced on the TikTok platform, some are related to cultural matters such as folk dances, folk songs, and entertainment. Content also features fashion, food, unique traditions, and tourist sites (The Sauce, 2020). Some of the celebrity TikTokers who post content on Kenyan culture include Bwakali David who posts content on Kenyan culture and history, Curll Bunny who identifies as a Kenyan Norwegian girl and blogs about multicultural issues, and Ivy Miricho who showcases tourist attraction sites (The Sauce, 2020). Indeed, social media platforms have offered an important lifeline to several Kenyan creatives interested in curating, marketing and monetizing their content (Ndaka, 2022).

The Maragoli people are part of the patrilineal Luhya Community which inhabit the Western Province and parts of the Rift Valley Province of Kenya. The Luhya are a diverse group of Bantu-speaking people whose sense of common identity seems to have grown largely out of the colonial experience and has gained momentum in the years following World War II. Based largely upon common social, cultural and linguistic identity, people who once considered themselves distinct groups came to also identify themselves as Luhya. According to the 2019 national census in Kenya, the Luhya constitute the second largest tribe in Kenya after the Kikuyu with a population of 6.82 million (Kenya National Bureau of Statistics, 2019). The Luhya speak a cluster of related dialects which includes Maragoli (Kabaji, 2005).

The Luhya community has a rich array of diverse cultural expressions (Abunza, 1991). Similarly, the Maragoli community also has a vibrant culture that includes naming, initiation rites, marriage ceremonies, and memorial ceremonies among others. To preserve the rich culture, an annual festival dubbed the Maragoli Cultural Festival is held every 26th of December in Vihiga County in Kenya. The festival showcases traditional foods and brews, dressing and dances. Cultural artefacts such as gourds, pots, and baskets are displayed and Maragoli history, cultural norms and taboos are also discussed during the ceremony (Akaranga, 1996).

Despite the rich cultural expression and heritage among the Maragoli, no study has highlighted the expression of this culture online. This chapter, therefore, highlights cultural content created and uploaded by Maragoli content creators on the TikTok platform. This chapter takes a cue from Yékú (2022) and Ligaga (2012) who insist on paying attention to online platforms and how they stage undismissable aspects of African social, political and cultural life. Ligaga (2012) sees the internet as a space where most people articulate their opinions and desires, perform their identities, present the unsaid, circulate informal information, and generally negotiate the meanings of cultural issues. Indeed, social media platforms provide a means to learn about alternative narrations and histories (Ogola, 2017).

THEORETICAL FRAMEWORK

The study is guided by the social construction theory. According to Berger and Luckmann's (1967) enunciation of the social construction of reality theory, individuals create their reality, based on their own experiences, even if this is not an objective reality. "Everyday life presents itself as a reality interpreted by men and subjectively meaningful to them as a coherent world," (p. 19). Adoni and Mane (1984) suggested the social construction of reality is composed of interactions among individuals, society, and culture. The construction is social, as it can only occur with social interaction, either real or symbolic. In addition, individuals play dual roles in the construction, as they are both the creators and the producers of their individual social world or reality.

Adoni and Mane (1984) defined three types of social reality. First, the objective social reality is made up of factual information. Second, the symbolic social reality is composed of art, literature, and mass media. The third type of social reality is the subjective social reality, which is both objective and symbolic. Subjective reality is organized by the individual's zones of reference or their distance from the factual or objective reality. The close zone is composed of social elements and experiences the individual is frequently exposed to; the remote zone is composed of general social elements that the individual does not have close access to, such as public opinion. Allen and Waks (1990) (as cited in Gruidl, K. M., 2001) examined the extent of media influence on social reality construction and found that exposure to mass media influences social issues. It is important to analyze today's new media apps, such as TikTok, through their media environment and content. This study examines the social construction of reality on how short video apps shape and influence the culture and behaviors of the Kenyan people, more particularly the Maragoli culture.

METHOD

Qualitative content analysis was employed to explore how microcelebrities used TikTok to produce the culture of the Maragoli community in Kenya. Content analysis has been widely used in communication research to describe the manifest content of communication phenomena (Treadwell & Davis, 2020). Content analysis adheres to the naturalistic paradigm to interpret meanings from the content of text data (Treadwell & Davis, 2020; Hsieh & Shannon, 2005). The researcher collected videos from seven content creators from the Maragoli community which were published on TikTok between January and June 2022. The content creators were Mama Kevin, The Musalia Mudambi, Maragoli Queen, Ngadi Comedy, Starboy Comedi, Musungu the Luhya Princess, and Maragoli the Trending King. They were selected because of their recognition and online presence. A total of 35 videos from the seven content creators were collected and analyzed in the study. At least five videos were randomly chosen from each content creator. The researcher also conducted in-depth semi-structured interviews with the seven microcelebrities from the Maragoli community. Interviews were conducted in person and recorded with participants' consent. Qualitative data was analyzed through the systematic classification process of coding and identifying themes.

PLATFORM ADOPTION

Results indicate that Maragoli content creators have adopted social media platforms to varying degrees (see Table 2.1). The Facebook platform has the highest adoption among content creators, followed by YouTube and TikTok. Although all the content creators had TikTok accounts, the majority of those sampled were recent entrants with a year's experience using the platform. All the content creators began posting content on Facebook before transiting to other platforms like TikTok. Some of the content creators interviewed reported numerous advantages of using TikTok for content creation and sharing:

> TikTok is convenient for me because it is quick to record and edit videos on the platform. If I post a video with good content, it is more likely to go viral on TikTok than the other platforms. I can also see notifications about my videos and determine their popularity with my audience (Ngadi Comedy, 2023 personal communication).

> "I prefer TikTok because it doesn't have a lot of critics like Facebook," (Musungu the Luhya Princess, 2023 personal communication).

Some, however, were ambivalent about the use of TikTok. Results show that some content creators found TikTok challenging to use:

> I started posting my content on Facebook. I didn't know much about TikTok. Although I have a presence on TikTok, I do not like it as much because I find it challenging to use (Starboy Comedi, 2023 personal communication).

Some stated that it was easier to find their audience on Facebook than on other platforms. One said "My audience can access Facebook easily. I have a huge following on Facebook compared to TikTok and YouTube," (Mama Kevin, 2023 personal communication).

Some content creators stated that they joined TikTok because of pressure from their fans. In an interview, Mama Kevin said, "I joined TikTok because my fans demanded it. After I joined, I discovered that I could monitor feedback from the audience. However, I'm still learning more about TikTok."

The Musalia Mudambi who has not joined TikTok, has a pseudo account created using his name with 338 followers. His content is also available on TikTok having been shared by his fans. In an interview, The Musalia Mudambi stated, "I chose to concentrate on Facebook because my largest and strongest target audience is on Facebook. I have 115 thousand followers."

Most content creators used a cross-platform sharing strategy. Most of them posted on TikTok, Facebook, YouTube, and WhatsApp. In an interview, Musungu the Luhya Princess stated that she posted content on various platforms and included links to her other platforms so that her audience could locate her

Table 2.1. Platform adoption

User Name	Gender	Facebook followers	YouTube subscribers	TikTok followers	Year started TikTok
Mama Kevin	Female	12.5k	2.45k	2.9k	2020
The Musalia Mudambi	Male	115k	9.08K	338 *	2021
Maragoli Queen	Female	355k	5.07k	16.8k	2021
Ngadi comedy	Male	40k	1.67k	5.6k	2021
Starboy Comedi	Male	5.6k	496	1k	2022
Musungu the Luhya Princess	Female	1.9k	570	480	2022
Maragoli the trending King	Male	5.7k	136	200	2022

*This represents a pseudo-account on TikTok

other content. Other content creators stated that TikTok was good for marketing because it created room for audiences to find you easily.

> What made me start TikTok videos I realized so many people were using my clips on TikTok just because I had no account on TikTok and they got more likes and so those who knew me kept on pushing me to open an account on TikTok which I did, and it is growing well, (Maragoli Queen, 2023).

Most content creators revealed that they targeted the general audience. This showed that the adoption of different platforms wasn't based on audience type and platform preference. The few who were specific hadn't narrowed their target audience enough. For example, Musungu the Luhya Princess identified her target audience as women and the youth.

Although most scholars singled out TikTok as easy to use compared with other social media platforms (Zhu et al., 2019; Yang et al., 2019), some of the content creators surveyed indicated a lack of knowledge in using the platform to maximize platform affordances. Of those who cited the ease of use of the platform, they noted the low threshold for the creation of videos. However, most content creators involved several talents in their shows hence requiring the services of a production crew. Owing to limited funds, most engaged amateur camera persons. In an interview, Ngadi Comedy stated that he doubled up as a producer, scriptwriter, and actor, requiring only a camera person. The lean production crew and a lack of budget affected the quality of the videos produced. There are two types of online videos produced on social media networks: professional and amateur. Amateur videos differ significantly from professional ones in various aspects such as content, production, and editing styles. Some content creators also noted that audiences located their content more easily on TikTok. Indeed, TikTok pushes content according to users' needs, preferences, and perspectives, greatly contributing to its wide usage and increasing popularity (Yang et al., 2019).

THEMATIC FRAMES

Analysis of the short videos from the content creators in the past year has shown the following themes: emphasis on Maragoli language and culture, relationship advice, commentary on social issues, moral dilemmas, and gender roles. Some content creators satirize local governments, corruption, religion, and unemployment. However, a majority of the content is about memory, where content creators explore childhood experiences, especially at the hands of insensitive parents. All content creators aim at entertaining their audiences. For instance, The Musalia Mudambi posts videos which centre on family melodramas. In an interview, the Maragoli Queen stated that she preserved the culture of the Maragoli people by reminding the audience about the practices parents and other elders held on to so dearly.

In an interview with Mama Kevin, she stated that there was a shortage of content from the Maragoli community online. "The Maragoli are part of the larger Luhya community. I saw there was an absence of content depicting the Maragoli culture online, yet the other Luhya sub-tribes had their content online. I, therefore, decided to build the Maragoli culture brand on social media," said Mama Kevin.

In an interview conducted with The Musalia Mudambi, he stated that few content creators were creating Maragoli content and felt compelled to do so to preserve the Maragoli culture. He said:

> I noticed Maragoli as a language was dying and some Maragolis thought speaking their language was not cool. So, I had to change the narrative by creating attractive short videos that would make Maragolis proud of their language.

Akaranga (1996) notes the need to preserve the culture of the Maragoli people. One such effort is the introduction of the Maragoli Cultural Festival to preserve indigenous values. The festival, which was introduced by Maragoli leaders, scholars and elders is held annually to display various indigenous cultural materials, artefacts, and cultural values, some of which have been watered down by factors of social change.

ONLINE IDENTITIES

Most content creators branded themselves using pseudonyms on TikTok. They also construct identity by posting pictures of themselves on TikTok and across other social media platforms. Online identities shown on TikTok are much more fluid. For example, Mama Kevin has a banner on Facebook that shows her photo and the name Mama Kevin Entertainment. However, on TikTok, she goes by the name sharonondego. Maragoli Queen also has multiple identities online. She is also known as Mama Kanaiza or Maragoli the Trending Queen. On Facebook and YouTube, she brands herself as Maragoli Queen while on TikTok she goes by the name maragoliqueen32.

In an interview, Maragoli Queen stated that most people know her as Mama Kanaiza. She creates her identity by dressing like a village woman because she represents the voice of village mothers. Often, she maintains a serious stance when making social commentary. Ngadi Comedy said, "I dress in shorts. This helps my audience to identify me easily online. I act as a man who has is struggling with family relationships." The Musalia Mudambi, who is a man, shows different versions of femininity by posting videos of himself dressed as an old village woman who is well-informed about the current affairs in her village.

Findings indicate that most content creators craft identities—versions of the self, based on the images and auto-biographical content. Scholars note that most content creators promote themselves as personal brands, sharing their curated identities (Abidin, 2016; Duffy & Hund, 2019; Marwick, 2015). The self-branding activities of creators become "a form of affective, immaterial labour that is purposefully undertaken by individuals to garner attention, reputation, and potentially profit" (Hearn, 2010).

Scholars note that authenticity is a guiding principle of self-branding on social media (Abidin, 2016; Marwick, 2015; Duffy, 2017). Content creators rely on authenticity to construct a sense of intimacy and connection with their followers. Content creators who were interviewed stated that they put authenticity as a priority. Musungu the Luhya Princess said "I act videos that are of real life situations, something that happened either to a family member, a friend or even me as a person. That makes my work relatable." Mama Kevin stated, "I don't fake, present something real, I target the Maragoli community with reality and humour."

Being authentic also works for bloggers and influencers as a form of distinction from traditional media celebrities, with their trappings of top-down influence (Duffy, 2017). Social media content creators construct an audience based on presenting themselves as authentic and affective consumers building a reputation qualifying themselves as brands of authentic lifestyle (Abidin, 2018; Duffy, 2017).

DIRECT COMMUNICATION STYLE

Analysis of TikTok videos showed low-context communication behavior which emphasize the direct communication style and explicit expression of thoughts and ideas. Individual celebrities featured in the study mainly use direct communication styles to communicate with audiences. Maragoli Queen, for example, used simple and explicit expressions to communicate with audiences. Each short video gave thought-provoking commentary on topical social issues in society. Creators of TikTok short videos need to express clearly and finish the story within a few minutes. Because of the time limit on TikTok, each video has to communicate messages directly to its audiences to achieve its desired effects.

Along with the direct communication style, strong emotional expressions and frequent use of instrumental talks are additional features that characterize TikTok's popular videos. In videos produced by The Musalia Mudambi, who is a male actor who has adopted the role of a female character, there is a presence of strong emotional expressions to create humor. It is through these direct and emotional expressive acts that the videos achieve the entertainment value.

According to Hess et al. (2016), there are emotional expressive and emotional restraint ways of communication. They further posit that men are usually associated with emotional restraint communication style, while women show more emotions during communication by using emotional expressive style. However, this analysis of videos from the Maragoli Content creators does not reveal obvious differences regarding masculinity and femininity ways of expression.

MONETIZATION OF CONTENT

Content creators were asked whether they monetized their content on TikTok. Only one content creator stated that he was able to monetize his content on TikTok. However, the revenue he received was negligible. All content creators stated that their main source of revenue was from direct donations from well-wishers. Others stated that they would have wished to monetize content on TikTok but they lacked knowledge on how to do it. In an interview, Maragoli Queen stated, "I would like to monetize my videos, but I do not know how to do it. Sometimes I get donations but not that much." Other content creators stated that they host live broadcasts of events on their online platforms to receive revenue since they were considered microcelebrities. Other content creators noted that they had become influencers owing to their large following online and brands pay for them to promote their products. Others took up roles such as emceeing events and motivational speaking to earn revenue.

Although in other contexts TikTok has produced microcelebrities who have experienced commercial success (Zhang, 2020; Xu, 2017), findings indicate that Maragoli content creators are struggling to monetize their content in the Kenyan context. According to Xu (2017), wanghong economy means the business chain of celebrities on the Internet to make profits by sharing their lifestyle, experience, and opinions, interacting with fans, and guiding them to shops, brands, goods, and services. Without agents, support teams and media platforms, online marketing strategies, and product selling methods, little can be achieved in the way of marketing.

In addition, content creators require knowledge on the efficacy of social media metrics (e.g., likes, shares, reproductions) that are subject to valuation by marketing agencies or other commercial entities (Gandini, 2016; Hearn & Schoenhoff, 2016). According to Brydges and Sjöholm (2018) content creators can turn their passion into an online business by promoting brands receiving freebies in exchange for shout-outs and mentions and engaging for endorsements and sponsorships.

CONCLUSION

Regarding online platforms used by Maragoli content creators, it was established that most content creators used a cross-platform sharing strategy where they post content on TikTok, Facebook, YouTube, and WhatsApp. Also, most content creators revealed that they targeted the general audience. Some content creators also noted that audiences located their content more easily on TikTok.

Regarding thematic frames, findings indicate an emphasis on Maragoli culture, advice on relationship issues, commentary on topical issues, moral dilemmas and gender roles. Some content creators satirize local governments, dressing, corruption, religion and other social issues like unemployment. However, a majority of the content was about memory, where content creators explore childhood experiences, especially at the hands of insensitive parents. All content creators aim to entertain their audiences.

The paper also sought to investigate the online identities of the Maragoli content creators, and it was established that most content creators branded themselves using pseudonyms on TikTok. They also create their identity through dressing with some adopting cross-dressing strategies. Findings also indicate that content creators employed direct communication styles that included explicit expression of thoughts and ideas and use of strong emotional expressions.

Regarding monetization of online content, only one content creator stated that he was able to monetize content on TikTok. Most content creators however stated that their main source of revenue was from direct donations from well-wishers. Others stated that they would have wished to monetize content on TikTok, but they lacked knowledge on how to do it. Although the main sources of revenue for content creators are donations from well-wishers, advertising and paid sponsorships opportunities are scarce and leave most content creators, who are freelancers, without financial lifelines. This calls into question the sustainability of Maragoli cultural content creation online.

REFERENCES

Abidin C. (2016). Visibility labour: Engaging with influencers' fashion brands and #OOTD advertorial campaigns on Instagram. *Media International Australia,* 161(1), 86–100. https://doi.org/10.1177/1329878X16665177

Abdin, C. (2018). Internet celebrity: Understanding fame online. Emerald Publishing.

Abwunza, J. M. (1991). *Logoli women of western Kenya speak: Needs and means* [Doctoral dissertation, University of Toronto/University of Nairobi].

Akaranga, S. I. (1996). A study of Logooli moral values: With particular reference to taboos, curses and oaths [Doctoral dissertation, University of Nairobi].

Berger, P. L., & Luckmann, T. (1967). *The Social Construction of Reality: A Treatise in the Sociology of Knowledge.* Anchor Books.

Bing, N. (2015). Kenya decides: Kiswahili, social media and politics in Kenya's 2013 general elections. *Journal of African Media Studies, 7*(2), 165–183.

Bloggers Association of Kenya (BAKE) (2015). *The State of blogging and social media in Kenya: 2015 report.* The Bloggers Association of Kenya.

boyd, d. (2014). It's complicated: The social lives of networked teens. Yale University Press.

Bucher, T. (2021). The allure of TikTok: A platform for creating, sharing, and discovering short videos. Information, Communication & Society, 24(2), 156-168.

Craig D. (2019). Creator management in the social media entertainment industry. In Deuze M., Prenger M. (Eds.), Making media: Production, practices, and professions (pp. 363–374). Amsterdam University Press.

Datareportal (2023). Digital 2023: Kenya. https://datareportal.com/reports/digital-2023-kenya

Duffy, B. E. (2017). *(Not) getting paid to do what you love: Gender, social media, and aspirational work.* Yale University Press.

Gandini, A. (2016). Digital work: Self-branding and social capital in the freelance knowledge economy. *Marketing Theory, 16*(1), 123–141. https://doi.org/10.1177/1470593115607942

Goffman, E. (1959). *The Presentation of Self in Everyday Life.* New York: Doubleda

Gruidl, K. M. (2001). The effects of television on the social construction of body images by five and six-year-old girls. https://digitalcommons.unomaha.edu/studentwork/260 such as public opinion. Allen and Waks (1990) examined Hall, M., & Caton, S. (2017). Am I who I say I am? Unobtrusive self-representation and personality recognition on Facebook. *PloS one,* 12(9), e0184417.

Hearn, A. (2010). Structuring feeling: Web 2.0, online ranking and rating, and the digital "reputation" economy. *Ephemera, 10*(3–4), 421–438.

Hearn, A., & Schoenhoff, S. (2016). From celebrity to influencer: Tracing the diffusion of celebrity value across the data stream. In P. D. Marshall & S. Redmond (Eds.), *A companion to celebrity* (pp. 194–212). John Wiley.

Herring, S. C., & Kapidzic, S. (2015). Teens, gender, and self-presentation in social media. *International encyclopedia of social and behavioral sciences,* 2(3), 1-16.

Hess, U., David, S., & Hareli, S. (2016). Emotional restraint is good for men only: The influence of emotional restraint on perceptions of competence. *Emotion (Washington, D.C.),* 16(2), 208–213.

Hogan, B. (2010). The presentation of self in the age of social media: Distinguishing performances and exhibitions online. Bulletin of Science, Technology & Society, 30, 377386. DOI:10.1177/0270467610385893

Hsieh, H. F., & Shannon, S. E. (2005). Three approaches to qualitative content analysis. *Qualitative health research,* 15(9), 1277–1288. https://doi.org/10.1177/1049732305276687

Kabaji, E. S. (2005). The construction of gender through the narrative process of the African folktale: A case study of the Maragoli folktale [Doctoral dissertation, University of South Africa]. https://uir.unisa.ac.za/bitstream/handle/10500/1798/thesis.pdf

Kenya National Bureau of Statistics (2019). 2019 Kenya population and housing census: Volume 1: Population by county and sub county. Retrieved February 2, 2024, from https://housingfinanceafrica.org/app/uploads/VOLUME-I-KPHC-2019.pdf

Leffer, L. (2022). Political disinformation is all over Kenyan TikTok. *Gizmodo.* Retrieved February 2, 2024, from https://gizmodo.com/tiktok-disinformation-kenya-social-media-1849033251

Ligaga, D. (2012). "Virtual expressions": Alternative online spaces and the staging of Kenyan popular cultures. *Research in African Literatures, 43*(4), 1–16. https://doi.org/10.2979/reseafrilite.43.4.1

Marwick, A. E. (2013). Online identity. In J. Hartley, J. Burgess, & A. Bruns (Eds.), *A companion to new media dynamics* (pp. 355–364). Blackwell Publishing. https://doi.org/10.1002/9781118321607.ch23

Marwick, A. E. (2015). Instafame: Luxury selfies in the attention economy. *Public Culture, 27*(1), 137–160. https://doi.org/10.1215/08992363-2798379

Marwick, A. E., & Boyd, D. (2011). I tweet honestly, I tweet passionately: Twitter users, context collapse, and the imagined audience. *New Media & Society,* 13(1), 114-133.

Manovich, L. (2020). Cultural Analytics. The MIT Press

Mukhongo, L. L. (2020). Participatory media cultures: Virality, humour, and online political contestations in Kenya. *Africa Spectrum, 55*(2), 148–169. https://doi.org/10.1177/0002039720957014

Ndavula, J. (2018). *Social Media and Political Campaigns in Kenya: An Examination of the Influence of Digital Networking Technologies on Election Processes.* California: Borderless Press.

Ndaka, F. M. (2022). *Wakurugenzi* networks: Reframing Kenyan vernaculars of gender/gendering in Abel Mutua's YouTube channel. *Eastern African Literary and Cultural Studies, 9*(1), 19–40. https://doi.org/10.1080/23277408.2022.2106609

Ndavula, J. O., & Mueni, J. (2014). New media and political marketing in Kenya: the case of 2013 general elections. *International Journal of Arts and Commerce 3*(6), 69–84.

Nieborg, D. B., & Poell, T. (2018). The platformization of cultural production: Theorizing the contingent cultural commodity. *New Media & Society, 20*(11),. 4275–4292. https://doi.org/10.1177/1461444818769694

Nieborg, D. B., Duffy, B. E., & Poell, T. (2020). Studying platforms and cultural production: Methods, institutions, and practices. *Social Media + Society, 6*(3). https://doi.org/10.1177/2056305120943273

Ogola, G. (2017). *Popular media in Kenyan history: Fiction and newspapers as political actors.* Palgrave Macmillan. https://doi.org/10.1007/978-3-319-49097-7.

Osiakwan, E. M. K. (2017). The KINGS of Africa's digital economy. In: B. Ndemo & T. Weiss (Eds.) *Digital Kenya: An entrepreneurial revolution in the making* (pp. 55–83). Palgrave Macmillan.

Qin, Y., Omar, B., & Musetti, A. (2022). The addiction behavior of short-form video app TikTok: The information quality and system quality perspective. *Frontiers in Psychology, 13,* 932805. https://doi.org/10.3389/fpsyg.2022.932805

Similarweb. (2022). Top apps ranking. Retrieved from https://www.similarweb.com/apps/top/apple/store-rank/ke/all/top-free/iphone/

Statista (2022). Most used social media platforms in Kenya as of Q3 2021. https://www.statista.com/statistics/1229091/most-popular-social-networks-in-kenya/

The Sauce (2022). Kenyans promote exciting cultural diversity on TikTok. Retrieved February 2, 2024, from https://www.capitalfm.co.ke/thesauce/kenyans-promote-exciting-cultural-diversity-on-tiktok/

Treadwell, D., & Davis, M. (2020). *Introducing Communication Research: Paths of Inquiry* (4th ed.). SAGE Publications.

van Dijck, J. (2013). 'You have one identity': Performing the self on Facebook and LinkedIn. *Media, Culture & Society,* 35(2), 199-215. https://doi.org/10.1177/0163443712468605

Vogel, E. A., Rose, J. P., Roberts, L. R., & Eckles, K. (2014). Social Comparison, Social Media, and Self-Esteem. Psychology of Popular Media Culture, 3, 206.
https://doi.org/10.1037/ppm0000047

Willems, W., & Mano, W. (2016). Decolonizing and provincializing audience and internet studies. In: W. Willems & W. Mano (Eds.) *Everyday media culture in Africa: Audiences and users* (pp. 1–21). Routledge.

Xu, K. (2017). What is "internet celebrity economy" in China? Target China: China Marketing Experts. Retrieved February 2, 2024, from https://targetchina.com.au/article/internet-celebrity/

Yang, S., Zhao, Y., & Ma, Y. (2019). Analysis of the reasons and development of short video application – Taking TikTok as an example. 2019 9th International Conference on Information and Social Science (ICISS 2019), 340–343.

Yékú, J. (2022). Cultural netizenship: Social media, popular culture, and performance in Nigeria. Indiana University Press.

Zhang, P. (2020). The interaction between internet celebrities and their audience through social media platforms – A case study on a Chinese food blogger. *Advances in Social Science, Education and Humanities Research*, *451*, 637–641.

Zhu, C., Xu, X., Zhang, W., Chen, J., & Evans, R. (2019). How health communication via TikTok makes a difference: A content analysis of TikTok accounts run by Chinese provincial health committees. *International Journal of Environmental Research and Public Health*, *17*, 192–205.

CHAPTER THREE

Content Creation and TikTok Influencers in Namibia

JOHANNES TUKONDJENI

INTRODUCTION

TikTok has emerged as one of the most popular social media apps across the world (Ohalete, 2023). It is believed to have over one billion monthly active users. This makes the app the biggest competitor of WhatsApp, which is owned by Meta. The growth of TikTok in Africa coincided with the arrival of the devastating COVID-19 pandemic. The app has taken the Namibian social market by storm. Unlike traditional social media platforms such as Facebook, Twitter, Instagram, and YouTube, short-form videos provide fun and easy-to-eat content (Cervantes, 2022). Known as Douyin in its home market, TikTok was launched in China in September 2016. It soon began gaining momentum in China. The parent company, ByteDance, launched an international version of TikTok in 2017. TikTok originally started as a short-form video-sharing platform, primarily for lip-syncing and dance videos, however, it has since evolved into a full-fledged video service with content accessible to all types of audiences (Iqbal, 2022). Although it is immensely popular with children and teenagers, it has also witnessed growth amongst the youth and older people in Africa. Compared to traditional social media platforms, TikTok offers new unique and interesting ways to interact with other users (Ohalete, 2023). It was around 2020 that this application began to infiltrate the Namibian market. Its growth was incited and accelerated by the lockdowns and remote working arrangements that accompanied the COVID-19 pandemic. With most people spending most of their time online, TikTok became the social media of choice amongst children and teenagers. Ever since the pandemic, the popularity of the app has grown in leaps and bounds in Namibia.

With an array of celebrities quickly joining the platform, the app became a source of attraction for teenagers and young adults worldwide.

TikTok can be described as a platform where users can make videos of about 15 seconds. These videos then run in a loop until you choose to move to the next video. It is also possible to merge video clips which then allows for 60-second clips. Videos can incorporate music samples, filters, quick cuts, stickers, and other add-ons. DSouza (2022), argues that TikTok has become a popular social networking app that allows users to create, view, and download videos captured on mobile devices or webcams. With its personalized feeds of original short video streams with music and sound effects, this app stands out for its addictive quality and high level of interactivity. Furthermore, DSouza (2022) notes that amateur and professional creators can add effects like filters, soundtracks, and stickers to their videos, and can collaborate on content and create split-screen duets regardless of locations. Evidently, the app can be used for a diverse range of purposes.

Although there are many emerging studies on how TikTok is used by children, teenagers and social media influencers in China, Indonesia, Philippines, Malaysia, and South Korea, very few studies have been published in Africa on the subject. Focusing on young social media influencers in Namibia, this study seeks to examine the motivations behind the creation of TikTok profiles by social media influencers. It will examine the types of social media influencers that have emerged on TikTok in Namibia. It will also investigate the content that is produced by these influencers and its reach amongst the audiences. Finally, the chapter will explore the monetization strategies that are being employed by social media influencers in Namibia. The next section presents literature review on the use of TikTok by social media influencers across the world. It will also articulate how social media influencers in Africa are using the app.

SOCIAL MEDIA USE IN AFRICA AND BEYOND

The growth of TikTok and its impact on other social media services present boundless opportunities for brands to share their products through influencers (Peterson, 2022). TikTok influencer marketing campaigns often include creating challenges where users are encouraged to create their videos based on a certain topic, audio clip, or dance. By creating a challenge around a particular product, brands can start their campaign with influencer marketing and then grow it among other users (Aguiar, 2022). The app has fueled the rise of "content houses" or "collab houses" where groups of young social media influencers are housed together in mansions to create an impressive backdrop for their branded viral content (Battisby, 2022). Influencers have become popular on TikTok due to their ability to quickly and easily build trust with their followers. This is why TikTok influencer marketing is a great investment as it allows influencers to introduce brand to their followers, making them more likely to trust them, want to follow them, and learn more about their product (Aguiar, 2022). Global brands such as Nike, Skittles, Fenty Beauty, Pepsi, Calvin Klein, Sony, and FIFA have recognized the importance of TikTok as a key technique to engage with young audiences, encourage user-generated content, and partner with relevant influencers (Battisby, 2022). A TikTok influencer marketing strategy can get a brand and product in front of a large new audience and potential customers. By strategically selecting an influencer partner, a brand can ensure that the right people from their target market will see the video (Aguiar, 2022).

Influencers are finding TikTok to be a terrific platform to develop their devoted following and engage with new people as the app's algorithm can place their content in front of consumers with similar interests (Peterson, 2022). TikTok allows users to plug their other social media accounts as links in the bio part, making the growth reciprocal. TikTok influencers can boost their following on YouTube, Instagram, Twitter, and other platforms in this manner (Peterson, 2022).

TikTok is available in 154 countries and has the highest penetration in Asia, with over one third of users in Asia aged 16–64 having an account. The rest of the world has relatively low penetration, with 12 percent in North America and 10 percent in Latin America and Europe respectively (Battisby, 2022). With 3 billion downloads (including 672 million downloads in 2022 alone) and 50 million daily active users, TikTok has had great impact in the app world since its launch in 2016 going to win over the hearts, minds, and screens of social media users (McLachlan, 2023). In addition to this, Insider Intelligence (2023) predicts that TikTok will have 834.3 million monthly users worldwide in 2023. As one of the Big Five global social networks (Facebook, Instagram, TikTok, Snapchat, and Twitter), it is currently the third largest. Ruby (2023) presents that as of 2023, TikTok is one of the most widely used social media networks, with 1.05 billion active members spread over 154 nations.

Also worth noting is that TikTok is currently the sixth most popular social media network worldwide (McLachlan, 2023). Moreover, TikTok, which is accessible in 150+ markets and 35+ languages, is the most downloaded app in more than 40 countries. Despite being the most downloaded app on the Apple App Store, TikTok was the second-most downloaded app overall in 2022, trailing only Instagram.

People across Africa are increasingly adopting social media as mobile internet coverage expands and smartphones drop in price (Ovuorie, 2022). Galal (2022) claims that African social media users have been steadily increasing reaching 384 million as of 2022. In comparison to other regions, northern and northern Africa have more people using social media. Research conducted by Meltwater (2023) indicates that, although Facebook continues to be the most popular social media network for businesses, the use of TikTok is growing quickly, having increased from 16% to 30% in 2021. Furthermore, 47% of respondents said they intended to use TikTok in 2023. When solely examining respondents from Africa, this percentage stayed constant at 46.98%. Facebook is the leading social media platform in Africa in terms of market share (Statista, 2022). However, Meltwater (2023) reasons that marketers need to think about which channels are appropriate for their marketing mix because every channel is expanding. Video content is still one of the biggest trends in 2023, and TikTok is the app that everyone is talking about.

THE STATE OF SOCIAL MEDIA USE IN NAMIBIA

Now that cellphones are more widely available in Namibia, more and more people can use social networking sites like Facebook, LinkedIn, Tumblr, Instagram, Twitter, WhatsApp, and a host of others. Young people that wish to be heard for their alternative viewpoints make up many those using these sites (Sam, 2019). Starting with Facebook, according to information found in Meta's advertising resources, at the beginning of 2023, Facebook had 578 thousand users in Namibia (Kemp, 2023). An investigating by the researcher revealed that Dellish Matthews, a local socialite and former Big Brother Africa Winner with more than 429 thousand followers is one of the biggest Namibian influencers on Facebook. She is followed by Dr. Job Amupanda who has 221 thousand followers. Dr Amupanda is an academician, former Mayor of Windhoek and a well-established social justice activist. At the same time, these influencers command the same respect on Instagram, with Dellish having 780 thousand followers and Dr. Amupanda having 164 thousand followers, respectively.

Statistics from Meta's advertising tools indicate that in early 2023 Instagram had 317.4 thousand users in Namibia. However, Instagram only allows users who are 13 years and older to access its platform, thus it's useful to know that in Namibia, 18.1% of the "eligible" audience, utilizes Instagram in 2023 (Kemp, 2023). Meanwhile figures published on LinkedIn indicate that in early 2023, the site had 310.0 thousand "members" in Namibia (Kemp, 2023).

Also, statistics found in Twitter's advertising resources revealed that at the beginning of 2023 Namibia had 94.4 thousand Twitter users. Given that Twitter only allows users who are 13 years and older to utilize its platform, these numbers indicate that in Namibia 5.4% of the "eligible" population were using Twitter in 2023 (Kemp, 2023). All in all, statistics by Kemp (2023) divulge that at the beginning of 2023, Namibia had 2.81 million active mobile connections, according to data from GSMA Intelligence.

However, it is essential to keep in mind that many individuals own more than one mobile phone;, one for personal use and another for business. Therefore, it is common for mobile devices to significantly outnumber the people. After all, has been said and done, Namibia's population is still at its infant stage just with a population of 2,653,657 as of December 2022 (Worldometer, 2022). Even though there are no detailed reports and statistics yet about TikTok users in Namibia, it is recorded that by 2022 there were 857.2 thousand social media users in the Land of the Brave (Kemp, 2022). Kemp (2023) also stated that at the beginning of 2023, when internet penetration was at 53.0 percent, there were 1.37 million users in Namibia. Moreover, in January 2023, there were 729.2 thousand social media users in Namibia which equals to 28.2 percent of the Namibian population. Kemp (2023) also maintains that in early 2023, there were 2.81 million active mobile phone connections in Namibia, which represents 108.7% of the country's population.

Since the introduction of TikTok, Namibians have registered a significant presence on the widely popular short video platform. Its popularity in Namibia coincided with the COVID-19 lockdowns prompting those working from home and those with nothing to do to flock to the app to produce, distribute and consume content. In the Namibian context, these TikTok influencers are not famous in physical spaces, but they have lionized their names on this platform. Individuals and corporate entities are utilizing these creators to add credibility and to promote their brands, products, and services. Agreeing with these sentiments, DSouza (2022) argues that marketing on TikTok is still maturing, but a growing number of agencies are eager to help brands create the kind of quirky content that gets clicks on TikTok.

THEORETICAL FRAMEWORK

This research employs Technological Appropriation Theory. The Technological Appropriation Theory describes the process by which users and groups adopt, adapt, and integrate technology into their lives, practices, and work routines (Gonzalez et al., 2009). It refers to the effort users make to make sense of the technology within their context (Janneck, 2009). After being introduced to the end-user, the intended use and meaning of a technology is sometimes altered by the user (Beenkens & Verburg, 2008).

The circumstances surrounding a technology's introduction into a use context, or recontextualization, are essential for a successful technology use (Janneck,

2009). Even if carefully introduced, the original situation is sometimes adapted. Regarding adaptation, appropriation has an accent on the fact that the user adjusts the technology for his own best practice, while adaptation relates to the fact that the use sometimes changes in general (Beenkens and Verburg, 2008). Users that utilize a technical artifact actively participate in the process by "appropriating" it, which means they investigate a new technology and decide how to incorporate it or not into their practices and work routines (Janneck, 2009).

METHODOLOGICAL APPROACH

The study adopted virtual ethnography which is a qualitative research methodology that adapts principles of traditional ethnographic research to study cultural manifestations of online groups (Floorschreurs, 2013). Virtual ethnography is a new form of ethnography, which was created in response to the need for studies of electronic communities provided by networks. Online or virtual ethnography means conducting ethnographic research on the Internet. It usually examines interactions on the Internet and in the online community (Kucharski & Torres, 2012). Caulfield (2023) contends that the main advantage of ethnography is that it gives the researcher direct access to the culture and practices of a group. It is a useful approach for learning first-hand about the behavior and interactions of people within a particular context. Caulfield (2023) also states that by becoming immersed in a social environment, the researcher may have access to more authentic information and spontaneously observe dynamics that they could not have found out about simply by asking.

In total, 31 TikTok channels were analyzed by the researcher over the period of three months, from September to November 2022. All the TikTok accounts selected had more than 20 000 followers and they were deemed to be influencers considering the number of followers they have. The researcher also looked at the number of engagements, likes, comments, number of shares, duets, and number of favorites. Age and gender were not a determining factor or a selection criterion. To collect the primary data the 31 content creators were asked to participate in either a telephonic or face-to-face interviews or complete a questionnaire. Of the 31 content creators identified, 11 agreed to participate in the study, while 20 did not indicate whether they were interested or not. In the end, only 4 participants responded to the questionnaire. 2 participants responded via WhatsApp message while 1 participated by filling out the questionnaire and 1 participant was interviewed over the telephone. In the survey, they were asked to answer a series of questions to talk about their overall involvement on social media, particularly on TikTok. They were asked to speak about the type of content they create and how they were using the platform to generate income. Ethical considerations were considered during this study. The participants were informed beforehand that they were free to decline being interviewed or fill out the questionnaire if they were not comfortable with the objectives of the study. In addition, the participants were assured of anonymity and confidentiality in the study. The section below focuses on content creation and the emergence of social media influencers on TikTok in Namibia. It maps out the identities of these influencers, thematic areas of their content, the reach and engagement on their short videos and their monetization strategies.

TYPES OF INFLUENCERS ON NAMIBIAN TIKTOK

This study found that TikTok has developed an entertainment home theatre for young people across the world. Namibian content producers on this app entertain each other through comedy, storytelling, dancing, and performance of spiritual hymns. Most of the creatives use lip syncing to sing along to a certain song or dance to the music. They have their own creative ways of creating stories that are funny or relatable to real life situations. There are also motivational speakers on the Namibian TikTok who create content aimed at inspiring others and giving hope to those feeling hopeless. These motivational TikTok influencers focus on inspiring the youth by addressing social issues such as unemployment, corruption, and gender-based violence, which are high in Namibia. These creatives believe that life should not just be judged based on one event but rather should be viewed from different perspectives. Some of the motivational influencers maintain that people should always think positively to yield positive results in their lives. They share stories, scenarios, and testimonies based on their own life experiences and how they overcame such difficulties.

The researcher also observed that there are also Namibian influencers on TikTok who relationship coaches are also. These creatives believe that relationships are the foundation of families, which gives birth to communities and communities birth a nation. Their argument is that unhealthy relationships make for an unhealth communities and ultimately end in a broken world. Thus, relationship coaches create content that focuses on teaching Namibians how they can take care of each other in relationships and learn how to demonstrate love to each other instead of the superficial "I love you". By doing this, they can have healthy, loving and thriving relationships. They advise individuals and couples on how to solve conflicts in their relationships by using effective communication skills. These influencers like@foibeblessygeorge, and @kukugwakapulwa are sometimes seen on vacation with their partners or on a date talking about how to renew their love, deepen intimacy and increase pleasure in their relationships on TikTok. Furthermore, they provide advice on financial matters within a relationship and parental advice on how to raise their children in way healthy way, so they subsequently become good citizens.

There are also religious TikTok influencers in Namibia like @pst_show_shakalunga and @andrewtegakakunde. Their purpose is to share their interests and things that resonate with them with the rest of the world. Particularly, these TikTok users are known for creating Christian-based messages. They share messages on how to be a good Christian and how to connect with the Creator through prayers and worship. Their content focuses on encouraging their followers to refuse defeat and to rise above life's challenges. Moreover, they also preach the message of gaining life after death through salvation.

Tidy and Galer (2020) argue that TikTok's rapid growth has put the app at the forefront of the minds of politicians as well. Recently, in Namibia, political parties like the South West Africa People's Organisation (SWAPO), Popular Democratic Movement (PDM), Independent Patriot of Change (IPC) and Landless Peoples Movement (LPM) have registered their presence on the app. Young individual politicians such as @vwmuvale have also created accounts on the app with the hope of mobilizing voters to support them during elections. This has given a green light to Namibians to use TikTok to contact their parties and politicians. The app has provided an avenue for citizens to speak the truth to power. These individuals initiate meaningful dialogues advocating for social and political change. They also criticize the ruling party (SWAPO) for failing to deliver services they promised to the people during the liberation struggle. At the same time, political influencers use the platform to criticize opposition leaders for not being effective in their office and for refusing to use their voices as law makers. These individuals have become political influencers, and they are using the platform to influence public opinion.

There are also human rights influencers in Namibia that use their accounts to advocate for freedom and justice for all. Influencers like @abisaihango, @talahgacosta and @omuyapuki1 are of the view that all citizens should be allowed to exercise their constitutional rights. They speak about what they consider to be important issues in the country such as gender-based violence, lesbian, gay, bisexual, transgender, queer or questioning (LGBTQ+), same-sex marriage, and abortion. Human rights influencers believe that there is no freedom if there is no equality. This observation is in line with Tidy and Galer's (2020) argument that TikTok is one of the first platforms that many young people will use to share social activism content.

The researcher observed the growth of what he calls Namibian 'cultural influencers' on TikTok. These are influencers who promote the country's cultural heritage. Some of them use the app to promote traditional products. This group of cultural content creators seek to educate Namibians about their cultural heritage as well as encouraging them to preserve their values, languages, and traditional beliefs. Cultural influencers like, @ginasamuels3, @gaptaxil and @malakiahaimbangu are all from the Ovawambo tribe. While @kashivi_20, is a multilingual but originally from the Okavango speaking people, but all in all, these influencers generate content narrating the history of their tribes. They, for example, explain why certain rituals are performed, the significance of gender roles and division of labor, the importance of arranged marriages and traditional food preparation skills.

COVID-19 AND THE RISE OF TIKTOK INFLUENCERS

TikTok has brought together many communities of people based on their interests, social identities and type of content they enjoy. (Tidy and Galer, 2020). TikTok format is suitable for entertainment and comedy. However, it is increasingly used for infotainment as well. So-called influencers gain a steady following on TikTok by offering tips and tricks as well as by promoting themselves. Beauty, fashion, personal finance, and cooking are all popular topics for informative videos. This format is increasingly used to promote and sell products (DSouza, 2022). Over time, the concept of fame has evolved to include new forms of fame created with each new technology. In today's increasingly digital world, we are witnessing an explosive growth of new idols of this generation who are popular on social media and are best known as social media influencers (Gómez, 2019). Social media influencers (SMIs) represent a new group of independent third-party advocates who shape public attitudes through blogging, tweeting, and using other social media platforms such TikTok (Freberg et al., 2011). As of 2022, TikTok has been downloaded over 3 billion times. As the platform grows, it is evolving and capturing the interest of both brands and celebrities (Midson-Short, 2022).

Considering what happened, It gives the impression that the pandemic created an opportunity for the popularization of TikTok in Namibia. The story of Matilde (@matildekulo), who is in the media and film industry and one of the participants in this study, demonstrates that joining TikTok was her coping mechanisms during COVID-19. It was a way of escaping the stories of hopelessness the pandemic brought, and limited social interaction brought by the lockdowns throughout Namibia. In an interview, Matilde said her journey on TikTok started immediately after the first COVID-19 case was reported. She said that at that time she had a lot of government activities she was filming. She found herself panicking and overwhelmed by the death cases due to the deadly virus. She said:

> "I then choose to keep myself busy" (Matilde, 24 November 2022, WhatsApp message).

Likewise, Tilda Uutsi (@tildauutsi1) joined the popular platform during that same period of the pandemic. Her story is quite different and emotional as she experienced personal trauma associated with the pandemic. It was during the process of overcoming this trauma that she decided to create an account on TikTok. She narrated it as follows:

> As much as work can be overwhelming, when you are home alone, you feel lonely and TikTok can keep you busy. Therefore, I was consoled just by watching other people's videos and creating my own contents helped me to overcome whatever I was going through (Tilda, 22 November 2022, Telephonic Interview).

Kulah (@kulah_mathews) one of the Namibian TikTok content creators said she joined the platform at the beginning of 2020 just shortly after the COVID-19 outbreak. She narrated that at the time she joined TikTok, she had a full-time job and sometimes found herself working shifts to minimize the spread of COVID-19 in the workplace.

> These were some of the measures our organization took to help keep the nation safe and the entire staff by adopting the 'work from home' new normal (Kulah, 15 November 2022, WhatsApp message).

Kulah added that during that period she was also a second-year student at NUST where face-to-face classes were discontinued to adapt remote teaching and learning. It was during this period that Kulah found herself spending a lot of time indoors and sometimes with nothing to do. Soon after, she accidentally discovered her peers creating content on TikTok and she observed that they were having so much fun. Consequently, she created an account on the app and started creating content which featured some famous politicians.

> People loved the very first video I did lip-syncing the governor of a specific region, and it went viral. I was trending on all social media platforms including Instagram. I had a lot of time on my hands that I could utilize to entertain the nation, even though we were losing so many people to the deadly virus, again, we needed to look at life from both sides of the coin and that's what motivated me to join (Kulah, 15 November 2022, WhatsApp message).

It should not be generalized that most Namibians joined TikTok at the height of the pandemic. However, it was during the pandemic that there was a significant increase in TikTok users in Namibia. A case in point is of Katrina Jacob (@cath_jac) who had the desire to join the platform back in 2019 while pursuing her studies in The Peoples Republic of China. Nevertheless, she could not join due to social media policies in that country. She believes that it would have given her a great advantage to create a TikTok account while in a foreign nation because she would easily reach a lot of Namibians in that country and the algorithm could also push it back to Namibia at the same time. But that did not work out. It was only when she returned home that she created her first TikTok account in November 2020. In her own words she said:

> I made a few gospel videos and two of them went viral, as far as South Africa, Kenya, Uganda, Nigeria, Zambia, Botswana, and Zimbabwe. The two videos that went viral were both created in the same day, and clocked about 305 400 views, with over 7000 shares, about 95628 likes, lots of comments and favorites. This is when I realized, there's potential in the niche I chose (Cathy, 14 November 2022, Questionnaire).

WHAT DOES IT TAKE TO BE A CONTENT CREATOR ON TIKTOK?

A social media content creator is a person responsible for creating and uploading content on social media platforms. They may create this content for fun, or they may have a job as a professional content creator, also known as an influencer (Gogoleva, 2021). Working as a content creator requires charisma, creativity, an understanding of what people care about, and being comfortable in front of the camera. Also, this job requires a lot of effort, time, and dedication (Woodcock, 2022). @kulah_mathews, a communication graduate from the Namibia University of Science and Technology (NUST) who doubles as a part-time TikTok content creator indicated that it takes a lot of work to make TikTok videos. Contrary to popular belief, content creation is not simply a matter of picking up a camera and then recording. Before recording, the creator needs to decide why they are creating that video and the potential effect on the viewers. This is what she had to say:

> I sometimes script my content and look for venues to record as well as outfits. That's how much effort I put into what I would like to share with the public because some videos I get over 300 thousand views and that itself is evident that the level of engagement on TikTok is quite high (Kulah, 15 November 2022, WhatsApp message).

Woodcock (2022) noted that content creators play a large and important role in the world of social media. Their work is stressful and requires a lot of time and effort, as well as wisdom and commitment. Chang (2024) argues that creating scroll stopping content that drives unicorn social media engagement through views, follows, likes, comments, shares, and saves is easier said than done. As Tidy and Galer (2020) write, TikTok users can choose from a huge database of songs, filters and movie clips to lip sync too. Interviews and observations showed that Namibian content creators use lip synchronization to ensure their contents stands out, creates buzz, engages, and delivers. For instance, @cath_jac, a com poser and performer of spiritual hymns, said that she uses lip syncing for gospel songs. This is because she grew up doing choir performances and rehearsals. The app allows her to do renditions of her favorite songs and choruses from other choirs. She explained it in the following words:

> Naturally, I love singing, I have been singing in church choirs since my childhood. I believe there are so many wonderful ways to praise and worship but my favorite way to express my love for the Lord is through singing and loving others, especially vulnerable children and old people. Singing for me is hopeful sound, and many times a joyful noise that can transform someone's life (Cathy, 14 November 2022, Questionnaire).
>
> In any case, choosing the right niche is just the first step. Next, one must create quality content daily tailored to his or her audience. If you cannot keep up with quality content daily, you might struggle to grow your social media account, TikTok channel. Moreover, different content creators produce content that speaks to their target audience and for that, it increases the engagement algorithm. This can be observed by the number of likes, shares, duet that a certain video gets or how the public engages with the creator in the comment section (Matilde, 24 November 2022, WhatsApp Message).

TikTok also allows content creators to self-study and improve their content by seeing which content gets the most views and comments on the platform. By doing this, content creators can decide which areas to focus on instead of investing resources into content ideas that are not effective and do not bring positive results. Routh (2021) argues that the biggest draw of TikTok is its ability to post about anything. Whether it be humor, hobbies, fitness, travel, music, photography, dance; each category is open and attracts a lot of attention. Each area provides visibility to people who can adapt their content into a short video template.

ENGAGEMENT LEVEL WITH THE PUBLIC

Generally, popular content creators on TikTok get millions of views. These views are corroborated with more engagement as the creative can choose to be more personal with their audiences. A good content creator should be able to create content that will be shared multiple times and get a significant reach (Woodcock, 2022). This is indeed the case in the Namibian context. As observed, the level of engagement on most TikTok accounts in Namibia was relatively high. Most accounts received a lot of views, likes, shares, downloads, favorites, and endless comments. Most content creators used the comment section to provide feedback to their audiences. The influencers responded or engaged with the public through writing or responding with a video as TikTok gives them that freedom. In addition, most Namibian TikTok influencers collaborated with other influencers in some videos to help each other to grow on the platform. In addition, some influencers hosted live videos where they engaged with their followers, either by hosting a question-and-answer session, a debate or simply talking about a subject that may be trending or relevant at that time. Some of the issues that were discussed include poverty, gender-based violence (GBV), divorce, and unemployment. In this case, Namibian TikTok influencers are playing a major role by giving people hope via comedy, hymns, motivation, dancing and other uplifting content. It is evident that influencers can make their followers forget about challenges they are facing through symbolic interactionism. The comments sections of these influencers speak volume about the reach and impact of their content on TikTok. Below are some of the comments by the audiences of social media influencers in Namibia:

> "You have made my day."
> "I watched this video for more than three times,"
> "I just needed to hear this,"
> "You gained a follower,"
> "You are my favorite TikToker,"
> "I will share this with my colleagues,"
> "We need more people like you in our nation."
> "Thank you for sharing this, you saved my life as I was about to give up" … etc.

These comments prove that TikTok is not merely an app to watch people lip-syncing and dancing, but it is an important platform that allows and facilitates the discourse of certain subjects.

Although most Namibian TikTok influencers are not famous in the real world (physical spaces), they are well-known on the app. The comment sections of their accounts show that some of the influencers are slowly becoming celebrities in the digital space. Their followers sometimes comment on how they finally met their favorite content creators at random places like at the shopping mall, place of worship, or in the bank. In fact, there are influencers who have communicated that their followers are free to request a photo or feature in their video whenever or wherever they meet them. @kulah_mathews indicated that content creation on TikTok has helped her to gain popularity to a certain extent. Although she does not regard herself as 'popular,' she observed that she is now recognizable. Kula said that:

> I am easy to spot out in a crowd, that 'oh it is that lady from TikTok, oh it is the lady that told so and so story'. The feedback is quite good though; however, it can be overwhelming when people stare at you and do not say a word. You start asking yourself if there is something wrong with you or you are not properly dressed. It only kicks in later that people could be staring because they must have seen your latest release (Kulah, 15 November 2022, WhatsApp message).

Meanwhile, @cath_jac admits that TikTok has increased her feeling of community and a sense of connection with her followers. She explained that this is important for people who might be geographically and socially isolated. She summarized these sentiments as follows:

> At church, a lot of people will be smiling and pointing at me. Also in the community, by the markets or in town, some people will greet you and say, 'we just see you on TikTok, we follow you and we love or admire you'. 'Nice to meet you in person'. But some people will just stare at you and smile or greet you by your name and pass. Then you know, it must be TikTok (Cathy, 14 November 2022, Questionnaire).

MONETIZATION OF CONTENT AND ALGORITHMIC LITERACY AMONG NAMIBIA CREATIVES

TikTok users have limited ways to monetize their popularity through the app. Since the view count is extremely high, most users will ask their audience to visit their other platforms or websites to monetize (Midson-Short, 2022). TikTok creators can share their Instagram and YouTube links in their profile, which makes it easier to have people follow the influencer on different platforms. Most Namibian TikTok influencers have linked their Instagram accounts to their TikTok's account where they promote products and services for a certain fee as their side hustle. Tilda Uutsi (@tildauutsi1), who has more than 100 thousand followers on Instagram has linked her Instagram account to her TikTok has seen both paid and unpaid influencer campaigns, so brands should use a tracker tool to identify relevant influencers (Battisby, 2022).

TikTok channel. She loads her Instagram stories with posters and promotion daily. She said that she is generating a decent income from her content creation. In the case of Tilda, she gets income through advertising and marketing of goods and services on behalf of her clients. This kind of influencer marketing has been gaining popularity in Africa. Likewise, @kulah_mathews noted that:

> I have been approached by small business owners to collaborate with them. Seeing that I am a micro influencer on Instagram, I work with small businesses and expose them to their intended audience. Some pay me monetary, and others give me goods to advertise for them for free. This is a win-win situation for me especially if I advertise someone's business and they make a sell or increase sales, that makes me fulfilled that I am doing something right (Kulah, 15 November 2022, WhatsApp message).

Some influencers are still searching for social media compensation plans, which are still a dream in most African countries, including Namibia. Unless one must use a Virtual Private Network (VPN). Midson-Short (2022) argues that one might think of TikTok for business is similar to using Instagram Stories, however, they are not meant to push for sales but rather to show the personality of the business. Evidently, Namibian TikTok influencers have grabbed the opportunity to advertise their businesses and those of others on their TikTok channels. Some influencers do commercial breaks of at least 30 seconds on their video contents while others may share business posters with an advertisement voiceover in the background. These videos might be one minute long or more. Since these Namibian TikTok influencers such as @foibeblessygeorge and @ndillypombili2808 are gaining popularity, they are being hired as Masters of Ceremonies (MC) or brand ambassadors of certain corporates. Some create their content and tweak their account to fit certain brands and services to increase their chances of being hired by those brands. Midson-Short (2022) maintains that the main goal for TikTok influencers is to gain enough traction and followers to partner with brands and other media outlets. In the Namibian context this study found that most TikTok influencers, like, @ndillypombili2808, @ndinah1, @popo999, @i.am.heinrich and @honorable_m_shuudeni often wear promotional items like t-shirts and caps of certain corporates while recording their content. Others even appear on video testimonials urging their audiences or followers to subscribe to a brand's channel.

It was also observed during this research that some TikTok influencers in Namibia include hashtags in their content captions to encourage users to use that specific hashtag. Whether these influencers use are actually users of the product or service they recommend is up to them. But one thing is certain, as they promote a brand's message that gets them paid. As the TikTok app matures, its ability to provide advertising and promotion opportunities will likely become an even more important part of how businesses market online (Midson-Short, 2022).

CONCLUSION

Digital media is the future. Social media has become heavily incorporated in our daily lives, shaping how we live, communicate, and even consume products and information. One can go online today and get immediate updates of the latest news, from climate change to entertainment. Having established that TikTok is one of the largest and most influential apps today, people should use this platform to network and market with the world at large. Becoming more conscious about how social media is generally used, and TikTok in particular, and the impact that it has on people's daily lives can motivate subscribers to use this powerful tool more effectively. TikTok is building communities and bringing people from all over the world closer together. Like any other individual in a democratic society like Namibia, social media or TikTok influencers have their personal opinions and beliefs, depending on what they have been exposed to or what they have experienced. Therefore, it is important to note that you might not always agree or resonate with their sentiments.

REFERENCES

Aguiar, R. (2022). *3 reasons why TikTok is pivotal for influencer marketing*. Pixlee TurnTo Blog. Retrieved April 9, 2023, from https://www.pixlee.com/blog/3-reasons-why-tiktok-is-pivotal-for-influencer-marketing

Battisby, A. (2022). *An in-depth look at marketing on TikTok*. Digital Marketing Institute. Retrieved April 9, 2023, from https://digitalmarketinginstitute.com/blog/an-in-depth-look-at-marketing-on-tiktok

Beenkens, F. H. C., & Verburg, R. M. (2008). Extending tam to measure the adoption of e-collaboration in Healthcare Arenas. *Encyclopedia of e-collaboration* (pp. 265–271). https://doi.org/10.4018/978-1-59904-000-4.ch041.

Caulfield, J. (2023). *What is ethnography?: Definition, guide & examples, Scribbr*. Retrieved April 9, 2023, from https://www.scribbr.com/methodology/ethnography/

Cervantes, E. (2022). TikTok: When was it created and who owns it? [online] Android Authority. Retrieved April 9, 2023, from https://www.androidauthority.com/who-owns-tiktok-3176134/

Chang, S. (2024). 12 must-have tools every social media content creator needs to drive engagement in 2024. *Customers.ai*. https://customers.ai/blog/social-media-content-creator.

D'Souza, D. (2022). *What Is TikTok?* Investopedia. Retrieved April 9, 2023, from https://www.investopedia.com/what-is-tiktok-4588933.

Floorschreurs. (2013). *What is virtual ethnography? Netnographies*. Retrieved April 9, 2023, from https://netnographies.wordpress.com/2013/11/02/what-is-virtual-ethnography/

Freberg, K., Graham, K., McGaughey, K., & Freberg, L. A. (2011). Who are the social media influencers? A study of public perceptions of personality. *Public Relations Review*, *37*(1), 90–92.

Galal. (2022). *Topic: Social media in Africa*. Retrieved April 9, 2023, from https://www.statista.com/topics/9922/social-media-in-africa/

Gogoleva, D. (2021). *Social media content creator: The best tools to use for creating content & habits of successful creators*. insense.pro. Retrieved April 9, 2023, from https://insense.pro/blog/social-media-content-creator-the-best-tools-to-use

Gómez, A. R. (2019). Digital fame and fortune in the age of social media: A classification of social media influencers. *aDResearch: Revista Internacional de Investigación en Comunicación 19*, 8–29. Retrieved April 9, 2023, from https://dialnet.unirioja.es/servlet/articulo?codigo=6785540

Gonzalez, V. M., Kraemer, K, L., & Castro, L. A. (2009). "Beyond safety concerns," *Handbook of research on urban informatics*, 131–143. Retrieved April 9, 2023, from https://doi.org/10.4018/978-1-60566-152-0.ch009

Insider Intelligence (2023). TikTok users worldwide (2020–2025). *Insider Intelligence*. Retrieved April 16, 2023, from https://www.insiderintelligence.com/charts/global-tiktok-user-stats/

Iqbal, M. (2022). TikTok revenue and usage statistics (2021). *Business of Apps*. Retrieved April 16, 2023, from https://www.businessofapps.com/data/tik-tok-statistics/

Janneck, M. (2009) Recontextualising technology in appropriation processes. *Handbook of research on socio-technical design and social networking systems* (pp. 153–166). https://doi.org/10.4018/978-1-60566-264-0.ch011

Kemp, S. (2022). Digital 2022: Namibia. *DataReportal – Global Digital Insights*. Retrieved December 16, 2022, from https://datareportal.com/reports/digital-2022namibia#:~:text=Social%20media%20statistics%20for%20Namibia%20in%202022&text=The%20number%20of%20social%20media

Kemp, S. (2023). Digital 2023: Namibia. *DataReportal – Global Digital Insights*. Retrieved April 16, 2023, from https://doi.org/10.4018/978-1-60960-762-3.ch005

Kucharski, M. V., & Torres, P. L. (2012). Educational research in virtual learning environments. In *Handbook of Research on Practices and Outcomes in Virtual Worlds and Environments* (pp. 75–96). https://doi.org/10.4018/978-1-60960-762-3.ch005

McLachlan, S. (2023). 50+ important TikTok stats marketers need to know in 2023. *Hootsuite*. Retrieved April 16, 2023, from https://blog.hootsuite.com/tiktok-stats/

Midson-Short, D. (2022). *What is Tik Tok used for, and why is it so popular? Brandastic*. Retrieved April 16, 2023, from https://brandastic.com/blog/what-is-tiktok-and-why-is-it-so-popular/

Ohalete, S. G. C. (2023, August). Rise in social media usage among Africa's young people raises concern. *Vatican News*. https://www.vaticannews.va/en/africa/news/2023-08/rise-in-social-media-usage-among-africa-s-young-people-raises-co.html.

Ovuorie, T. (2022). *Increased social media use puts African leaders on edge*. Retrieved April 9, 2022, from https://corporate.dw.com/en/increased-social-media-use-puts-african-leaders-on-edge/a-61303854

Peterson, A G. (2022). *How TikTok is effectively being used by influencers, Quotient*. Retrieved April 9, 2023, from https://www.quotient.com/blog/how-influencers-use-tiktok/#:~:text=Influencers%20are%20finding%20TikTok%20to,links%20in%20the%20bio%20section

Routh, E. (2021). The history of TikTok. *The Prospectus*. Retrieved April 13, 2023, from https://www.prospectusnews.com/2021/10/20/the-history-of-tiktok/

Ruby, D. (2023). *TikTok statistics 2023 – (users, revenue and trends), Demand Sage*. Retrieved April 9, 2022, from https://www.demandsage.com/tiktok-user-statistics/

Sam, T. (2019). *Social media and its impact on communication*. Retrieved April 9, 2023, from https://www.namibian.com.na/social-media-and-its-impact-on-communication-2/

Statista. (2022). *Topic: Social media in Africa*. Retrieved April 9, 2023, from https://www.statista.com/topics/9922/social-media-in-africa/#topicOverview

Tidy, J., & Galer, S. S. (2020). TikTok: The story of a social media giant. *BBC News*. Retrieved April 13, 2023, from https://www.bbc.com/news/technology-53640724

Woodcock, M. (2022). What is a social media content creator? *Lickd*. Retrieved December 17, 2022, from https://lickd.co/blog/advice-for-content-creators/what-is-a-social-media-content-creator

Worldometer. (2022). Namibia Population (2021). *Worldometer*. Retrieved December 16, 2022, from https://www.worldometers.info/worldpopulation/namibia-population/#:~:text=The%20current%20population%20of%20Namibia

CHAPTER FOUR

The Commodification of Popularity on Social Media: Mega Influencers and Content Monetization on TikTok in Ghana

GIFTY APPIAH-ADJEI, ELIZABETH OWUSU ASIAMAH, RAINBOW SACKEY AND BELINDA OSEI-MENSAH

INTRODUCTION

The Internet and social media wield significant influence in shaping public discourse; hence, they are now considered essential platforms for public discourse (Agana & Prempeh, 2022). Thus, they empower the citizenry with opportunities for creating and disseminating content and afford them the audience for engagements (Kalyango & Adu-Kumi, 2013). Although the original purpose of social media platforms was for entertainment and to bridge social interactions, they are now used for business purposes (Purwandari et al., 2022). This phenomenon is not lost on social media influencers who use the influencer-follower relationship to earn money.

The networking feature of social media and specific characteristics of content creators enable them to build up a substantial network of followers by posting media content of their everyday lives (De Vierman et al., 2017) and gain popularity from followers to commodify attention. Social media influencer (SMI) literature indicates that traits like attractiveness, similarities, authenticity, and trustworthiness empower content creators to attract, maintain and influence the buying intention of followers (Brown & Hayes, 2015). To Lou and Yuan (2019), the physical attractiveness of content creators causes followers to recognize and remember a brand or a product. Leparoux et al. (2019) further indicates that

SMIs can also create attractiveness when they act naturally and are themselves in their content. The similarity traits bother on connectedness through parasocial relations because followers are attracted to and become loyal followers of SMIs when they can identify with them (Lou & Yuan, 2019).

Childers et al. (2019) argue that as SMIs genuinely and passionately communicate the subject matter of their content, they create credibility on the subject matter. Thus, the congruence between an SMI and the products/issues is a crucial factor that indicates authenticity for followers, especially the Z generation. Trustworthiness is the belief followers have in the content posted by SMIs, and this belief is due to the expertise SMIs exhibit about the issue/product. The foregoing results in a relationship whereby the content creators hold some influence over their followers (Abidin, 2016) and become influencers on social media platforms. Also, the popularity of SMIs enables them to create a human brand and profit from it (Taillion et al., 2020). Thus, SMIs become brand ambassadors who promote products and services on social media platforms through collaboration with brands (Belanche et al., 2021).

SMIs carry out their brand ambassador role by carefully integrating brand-sponsored messages into their posts (De Veiman et al., 2017). Hence, the content they create for dissemination becomes commodities/services they sell to potential media consumers (McQuail, 2010). Jin and Feenberg (2015) indicate that social media platforms enable influencers to commodify media content through traffic caused by followers on social media. Thus, the popularity and influence gains come with the exposure that the influencers turn into a marketing tool and monetize (Taillion et al., 2020) to brand managers/companies that use influencer marketing as a digital marketing avenue (Hall, 2015).

The influencer marketing industry is thriving, boasting hundreds of thousands of influencers globally, with a projection of USD 6.5 billion as of 2019 (Stokel-Walker, 2019). This thriving industry and the benefits that come with it are not lost to researchers. As such, they have given attention to this phenomenon. A plethora of studies have investigated the public perception of influencers (Coco & Ecket, 2020), influencer marketing strategies (Ponirah, 2020) and influencer-follower relationship (Tafesse & Wood, 2021). Other studies have focused on the underpinnings of theories of social media influencers (More & Lingman, 2019), conceptualisation of the various dimensions of social media influencers (Ferberg et al., 2011; Pang et al., 2016) among others. Within the African context, studies on social media abound; however, those on SMIs are scarce. Ezenwafor et al. (2021) have studied social media influencers and the purchasing intention among social media users. The authors posit that SMI studies are "sparse and lacking in a typical sub-Saharan Africa which has a sally promising growth in social media usage" (p. 218). This justifies the need for researchers in Africa and Ghana to pay more attention to this phenomenon.

Within the Ghanaian context, attention has been given to the role of SMIs and consumer purchases (Frimpong & Alam, 2020; Odoi, 2021). Though extant literature on SMIs exists in the Global North, vice versa is the case in Ghana. Hence, this study investigates social media influencing in Ghana using selected Ghanaian mega influencers on TikTok as case studies. In this paper, we reflect on SMIs and the commercialization of their popularity. We examine the suppositions of the 4 P's marketing mix and the mere exposure effect theory. Finally, findings on the nature of the content the influencers used to attract and maintain followers and how they monetize their popularity are presented and discussed.

SOCIAL MEDIA INFLUENCERS

Duffy (2020) describes SMIs as a group of online content creators with a considerable number of social media followers, outstanding brand persona, and some form of relationship with commercial sponsors. These influencers are sometimes called third-party endorsers/social media opinion leaders who contribute to consumers' attitudes towards specific brands on Social Networking Sites (SMSs) and blogs (Dangl, 2017; Freberg et al., 2011).

There is a contention in the literature concerning the types of influencers: some scholars identify three, whereas others recognize four. According to Dangl (2017), SMIs can be classified as mega, macro and micro-influencers. Mega-influencers have more than one million followers on any social media platform. They are often the typical celebrities like musicians, actors, sportspersons and other ordinary people who rise to influencer status through social media. These groups can also reach a high number of people in terms of advertisement; however, they cannot reach a specific target group for a particular brand. Conversely, macro-influencers have between 10,000 and 1, 000,000 followers and can reach more specific target groups than mega-influencers. Micro-influencers have between 500 and 10,000 followers, yet they are deemed the best at reaching targeted groups in a particular brand because they are known to possess faithful followers, making them more trustworthy than the other categories of influencers (Dangl, 2017). The other school of thought also categorizes SMIs into mega, macro, micro and nano; nano influencers have less than 1,000 followers; micro-influencers have between 1,000 and 100,000 and macro influencers have followers ranging from 100,000 to 1 million (Wibawa et al., 2021). However, the number of followers for mega influencers remains the same for all scholars – above 1 million followers.

According to Duffy (2020), 'tobesocial' (a social media company) also classifies social media influencers into up-to-date lifestylers, entertainers, activists, experts, and artists. The up-to-date influencer provides current information to their audience with their own opinions featured in their presentation. The lifestyler sets trends in terms of fashion and popular culture in general through the media. The entertainer infuses creativity, humour, and individuality into the content they provide to their audience. The activist uses their social media platform to create awareness and advocate for specific causes. The expert offers information about their expertise, whereas the artists create their content using their talent. These can be musicians and actors (Duffy, 2020).

Most internet users prefer endorsements by SMIs because they are more relatable and can build and maintain strong relationships with their followers (Szczurski, 2017). The activities of SMIs concerning advertising and marketing for brands can be linked to the earliest form of marketing, which was through word of mouth (Duffy, 2020). Consumers perceive influencers' advertisements and other persuasive communication as "authentic or organic" than those made by the traditional media because these influencers infuse commercial content into their existing videos, texts, and other narrative content they create (Duffy, 2020, p. 1). Advertising goods and services to followers through constant information and inspiration is a means of earning income for most SMIs. Abidin (2016) avers that some characteristics of SMIs include their relentless craving for more followers, constant interactions/engagements with followers, and eagerness to monetize their activities/content on social media. According to Duffy (2020), influencers operate in a currency of exchange exclusive to the attention economy: social media metrics. Hence, to monetize their following, SMIs must demonstrate their ability to wield sway with verifiable evidence – YouTube subscribers, Instagram/Twitter followers, Facebook Likes, and Weibo comments – along with more elusive symbols of "engagement" or "impact" (p. 2).

People follow SMIs because they (followers) are interested in what they (SMIs) represent or promote on their pages (Jarrar et al., 2020). SMIs deliberately engage in careful impression management and self-branding (Duffy, 2020) to attract more followers whom they can sell to brands and companies. This chapter, therefore, focuses on how four mega SMIs in Ghana – @erkuahofficial, @wesleykessegh, @asantewaaaaa, and @say.logan – cautiously engage in impression management and self-branding on TikTok to attract more followers and economize the attention from their followers. These four mega influencers are ordinary people who gained popularity through their constant engagements on TikTok. @erkuahofficial, known as Janet Offei, is a political science graduate from the University of Ghana, while @wesleykessegh, known as Wesley Kesse, is a Public Relations graduate from the Ghana Institute of Journalism. @asantewaaaaa, called Martina Dwamena, is a married nurse with a son. @say.logan, also known as Charles Logan, is a dancer and a student at the University of Ghana. The influencers started creating content on TikTok during the COVID lockdown era out of boredom and became popular due to their videos. They all have over a million followers and are the top four Ghanaian TikTokers in Ghana.

THE COMMERCIALIZATION OF POPULARITY ON SOCIAL MEDIA

According to Gaenssle and Budzinski (2021), SMIs can influence the everyday decisions of their followers. Hence, they become a marketing tool that organizations use to advertise products/services and endorse institutions and ideologies through their social media profiles. De Veiman et al. (2017) refer to this process as influencer marketing. Business Insider (2019) predicted that the worth of influencer marketing would reach 15 billion dollars in 2022 because it has recently become the most regularly used marketing tactic. Consequently, the growth of scholarly works around this phenomenon has increased exponentially (Hudders et al., 2021). The authors further assert that the increase in SMIs is motivated by the fame/popularity they garner and the benefits they derive from companies in the form of free products and endorsement revenues from promoting organizational products/services.

Campbell and Farrell (2020) contend that the commercialization of social media popularity results from the weakness and inefficiency of conventional forms of persuasive communication coupled with the growing debate favoring online user-generated content as a more appropriate channel to achieve behavioral change in people. Hence, SMIs are compensated through both financial and material means when they endorse products, services, brands, and ideologies through their posts on social media.

The commercialization of popularity on social media manifests in different folds, ranging from influencer endorsement to sponsored content (Hudders et al., 2021). A new trend discovered in the commercialization process is using live-streaming videos by influencers to promote sponsored content (Woodcock & Johnson, 2019). Using SMIs to promote products/services is seen as cost-effective because they create compelling sponsored content and share it with their numerous followers (Borchers & Enke, 2021). Lin et al. (2018) posit that SMIs can increase the epicurean value of a product by establishing a link between their status and affection for the product. Thus, the product's usefulness can increase when the influencer discusses the product in detail.

Hudders et al. (2021) reveal that SMIs strategically create content that continues to enhance the growth of their social media followers. This is done to ensure the sustainability of relevance and the commercialization of their popularity in that space. Studies have identified the kinds of content posted by SMIs and have concluded that influencers are more obsessed with the creation of content that promotes personal intimacy with their followers (Abidin & Thompson, 2012; Duffy & Kang, 2020; Pilgrim & Bohnet-Joschko, 2019). For instance, Duffy and Kang (2020) found that travel bloggers use the 'About Me' section on their pages to build a favorable image. Thus, they marketed themselves as brands, emphasizing branding as daring and risk-takers to distinguish themselves from other bloggers. This is similar to Abidin and Thompson's (2012) articulation that these users show compliments and show them what happens behind the scenes. Jorge et al. (2018) also discovered that renowned Portuguese vlogger, SofiaBBeauty, used personal storytelling to explain her appreciation of particular products and further gave her viewers a glimpse into her personal life to strike a balance between genuineness and commercialism. For Abidin and Thompson (2012), these influencers promote products in their content and set standards for ideal beauty. For example, Pilgrim and Bohnet-Joschko (2019) identified content that shows perfect body size and habits, such as exercising and low-fat diets.

These studies revealed that SMIs' use of their content to advertise products has become more frequent lately than in the past. Schwemmer and Ziewiecki (2018) conducted an automated content analysis of the 100 most popular German YouTube channel videos between 2009 and 2017. The findings showed a sharp rise in the use of referral links in the video descriptions of these popular YouTube channels and the number of product promotions mentioned in videos. Likewise, Pilgrim and Bohnet-Joschko (2019) established in their study that 71% of social media influencer posts analyzed featured at least one brand and 90% of these companies were explicitly named and tagged in the posts. This data demonstrates the importance of branded content in SMI postings. From these narratives, it can be stated that SMIs mainly endorse sponsored content on their profiles through real-life stories. This establishes credibility and ensures their online image is carefully preserved (Hudders et al., 2021).

THE 4PS MARKETING MIX

The essence of marketing entails creating, providing, and exchanging services of value with others through the performance of activities (Kotler, 2001). This marketing function depends on the marketing mix, which describes the various actions required to develop and implement an all-encompassing marketing strategy to increase the value of a product/service (Kotler, 2001). McCarthy (1981) is known to have summarized the components of the marketing mix into the 'four Ps': product, price, place, and promotion. Product refers to intangible services or market offerings that a client can purchase. Regarding influencer marketing, the popularity and influence over followers gained through SMIs' content become the product they offer to the companies or brands who want to sell their services or market offering to their followers. Price is determined by the expenses incurred while purchasing an item based on its perceived value and demand (Kotler & Armstrong, 2010). Kotler and Armstrong (2010) say that price in the marketing mix presents revenue to the brand. Hence, content monetization becomes the revenue for the human brand of TikTok influencers. How an influencer's content is monetized or priced is based on followers' appreciation of the content offered to them. For influencers to benefit, they must present themselves as relatable and tailor their offerings to the customer's demands (Kelly et al., 2010). Only then will the customer/followers be willing to pay for the value they perceive they receive (Wind, 2014).

Besides, promotion encircles advertising and other communication tactics used to inform, persuade, or remind the target market of the product's availability and benefits (Kotler, 2001). Promotion of a product or place is one such action in which influencers advertise products/services through their content to their large following or captive audiences (Gomez-Arias & Genin, 2009). In influencer marketing, creating compelling sponsored content with a strategic endorsement of a product is one of the tactics used by SMIs to promote specific brands and influence consumers' attitudes towards such brands on a social media platform like TikTok. When SMIs speak in detail about the product they are endorsing, they establish the link between their status, affection and the product, persuading their followers to appreciate the product.

SMIs obtain revenue by utilizing social media insights and cultivating and monetizing their following (Benedict, 2013; Gomez-Arias & Genin, 2009). Benedict (2013) explains that content creators base their marketing on insights they receive from social media trends, viewership and responses to promotional campaigns. Content creators can maximize the value of their relationships with their audiences to augment the benefit of social media (Gomez-Arias & Genin, 2009) when they share sponsored content on their accounts, [engage in live video streaming], and advertise for brands (Campbell & Grimm, 2019).

For instance, Johnson and Woodcock (2019) studied live streaming and methods of monetization of content by users of the Twitch.tv platform. They pointed out that live streamers make money by introducing games and competitions and, in turn, recognize the viewers who donate to them. On the other hand, the live video streaming feature on the TikTok application allows users to interact with their followers, play games and gain monetary benefits. This indicates that the content is not sold to an outside party but is used internally to generate revenue for the influencer through competition and games. This might be observed in how they use their live streams and make their broadcasts more engaging for live audiences. In summary, the marketing mix highlights the factors contributing to monetizing content and the marketing strategies used to achieve that objective, making it pertinent to this study.

MERE EXPOSURE EFFECT (MEE) THEORY

Robert Zajonc propounded the Mere Exposure Effect (MEE) theory in 1968 (Bornstein & D'Agostino, 1992). The MEE theory is often applied in product sales and marketing research to explain how the repeated exposure of consumers to specific brand advertisements influences them (consumers) to have a positive interest in those brands (Bornstein & Craver-Lemley, 2017). Wang et al. (2013) aver that consumers' exposure to advertisements occurs incidentally when their attention is geared towards something else (such as surfing the internet or socializing on Social Networking Sites, among others). Any advertisement that comes into contact with the consumer is regarded as secondary and not actively processed. However, since most emotional reactions and learning occur outside one's awareness, such advertisements may change the subconscious minds of these consumers' merely' because the consumers are conversant with them (Zajonc,1968).

The MEE is why content marketing excels (Kaltwasser, 2019). There have been contentions about whether recognition impedes the MEE or facilitates the effect (Grimes & Stafford, 2012). Robinson and Elias (2005) contend that as people get exposed to a particular stimulus (product or person), they learn more about it, which reduces their uncertainty level and further brings about a positive attitude towards the said stimulus. This supports the claim that, indeed, recognition facilitates the MEE. Since the selected TikTok influencers commodify their popularity to their followers through their posts, the MEE theory will help explain the rationale for their consistency in sharing the kinds of content they post on their pages.

The mere exposure effect theory aligns with the promotion component of the 4Ps marketing mix. Thus, as SMIs consistently share content on their TikTok pages for their followers, they automatically promote their human brands, which can positively influence their followers' perceptions of their brands.

METHODOLOGY

This study employs a qualitative research approach to understand the significance and meanings of the phenomenon under investigation (Creswell & Creswell, 2018). This is consistent with Brennen's (2021) claim that the qualitative research approach enables researchers to get a more in-depth and detailed understanding of the themes being examined, allowing the researcher to gather and analyze non-numerical data about the investigation's emphasis. Anchored on the case study design, the study adopted content analysis to examine the posts of four selected TikTok influencers and establish the nature of the content the influencers posted. This was to explore the social constructs surrounding the material generated throughout the study period. Interviews were also conducted to discover how these influencers monetize or commercialize their content. The case study helped the researchers to conduct an extensive analysis of the phenomenon using the selected subjects. This allowed the researchers to employ multiple data collection methods to gain more appreciation of the commodification of popularity on social media within the Ghanaian context and ensure data corroboration (Yin, 2014). In furtherance, Quan-Haase and Sloan (2017) argue that in social media research that involves big data, qualitative researchers should not focus on the breadth of data; instead, the focus should be on using small but thick data by adding other sources of data collection methods to augment the data.

Consequently, four Ghanaian mega influencers on TikTok – @erkuahofficial, @wesleykessegh, @asantewaaaaa, and @say.logan – were purposively selected for the study. These mega influencers were selected because they were among the most followed TikTok influencers in Ghana, with over one million followers (Dangl, 2017). Videos posted by the influencers with 500 thousand and over views were analyzed. The study period is from August to October 2022, and the selection of the study period was informed by data saturation (Creswell, 2014) and the data currency. To ensure that the gathered data is thick enough to aid the researchers in collecting enough data for this study, interviews were conducted with three of the selected influencers, who agreed to be part of the study to provide more context to the videos they posted (Airoldi, 2018; Latzko-Toth et al., 2017), and to capture their experiences and the meanings they attribute to them (Sloan & Quan-Haase, 2017). These interviews were conducted after the researchers had collected data from the qualitative content analysis of the selected videos posted by the four influencers (Sloan & Quan-Haase, 2017). The posts helped the researchers access the actual practices of the four chosen influencers on TikTok to capture and analyzed the traces of their TikTok activities (Howison et al., 2011). The data gathered from the qualitative content analysis and interviews were analyzed thematically to identify similar patterns across the data sets and form themes that answer the research questions (Braun & Clarke, 2018).

Per ethical standards, participants' consent was obtained before the interviews. Due to the researchers' pledge of anonymity, the pseudonyms Interviewer A, B and C were used to represent the influencers sampled for the study.

Table 4.1. Total number of videos posted within the study period by the influencers (Source: the author)

Month	Total Videos Posted N (%)	@asantewaaaaa N (%)	@wesleykessegh N (%)	@erkuahofficial N (%)	@say.logan N (%)
Aug	330 (41.8%)	192 (24.3%)	56 (7.1%)	41 (5.2%)	41 (5.2%)
Sept	203 (25.7%)	118 (15%)	34 (4.3%)	21 (2.7%)	30 (3.8%)
Oct	256 (32.5%)	156 (19.8%)	35 (4.4%)	30 (3.8%)	35 (4.4%)
Total	*789 (100%)*	*466 (59.1%)*	*125 (15.8%)*	*92 (11.7%)*	*106 (13.4%)*

FREQUENCY OF VIDEOS POSTED BY THE INFLUENCERS TO ATTRACT AND MAINTAIN FOLLOWERS

Though one of the objectives of this study was to examine the nature of the content posted by the influencers to attract and maintain followers, the study first sought to establish the frequency of videos posted within the study period and videos with 5k and over views. This is because Brown and Hayes (2015) have identified high frequency of publishing content as an important factor for SMIs to create attractiveness towards them. Thus, it is out of the ability of SMIs to create attractiveness that ensures that their followers are maintained.

Table 4.1 revealed that the four mega influencers posted 789 videos within the study period. From this number, 466 videos (59.1 per cent) were posted by @asantewaaaaa, 125 videos (15.8 per cent) by @wesleykessegh, 106 videos (13.4 per cent) by @say.logan, and 92 videos (11.7 per cent) by @erkuahofficial. Also, @asantewaaaaa posted 191 (24.3%), 118 (15 per cent) and 156 (19.8 per cent) videos in August, September and October, respectively; likewise, @wesleykessegh with 56 (7.1 per cent), 34 (4.3 per cent), and 35 (4.4 per cent) videos within the study period. Besides, @ekuahofficial posted 41 (5.2 per cent), 21 (2.7 per cent) and 30 (3.8 per cent) videos, respectively, whereas @say.logan posted 41, 30, and 35 videos during the study period. Data gathered showed that most videos posted within the study period (59.1 per cent) were by @asantewaaaaa, and @ekuahofficial had the least number of videos (11.7 per cent).

In Table 4.2, data gathered showed that out of the 789 videos posted, 94 (12 per cent) had 50k and over views, whereas 701 (88 per cent) had less than 50k views. Regarding the influencers, findings established that @asantewaaaaa had 35 videos (4.45 per cent) with over 50k and above views, while @wesleykessegh, @ekuahofficial, and @say.logan had 10 (1.3 per cent), 41(5.2 per cent), and eight (1 per cent) videos in this category respectively. Even though @ekuahofficial had the least number of videos posted within the study period, most of her videos had

Table 4.2. Videos with 5k and over views and with less than 50k views (Source: the author)

Videos	@asantewaaaaa N (%)	@wesleykessegh N (%)	@erkuahofficial N (%)	@ say.logan N (%)	*Total*
5k and over views	35 (4.45%)	10 (1.3%)	41(5.2%)	8 (1%)	94 (12%)
Less than 5k views	431(54.6%)	115 (14.5%)	51 (6.5%)	98 (12.4%)	701(88%)
Total	*466(59.1%)*	*125 (15.8%)*	*92 (11.7%)*	*106(13.4%)*	*789 (100%)*

50k and over viewers compared with the other three influencers. @say.logan had the least videos with 50k and over views within the study period.

In Table 4.3, data analysis established that in August 2022, a total of 29 videos posted by the influencers had 50k and over views, out of which 14 were from @asantewaaaaa, 11 from @ekuahofficial and two each from @wesleykessegh and @say.logan. Twenty-three videos in this category were also posted in September, and ten videos each were from @asantewaaaaa and @ehuahofficial, while @say.logan, and @wesleykessegh posted two and one videos, respectively. In the final month, 20 of the videos posted by @ekuahofficial had 50k and over views, with @asantewaaaa, @wesleykessgh, and @say.logan having 11, seven and four videos within the same category.

It has been indicated that SMIs persistently crave followers, interactions, and engagements with them (Abidin, 2016). This is usually done by consistently creating and sharing content that ensures an encounter with their followers and potential followers. Consistency in posting videos is meant to attract and maintain followers (Brown & Hayes, 2015), enabling SMIs to acquire resources/capital from the attention economy (Duffy, 2020) that they finally monetize. Upon critical analysis of data in Tables 4.1; 4.2 and 4.3, findings reveal that within the study

Table 4.3. Monthly distribution of videos with 5k and over views (Source: the author)

Month	Total Videos Posted N (%)	@asantewaaaaa N (%)	@wesleykessegh N (%)	@erkuahofficial N (%)	@say.logan N (%)
Aug	29 (%)	14 (%)	2 (%)	11 (%)	2 (%)
Sept	23 (%)	10 (%)	1 (%)	10 (%)	2 (%)
Oct	42 (%)	11 (%)	7 (%)	20 (%)	4 (%)
Total	*94 (100%)*	*35 (%)*	*10 (%)*	*41 (%)*	*8 (%)*

period, the selected influencers frequently posted videos on TikTok to engage with their followers. On average, @asantewaaaaa posted over 100 videos monthly, whereas the remaining three influencers posted about 30 videos monthly. It was also discovered that @asantewaaaaa was the influencer with the highest number of videos, but @erkuahofficial had the most videos with 5k and over views. Thus, 466 out of 789 of the total videos within the study period were posted by @asantewaaaaa, and out of the 94 videos with 5k and over views, 41 were from @erkuahofficial even though she posted the least number of videos than all the selected influencers. This implies that within the study period, @asantewaaaaa and @erkuahofficial created more attractiveness (Brown & Hayes, 2015) and had more attention capital (Duffy, 2020) than @wesleykessegh and @say.logan.

NATURE OF CONTENT OF VIDEOS POSTED TO ATTRACT AND MAINTAIN FOLLOWERS

To Borchers and Enke (2021), the effectiveness of SMIs lies in their ability to create compelling content. It is one of the tactics they use to attract and maintain their followers because the content of the videos serves as the focus of attention for the followers. Hence, this study sought to examine the nature of the content of videos posted by the influencers within the study period to establish topics that followers of the selected influencers found compelling. After the review of the 94 videos with 5k and over views, themes that emerged indicated that the nature of the videos was that of funny dance drama (comical dance moves where the influencers dramatized or acted out scenes based on music lyrics or trending music videos), or lip syncing (moving one's lips in synchronization with pre-recorded videos or music by other content creators), or promotions (publicity for a song, product or place) or personal/family videos (content about the influencer's life or response to comments from followers) or duet (creation of content based on another video produced by another creator and placing such videos side by side the original video). The frequency of the themes is presented in table 4.4.

In Table 4.4, findings established that out of the 94 videos with 5k and over views, 47, representing 50 percent, were videos of the influencers engaging in the funny dance drama. In 27 of the videos representing 28.7 percent, they lip-synced, whereas Eight of the videos, representing 8.5 percent, were about promotions. Also, seven of the videos were personal, while the remaining five videos, representing 5.3 per cent, were duet videos of other content creators.

The findings showed that funny dance drama was the most dominant subject matter used by the selected influencers in creating their content. Twenty three (24.5 per cent) out of the 41 videos from @erkuahofficial were funny dance dramas,

Table 4.4. Nature of content of videos with 5k and over views (Source: the author)

Nature of Video Content	@asantewaaaaa N (%)	@wesleykessegh N (%)	@erkuahofficial N (%)	@say.logan N (%)	*Total*
Promotion	0 (0%)	0 (0%)	7 (7.4%)	1(1.1%)	8 (8.5%)
Funny Dance Drama videos	16 (17%)	3 (3.2%)	23 (24.5%)	5 (5.3%)	47 (50%)
Lip-syncing	10 (10.6%)	6 (6.4%)	9 (9.6%)	2 (2.1%)	27 (28.7%)
Personal/family	6 (6.4%)	1 (1.1%)	0 (0%)	0 (0%)	7 (7.4%)
Duet videos	3 (3.2%)	0 (0%)	2 (2.1%)%	0 (%)	5 (5.3%)
Total	*35 (37.2%)*	*10 (10.7%)*	*41(43.6%)*	*8(8.5%)*	*94 (100%)*

and this was followed by @asantewaaaaa, @say.logan, and @wesleykessegh with 16 (17 per cent), five (5.3 per cent), and three (3.2 per cent) videos respectively. The next dominant theme was lip syncing comprising ten videos (10.6 percent) from @asantewaaaaa, followed by @erkuahofficial with nine videos (9.6 percent), whereas @wesleykessegh, and @say.logan had six videos (6.4 percent) and two videos (2.1 percent) correspondingly. Videos that advertised songs, products or places were the next dominant theme. Out of the eight (8.5 percent) videos on promotion, seven (7.4 percent) of them were from @erkuahofficial, whereas one (1.1 percent) was from @say.logan. Findings revealed that while @erkuahofficial promoted songs and products, @say.logan promoted a place.

For instance, it was realized that @erkuahofficial engaged in song promotion for some musicians whom she either tagged in the captioned posts or acted with the artists. Notable among the song promotion is her 2.0M (September 22, 2022) viewed song promotion for Mr. Eazi on his song 'Patek flex'. She also collaborated with musician Zlatan in one of her videos to hype his newly released song (547.2K views/ October 19, 2022). In other instances, @erkuahofficial casually held or drank Kalyppo juice while dancing or placed the product beside her as she created her content without referring to the product. It was also observed that she usually tags the TikTok pages of the brands she advertises for in her caption. In the only promotion video posted by @say.logan (October 9, 2022/ 1.8M views), he advertised a hotel (GC Royal Hotel) when he mentioned the details of the place, and he tagged the name of the hotel in his main caption and also in the comment section. Within the study period, @asantewaaaaa and @wesleykessegh did not have any video with 5k and over views on promotion.

It is important to note that while traits of attractiveness and similarities run through all the 94 videos with 5k and over views, authenticity and trustworthiness were observed in only the promotion videos. Also, the themes generated from the videos concern subject matter that Generation Z in Ghana can easily relate to. For instance, on October 7, 2022, the video posted by @asantewaaaaa exhibited her being herself as she danced to the popular song 'Attention' by Sped Up Mage. Also, actions by @wesleykessegh in his video posted on October 3, 2022, indicated his acting in a manner that anyone could relate to. The interview data affirmed this because the influencers admitted to creating content their followers could relate to and appreciate. For instance, Interviewee A disclosed that:

> Because the content I create is for my fans, I do things they can relate to and appreciate and put my comment section on so that I can also get their feedback on the content I share.

Another interviewee also indicates that the aim is "to create relatable contents so it becomes easier for my audience to engage with them" (Interviewee B). These show the authenticity and trustworthy traits in the videos and establish conscious efforts by @erkuahofficial, and @say.logan to promote Mr. Eazi's music and the hotel to their followers, respectively.

The argument underpinning the authenticity trait is that when SMIs show a genuine and passionate interest in the brand/subject matter they promote, they create credibility (Childers et al., 2019), while the trustworthiness trait has to do with the belief followers have in SMIs due to the exhibition of their expertise on the issue or product (Lou & Yuan, 2019). These assertions align with findings from the content analysis and the interview data. It was discovered that the influencers exhibited a lot of energy and commitment in their videos. For example, the videos posted by @erkuahofficial and @say.logan on September 22, 2022, and October 9, 2022, showed that @erkuahofficial was passionate about Mr. Eazi's song, Patek Flex, whereas @say.logan did the same in his video about GC Royal Hotel. As an affirmation of the interview data, the participants noted that much time, energy, and investment go into the content they create to enable their followers to engage and believe in it. Therefore, one of the interviewees posited that "it takes a lot of energy and time to create something you believe your fans would love because they are the ones that make us popular on the app [TikTok]" (Interviewee A).

The above findings agree with assertions in SMI literature. While attractiveness and similarities are linked to the ability to attract and maintain followers, authenticity and trustworthiness influence the buying intention of followers (Leparoux et al., 2019). Upon careful observation of the nature of videos from the selected influencers, it was discovered that the influencers were naturally being themselves and acted in a manner that made it easy for their followers to relate and associate with their actions and attitudes. SMI literature indicates that these traits enable influencers to attract and maintain followers and influence their buying intentions. Hence, the presence of these traits in the videos posted by @asantewaaaaa, @erkuahofficial, @say.logan and @wesleykessegh explains why the influencers were able to attract 5k and over views (Brown & Hayes, 2015; Childers et al. 2019; Leparoux et al., 2019; Lou & Yuan, 2019). Also, the findings align with the MEE theory because the repeated exposure of content posted by @asantewaaaaa, @erkuahofficial, @say.logan, and @wesleykessegh on TikTok automatically promoted their human brands that positively influenced their followers' perception of their brand (Kaltwasser, 2019; Le Bon & Merunka, 2017).

MONETIZATION OF CONTENT AND POPULARITY

Upon analysis of the data gathered, it was discovered that the influencers earn money from TikTok in two main ways: through services or activities on the app and outside the app. Three main themes were derived: earning through live gifting, endorsements of products and advertisement of their human brand. Thus, live gifting and brand endorsements were the primary means of making money from the app, whereas they sometimes earned money by selling their services (popularity) to people or organizations.

Through Live Gifting

Upon analysis of the interview data, the influencers disclosed that one of the means they earn money on TikTok is through live gifting. This is the primary means of making money for the selected influencers. Live gifting is a feature on TikTok that allows content creators with more than 1000 followers to have live online sessions where their followers/fans appreciate them with virtual gifts (Geyser, 2022). These digital gifts are converted to a TikTok currency known as diamonds, enabling influencers to cash out and earn money. Hence, the influencers admitted that some of their followers offer them digital gifts such as roses, dogs, and lions during such live sessions. The influencers indicated that these gifts were then cashed out in the form of money through PayPal. All the interviewees admitted that they earn money from their followers through live online sessions. Therefore, one of the interviewees notes, "when we go live, some followers gift us which are all monies in dollars" (Interviewee B).

Also, another means for making money through live gifting was through a game launched on TikTok in 2021, where two content creators compete for rewards of gifts from their followers for a stipulated time, after which the influencer with the most gifts at the end of the competition cashes out for money. Analysis of the data showed that upon initiating this game, the influencers call out to their followers to come out in their numbers and help them win the competition through gifts. They (influencers) then acknowledge, commend or praise their followers for donating gifts. One of the interviewees notes that "almost all the time, there is competition with another influencer, or a known person and people will not give you gifts if you are not popular" (Interviewee C).

The giving of virtual gifts by followers is due to the influencers' popularity and influence over their followers. Thus, they appreciate the content created by these influencers by sending virtual gifts to them. This aligns with the assertion by Taillion et al. (2020) that the popularity and influence of TikTok influencers give them a kind of exposure that they use to earn money. It can be argued that in such instances, the popularity and influence of the influencers become a product that is promoted through compelling and engaging content and indirectly monetized on the TikTok app (Benevento et. al 2025).

Through Brand Endorsements

The interview data revealed that another way influencers earn money on the app is through endorsements. Since the app permits users to create and upload their content, the influencers create content through which they directly or indirectly promote a company or individual's product or service(s) and get paid. Thus, the influencers strategically integrate information about the product or service they are promoting into their videos and market it to their followers who watch their videos. The influencers also tag the TikTok page of the brand/product they promote.

For instance, in the video posted on October 1, 2022, @erkuahofficial directly markets Kalypo juice when she casually holds the juice with comic exaggerations and facial expressions and tags the page of Kalypo juice, as indicated in the screenshot in Figure 4.1. The same can be said of @say.logan when he directly markets the services of G C Royal Hotel in his video posted on October 9, 2022. There were other instances where the influencers indirectly marketed companies' products or services by strategically situating the product/service into their videos without any reference to them.

For example, in the video posted by @erkuahofficial on August 30, 2022, she placed Kalypo juice beside her as she created her content without referring to the juice (Fig, 4.2).

The interviewees admitted that through such endorsements, they were paid well by the companies or individuals they get the deals from them. So, an interviewee avers that "I mostly advertise for brands on my page who in turn pay me good monies for my services" (Interviewee A).

Another interviewee also indicated that

> With my publicity, brands and musicians that come to me for advertisement pay, because that is another way we make our money (Interviewee B).

Figure 4.1. Screenshot of @ekuahofficial and @say.logan endorsing Kalypo juice and G C Royal Hotel (Source: erkuahofficial and Baby Boy TikTok).

Through Advertisement of popularity/human brand

Our analysis also discovered that some of the selected influencers (two out of four) advertise their human brand on their TikTok profiles. Thus, these influencers display their contacts so that potential clients can contact them for business. Hence, @say.logan indicates on his TikTok profile that he does promotion/advertisement and leaves his contact information, and @asantewaaaaa has left her contact on her profile for the sake of business.

It was established via the interview data that some influencers also get invitations to events due to their popularity on TikTok. This comes with an opportunity to be paid due to their attention capital. Thus, event organizers also patronize the popularity of these influencers to drive or hype their programs and get more of their followers to attend such programs. Interviewee C denotes that

> I know of some colleagues who get opportunities to be invited to programs and get paid. I haven't had such opportunities even though I have the numbers.

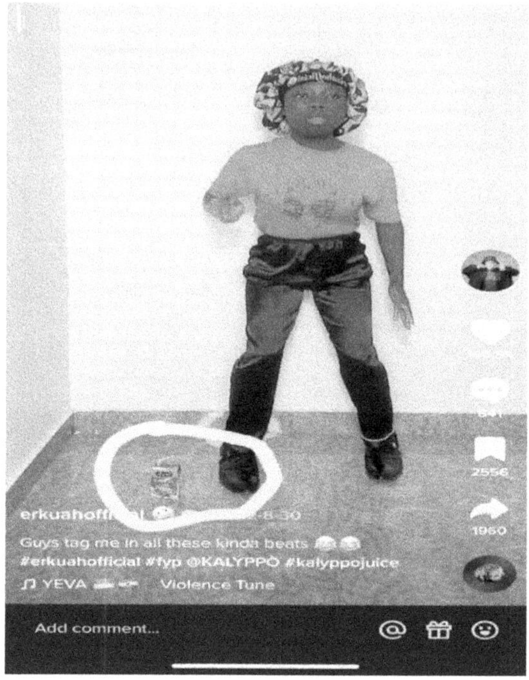

Figure 4.2. Screenshot of @ekuahofficial indirectly promoting Kalypo juice in her video (Source: erkuahofficial TikTok).

Upon critical analysis of the above findings and the marketing mix strategy, a complex situation of attempts by both the influencers and entities offering the endorsement deals to the influencers "to boost sales of products" unfolds (Benevento et al 2025). Findings established three means through which the influencers in Ghana earn money on TikTok (through live gifting, endorsement and commercialization of human brand) and the money earned by the influencers via the three means is due to their popularity and the influence they weld over their followers. This implies that through their popularity on the app, they develop a human brand that becomes a product they sell to organizations and individuals. For instance, it is realized that whereas Kalypo fruit juice, music and GC Royal Hotel are the products that @erkuahofficial and @say.logan indirectly promote to their followers, the popularity of the influencers (which is their human brand) also become the intangible services or market offering they sell to the organizations or individuals that need it (Kotler, 2001; Twin, 2021). Also, the invitation to be characters in advertisements aired on other media platforms and to attend and hype events is a result of their ability to influence their followers due to their popularity. Therefore, the influencers become customer service employees for the organizations and individuals and present the products/

services promoted appealingly to their followers (Benevento et al 2025). In doing so, the influencers present themselves as relatable (the attractive and similarities traits), exhibit their expertise about the product/service (the authenticity and trustworthiness traits) and tailor their offerings to the demands of the customer (Kelly et al., 2010).

CONCLUSION

The study establishes the nature of the content selected mega TikTok influencers posted and how they monetize their content. The nature of videos posted within the study period was dominantly about dance and drama, where the influencers dramatized the lyrics of some Ghanaian songs via dancing in a comical manner. This was followed by lip-syncing videos where they re-enact videos from other content creators. They also posted promotional videos that directly and indirectly sold products, places, and content on personal issues to their followers. These were done to create fun and engage with their followers on relatable issues as they employ the attractiveness, similarities, authenticity and trustworthiness traits to attract and maintain followers and to influence their followers' intentions to patronize goods and services of some organizations and individuals (Brown & Hayes, 2015; Childers et al. (2019); Leparoux et al., 2019; Lou & Yuan, 2019). They also promote their human brands through repeated exposure to such content (Kaltwasser, 2019; Le Bon & Merunka, 2017).

Also, the study revealed that although TikTok offers various means for monetizing content, the selected influencers monetized their content via only three primary means due to jurisdiction restrictions. This implies that, by their jurisdiction, the influencers are limited in how they can earn money on TikTok. For instance, Creator Next is a program on TikTok that enables content creators to make money through creator funds, creator marketplace, video gifts, live gifts, and tips, but access to these features is jurisdiction-specific. Hence, creators fund is accessible to TikTok influencers in the US, UK, France, Germany, Spain, and Italy. The absence of Africa in these jurisdiction-specific features limits how the selected mega influencers can monetize their content on TikTok.

REFERENCES

Abidin, C. (2016). Visibility labour: Engaging with influencers' fashion brands and #OOTD advertorial campaigns on Instagram, *Media International Australia*, *161*(1), 86–100.

Abidin, C., & Thompson, E. C. (2012). Cyber-femininities and commercial intimacy in blogshops. *Women's Studies International Forum 35*(6), 467–477. https://doi.org/10.1016/j.wsif.2012.10.005

Agana, N., & Prempeh, C. (2022). Of farms, legends, and fools: Re-engaging Ghana's development narrative through social media. *Media, Culture & Society*, *44*(7), 1290–1306 https://doi.org/10.1177/01634437221111918

Airoldi, M. (2018). Ethnography and the digital fields of social media. *International Journal of Social Research Methodology*, *21*(6), 661–673.

Belanche, D., Casalo, L. V., Flavian, M., & Ibanez-Sanchez, S. (2021). Building influencers' credibility on Instagram: Effects on followers' attitudes and behavioural responses toward the influencer. *Journal of Retailing and Consumer Services*, *61*(102585), 1–11.

Benedict, J. P. (2013). Embracing the power of social media for broadcast business insight. *Cognizant Insight*. Retrieved April 20, 2024, from https://www.scribd.com/document/155635564/Embracing-the-Power-of-Social-Media-for-Broadcast-Business-Insight

Benevento, E., Aloini, D., Roma, P., & Bellino, D. (2025). The impact of influencers on brand social network growth: Insights from new product launch events on Twitter https://doi.org/10.1016/j.jbusres.2024.115123

Borchers, N. S., & Enke, N. (2021). Managing strategic influencer communication: A systematic overview on emerging planning, organization, and controlling routines. *Public Relations Review*, *47*:3, 1–13 https://doi.org/10.1016/j.pubrev.2021.102041

Bornstein, R. F., & Craver-Lemley, C. (2017). Mere exposure effect. In R. F. Pohl (Ed.). *Cognitive illusions: intriguing phenomena in judgement, thinking and memory* (2nd ed.) (pp. 256–275). Routledge.

Bornstein, R. F., & D'Agostino, P. R. (1992). Stimulus recognition and the mere exposure effect. *Journal of Personality and Social Psychology*, *63*(4), 545–552.

Brennen, B. S. (2021). *Qualitative research methods for media studies*. Routledge.

Brown, D., & Hayes, N. (2015). *Influencer marketing: Who really influences your customers?* (1st ed.) Routledge.

Business Insider (2019). Influencer Marketing: State of the social media influencer market in 2020. Online Report. https://www.businessinsider.com/influencer-marketing-report?r=US&IR=T

Campbell, C., & Farrell, J. R. (2020) More than meets the eye: The functional components underlying influencer marketing. *Business Horizons*, *63*(4), 469–479. https://doi.org/10.1016/j.bushor.2020.03.003

Campbell, C., & Grimm, P. E. (2019). The challenges native advertising poses: Exploring potential Federal Trade Commission responses and identifying research needs. *Journal of Public Policy & Marketing*, *38*(1), 110–123.

Childers, C. C., Lemon, L. L., & Hoy, M. G. (2019). #Sponsored #Ad: Agency perspective on influencer marketing campaigns. *Journal of Current Issues and Research in Advertising*, *40*(3), 258–274.

Clarke, V., & Braun, V. (2018). Using thematic analysis in counselling and psychotherapy research: A critical reflection. *Counselling and Psychotherapy Research*, *18*(2), 107–110. https://doi.org/10.1002/capr.12165

Coco, S. L., & Eckert, S. (2020). #sponsored: Consumer insights on social media influencer marketing. *Public Relations Inquiry 9*, 177–194. https://doi.org/10.1177/2046147X20920816

Creswell, J. W., & Creswell, J. D. (2018) *Research design: Qualitative, quantitative, and mixed methods approaches*. Sage publications.

Creswell, J. W. (2014). *Qualitative, quantitative and mixed methods approaches* (4th ed.).California, United State of America.: Sage Publications

Dangl, V. (2017). Social media influencer marketing: An empirical study on brand sponsorships and the effects on credibility of social media influencers in the fitness industry (Master Thesis). Institut für Handel, Absatz und Marketing.

De Veirman, M., Cauberghe, V., & Hudders, L. (2017). Marketing through Instagram influencers: the impact of number of followers and product divergence on brand attitude. *International Journal of Advertising*, *36*(5), 798–828. https://doi.org/10.1080/02650487.2017.1348035

Duffy, A., & Kang, H. Y. P. (2020). Follow me, I'm famous: travel bloggers' self-mediated performances of everyday exoticism. *Media, Culture and Society*, *42*(2), 72–190. https://doi.org/10.1177/0163443719853503

Duffy, B. E. (2020). Social media influencers. In E. Ross (Ed.), *The international encyclopedia of gender, media, and communication*. https://doi.org/10.1002/9781119429128.iegmc219

Ezenwafor, E. C., Olise, C. M., & Ebizie, P. I. (2021). Social media influencer and purchase intention amongst social media users in developing African economy. *Quest Journal of Management and Social Sciences*, *3*(2), 217–228.

Freberg, K. et al. (2011). Who are the social media influencers? A study of public perceptions of personality. *Public Relations Review*, *37*(1), 90–92

Freberg, K., Graham, K., McGaughey, K and Frberg, L.A. (2011). Who are the social media influencers? A study of public perceptions of personality. Public Relations Review, 37(1), pp90–92

Frimpong, A. O., & Alam, K. (2020). The impact of online marketing influencers on consumer purchase decision: A case study of Ghana. https://www.diva-portal.org/smash/get/diva2:1436730/FULLTEXT01.pdf

Gaenssle, S., & Budzinski, O. (2021). Stars in social media: New light through old windows? *Journal of Media Business Studies*, *18*(2), 79–105. https://doi.org/10.1080/16522354.2020.1738694

Geyser, W. (2022). What are TikTok live gifts and how do they work? Retrieved December 20, 2024, from https://influencermarketinghub.com/TikTok-live-gifts/

Gomez-Arias, J. T., & Genin, L. (2009). Beyond monetisation: Creating value through online social networks. *International Journal of Electronic Business Management*, *7*(2), 79–85.

Grimes, A., & Stafford, T. (2012). Memory enhances the mere exposure effect. *Psychology and Marketing*, *29*(12), 995–1003.

Hall, J. (2015). Build authentic audience experiences through influencer marketing. Retrieved December 20, 2024, from www.forbes.com/sites/johnhall/2015/12/17/build-authenticaudience-experiences-through-influencer-marketing/#1cf07dda4ff2

Howison, J., Wiggins, A., & Crowston, K. (2011). Validity issues in the use of social network analysis with digital trace data. *Journal of the Association for Information Systems*, *12*(12), 768–797. https://scispace.com/pdf/validity-issues-in-the-use-of-social-network-analysis-with-3o5la3vq8f.pdf

Hudders, L., De Jans, S., & De Veirman, M. (2021). The commercialisation of social media stars: a literature review and conceptual framework on the strategic use of social media influencers. *Social Media Influencers in Strategic Communication*, *40*(6), 24–67. https://doi.org/10.1089/cyber.2020.0478

Jarrar, Y., Awobamise, A. O., & Aderibigbe, A. A. (2020). Effectiveness of influencer marketing vs social media sponsored advertising. Utopía y praxis latinoamericana: revista internacional de filosofía iberoamericana y teoría social, (12), 40-54. (This citation replaces yosra)

Jarrar, Y., Awobamise, A. O., & Aderibigbe, A. A. (2020) Effectiveness of influencer marketing vs social media sponsored advertising. *Revista Internacional de Filosofía Iberoamericana y Teoría Social, 12*, 40–54. https://doi.org/10.5281/zenodo.4280084

Jin, D. Y., & Feenberg, A. (2015). Commodity and community in social networking: Marx and the monetisation of user-generated content. *The Information Society, 13*(1), 52–60.

Johnson, M. R., & Woodcock, J. (2019) "And today's top donator is": How live streamers on Twitch. tv monetise and gamify their broadcasts. *Social Media+ Society, 5*(4), 1–11.

Jorge, A., Marôpo, L., & Nunes, T. (2018). 'I am not being sponsored to say this': a teen youtuber and her audience negotiate branded content. *Observatorio* (OBS*), *2018*(Special Issue), 76–96. https://doi.org/10.15847/obsOBS0001382

Kaltwasser, K. (2019). The mere-exposure effect – Why content marketing works. *Marketing and Media*. Retrieved December 20, 2024, from https://dmexco.com/stories/the-mere-exposure-effect-why-content-marketing-works/

Kalyango, Y., & Adu-Kumi, B. (2013). Impact of social media on political mobilization in East and West Africa. *Global Media Journal, 12*(22), 1–20.

Kelly, L., Kerr, G., & Drennan, J. (2010). Avoidance of advertising in social networking sites: The teenage perspective. *Journal of Interactive Advertising, 10*(2), 16–27.

Kotler, N. (2001). New ways of experiencing culture: the role of museums and marketing implications. *Museum Management and Curatorship, 19*(4), 417–425.

Kotler, P., & Armstrong, G. (2010). *Principles of marketing*. Pearson Education.

Latzko-Toth, G., Bonneau, C., & Millette, M. (2017). Small data, thick data: Thickening strategies for trace-based social media research. In A. Quan-Haase & L. Sloan (Eds.) *The SAGE handbook of social media research methods* (pp. 199–214). Sage Publications.

Le Bon, C., & Merunka, D. (2017). Uncovering and understanding the influence of repeated exposure on Fashion Products Adoption. *Journal of Marketing Development and Competitiveness, 11*(3), 21–31.

Leparoux, M., Minier, P., & Anand, A. (2019). The online influencers strategies and their impact on consumers decision process. *Vestnik of Saint Petersburg University. Management, 18*(3), 419–447.

Lin, H. C., Bruning, P. F., & Swarna, H. (2018). Using online opinion leaders to promote the hedonic and utilitarian value of products and services. *Business Horizons, 61*(3), 431–442. https://doi.org/10.1016/j.bushor.2018.01.010

Lou, C., & Yuan, S. (2019). Influencer marketing: How message value and credibility affect consumer trust of branded content on social media. *Journal of Interactive Advertising, 19*(1), 58–73.

McCarthy, J. (1981). *Basic marketing – A managerial approach*. Irwin McGraw Hill.

McQuail, D. (2010). McQuail's Mass Communication Theory (6th ed). London: Sage Publications.

Odoi, J. (2021). *The role of social media influencers in offline consumer purchase decision in Ghana*. Retrieved December 20, 2024, from https://repository.unimac.edu.gh/server/api/core/bitstreams/30159613-8ab9-40c8-8eee-9c6b3cef2549/content

Pilgrim, K., & Bohnet-Joschko, S. (2019). Selling health and happiness how influencers communicate on Instagram about dieting and exercise: Mixed methods research. *BMC Public Health, 19*(1), 1–9. https://doi.org/10.1186/s12889-019-7387-8

Ponirah, A. (2020). Influencer marketing as a marketing strategy. *Journal of Economicate Studies* (JoES) *4*(1), 11–16, https://journal.islamicateinstitute.co.id/index.php/joes/article/view/649

Purwandari, B. et al. (2022). The effect of interaction between followers and influencers on intention to follow travel recommendations from influencers in indonesia based on follower-influencer experience and emotional dimension. *Information*, *13*(8), 13, 384, https://www.mdpi.com/2078-2489/13/8/384

Quan-Haase, A., & Sloan, L. (Eds.) (2017). *The SAGE handbook of social media research methods*. Sage.

Robinson, B. M., & Elias, L. J. (2005). Novel stimuli are negative stimuli: evidence that negative affect is reduced in Mere Exposure Effect. *Perceptual and Motor Skills*, *100*(2), 365–372. https://doi.org/10.2466/PMS.100.2.365-372

Schwemmer, C., & Ziewiecki, S. (2018). Social media sellout: The increasing role of product promotion on YouTube. *Social Media+ Society*, *4*(3), 1–20. https://doi.org/10.1177/2056305118786720

Stokel-Walker, C. (2019, February 3). 'Instagram: beware of bad influencers … *The Guardian*. Retrieved December 20, 2024, from www.theguardian.com/technology/2019/feb/03/instagram-beware-bad-influencers-product-twittersnapchat-fyre-kendall-jenner-bella-hadid

Szczurski, M. (2017). Social media influencer: A lifestyle or a profession of the XXIst century? *International Journal of Management and Applied Science*, *3*(10), 4–7.

Tafesse, W., & Wood, B. P. (2021). Followers' engagement with Instagram influencers: The role of influencers' content and engagement strategy. *Journal of Retailing and Consumer Services*, *58*(102303), 1–9, https://doi.org/10.1016/j.jretconser.2020.102303

Taillon, B. J., Mueller, S. M., Kowalczyk, C. M., & Jones, D. N. (2020). Understanding the relationships between social media influencers and their followers: the moderating role of closeness. *Journal of Product & Brand Management*, *29*(6), 767–782.

Wang, K. Y., Shih, E., & Peracchio, L. A. (2013). How banner ads can be effective: Investigating the influences of exposure duration and banner ad complexity. *International Journal of Advertising*, *32*(1), 121–141.

Wibawa, R. C., Pratiwi, C. P., & Lasarati, H. (2021). The role of nano influencers through Instagram as an effective digital marketing strategy. *Advances in Economica, Business and Management Research*, *198*, 233–238.

Wind, Y. J. (2014). Toward a new marketing paradigm. In L. Moutinho, E. Bigné & A. K. Manrai (Eds.) *The Routledge companion to the future of marketing* (pp. 38–59). Routledge.

Woodcock, J., & Johnson, M. R. (2019). The affective labor and performance of live streaming on Twitch.tv. *Television and New Media*, *20*(8), 813–823. https://doi.org/10.1177/1527476419851077

Yin, R. K. (2014). *Case study research: Design and methods* (5th ed.). Sage

Zajonc, R. B. (1968). Attitudinal effects of mere exposure. *Journal of Personality and Social Psychology*, *9*(22), 461–472.

SECTION TWO

IDENTITY CONSTRUCTIONS, PERFORMANCES AND PERCEPTIONS

CHAPTER FIVE

'Chilling With the Big Boys': Self-Identity, Microcelebritism and the 'Bigger Picture' in Zimbabwean TikTok Culture

OSWELLED UREKE

INTRODUCTION

The exponential growth and proliferation of visual social networking sites (SNS) such as Instagram, TikTok, Facebook and X (formerly Twitter) necessitate studies of how people interact with and on them. Lately, it has become almost obligatory for everyone to have a digital presence, resulting in the rise of a 'profile economy' in which communication of the 'self' to others is paramount. The communication process entails letting others know what one is up to, stirred by design prompts such as Facebook's "what's on your mind?" While this presents tremendous networking opportunities, the downside is that addictive use of social networking sites sometimes causes stress, anxiety, and a sense of being overwhelmed such that some users require a 'digital detox' to get back to their normal lives (Mutsvairo, Ragnedda & Mabvundwi, 2022). Addictive use of SNS is characterized by a compulsive desire to post something regularly or to check what everyone else is up to, culminating in a 'fear of missing out' (FOMO) (Oberst et al., 2016). For these reasons, social media activities that involve sharing images of the self, are regarded as banal, narcissistic routines of self-curation fueled by an endless human desire for attention (Ibrahim, 2018).

This chapter focuses on TikTok, an SNS created by Chinese developer, ByteDance, in 2016, which people use to create, publish, and consume short, usually witty, fleeting moments of their lives. TikTok is both a performative and exhibitionistic platform whose content is created simultaneously for the benefit of other people (consumers) and self-gratification (of the creators). TikTok users film and exhibit themselves in a preferred manner to attract attention, likes, following, and sometimes monetary benefits. This evinces Tufekci's (2013) conceptualization of attention as a resource and opinion leaders as key mediators of attention. Higher likes and following metrics motivate users to produce more and similar content, making this an example of what Ureke (2021) has called 'audience commissioning'. Fundamentally, as TikTok creators play on the platform, they perform work for which they are rewarded with likes while financially enriching the platforms hosting the content. This unites the diametric opposites of play and labor into 'playbor' (Ferrer-Conill, 2018). This chapter explores how selected protagonists in the Zimbabwean TikTok community (ZimTikTokers) perform this playbor in the process of curating themselves. Put simply, the chapter examines what ZimTikTokers are 'up to'.

Created as Douyin, the application was launched as TikTok for international users in 2017. It became popular in 2020 as people used it to escape boredom during lockdowns imposed at the height of the Covid-19 pandemic (Kennedy, 2020). Since then, TikTok has become one of the most downloaded apps of the decade (Bazen, 2022; Schellewald, 2021; Zuo & Wang, 2019) with over a billion users as of July 2021 (O'Connor, 2021). Its content revolves around themes of beauty, fashion, dance trends, humor, testimonials, instructional videos (O'Connor, 2021; Zuo & Wang, 2019), and (mostly female) Generation Z culture (Bazen, 2022; Kennedy, 2020). Its content is sometimes regarded as "childish", "simple", "silly" and generally "lacking depth and complexity" (Schellewald, 2021, p. 1437). Because its videos are fleeting and random, giving self-interested, momentary pleasure, TikTok has been labeled "digital crack cocaine" (Schellewald, 2021; Koetsier, 2020). This suggests that the platform is never used for anything serious and is tantamount to what Ibrahim (2018, p. 39) calls the "aestheticization of the mundane and trivial in our everyday lives". There are also concerns about the use of TikTok for surveillance and a tendency to encroach into or reveal private spaces. Using the case of popular TikToker Charli D'Amelio, Kennedy (2020, p. 1070), argues that the platform has transformed girls' bedrooms "from a space previously conceptualized as private and safe from judgment to one of public visibility, surveillance, and evaluation" and that it "invites and rewards, via the logic of its metrics, the viral spectacle of girls' bedroom culture" (ibid). However, Schellewald (2021) regards such negative views of TikTok to be patronizing and top-down as they are often enunciated by conservative people who have fears about privacy and perceived addictiveness of digital media. Similarly, Markham

(2020, p. 2) rejects the idea that the digital age corrupts, corrodes, or dilutes what it means to be human, arguing that "Whatever the digital brings into being is as real as anything else".

The exponential growth in internet coverage and access to digital technology such as mobile phones has led to a corresponding growth in digital economies, including digital arts. TikTok content performances deserve interrogation because there is growing evidence that they have 'serious' use in society. In the US, TikTok was used by politicians to convey campaign messages in the run-up to the 2020 elections after the realization that it could reach a younger demographic (Bazen, 2022; Vaccari & Valeriani, 2021). The application was similarly used by politicians in the run-up to Zimbabwe's 2023 elections (Ureke, 2024). The social media platform has also been used to promote hatred and extremism, such that in the first three months of 2021 alone, it pulled down 300,000 videos for encouraging violent extremism (O'Connor, 2021, p. 7). Similar studies of many forms of popular culture such as music, memes and jokes show that they are not a simple laughing matter, but are important avenues for social commentary, which allow people to confront their everyday pressures (Msimanga, Tshuma & Matsilele, 2022; Källstig, 2021; Ureke & Washaya, 2016; Chiumbu & Musemwa, 2012; Willems, 2008). In spite of TikTok's popularity and ubiquity, there is sporadic literature on it, with very little scholarly attention paid to the SNS in an African, and specifically Zimbabwean context (Ureke, 2024; Machirori, 2023). This is in stark contrast to the abundance of studies on the use by Zimbabweans of SNSs such as Facebook and X (Mare, 2018; Chibuwe & Ureke, 2016; Mututwa & Mare, 2021; Mpofu & Mare, 2020).

Zimbabwe TikTok is selected as a case because studying (African) popular culture content can be greatly aided by an understanding of the broader context in which such content is created, shared, and consumed (Schellewald, 2021). Thus, the researcher's own lived realities are at the core of the interpretive endeavor of the study. The scope of the study is between January 2021 and July 2022. The researcher joined TikTok in January 2021.

ONLINE PERFORMANCE, MICROCELEBRITISM AND THE CONCEPT OF 'BEING ZIMBABWEAN'

TikTok videos can be read as performances, which Goffman (1956, p. 13) defines as "the activity of an individual which occurs during a period marked by his continuous presence before a set of observers, and which has some influence on the observers". Similarly, Marshall (2010, p. 40) views online performances as a "staging of the self" to a wider public. The 'self' presented online is highly aware of an audience thus they deliberately construct a character for their performance of the self (Marshall, 2010). In the process, the notion of what is 'public' and what is 'private' is lost as users share their selves "as commodities for the consumption of others" (Ibrahim, 2018, p. 2). Thus, private places such as bathrooms and bedrooms and even private body parts are exhibited for public amusement. TikTok creators construct a persona for online use, which is why they dress/undress in costumes and make-up that suits their self-assigned roles. They can become famous for this, in the process, becoming 'micro-celebrities'. A microcelebrity is an ordinary person who "amps up" their popularity through a unique style of online performance (Johnston, 2020, p. 509), or a person who attains celebrity status or popularity via strategic and concerted cultivation of an audience through social media (Khamis et al., 2017).

This chapter deploys as its theoretical premise, the concept of 'being Zimbabwean', which relates to the theory of identity. Admittedly, identity is always in flux, depending on the conditions surrounding a person. People manifest different identities at work, at home, at places of worship, at school etc. As such, TikTok performances are one of the several possible iterations of identities which, according to the moment, amplify or conceal certain traits. According to Stuart Hall (1989), specific cultural and historical contexts shape or construct how one enunciates themselves. Yet, the way people express themselves is central to any quest to understand who they are. danah boyd (2011) argues that people rarely narrate their history before telling a story, yet that history is important to the significance of the story. boyd (ibid) further argues that when people perform online, they may be aware of the immediate audience, yet their performances may become accessible and may indeed be searched for by other unforeseen audiences who may or may not be aware of the context of the performance. Thus, context is always important when interpreting online self-enunciations. As Källstig (2021, pp. 49–50) contends on Zimbabwean stand-up comedy, performance occurs within society and is an iteration of that society's norms thus "in articulating their experiences on stage, Zimbabwean stand-up comedians enact the society they are in". The individual on TikTok reveals the 'self' through performance, just as Chibuwe, Mpofu & Bhowa (2021, p. 1) observe of anonymous individuals on Twitter, that: "The individual inadvertently inscribes himself or herself in what s/he writes." Thus, online identity is both a construction and a perception. Individuals construct their identity initially around the user profile which reveals personal information about themselves. In this process, users selectively and coherently organize their online experiences into meaningful narratives (Gilpin, 2011). As noted by Zizzi Papacharissi (2011, p. 304), self-presentation is ever-evolving through a series of presentations, comparisons, adjustments, and defenses "against a constellation of social, cultural, economic or political realities". Thus, the aesthetic of one's online performances becomes enmeshed with their identity. What we see on TikTok are not the actual people, but their digital manifestations or the 'semiotic self' (Wiley, 1994) which can be reproduced and shared. At the same time, these apparitions derive from real people who reside in *real spaces* and *real time* and perform using their *real bodies*.

TikTok is an important platform in the formation and maintenance of the self-identity because users deliberately project their personal experiences but also experience self-worth from the validation they get from other users' reactions to their content. High numbers of likes, shares, and follows reinforce some online behavior. Thus, TikTokers use the evaluation and interaction of networked others to complete their identity construction. In line with this Khamis et al. (2017, p. 196) contend that "Social media is driven by a specific kind of identity construction – self mediation – and what users post, share and like effectively creates a highly curated and often abridged snapshot of how they want to be seen" and equally, what they want to conceal. It is further argued here that, when considered collectively, the videos ascribed to a specific region, for example #zimtiktok reveal some pattern or a cultural mural that shows the 'bigger picture' or group identity of 'being Zimbabwean'. This is done with caution, noting Kashope Wright's (2002) problematics of affixing different performances to a singular identity. In so doing, the contested nature of *being Zimbabwean* needs to be acknowledged. Such contestation manifests in different ways such as ethnic, linguistic, racial, and cultural differences. I am cautious that 'Zimbabweanness' is taken for granted and often constructed around perspectives that privilege the Shona ethnic group (Ndlovu-Gatsheni, 2009; Ncube, 2014). Therefore, #zimtiktok is analyzed while appreciating the limitation that it is a grouping of content posted by different people in different spaces and with different intentions. Thus, the double bind of this research endeavor lies in the methodological compulsion to deal with a geo-cultural delimitation that reduces spontaneity while conscious of the mobility and cosmopolitanism fostered by SNSs which disembeds people's digital experience from physical locations. As Gustafson (2001) argues, place and place attachment are increasingly losing significance when trying to understand everyday experiences. To use Hall's (1995) explanation, identity can be either 'rooted' or 'routed'. In terms of the 'rooted', the natural bond that exists between people and the places of their belonging, is central to their identity formation. It represents their identity in terms of their 'roots', which suggests belonging to a particular place and a particular way of doing things within that space. This is an essentialist definition of identity as a personality or combination of traits linked to a specific territory which yields universalized statements such as 'This is not the way Africans behave' or 'An African man is supposed to do a, b, c'. Thus, those without proper 'rooting' deviate from the norm. Hall (1995) argues that, instead of being 'rooted', identity is becoming 'routed' which means that instead of linking people to places, we may also consider their exchanges, encounters, and movements. Developments in communication technology mean people are increasingly becoming mobile and not attached to places (Gustafson, 2001). Instead of seeing identity as either 'rooted' or 'routed' I use an eclectic approach to identity where people's performances, though linked with certain territories, are understood as part of their interconnectedness in the digital world. My interpretation may impose stereotypes on the activities of TikTok creators, which may be tangential to their offline lives. At the same time, these users do not use the App in similar, uniform, or coherent ways. Furthermore, the polysemy of images makes analysis of TikTok performances complex unlike for discursive platforms.

There are now entrenched or rooted ways of perceiving and imagining Zimbabweans, stemming from the well-documented 'Zimbabwean crisis'. The term 'Zimbabwean crisis' has been used extensively to describe a myriad of challenges, obstacles and threats that face ordinary Zimbabweans (Mhiripiri & Ureke, 2019; Chiumbu & Musemwa, 2012). Thus, Zimbabwe has morphed beyond being merely the name of a country to an appellation synonymous with crisis and strife. One of the manifestations of this crisis is a massive exodus of Zimbabweans to other countries in search of better economic fortunes. In those countries, Zimbabweans are looked down upon and often given derogatory names. For example, in the United Kingdom (UK), care workers of Zimbabwean origin are dubbed BBC, meaning 'British Bottom Cleaners', 'bum technicians' or 'ma.dot.com' ("dot implying dirt" or human excretion), which has left them "stressed and frustrated" (McGregor, 2007, p. 802). Those who have migrated to neighboring countries such as Botswana and South Africa -where they are derogatively called *Makwerekwere* – are also inhumanely treated (Marr, 2012) or, in worst cases, killed in xenophobic riots (Hiropoulos, 2019). Against this background, *being* Zimbabwean is tantamount to *being* desperate, unhappy, forlorn, humiliated, brooding, ailing, and many other things associated with an unhappy place. Zimbabwe features among the most unhappy countries in the world, in the United Nations (UN) -sponsored World Happiness Report (Helliwell et al 2021). Although the report also takes the Covid-19 pandemic into consideration, it comes as no surprise, as Zimbabwe already ranks lowly on other indices such as corruption, indebtedness, and life expectancy (see Transparency International, 2021; WHO, 2020). One can debate the nature of such reports from a contextual standpoint, but they do provide an idea of what 'being Zimbabwean' means theoretically. This chapter, therefore, analyzes performances by some zimtiktokers to examine whether or not their acts are consistent with the common perception of a Zimbabwean. Because TikTok thrives on performance, it is possible to decode things like dances, gestures, and language in the context of cultural identity. As Stuart Hall (1989) argues, cultural identity reflects the shared historical experiences and cultural codes that provide continuous frames of reference and meaning. Thus, each performance on Zimbabwean TikTok has common frames of reference that, when considered together, constitute the cultural identity of that digital community. As Christensen (2003) contends, digital technologies only assert those identities that already exist offline.

METHODOLOGY

According to Rose (2014), images represent symbolic and communicative activities, which suggests that visuals must be interpreted within the context which they are created and shared. Socio-cultural appreciation of the context in which images are made is fundamental to the unpacking of any visual culture. For one to interpret online performances, one needs to have some lived experience or knowledge about what is happening within that geo-political space. The immediate methodological challenge that arises is on what basis to categorize individual videos by different users as "Zimbabwean". The TikTok algorithm normally suggests content to users under the 'For You' section, based on several factors including the user's geolocation, liked videos as well as viewing patterns. The application's traffic distribution is largely based on "neighborhood and attention" (Zuo & Wang, 2019, p. 2), which means that a user is likely to get on their timeline, content within their geographic location or that to which they normally pay attention. These factors feed into a recommendation algorithm that suggests videos that one might watch or users that one might follow. This means the TikTok feed that one encounters is not automatically from a particular country, thus, there is need for further background research before ascribing social media content a territorial tag.

In this study, data was collected under the hashtags #zimtiktok and #zimbabweantiktok. Hashtags represent niche communities that unite creators with the same interests (routes) or geolocation (roots). The challenge with this method is that a hashtag only shows to which discourse content belongs, not always the geo-location. For example, the Nel twins, who have a Zimbabwean father but live in Southampton, UK (The Nel Twins, n.d) sometimes appear under #zimtiktok. Schellewald (2021, p. 1440) cautions that "An overinterpretation of individual videos needs to be avoided, and instead, focus should be set on their embeddedness within the broader background of shared trends, memes or platform-specific language". After doing a scronalysis (Ureke, 2024) videos were selected purposively based on the corpus of data that is known i.e. performances from, about, or relating to Zimbabwe, broadly contained under the hashtag #zimtiktok and #zimbabweantiktok. Top accounts were sought, focusing on those with more than 50000 followers. Using scronalysis, the researcher then searched for and selected "most followed videos" and considered how many times these videos had been liked. The researcher considered what the videos' subjects were and what soundtrack had been used. Desktop research was conducted on the soundtracks and other contextual detail.

When users reach a certain number of followers on social media platforms, they become 'influencers' – "individuals with big followings online which attract a large amount of engagement" (Kay, Mulcahy & Parkinson, 2020, p. 250). Influencers can be classified as micro-influencers (those with a low following) and macro-influencers (high following) (Kay et al., 2020). Sofia Correa de Sousa (2020) further breaks down influencer categories into six tiers, namely nano, micro, mid-tier, macro, mega and celebrity influencers. According to de Sousa, the numbers of followers/likes vary according to the platform (e.g. Instagram, YouTube etc.), but generally, mid-tier influencers range between 50 000–100 000 likes. Building on this influencer segmentation, the study selected those TikTokers with at least 50 000 followers. This is a high number considering that in Zimbabwe, internet access is severely limited (Freedom House, 2021) compounded by the fact that TikTok is a fairly recent innovation. The TikTokers were ranked into a top 30 by follow metrics assuming that the higher the number of followers a user had, the higher their popularity. Secondly, the higher the likes for a video, the higher its popularity. Using the most followed videos meant they were possibly the ones that resonated with Zimbabwean users/followers' tastes. Below is a table that illustrates the data captured (Table 5.1).

Hermeneutics was used to analyze the content. Most TikTok content requires an awareness of context in order to get their meaning. Some of the performances revolve around local occurrences which may appear meaningless to an 'outsider' without context. Dramatizations are usually in indigenous language and may be about local occurrences that have only local significance.

'TWERK-TOK', PUB-LIKE SPHERE: ZIMTIKTOKERS DANCING THROUGH THE CRISIS

Dancing is one of the most common performances by Zimbabwean TikTok creators. At the time of writing, the five most followed creators were Victor Ivyic (@victor_ivyic), Nel twins (@shanaeandrenae), Tee (@tiann222), Madamboss Zim (@madambosszim), and Lonlisha98 (@lonlisha98), whose videos had the common theme of dancing. The five most viewed videos were the Nel twins' video dancing to 'What's up everybody', Ivyic's video reacting to a trending 'Kelly dance', Madamboss Zim's 'Vulindlela' dance, Justcookiedough's (@justcookiedough1) dramatization of 'When he asks me to go on top' [during sex] and Bigbabyamy's (@bigbabyamy) complaint about lengthy TikTok videos. The five most liked videos were the Nel twins' dancing video, Bigbabyamy's complaint,

Table 5.1. ZimTikTok influencers (Source: the author)

Account	Followers	Most viewed video	Views	Likes	Date posted	Act	soundtrack contained
Roshney Kellendria Jussah @queen_of_skits	181.4k	African haidressers be like	504k	45k	16-Jun-21	Mimicing a West African hairdresser	beverly adaeze 136 vids
Mama Vee @ mamavee_zw	87.2k	my biggest mistake in johannesburg	300k	8.3K	02-Apr	Situational drama bragging about prostitution in SA	original sound 4 vids
Ella_zw @ella_zw	57.5k	Untitled	377.8k	12.9k	13-Sep-21	Mimicing Emmanuel Makandiwa sermon	ruvarashe096 – 477 vids
Tee @tianr.222	409.5k	Baba inzwaika munamato wangu	409.6k	10.4k	26-Sep-21	Lip syncing over Christian hymn "inzwai munamato wangu"	ameno and lion of judah (Lebo Sekgobela)
Patiencetapiwa @ patiencetapiwa	59.9k	This kid	384k	13.8k	01-Apr-22	Mimicing "ndaitoda kudhigidha" viral video	from original clip Van Choga – 3474
Skits By Kingsley @ kingsleezw	122.7k	when you run with big boys	421.9k	26.8k	24-Dec-21	Lip syncing to 'Ameno' then 'Lion of Judah'	
Lonlisha @lonlisha98	270.5k	Untitled	442.4k	21.7k	02-Feb-22	Dancing to 'Zula zula'	Zula zula – 138.5k
Madamboss Zim @ madambosszim	351.7k	untitled	2.8M	234.2k	21-Apr-21	Dancing to 'Vuli ndlela'	Vulindlela, b fassie - 13.8k vids

Continued

Table 5.1. Continued

Account	Followers	Most viewed video	Views	Likes	Date posted	Act	soundtrack contained
Mai Tt @ maitsdiaries1	91.7k	Ndaitoda	537.8k	16.4k	15-Apr-22	Mimicing “ndaitoda kudhigidha” viral video	vanchoga1 -3361 vids
Lin dah @ itsyogallin353	126.9k	untitled	184.1k	6.2K	03-Jan-22	Mimicing Emmanuel Makandiwa sermon	Emmanuel Makandiwa sermon – 205 vids
tanny tanny @ tannytanny24	84.6k	challenge went wrong	1.1m	43.4k	10-Dec-21	Situational drama of pregnant woman	Love nwantiti Ckay ft Joeboy – 169k vids
Mel @meltasha96	169.1k	untitled	372.3k	19k	27-May-22	Dancing to Buga	Buga – Kizz Daniel and Tekno -167k vids
Michellenativel @ michelle.nativel	95.1k	Millenials where you at????	1.5M	304.3K	23-Jun-21	Dancin and dramatizing to a song	Nado Wick – Who want smoke – 188 vids
Astra @astra632	188k	Me seeing people suffering the wrath of Umjolo	804.5k	40.5k	13-Oct-21	Enacting singing to a Shona adaptation of Joe Boy’s Alcohol	Achim McG – Mjolo - 1464 vids
Caddie C @caddiec	55.4k	How Zimbabwean Ladies were made	764.4k	47.2k	15-Feb-21	Dramatizing her rejection of all ‘bad’ things about Zimbabwean women	755.7k vids

Account	Followers	Most viewed video	Views	Likes	Date posted	Act	soundtrack contained
Justcookiedough @ justcookiedough	94.9k	When he asks me to go on top	2.3M	130.2K	26-Jun-21	dressing up after sex "I came to get D, not to give P"	Male voice – 3536 vids
Zvoboks @zvoboks	136.9k	When she … wants to	1M	50.9K	28-Apr-21	except from Estate Fever Nigerian comedy	Original sound from the comedy – 323 vids
Carlton Mandaza @ carl_official.zw	90.2k	No blinking	1.2M	88.1K	21-Jan-22	Shaking to music and not blinking	Emergency Call ft Welle SA, Lusha & Major Keys – 160.3k vds
Bigbabyamy @bigbabyamy	80k	Ah ah I rebuke/ We lik spending money	1.7M	403.4k	Aug 20/28 April 22	complaining about TikTok 3 min vids	hers 7 vids/86.8k vids
Tarrie and Martin @ tarriemartin	123.5k	untitled	1.7M	57.7K	10-Jun-22	Lady struggling to walk in high heels, with her partner	Laugh – Theif
KurtsyNkomo @ kurtsynkomo	64.6k	When you are Zimbabwean, but you get invited to a Congo party	96.3k	30.62k	27-Apr-22	Dancing to Rhumba track	Acceleration (Seben) – Super Tshim

Continued

Table 5.1. Continued

Account	Followers	Most viewed video	Views	Likes	Date posted	Act	soundtrack contained
Tadiwa @wyktadiwa	86.7k	I wanted to do the challenge but all eyes were on me	493.7k	17.0k	26-Dec-21	Dancing to Enzo Ishall's Siki	Siki – Enzo Ishall – 9180 vids
Axecure Sneakers @ magic_wacho	104.6k	When Tadiwa posted that she is now single on Instagram story	15.8k		22-May	Lip sync to Wakambondidirei	Karamba kurambwa – 2507 vids
Nyasha @yyolash_	124.4k	untitled	340k	18.4k	02-Feb-21	Lip syncing to Herman's Zvandofarira	Zvandofarira – Herman – 3033 vids
Emmanuel Makandiwa	53.7k	Is saying sorry enough?	437.k	17.5k	24-Feb	Sermon teaching people on propert apology and thanking ettiquette	original 20 vids
Chipo the trouble causer @ chipothetroublecauser	88.1k	untitled	135.4k	4059	04-Jun	Dancing to Jah Prayzah's Chinamira	Chinamira – Jah Prayzah – 28 vids

Account	Followers	Most viewed video	Views	Likes	Date posted	Act	soundtrack contained
Nel Twins @ shanaeandranae	1.4m	Hey what's up everybody	8.2M	800K	05-Sep-18	Dancing to whats up everybody	
Victor Ivyic @victor_ ivyic	2.3m	Guys after discovering the Kelly trend	4.6M	300k	25-Jun-22	Dramatisation of surprise	Gwijoavenue

Nel twins have Zimbabwean dad. They are from Southampton, UK. They interviewed him on Youtube: https://www.youtube.com/watch?v=OgVMmd9VK90 accessed 22 June 2022

nel twins dating a s a zimbanwean girl 30.2k likes, watched 360.9k times

TikTok micro influencer 50000–150000 followers: https://www.viralnation.com/blog/micro-macro-celebrity-get-to-know-your-influencer-tiers/#:~:text=This%20is%20why%20macro%2Dinfluencers,750%2C000%20%E2%80%93%202%2C500%2C000%20followers%20on%20TikTok.

Michelle Nativel's (@michelle.nativel, formerly Thug and cupcake) dance, Ivyic's reaction to a dance and Madam Boss' *Vulindlela* dance.

Dancing was a recurring performance even for those TikTokers whose most popular videos were not dances. In many instances, the performances featured scantily dressed (mostly female) creators twerking, gyrating, wining or otherwise seductively exhibiting their anatomies. They joined in the fun of popular global dance challenges but often the effort and attention was placed on the uniqueness of their bodies or sense of fashion. The evident expenditure on wardrobe, make-up and props to maximize attention, shows an entrepreneurial persistence to boost popularity, which is a consistent trait of most TikTok performances. For example, many videos by Lonlisha, Justcookiedough and Mel (@meltasha96) showed off the body, make-up and designer regalia. Justcookiedough was in many videos dressed in revealing or figure-hugging attire. Similarly, Lonslisha was consistently dressed in crop-tops, short dresses or tight-fitting jeans. She invariably liked to gyrate and turn her back to the camera to show off her backside. This seemed clearly intended, as she constantly deployed medium or full body 'upskirt' shots that could show this detail. In her most popular video, she was dressed in a tight-fitting black dress and sandals in an open space where she danced to the popular South African track *Zula Zula* (Khanyisa, Villosoul and Focalistic) first facing the camera, then turning to show her side view with a self-conscious smack on her face.

Like Lonlisha and Justcookiedough, Mel frequently exhibited her body by performing in revealing clothes, including swimwear. In her most popular video, she was dressed in a military green vest and a checkered mini-skirt wining to Nigerian pop track *Buga* (Kizz Daniel ft Tekno). The sexually suggestive dance trope, to some extent, makes Zimbabwean TikTok a *TwerkTok* [author's term] where creators compete on twerking and showing off flesh. This sets TikTok apart from other SNSs that thrive on discourse and debate, such as Twitter and Facebook, which have been lauded for their potentials of fostering a public sphere of ideas. TikTok performances, it can be argued, instead foster a 'pub-like sphere' where users are carefree and epitomize a sense of *joie de vivre* (joy of living), punctuated with vanity and attention-seeking narcissism, which Khamis et al. (2017, p. 199) liken to an "epidemic of self-obsession". From this point of view, TikTok usage has gone beyond Graeme Turner's (2004) 'demotic turn' and has since morphed into what Ibrahim (2018) calls a 'curatorial turn' marked by an obsession with the commodification of the self. While dancing and showing off are consistent with the uses of TikTok elsewhere, given the context provided about Zimbabwe, the dance routines give the impression that Zimbabweans on TikTok are dancing through their crisis. This is in sharp contrast to the gloomy image of a Zimbabwe in crisis that has been documented widely. These performances resonate with traditional uses of dance in Zimbabwean society, where it has previously been associated with therapy (Thram, 1999) and where the body is used as the focal point of performance subverting the disadvantage of not always having technological props such as lights and scenery (Ravengai, 2013).

When a user produces a TikTok video, especially when they turn the camera on themselves, they have production and performative decisions to make. The process is informed by choice and self-reflection – from the creator's own appearance to their set. In their mind, they already have a 'script' of what they want to perform, how they want to capture it, and what meaning they intend to convey. The difference between a photograph or video of someone taken by another, and one taken by oneself, is that, in the first instance, the image communicates what the photographer *intends to show* while in the latter instance, the image communicates how the content creator *intends to be seen*. For example, in her most popular post Tadiwa (@wyktadiwa), wearing a red basketball top and jean shorts, coyly dances to Zimbabwe dancehall artist Enzo Ishall's *Siki* in an open parking space. She performs a few moves, looks around self-consciously, and gives up. The caption reads: "I wanted to do the challenge, but all eyes were on me (laughing emojis) *zvaramba* [I give up]". This, together with Lonlisha's 'I had to embarrass myself' admission, reflects self-consciousness on the part of the performers. Thus, the dance performances by the TikTokers are deliberate, not by happenstance. Given the background of Zimbabweans' use of other SNSs, one would assume that TikTok could be, yet another platform used by citizens to predominantly portray and interact about their political and socio-economic troubles. Yet many ordinary Zimbabwean TikTokers seem to avoid political subjects because they are aware of the 'gaze' of observers. Perhaps they are equally aware of the well-documented harassment of influencers who have used social media for political messaging that goes contrary to the ruling ZANU PF party ideology.

TO BE OR NOT TO BE ZIMBABWEAN ONLINE

Many people shun their Zimbabwean roots as a result of the negativity increasingly associated with the country, reigniting Ndlovu-Gatsheni's (2009), do Zimbabweans exist? Unlike on Twitter and Facebook where topics of discussion indicate participants' origin, the banality of TikTok performances is oftentimes used to mask user identity. The masking of identity is in itself, a performance because it entails 'becoming' someone or something that one is actually not. Such a performance is classified by Goffman (1956) as cynical because only the performer obtains pleasure from his/her masquerade. In some cases, followers ask creators about their identity if they notice that their performances are rooted in Zimbabwean culture or are using Zimbabwean music. Such appearances and props constitute what Goffman (1956, p. 13) classifies as a 'front', "that part of the individual's performance which regularly functions in a general and fixed fashion to define the situation for those who observe the performance". For instance, Caddie C's (@caddiec) most viewed post is in response to a fan comment "please do how Zimbabwean ladies are made" which was a reaction to her earlier video on "how lesbians were created". She has Zimbabwean, Australian, South African and LGBTIQ+ movement flags on her profile to symbolize her multiple identities. As argued by Ureke (2024) these signs on a user's bio represent their ethos, in this case Caddie C as Zimbabwean and LGBTIQ+. In contrast, Victor Ivyic, who is reportedly Zimbabwean born (IOL, 2022) has rejected this alleged identity. According to widely circulated reports, Ivyic, who identifies as South African, told a follower who had messaged him directly, that only one of his parents hails from Zimbabwe. One of the reports quotes him as having said to the follower: "Hi, how are you? I saw your comment about why I don't want people to know. I did not say that. I am just not from Zimbabwe. One of my parent (sic) is. Thank you for your concern though, I appreciate" (Editor, 2022). In some of Ivyic's performances he lip synced to music by Zimbabwean artists such as Oliver Mtukudzi, Ally Mapiye and Leonard Dembo which naturally made his followers curious about his identity. Ivyic's example lies at the heart of Hall's rooted/routed identity. It shows the problems associated with essentialist definitions of identity as rooted.

Yet, in some cases, creators included Zimbabwean brands and such other props in their performances as a way of declaring their allegiance to Zimbabwe as a place and brand. For instance, in Mel's video "show me you are Zimbabwean without saying", she displayed Zimbabwean brands Nestle Cerevita, Mazoe Orange Crush, and Colcom pork pie with the caption "gifts from my mom back in Zimbabwe". These products are quite popular among Zimbabweans in the diaspora. In another video, she eats Sadza (Zimbabwe's staple starch) and Okra, which is also a common relish in Zimbabwe. By using as props brands that have demonstrated resilience and magnetic appeal in the face of the general de-marketing of Zimbabwe, Mel might be showcasing pride in her cultural identity in the face of adversity. As if to prove this, Mel captions one of the videos #proudlyzimbabwean. Likewise, in Patiencetapiwa's (@patiencetapiwaa) most popular performance, she holds a Dairiboard Pfuko Maheu, an equally popular Zimbabwean drink. The UK-based Nel twins also regularly post videos that link to their Zimbabwean roots. In one of the videos, they enact "dating as a Zimbabwean". Many users include the Zimbabwean flag in their profiles to make their identity apparent and thus brand themselves around national identity. The Zimbabwean flag was creatively appropriated by the cyberprotest movement #ThisFlag to mount opposition against the ruling ZANU (PF) party (Mpofu & Mare, 2020). This use of the Zimbabwean flag is patriotic symbolism that could be seen as a yearning for Zimbabwean roots in the face of negative perceptions of the country and the dehumanizing conditions that citizens experience at home and abroad.

CHILLING WITH THE BIG BOYS: CURATION OF ELEGANCE, BEAUTIFUL BODIES, AND POPULAR MUSIC

ZimTikTok videos also cover a variety of other subjects including exhibiting opulent places, cosmetics, designer clothes, high-end technology, nutritional supplements, physical workouts, and imitation of celebrity lives. The home interior, especially the bedroom, is one of the most featured spaces in TikTok videos. In their videos, Zimbabwean TikTokers Pamela Ella (@ella_zw), Mel, Nyasha (@yyolash_), Madam Boss and Victor Ivyc are always elegantly dressed and made up. In some cases, they endorse international products and popular culture. For example, in her most viewed video, Madam Boss is dressed in a Zulu bead outfit over a tight-fitting white dress while dancing to yesteryear South African hit song *Vulindlela* (Brenda Fassie). In a related video, Astra enacts a singing act, using a brush hung from the ceiling as a 'mic'. The song is a Shona remix to Joe Boy's *Alcohol* but is about '*umjolo*', South African slang for 'love'. Related to this is a video by KurtsyNkomo (@kurstynkomo), 'When you are Zimbabwean, but you get invited to a Congo party' in which she dances to a Congolese Rhumba track dressed in a pink crop top. This suggests that TikTok is one cosmopolitan community that provides a route for the expression of transnational cultures. At the same time, it demonstrates the concept of playbour discussed earlier. While the creators are 'playing' they are providing free labor for the marketing of the wardrobe and music they use in their performances.

The use of globally appealing soundtracks and settings by ZimTikTokers is designed to maximize visibility. As Johnston (2020, p. 509) contends, "garnering attention is work that relies on the management of the self and interpersonal engagements with followers". To create a profile and share content is to become part of the digital world, such that one's validation is not simply a matter of self-love but also depends on how one is rated by other online peers. This is why TikTokers invoke popular trends such as viral jokes and hit songs. In some of the studied cases, performers used soundtracks made by Zimbabwean artistes, which made the music go viral too, amplified by the popularity of the TikTokers' performances. Thus, there was a global cultural exchange in which Zimbabwean popular culture interacted with the dominant players in the global cultural industry. The export of both Zimbabwean popular music and TikTok performances onto the global scene can be metaphorically described as 'chilling with the big boys', adopted from Goya Menor and Nektunez's Amapiano track *Ameno*, one of the songs that went viral on TikTok around 2021–22. Goya Menor is a Nigerian artist who partnered with a Ghanaian music producer to remix the song on an Amapiano soundtrack. Amapiano is a music genre that originated and was popularized in South Africa. *Ameno* has become a worldwide hit with more than 18 million views on YouTube in about three months at the time of writing (Vibe Music, 2021), possibly as a result of its popularity on TikTok.

In many cases the creators danced to the accompanying music, often complementing the performance with gestures and mimicry that acted out the meaning of the lyrics. This unpacked the meaning of the music to non-native speakers and helped not only the music but the performances to go viral. Soon, other users would pick on the performance and join the "challenge" of mimicry, resulting in a *perfor-demic* [author's term]– a performance that goes viral to pandemic proportions. While performance may be personal and specific to a location, the universal reach of TikTok and the viral nature of online content globalizes performances. By 'challenging' others to repeat or mimic certain performances, content reach is multiplied within and through networks. As Lizelle Bischoff (2017, p. 263) observes the "'glocalization' of culture enabled by the use of digital technologies has given us unprecedented access to voices, stories, ideas, and views from cultures other than our own". Thus 'unhappy Zimbabweans' took to TikTok to participate in global digital culture, not only mimicking the culture of places abroad but also adding their own strokes on the global digital culture mural. Therefore, as Bischoff further points out, the ubiquity of digital technology means the world is, on one hand, deterritorialized through the broadening of cultural horizons such that there is a "disappearance of the relation between culture and its social and geographic territories" but, on the other hand, there is a reterritorialisation in the sense that the same digital arts relate to "specific socio-cultural and historical experiences and contexts of the geographical locations the art was produced in" (Bischoff, 2017, p. 263). Hence, art expressed through Zimbabwean performance, which in itself borrowed heavily from the nation's (rooted) culture(s), shared the same spaces and sometimes dueted (was routed) with other global performances and cultures. In the process, TikTok became the happy place where ZimTikTokers could reclaim their humanity trodden upon in other spheres of life. It became their place to 'chill' and exhibit 'being Zimbabwean' that markedly contrasted with stereotypical frames of 'being Zimbabwean' as represented in mainstream popular cultural outlets.

JUST FOR LAUGHS? THE BANAL, MIMICRY AND DRAMATIZATION OF THE EVERYDAY

Because of its trendy tendency, TikTok can be regarded as a 'memefication of everyday life' drawing from social and cultural elements common in some spaces. It promotes not only meme culture but also mimic culture. With mimicry, creators imitate speech, accent, gestures, and facial expressions. The acts of mimicry might be adaptations of topical news, public pronouncements, church sermons or trending dance routines. Because it does not depend on textual registers for communication, TikTok accommodates those who are unable to write. The originality of the videos is relatable, from people lip-syncing to popular music tracks to someone sprinting on a gym treadmill, to an imitation of political leaders' speeches. TikTok videos are often banal, quotidian, and mundane in their construction and subject. Instead of trivializing them for that, the ordinariness is what makes them an important window to society. The seemingly silly and unrefined performances reflect everyday life. Some of the analyzed ZimTikTok videos utilize socio-realism to show things that may be occurring in society. Such enactments include topics that would otherwise be regarded as taboo in Zimbabwe's relatively conservative cultures. Mama Vee (@mamavee_zw) is one of the creators that deploy situational drama quite often. Mama Vee is a man who dresses himself as a female character. In his/her most popular video 'My biggest mistake in Johannesburg' –Mama Vee is seated on the passenger's side of a car driven by a 'South African' man. She is engaged in a phone conversation, speaking in Shona language, that she assumes the driver cannot comprehend. In the tele-conversation, she brags that she is engaged in prostitution in South Africa while her husband thinks she is selling wares. This enactment touches on the topical subject of Zimbabwean entrepreneurs who frequently travel to neighboring countries for informal trade. In those countries, they sell a variety of wares and with the proceeds, buy relatively cheaper groceries and clothing items for their families back in Zimbabwe. Media reports suggest that some of these migrants, without reliable sources of income, sometimes resort to commercial sex work among other things (Staff Reporter, 2014; External Writer, 2011). In a related performance, Justcookledough's most viewed video, a lady is midway through dressing up after a sexual act. Mimicking a viral soundtrack, she says "I am not here to suffer. I am not here to … to … [laughs]". The video is captioned. "I came to GET D, not to give P. Thanks".

Mai Tt is another performer who dramatizing viral memes. In her most viewed video, she is dressed in bikini top and jean shorts standing in a swimming pool. She mimics a commonplace seemingly meaningless exchange between two people, which goes along like this:

Voice: *hee*? [what?]
Voice 1: *Ndaitoda kudhigidha mufana wangu* [I really wanted to swim, young man]
Voice: *kudhigidha payi?* [swimming where?]
Voice 1: *Ah zveipapo ndaitoda* [At that moment I really wanted to]
Voice: *kudigidha payi*? [swimming where?]
Voice 1: *ah uri kuona chii*? [you see?]
Voice: *ehe* [Yes]
Voice 1: *uri kuona iwewe*? [You see?]
Voice: *ehe* [yes]
Voice 1: *uri kuona ini*? [you see me?]
Voice: ehe [yes]
Voice 1: *kudhara* [long time ago-laughter].

The conversation is a man confiding in his friend that he wanted to have sex with an unnamed partner. The conversation went viral in Zimbabwe because of its sexual innuendos. Patiencetapiwa used the same audio track to enact her most viewed video as well. The dialogue lines have since been used in a recent song by Boom Beto, a Zimbabwean dancehall music artist. These interconnected performances and their popularity show that they touch on subjects that are not only interesting to other TikTok users but have wider cultural relevance among Zimbabweans. In Mai Tt's case, she uses the swimming pool as a front to reverse the metaphor of swimming as having sex. Performers like Mai Tt, Patiencetapiwa, Mama Vee and Justcookiedough, among others act as jesters who create humor around otherwise serious subjects to make them more palatable. Similar characters called *sahwiras* (friends) often feature at Shona public functions like funerals where they make jokes about the deceased. This is believed to lighten the somber mood engulfing the occasion. But while people laugh at the humor, they also reflect on the underlying critical issues raised by the performances. Therefore, it can be argued that TikTok plays a didactic function masked by its humorous presentation.

Other performances analyzed are based on mimicry and punchlines also deriving from actuality. For example, Ella frequently mimics forms of public speech such as church sermons and radio announcements. She famously mimics soundbites by Dee Jays, delivered over popular soundtracks. She might brandish a remote control, or an empty container as a prop to represent a microphone. She 'starts' a track, dances to it, pauses it to make an announcement and resumes the track and dancing. In her most viewed video, she mimics one of Zimbabwe's popular charismatic religious leaders Emmanuel Makandiwa (who is also among the top 30 TikTok influencers). Lin dah's (@itsyogallin353) most viewed video is also a mimicry of another Makandiwa sermon which she performs donning a blazer and straw hat. In Tee's most popular video, she lip syncs to a popular Christian hymn, 'Baba inzwai munamato wangu' (Lord hear my prayer). At the bottom is a caption "*Uyu munamato wangu kwamuri zvinonzi ndinamatire ndigokunamatirawo*" (This is my prayer for you. It is said if you pray for me, I will also pray for you). Let's pray time *yatiri yakaoma* (we are living in difficult times). The caption is followed by a prayer and heart emoji. In the performance, Tee is dressed in a doek and wrapper, which is common attire for Zimbabwean women. Both the singing and dressing are of significance. The song is dedicated to Zimbabweans going through difficult times. At the same time, she is appealing to God to answer her prayer and change the circumstances for the better. This performance exemplifies the critical role of religion in Zimbabwe's cultural cosmology. Pentecostal Christianity has had significant influence on Zimbabwean popular culture, chiefly because of its use of communication technologies such as television and mobile phones as well as its influence on everyday cultures such as music and dress (Togarasei, 2018). Read together with other mimicry performances, it can be argued that Zimbabwean TikTok performances are not just for laughs but also address critical issues affecting ordinary Zimbabweans and are a mirror of contemporary realities.

At the extreme end of the spectrum are performances that are abstract and may seem meaningless and not worthy of attention. These include face morphing, mugging for the camera (making faces). Carlton Mandaza (@carl_official.zw) and Chipo the trouble causer (@chipothetroublecauser) are examples of performers who frequently deploy this type of performance. In his most popular video, Carlton Mandaza rhythmically shakes his head to music, while not blinking, as a response to a "no blink challenge". Similarly, Chipo the trouble causer usually posts face-morphing videos where she exaggerates the size of her mouth, accompanied by voice alteration for a cartoon-like effect. Such banal, commonplace vernacular performances are only relatable to someone living in Zimbabwe. They enact the everyday, creating a mega-play portraying both the simplicity and absurdity of life. The mimicry and jokes are unrefined, leaning on the grotesque and obscene – the ugly. They go against the norm of elegantly dressed performers in luxurious places dancing to global pop music. This is important because in 2020, TikTok instructed its moderators to "algorithmically suppress posts by users deemed to appear 'abnormal, 'ugly' (indicating factors including wrinkles and obesity) and 'slummy' and to censor politically 'defamatory' and ideologically 'vulgar' content" (Kennedy, 2020, p. 1072). Therefore, these unrefined performances resist canonical ways of portraying the self as beautiful and of high culture. At the same time, the laughter that they generate might be therapeutic to both creator and user, much like the Hauka performance in Jean Rouch's *Mad Masters*. In that sense, one can argue that TikToking is a therapeutic practice that helps users cope with the everyday vagaries of life in Zimbabwe.

CONCLUSION

The chapter shows the variety of performances on Zimbabwean TikTok. These range from trivial, playful performances to those that are more serious and relatable to the everyday life of the average Zimbabwean. The study shows that even though the creators belong to a common online community, Zimbabwean TikTok, some of their performances show routed rather than rooted identities, to use Stuart Hall's (1989) distinction. Such performances have a cosmopolitan outlook in which performers do not make explicit their association with the Zimbabwean geo-political terrain. Their Zimbabwean identity is a matter of conjecture. This shows how complex identity is and how difficult it is to ascertain one's identity just by their performances. The findings also suggest that in some cases TikTok users play out certain identities and deploy props that define those identities as rooted. In other words, some performances give away or are meant to associate the performers with their Zimbabwean roots. In cases where users deliberately reveal their rooted Zimbabwean identities, they create narratives that resonate with other Zimbabwean users but at the same time showing pride in belonging to the community, making such performances a good example of vernacular creativity and expression. The chapter further shows that, in cases where performers reveal their Zimbabwean identity, they exhibit a digital patriotism that suggests that they are proud to be from that nation. Where Zimbabweans are generally regarded as unhappy people, such zimtiktokers curate their 'Zimbabweanness' in ways that cancel out the negative popular stereotypes about Zimbabwe.

REFERENCES

Bazen, L. (2022). *Fighting conspiracy theories on TikTok*. Green European Foundation.

Bischoff, L. (2017), The future is digital: An introduction to African digital arts, *Critical African Studies*, *9*(3), 261–267.

boyd, d. (2011). Social networking sites as networked publics: Affordances, dynamics and implications. In Z. Papacharissi (Ed.), *A networked self: Identity, community, and culture on social network sites* (pp. 39–58). Routledge.

Chibuwe, A., Mpofu, P., & Bhowa, K. (2021). Naming the ghost: Self-naming, pseudonyms and identities of phantoms on Zimbabwean Twitter. *Social Media and Society*, July-September 2021, 1–12

Chibuwe, A., & Ureke, O. (2016). "Political gladiators" on Facebook in Zimbabwe: A discursive analysis of intra-Zimbabwe African National Union – PF cyber wars; Baba Jukwa versus Amai Jukwa. *Media, Culture and Society*, *38*(8), 1247–1260

Chiumbu, S., & Musemwa, M. (2012). Introduction: Perspectives of the Zimbabwean crisis. In S. Chiumbu & M. Musemwa (Eds.), *Crisis! what crisis? The multiple dimensions of the Zimbabwean crisis* (pp. ix–xxiii). HSRC Press.

Christensen, N. B. (2003). *Inuit in cyberspace: Imbedding offline identities online.* Museum Tusculanum Press.

de Sousa, S. C. (2020). *Influencer tiers: How different categories of influencers impact the attitude of young Portuguese women* [Masters Thesis], Universidade Católica Portuguesa.

https://newsblaze.com/world/africa/zimbabwean-women-turn-to-prostitution-in-south-africa_21536/

Ferrer-Conill, R. (2018). Playbour and the Gamification of work: Empowerment, exploitation and fun as labour dynamics. In P. Bilić, J. Primorac, & B. Valtýsson (Eds.), *Technologies of labour and the politics of contradiction* (pp. 193–210). Palgrave Macmillan.

Gilpin, D. R. (2011). Working the Twittersphere: Microblogging as professional identity construction. In Z. Papacharissi (Ed.), *A networked self: Identity, community, and culture on social network sites* (pp. 232–250). Routledge.

Goffman, E. (1956). *The presentation of self in everyday life.* University of Edinburg

Gustafson, P. (2001), 'Roots and Routes: Exploring the Relationship between Place Attachment and Mobility', *Environment and Behaviour,* 3:5, pp667-686

Hall, S. (1995). Newcultures for old. In D. Massey&P. Jess (Eds.), *A place in the world? Places, cultures and globalization* (pp. 175-211). Oxford, UK: Open University/Oxford University Press.

Hall, S. (1989). Cultural identity and cinematic representation. *Framework: The Journal of Cinema and Media, 36*(1989), 68 81.

Helliwell, J.F., Layard, R., Sachs, J.D., De Neve, J., Aknin, L.B and Wang, S. (2021), World Happiness Report, New York: Sustainable Development Solutions Network

Hiropoulos, A. (2019). South Africa, migration and xenophobia. Deconstructing the perceived migration crisis and its influence on the xenophobic reception of migrants. *Contemporary Justice Review, 23*(1), 104–121.

Ibrahim, Y. (2018). *Production of the 'Self' in the digital age.* Palgrave Macmillan.

Johnston, J. E. (2020). Celebrity, Inc.: the self as work in the era of presentational culture online. *Celebrity Studies, 11*(4), 508–511.

Kennedy, M. (2020). "If the rise of the TikTok dance and e-girl aesthetic has taught us anything, it's that teenage girls rule the internet right now": TikTok celebrity, girls and the Coronavirus crisis. *European Journal of Cultural Studies, 23*(6), 1069–1076.

Kallstig, A. (2021). Laughing in the face of danger: Performativity and resistance in Zimbabwean stand-up comedy. *Global Society, 35*(1), 45–60

Kay, S., Mulcahy, R., & Parkinson, J. (2020). When less is more: The impact of macro and micro-social media influencers' disclosure. *Journal of Marketing Management, 36*(3–4), 248–278

Kashope Wright, H. (2002). Editorial: Notes on the (Im)Possibility of Articulating continental African Identity. *Critical Arts, 16*(2), 1–18.

Khamis, S., Ang, L., & Welling, R. (2017). Self-branding, 'micro celebrity and the rise of Social Media influencers. *Celebrity Studies, 8*(2), 191–208.

Koetsier, J. (2020), 'Digital Crack Cocaine: The Science Behind TikTok's Success', *Forbes. https://www.forbes.com/sites/johnkoetsier/2020/01/18/digital-crack-cocaine-the-science-behind-tiktoks-success/* Accessed 4 April 2025

Machirori, F. (2023). This is Africa. How Young African TikTok Trends Challenged Afropessimism During Covid-19. *Journal of African Media Studies, 15*(2), 161–177

Markham, T. (2020). *Digital life.* Polity Press.

Mare, A. (2018). Politics Unusual? Facebook and Political Campaigning during the 2013 Harmonised Elections in Zimbabwe. *African Journalism Studies, 39*(1), 90–110

Marr, S. (2012). They Treat Us Like Dogs': Demographic Claustrophobia and the Zimbabwean Struggle for Space on the Streets of Gaborone, Botswana, *African Historical Review*, *44*(1), 80–108.

Marshall, P. D. (2010). The promotion and presentation of the self: celebrity as marker of presentational media. *Celebrity Studies*, *1*(1), 35–48.

McGregor, J. (2007). 'Joining the BBC (British Bottom Cleaners)': Zimbabwean migrants and the UK care industry'. *Journal of Ethnic and Migration Studies*, *33*(5), 801–824.

Mhiripiri, N.A and Ureke, O. (2019), 'Theoretical paradoxes of representation and the problems of media representations of Zimbabwe in crisis', in *Critical Arts*, 32(5-6), p87-103. DOI: 10.1080/02560046.2018.1548026

Mpofu, S., & Mare, A. (2020). #ThisFlag: Social Media and Cyber-protests in Zimbabwe. In M. N. Ndlela & W. Mano (Eds.). *Social media and elections in africa, vol. 2: Challenges and opportunities*. (pp. 153–173). Palgrave Macmillan.

Msimanga, M. J., Tshuma, L. A., & Matsilele, T. (2022). The *why* of humour during a crisis: An exploration of COVID-19 memes in South Africa and Zimbabwe. *Journal of African Media Studies*, *14*(2), 189–207.

Mutsvairo, B., Ragnedda, M., & Mabvundwi, K. (2022). "Our old pastor thinks the mobile phone is a source of evil': Capturing contested and conflicting insights on digital wellbeing and digital detoxing in an age of rapid mobile connectivity', *Media Australia International*, 1–15.

Mututwa, W. T., & Mare, A. (2021). Competing or complimentary actors in the journalistic field? An analysis of the mediation of the covid-19 pandemic by mainstream and peripheral content creators in Zimbabwe. *African Journalism Studies*, *42*(4), 82–98.

Ncube, L. (2014). The interface between football and ethnic identity discourses in Zimbabwe. *Critical African Studies*, *6*(2–3), 192–210.

Ndlovu-Gatsheni, S. J. (2009). *Do 'Zimbabweans' exist? Trajectories of nationalism' national identity formation and crisis in a postcolonial state*, Peter Lang.

O'Connor, C. (2021). *Hatescape: An in-depth analysis of extremism and hate speech on TikTok*. Institute of Strategic Dialogue.

Oberst, U., Wegmann, E., Stodt, B., Brand, M., & Chamarro, A. (2016). Negative consequences from heavy social networking in adolescents: The mediating role of fear of missing out. *Journal of Adolescence*, *55*(2017), 51–60

Papacharissi, Z. (2011). Conclusion: A networked self. In Z. Papacharissi (Ed.), *A networked self: identity, community, and culture on social network sites*. (pp. 304–318). Routledge.

Ravengai, S. (2013). The political-aesthetic function of song and dance in Zimbabwean theatre 1980–1996. *Muziki: Journal of Music Research in Africa*, *10*(1), 1–18.

Rose, G. (2014). 'On the relation between 'visual research methods' and contemporary visual culture', *The Sociological Review*, *62*, 24–46.

Schellewald, A. (2021). Communicative forms on TikTok: Perspectives from digital ethnography. *International Journal of Communication*, *15*(2021), 1437–1457.

Staff Reporter. (2014, January 5). More Zim women resorting to prostitution in SA', *Bulawayo24 News*.https://bulawayo24.com/index-id-news-sc-africa-byo-40939.html. Accessed 4 April 2025

Thram, D. J. (1999). *Performance as ritual-performance as art: Therapeutic efficacy of Dandanda song and dance in Zimbabwe* [D.Phil Thesis], Indiana University

The Nel Twins. (n.d). Q&A with Zimbabwean Dadzw. Retrieved June 22, 2022, from https://www.youtube.com/watch?v=OgVMmd9VK90

Togarasei, L. (2018). 'Introduction'. In L. Togarasei (Ed.), *Aspects of Pentecostal Christianity in Zimbabwe* (pp. 1–14). Springer.

Tufekci, Z. (2013). "Not this one": Social movements, the attention economy, and microcelebrity networked activism, *American Behavioural Scientist, 57*(7), 848–870

Ureke, O., & Washaya, Y. (2016). Social commentary, subaltern voices and the alternative medium of Zimdancehall music: Unpacking the music of Winky D and Sniper Storm. *Muziki, 13*(1), 68–88

Ureke, O. (2024). Politics at play: TikTok and digital persuasion in Zimbabwe's 2023 general elections. *Africa Spectrum, 59*(2), 254–278.

Ureke, O. (2021). Aesthetic norms and motivations of subaltern video-filmmaking: Comic skits and mobile journalism of the everyday in Zimbabwe. In A. Vailati & G. Z. Villareal (Ed.), *Ethnographies of 'On Demand' films: Anthropological explorations of commissioned audio-visual productions* (pp. 219–241). Palgrave Macmillan.

Vaccari, C., & Valeriani, A. (2021). *Outside the bubble: Social media and political participation in western democracies.* Oxford University Press

Vibe Music. (2021). *Ameno Amapiano Remix* (Goya Menor & Necktunez). Retrieved March 25, 2022, from https://www.youtube.com/watch?v=3Un6uCY15_4

Wiley, N. (1994). *The semiotic self.* University of Chicago Press

Willems, W. (2008) Mocking the state: Comic strips in the Zimbabwean press. In J. Abbink & A. Van Dokkum (Eds.). *Dilemmas of development: Conflicts of interest and their resolutions in modernizing Africa.* (pp. 151–162). African Studies Collection.

World Health Organisation. (2020). *Life expectancy at birth.* https://data.who.int/countries/716. Accessed 4 April 2025

Yang, P. (2022). TikTok and microcelebrities: An analysis of the impact of short video apps on Chinese culture and communication. *China Media Research, 18*(1), 23–37.

Zuo, H., & Wang, T. (2019). Analysis of TikTok user behaviour from the perspective of popular culture. *Frontiers in Art Research, 1*(3), 1–5.

CHAPTER SIX

Digital Self-Representation, African Youth and the Question of Performative Authenticity in a Globalized World

CHIKEZIE E. UZUEGBUNAM, JOB MWAURA AND RICHARD CHINEDU ONONIWU

INTRODUCTION

Youth in the globalized digital age are shifting away from being passive users of media and instead taking an active role in creating their own meanings and identities through their interactions with various forms of media. Over the last few decades, digital technologies have become an integral aspect of young people's[1] lives across regions of the world. As of April 2024, the global internet user population had reached 5.44 billion, equating to 67.1 percent of the world's total population (Statista, 2024)[2]. Furthermore, there are now 5.07 billion social media users around the world, or 62.6 percent of the total global population (Statista, 2024). On the African continent, digital media technologies have changed the communicative, social, economic, political, and cultural experiences of young

1 In this chapter, youth and young people are used interchangeably to refer to young adults who are straddled between the ages of 18 and early 30s. This aligns with the definition of youth supported by the African Youth Charter (2013): https://au.int/sites/default/files/treaties/7789-treaty-0033_-_african_youth_charter_e.pdf

2 https://www.statista.com/statistics/617136/digital-population-worldwide/#:~:text=As%20of%20April%202024%2C%20there,population%2C%20were%20social%20media%20users.

people. Digital media expands the communication opportunities available to users, transcending geographic, temporal, physical, and social barriers (Uzuegbunam, 2024). The widespread use of digital and smart devices, computers, digital cameras, and video games, as well as socially networked apps and platforms, has altered the ways in which young people interact with their physical and social environments. The advent of digital technologies, particularly Web 2.0, has significantly influenced this process. Web 2.0, with its heterogeneous and accessible platforms and services, offers opportunities for individuals to replicate, simulate, and represent themselves in the digital world. These platforms include blogs, social media, podcasting, and photo- and video-sharing services, which have provided users with tools and spaces to connect, share, influence, market ideas, and self-present based on interests and personality. Social media platforms, a key component of Web 2.0, provide new, alternative, and empowering spaces for virtual identities to be constructed, visually presented, narrated, and consumed due to their "structural affordances such as anonymity, visibility, and persistence or durability" (Hollenbaugh, 2021, p. 84).

The digital revolution and its exponential spread are adjudged the greatest manifestations of globalization processes today. As digital technologies proliferate and become more widely used, debates and concerns regarding the impact of global media on young lives have multiplied. Concepts like 'transnational youth,' 'global world youth,' and 'neoliberal media globalization' have shaped viewpoints that highlight processes of global cultural flows, values, and goods from one region of the world to another (Uzuegbunam, 2020). Young people in sub-Saharan African countries are responding to globalization processes in the digital age in complex and nuanced ways. Scholars (for example, Cabán, 1998; Kraidy, 2002; Samper, 2010; Ssewakiryanga, 2004; Cohen, 2007; Hurst, 2009; Omoniyi et al., 2009; Farber, 2010; Uzuegbunam, 2020) have explored the notion of hybridized, domesticated, and appropriated identities, illustrating the ways in which globalized culture and ways of being are transported to different regions of the world and then integrated into local cultures and environments in ways that are appropriate for the unique histories, artefacts, and practices of those regions.

Scholars like Wasko (2008) and Uzuegbunam (2020) have argued that young individuals are especially susceptible to the perils and possibilities of globalization because they have greater access to varied cultural products and multiple media outlets. Young people frequently consume consumer goods, cultural products, and popular culture—including films, books, music, social media, podcasts, literature in vernacular languages, fashion and beauty products, and digital and legacy media (see Ugor, 2021). In this chapter, we move away from the persistent exemplification of the relationship between globalization and young lives as precarious, and rather highlight a more nuanced understanding of how identity, self-presentation, and digital culture interact. Stated differently, the chapter explores how young people in sub-Saharan African contexts utilize social media and digital platforms for self-presentation[3] and self-performance, as well as how these digital practices define or redefine what it means to be authentic. The chapter equally provides an analysis of the political, social, economic, and cultural implications of digital self-representation in the context of Africa.

One of the most significant consequences of youths' exponential immersion in digital lifeworlds is the rise of complex digital identities and cultures in the digital age. Online platforms and networked apps are transforming the ways in which we understand human identity, representation, and social interaction. Contemporary youth culture is, therefore, marked by the act of creating and maintaining profiles on these online platforms, serving as an 'initiation rite' into these spaces for young people (boyd, 2007) and to participate in a form of global citizenship, meaning that with the Internet and social media, young people are able to move across the local and successfully connect with users globally (Machirori, 2023). Beyond the concepts of 'cyberculture,' 'information society,' and 'new media,' the phrase 'digital culture' embodies a more comprehensive understanding of culture. It suggests that the limitations and advantages imposed by digital technologies influence all aspects of daily life, just as conventional media and old technologies like electricity were perceived to do in earlier eras (Thumim, 2012). Web-based platforms enable information to be produced, shared, and consumed in what is described as a 'democratic' (the term is in productive tension because, despite being a democratized space, digital platforms exacerbate inequality and marginalities in various ways) digital environment. This democratization of information has been facilitated by the global increase in internet usage. Participating in these platforms is about sharing oneself—or one's constructed and platformized identity—with others.

THEORIZING DIGITAL SELF-PRESENTATION, YOUTH IDENTITIES, AND PERFORMATIVE AUTHENTICITY

We adopt a postmodernist outlook in our attempt to find theoretical grounds within which to theorize how we understand youth identities in the digital age, particularly within the context of self-representation. According to Rayner, Wall, and Kruger (2004), postmodernism, a term reminiscent of Marshal McLuhan's concept of the global village that emerged in the 1970s and continues into the twenty-first century, is based on a view of contemporary society that is increasingly

3 We use the terms "self-presentation", and "digital self portraits" interchangeably since they mean virtually the same thing and to reflect the fluidity of usage in academic literature.

characterized by the rapid flow of images, information, popular culture, technology, consumerism, and live transmission of information. Young people's digital self-making may be interpreted as "technologies of the self" (a term popularized by Foucault, 1982) which generates unique identities, embodiments, or subjectivities and is inextricably linked to particular structures of power. According to Thumim (2012), self-representation, a term that was first identified by the author in the 1990s, is no longer considered a marginal activity or practice. In fact, scholarly attention to this practice is concomitant with the proliferation of what appear to be opportunities for self-representation in cultural and media spaces. As a result, the phrase 'self-representation' is currently employed frequently to denote the actions of engaged audiences in digital culture, in conjunction with other pertinent terms such as 'performance of the self' and 'presentation of the self.'

Nevertheless, the systematic study of self-representation began with the work of sociologist Erving Goffman (1959), at about the same time in psychology and sociology. Goffman's seminal work on the presentation of the self, which, when applied to today's realities, challenges the notion of a clear distinction between one's offline and online selves. Goffman's theorizing on the presentation of the self—in his work on *"The Presentation of Self in Everyday Life"*—first articulated in 1959 and later refined in 1990—provides a robust dramaturgical framework for understanding the complexities of self-representation. He posits that when an individual presents themselves before others, they engage in a performance, much like an actor on a stage. This performance is influenced by a variety of factors, including the individual's desire for others' approval, their need to conform to societal expectations, and their intent to control others' perceptions of them. Central to Goffman's analysis is the concept of 'front', which refers to the various props, costumes, and gestures used to facilitate a performance. These elements, which can be both physical and personal, communicate a performer's social status and set the tone for how an interaction will proceed.

In the context of African youth identities, digital platforms serve as the stage where these performances take place. The carefully curated digital personas that youth create and maintain online serve as a representation of the 'front.' Through their online interactions, they negotiate their identities, grappling with the tension between authenticity and performance. Self-disclosure, the revelation of personal information (i.e., thoughts or feelings) to others, is a core component of self-presentation (Hollenbaugh, 2021), especially in online and digital spaces with their multimedia features where text, visual, audio, and images proliferate and contend with each other in a struggle for communication, impression management, identity, and performance. By applying Goffman's theory to the African context, we aim to shed light on the intricate dynamics of digital self-representation and the question of performative authenticity in the digital lifeworlds of young Africans. This is not only relevant to understanding the experiences of sub-Saharan African youth in the digital age but also contributes to broader discussions on identity, authenticity, and the impact of digital technologies on sociality and connection and their wider continuities, discontinuities, and implications.

Questions such as 'Who am I?' and 'What is my role in society?' serve as central subjects of contemplation, influencing the thoughts, actions, and commitments of young individuals (Davis and Weinstein, 2017, p. 1). We, thus, also situate our discourse within Bauman's (2013) conceptualization of identity as a rich tapestry for understanding the fluidity and multiplicity of identities in the digital age. Their work underscores the impact of rapid global change on personal and social identities, emphasizing the fluid and uncertain nature of identity in contemporary society. Bauman's notion of 'liquid modernity' posits that identities are no longer fixed but are constantly in flux, elusive, and shaped by the rapid changes in society in such a manner that digital users could feel that they belong everywhere and nowhere at the same time. This perspective is particularly relevant to African youth, who are navigating their identities amidst the dual forces of traditional cultural norms and the globalizing influence of digital media. The digital sphere offers African youth a platform for self-representation, allowing them to articulate their identities in ways that may not be possible in their physical realities. However, this digital self-representation also raises the question of performative authenticity. Are these online identities genuine expressions of the self, or are they performances tailored to fit the expectations of the digital audience? Bauman's work prompts us to consider that these digital identities, while possibly performative, are no less 'real' than their offline counterparts. They represent a facet of the individual's identity, shaped by the unique dynamics of the digital environment.

DIGITAL SELF-REPRESENTATION, SUB-SAHARAN AFRICAN YOUTH AND THE QUESTION OF AUTHENTICITY

In the digital era, African youth navigate the complex landscapes of identity and community through social media and digital platforms, crafting self-representations that echo their multifaceted lives. Pfeiffer et al. (2014) expand on this narrative by highlighting the role of social media as arenas for the representation and shaping of popular youth culture among African youth. These digital platforms become spaces where youth can express their identities, interests, and values, selectively embracing certain aspects of the internet while discarding others. Bosch (2020) further elaborates, emphasizing social media's role in documenting life and fostering democratic practices within leisure and culture in South Africa. Bosch (ibid) suggests that these platforms reflect a blend of online and offline realities, contributing to public debates and showcasing the impact of digital technologies on social life. The motivation behind engagement with platforms like Facebook, Instagram, TikTok, and X (formerly Twitter) is underscored by the ease of accessing information and connecting with broader communities, often mediated through the strategic use of photos of popular figures to enhance engagement with content, including sexual and reproductive health messages. The content preferences of African youth lean towards the entertaining and educational, with a penchant for drama, sports, and humorous content that not only capture their attention but also compellingly conveys critical messages. Through these digital self-representations, sub-Saharan African youth negotiate and perform their identities, engaging in a continuous iterative process of self-expression and community interaction that reflects their evolving interests and values in the digital age.

Examples of digital self-representational practices among sub-Saharan African youth reveal that they are adept at navigating the digital realm to express themselves, challenge stereotypes and hegemonic structures, and build connections. Some notable examples include 21-year-old South African, Zingisa Socikwa, who highlight the proactive role of social media in redefining African youth identity and promoting a positive narrative through movements such as Blackboard Africa; and Charity Ekezie, a 30-year-old Nigerian who has become well-known for creating content that mocks stereotypes and tropes about Africa. Similarly, in Kenya, social media platforms serve as crucial spaces for youth to engage in societal discussions, maintain relationships, and derive satisfaction from feeling connected. Research by Ndlela and Mulwo (2017) has shown how young Kenyans utilize digital spaces to tackle societal issues and stay engaged with community and family, fostering a strong sense of belonging. Similarly, Ntarangwi (2023) discusses the role of youth and popular culture in Kenya as a counter move to political exploitation, using social media as a platform for self-determination and social critique. The case of Kenyan rapper, King Kaka, exemplifies how young artistes use their platforms to voice frustrations and engage in social commentary, thereby demonstrating the power of social media to foster a generation that is both critical and engaged with societal issues, in contrast to previous generations that were handicapped from contributing meaningfully to democratic citizenship due to political marginalization and little access to the media. Okesola and Oyebode (2023) examined how young Nigerian social media users used memes on WhatsApp and X (formerly Twitter) during the 2020 #EndSARS protest to express intersubjective opinions about the civil unrest and the roles some stakeholders played during the period, capturing one recent instance of digital self-representation in political action in the Nigerian context. The study demonstrates how social media memes used visual and verbal resources as forms of self-representation to express various types of attitudes, intersubjectivity, and judgement about the main participants in the #EndSARS protest, including public figures and government organizations, particularly the Nigerian army and police.

The views of scholars such as Granic et al. (2020) and McInroy et al (2019) imply that the networks and practices promoted by digital platforms appear to help marginalized and isolated youth, including those who identify as LGBTQ+ (Lesbian, Gay, Bisexual, Transgender, Queer) and who look for safe spaces to express beliefs and behaviors that defy accepted social norms. For example, in Nigeria, according to Onanuga (2020), moving beyond the often-unwelcoming physical public spaces, the digital realm has emerged as a haven for Nigerian queers who are striving to live authentically and shape their own narratives. By exploring how queer men navigate the digital media landscape and engage in advocacy against homophobia on X (Twitter), the study argues that queer Nigerian men are not only using digital platforms to express their sexual identities, but also to intentionally shape their identities in ways that are evident in both in-group and out-group advocacy efforts. The same is true in South Africa, where YouTube has enabled numerous LGBTQ+ vloggers to reach audiences and express queer life in a public media (Andrews, 2021).

Abubakar and Abubakar (2017) delineate the various strategies employed by African students in the diaspora for self-presentation on digital platforms. Predominantly, self-representational images featuring smiles and expressions of joy serve as a bridge to maintain connections with friends and family back home and as a means of attracting attention within their digital circles. This dynamic of impression management is further elaborated through the periodic updating of profile images with photos capturing significant places, people, and events, aiming to garner attention and comments from peers, thus reinforcing social standing and self-esteem. Additionally, sharing experiences via social media profile images becomes a tool for African students abroad to manage their self-image while preserving ties with their roots and seeking validation and admiration within their online communities. Moreover, Facebook, Instagram, and X (formerly Twitter) can also help young Africans and their likes in other parts of the world to, through self-representation, host meaningful discourses around career or education choices (Attah and Sule, 2022); use used language, fashion, and sports to express and identify themselves, sharpen their communication skills, establish relations with others, craft their gender expressions online, and foster collective social activity (Morwe et al., 2015). Ndlela and Mulwo (2017) found that social media platforms such as closed WhatsApp and Facebook groups enabled youth to discuss issues that they often found difficult to talk about in face-to-face interactions. In their study, one of the participants described how a friend in a private WhatsApp group was able to inform other users about her sexual orientation. The participant had realized she was attracted to a woman, but she struggled to tell her friends in person. It is evident from such incidents that the physical distance created by social media interactions offers a near comfortable environment in which participants find it easier to discuss topics that they may feel uncomfortable discussing in face-to-face interactions.

This fosters genuine self-expression in contrast to performative authenticity; which in the context of this chapter refers to the act of intentionally expressing or presenting oneself on digital media in a way that aligns with societal or cultural expectations rather than reflecting one's true self; or as Taylor (2022) argues, the strategic enactment of authenticity that is more about creating the appearance of authenticity rather than truly embodying it. Taylor (2022) notes that authenticity on social media is inherently performative and fleeting, challenging the traditional notion of fixed authenticity. According to Taylor, authenticity momentarily emerges through social interactions, underscoring its performative nature shaped by cultural and social frameworks, thus enriching our understanding of digital self-presentation among African youth.

These examples highlight the transformative power of digital self-representation practices among African youth, showcasing how they leverage social media and digital platforms for personal expression and to challenge existing narratives and stereotypes, thereby nurturing a more inclusive and dynamic understanding of African identity in the digital age. African youth construct their identities in a complex narrative that unfolds across both online and offline realms. They use digital platforms to explore aspects of their identities that might be less visible or accepted in their physical environments. This exploration is often driven by a desire for authenticity, activism, experimentation, and community. Digital spaces allow these youths to create nuanced self-representations that challenge traditional norms. They experiment with different personas online, reflecting the fluid nature of identities. However, as Granic et al. (2020) would argue, one of the most often cited criticisms of self-representation on digital platforms (social media platforms, especially) is that they curtail deeper conversations because they are designed to amplify performative aspects of personal storytelling. On the contrary, we argue that digital platforms in the conservative sub-Saharan African context enable the performance of an 'authentic' self, which fosters deeper, alternative conversations and identity development in safe, culturally dissonant digital spaces such as those explored by young, same-sex persons in the study conducted by Ndlela and Mulwo (2017) and Onanuga (2020).

Furthermore, the concept of authenticity in digital self-representation can be looked at against the backdrop of growing celebrity culture and gender presentation on social media, offering a complex view of performative practices. On the one hand, according to Uzuegbunam (2017), celebrity culture significantly sways young Nigerians' identity, aspirations, and behaviors. Celebrities craft ideas of success, relationships, and self-image through media portrayals that young individuals often aspire to emulate (see Omenugha, Uzuegbunam and Ndolo, 2016). Emulation in the broader context of digital practices reveals a performative layer to authenticity, where the real self frequently interacts with aspirational identities shaped by celebrity influences. Such dynamics highlight the impact of global media and celebrity culture on youth identities and signal the intricate relationship between performative authenticity and the construction of self in the digital age, underscoring the importance of media literacy to navigate these waters effectively. On the other hand, Kondakciu and Souto (2022) explore performative authenticity in digital practices within the context of gender presentation and self-expression among Millennials on social media. They identify four strategies—Empowering, Keeping It Real, Bracketing, and Online Masking—that individuals employ to manage their gendered self-presentation online. These strategies reflect diverse approaches to balancing authenticity with societal norms, highlighting the performative aspect of authenticity in digital practices. Performative authenticity as a form of self-presentation involves the use of specific visual cues, content production methods, and communication strategies to project an image of authenticity to the audience (Taylor, 2022).

BROADER IMPLICATIONS OF DIGITAL SELF-REPRESENTATION AMONG SUB-SAHARAN AFRICAN YOUTH

There seems to be a scholarly consensus that digital self-representation has become a significant aspect of contemporary culture, especially among young people who are increasingly engaging with various online platforms. This phenomenon raises questions about the cultural, social, economic, and political implications of digital self-representation, especially in today's world, where the lines between the physical and digital realm seem to have disappeared.

Cultural Implication

Digital self-representations which have filled digital spaces, are increasingly forging and reinforcing culture. Research (Machirori, 2023; Ndlela and Mulvo, 2017; Ntarangwi, 2023) suggests that digital self-representation gives African youth the opportunity to express their unique cultural identities and challenge stereotypes. Social media, especially, allows them to showcase their traditions, art, music, and fashion to a global audience; and this form of empowerment enables individuals to take control of their narratives which could foster a sense of pride and self-confidence. Digital self-representation facilitates cultural exchanges and fosters connections between African youth and their global counterparts. This interaction breaks down stereotypes and promotes a more nuanced understanding of diverse cultures. Yeku's (2022) concept of 'cultural netizenship' – social media-based cultural productions that serve as the visual repertoire for self-performances and activist speech – presents an important feature when considering the cultural implications of digital self-presentation. Social media is viewed as both a creative environment where marginal voices can be heard and a venue for cultural productions and expressions. However, there are assertions that the digital space may perpetuate commodification of identity (Udoinwang, 2022). Also, scholars (e.g., Koles et al., 2022; Sastimdur, 2023) suggest that in the pursuit of social media likes, shares, and followers, individuals might focus on superficial elements of their culture, potentially diluting its richness and complexity.

Social Implication

Digital platforms have become integral in shaping social practices and networks, particularly among young people. For instance, platforms such as Snapchat, TikTok, Instagram, and X (formerly Twitter) offer opportunities for the social practices of short bursts of comments and mutual engagement among young people. Scholars argue that despite some design constraints, many young users, including those in African contexts, are finding themselves in social networks where they engage in thoughtful conversations and meaningful identity explorations (Castellanos-Reyes et al., 2024). Social practices and networks fostered through digital platforms, which provide individuals with safe and empowering spaces to actualize the kinds of socialities and identities they hope for but are unable to consolidate in offline contexts. In African societies with extremely conservative viewpoints on sexual and gender expressions, digital social spaces are perceived as secure and liberating (Francis and McEwen, 2024; Saheed, 2023).

Political Implication

Digital self-representation provides a platform for African youths to engage in political discourse, express dissent, and challenge established power structures (see Bosch, 2020; Ugor, 2021). Social media, in particular, has played a pivotal role in amplifying marginalized voices and shedding light on issues that may be overlooked by traditional media. Young people's use of social media platforms and access to technologies enhance their freedom to express their ideas and demand for social change. Resistance movements led by young people in sub-Saharan Africa (cases in point – EndSARS in Nigeria; Fallist movement in South Africa; youth demonstrations in Sudan, Mozambique, Ethiopia, Uganda) have used a degree of digital technologies and self-representation to challenge mainstream narratives, foster a more diverse and inclusive discourse, and foster a sense of belonging and solidarity within certain groups. Political self-representation is an important tool for political contestation in African contexts marked by oppressive political spheres (Clarno and Vally, 2023). However, power imbalances can arise; there are those with restricted access to technology; and political polarization can occur, leading individuals to retreat into echo chambers that reinforce their existing opinions, thereby preventing constructive political dialogue (Tucker et al., 2018).

Economic Implication

The economic dimension to young Africans' digital self-representations can be understood in the context of the growing influencer culture or influencer marketing. According to Duffy (2020), influencers are a group of digital content creators characterized by their large online following, unique brand persona, and consistent partnerships with commercial brands. These influencers and content creators have become the new Word-of-Mouth (Kupemba, 2024). Many African Millennials and Gen-Zs are seizing the opportunity provided by big platforms such as TikTok, Instagram, YouTube, and Facebook to produce content that are both locally and globally consumed. According to UNESCO, in Africa – the world's youngest continent, where social media and mobile use has surged in recent years – this new career is attracting an increasing number of young people who commercialize the popularity they have achieved on Instagram, YouTube or Twitter (Ebale, 2023). The monetization policy of these platforms enables young influencers to earn income from the platforms as well as get paid by popular brands who contract them to promote their products and services.

CONCLUSION

This chapter has explored the ways in which young people in sub-Saharan African contexts use digital and social media for self-presentation and self- performance, aiming to provide an understanding of how social media self-representations offer insights into concurrent online and offline societal dynamics and ultimately examined how the notion of performative authenticity has become a variable in all of this, and with what social, political, economic, and cultural implications. The chapter argues that the process by which young people in Africa make sense of their life events, share them within their social and wider circles, connect them to accepted values, and integrate them with societal values is a conscious act of building an identity. Young Africans' self-representation and performance of authenticity in the digital era are evidenced by the ways in which they embody mediated versions of themselves and group expressions; are preoccupied with telling their life stories; navigate the socioeconomic, cultural, and political aspects that affect their lives; and get feedback on their online performance and identities.

Our discussion of digital self-representation is in line with the concept of postmodernism within the context of a neoliberal world. According to Strinati (2004), postmodernism is characterized by the growing dominance of media images in shaping our perception of reality and self-identity. It also emphasizes style, packaging, and branding, often at the expense of substance and content. Additionally, postmodernism involves a blurring of the boundaries between high culture and popular culture. The discourse also confirms various theoretical positions introduced earlier: 'performance of the self' (Thumin), 'presentation of the self' (Goffman), 'technologies of the self' (Foucault) and 'performative self' (Bauman). While past scholarship has delved into the digital self-representation of young people, as well as their performance of authenticity, this discussion presents the digital media as more empowering and liberating for young Africans, as it has helped them engage in more daring self-representations and present a more 'authentic' and individualized self, given their conservative environment. Sub-Saharan African youth navigate authenticity and self-performance on social media through an interplay of personal expression and societal expectations. They leverage digital platforms to craft identities that resonate with their experiences while engaging with global and local cultural narratives. This balancing act allows for exploring diverse aspects of their identities, including gender, ethnicity, and social status, in personally authentic and socially relevant ways. However, these discussions raise questions about the digital divide and access to digital platforms, highlighting issues of inequality and marginalization. At the same time, it underscores the importance of media and digital literacy required for young audiences to navigate the complex digital lifeworlds of today.

A limitation of the discussion in this chapter is that it seems to lump sub-Saharan African youths together as a homogeneous whole without explicitly considering other sub-divisions regarding gender, ethnicity, income level, social status, educational background, occupation, and place of residence; thereby tending to oversimplify the rich diversity and complexity that could exist in their digital self-representation and performance of authenticity.

REFERENCES

Abubakar, Y., & Abubakar, A. A. (2017). African students' self-presentation through social media profile images in University of Nicosia, Cyprus. *MCC: Media and Communication Cultures, 1*(2), 19–38.

Andrews, G. (2021). YouTube queer communities as heterotopias: Space, identity and "realness" in queer South African Vlogs, *Journal of African Cultural Studies, 33*(1), 84–100.

Attah, N. E., & Sule, B. (2022). Social media and social change in Africa. In: R. Baikady, S. Sajid, V. Nadesan, J. Przeperski, M. R. Islam, J. Gao (Eds.), *The Palgrave handbook of global social change* (pp. 1–20). Palgrave Macmillan.

Bauman, Z. (2013). *Identity: Conversations with Benedetto Vecchi*. Polity.

Kupemba, D. N. (2024, May 27). The influencers rallying South Africa's youth to vote. BBC News. Retrieved June 12, 2024, from https://www.bbc.com/news/articles/c51151lykzlo

Bosch, T. E. (2020). *Social media and everyday life in South Africa*. Routledge.

boyd, d. (2007). Social network sites: Public, private, or what? *Knowledge Tree, 13*(1), 1–7.

Cabán, P. (1998). The new synthesis of Latin American and Latino studies. In F. Bonilla, M. Edwin, R. Morales, & M. de los Angeles Torres (Eds.), *Borderless borders: U.S. Latinos, Latin Americans, and the paradox of interdependence* (pp. 195–215). Temple University Press.

Castellanos-Reyes, D., Richardson, J. C., & Maeda, Y. (2024). The evolution of social presence: A longitudinal exploration of the effect of online students' peer-interactions using social network analysis. *The Internet and Higher Education, 61*, 100939. https://doi.org/10.1016/j.iheduc.2024.100939

Clarno, A., & Vally, S., 2023. The context of struggle: Racial capitalism and political praxis in South Africa. *Ethnic and Racial Studies, 46*(16), 3425–3447.

Cohen, R. (2007). Creolization and cultural globalization: the soft sounds of fugitive power. *Globalizations 4*(3), 369–384. https://doi.org/10.1080/14747730701532492

Davis, K., & Weinstein, E. (2017). Identity Development in the Digital Age: An Eriksonian Perspective. In M. Wright (Ed.), *Identity, sexuality, and relationships among emerging adults in the digital age* (pp. 1–17). IGI Global.

Duffy, B. (2020). Social media influencers. In K. Ross, I. Bachmann, & V. Cardo (Eds.), *The international encyclopaedia of gender, media, and communication* (pp. 1–4). John Wiley & Sons.

Ebale, K. (2023, June 28). Africa's youth. Influencers make a big impact. *The UNESSCO Courier*. Retrieved July 1, 2024, from https://courier.unesco.org/en/articles/africas-youth-influencers-make-big-impact

Farber, L. (2010). Africanizing hybridity? Toward an Afropolitan aesthetic in contemporary South African fashion design. *Critical Arts: A Journal of South-North Cultural Studies 24*(1), 128–167.

Foucault, M. (1982, October). "Technologies of the Self: Lectures at University of Vermont". Retrieved July 1, 2024, from https://foucault.info/documents/foucault.technologiesOfSelf.en/

Francis, D., & McEwen, H. (2024). Normalizing intolerance: the efforts of Christian Right groups to block LGBTIQ+ inclusion in South African schools. *Culture, Health & Sexuality, 26*(2), 236–247.

Goffman, E. (1959/1990). *The presentation of self in everyday life*. The Penguin Press.

Granic, I., Morita, H., & Scholten, H. (2020). Beyond Screen Time: Identity Development in the Digital Age. *Psychological Inquiry, 31*(3), 195–223.

Hollenbaugh, E. E. (2021). Self-presentation in social media: Review and research opportunities. *Review of Communication Research, 9*, 81–98.

Hurst, E. (2009). Tsotsitaal, global culture and local style: identity and recontextualization in twenty-first century south African townships recontextualization in twenty-first century South African townships. *Social Dynamics: A Journal of African Studies 35*(2), 244–257.

Koles, B., Audrezet, A., Moulard, J. G., Ameen, N., & McKenna, B. (2022). The authentic virtual influencer: Authenticity manifestations in the metaverse. *Journal of Business Research, 170*(114325).

Kondakciu, K., Souto, M., & Zayer, L. T. (2022). Self-presentation and gender on social media: an exploration of the expression of "authentic selves". *Qualitative Market Research: An International Journal, 25*(1), 80–89

Kraidy, M. M. (2002). Hybridity in cultural globalization. *Communication Theory 12*(3), 316–339.

Machirori, F. (2023). This is Africa: How young African TikTok trends challenged afropessimism during COVID-19. *Journal of African Media Studies, 15*(2), 161–177.

McInroy, L. B., McCloskey, R. J., Craig, S. L., & Eaton, A. D. (2019). LGBTQ+ Youths' Community Engagement and Resource Seeking Online versus Offline. *Journal of Technology in Human Services,* 37(4), 315–333. https://doi.org/10.1080/15228835.2019.1617823

Morwe, K., Mulaudzi, T.T. P., Tugli, A. K., Klu, E. K., Ramakuela, N., & Matshidze, P. (2015). Youth, youth culture and socialization in the present technological era in a rural village of Limpopo Province, South Africa, *Journal of Social Sciences, 44*(1), 1–7.

Ndlela, M. N., & Mulwo, A. (2017). Social media, youth and everyday life in Kenya. *Journal of African Media Studies, 9*(2), 277–290.

Ntarangwi, M. (2023). Music, identity, and performance in East Africa. In L. Miller & D. Syring (Eds.), *The Routledge companion to the anthropology of performance* (pp. 238–249). Routledge

Okesola, S. O., & Oyebode, O. O. (2023). "The Soro-Soke [speak up] generation": multimodality and appraisal choices in selected #EndSARS civil protest-related memes in Nigeria. *Lang. Semiot. Stud, 9*(2), 290–312.

Omenugha, K. A., Uzuegbunam, C. E., & Ndolo, I. S. (2016). Celebrity culture, media and the Nigerian youth: negotiating cultural identities in a globalised world. *Critical Arts, 30*(2), 200–216. https://doi.org/10.1080/02560046.2016.1187791

Omoniyi, T., Scheld, S., & Oni, D. (2009). Negotiating youth identity in a transnational context in Nigeria. *Social Dynamics: A Journal of African Studies 35*(1), 1–18.

Onanuga, P. (2020). Coming out and reaching out: Linguistic advocacy on queer Nigerian Twitter. *Journal of African Cultural Studies, 33*(4), 489–504. https://doi.org/10.1080/13696815.2020.1806799

Pfeiffer, C., Kleeb, M., Mbelwa, A., & Ahorlu, C. (2014). The use of social media among adolescents in Dar es Salaam and Mtwara, Tanzania. *Reproductive Health Matters, 22*(43), 178–186.

Rayner, P., Wall, P., & Kruger, S. (2004). *AS media studies: The essential introduction.* Psychology Press

Saheed, R. O. (2023). Globalization and the emerging sexual trends in Africa. *ABUAD Journal of Social and Management Sciences, 4*(1), 75–91.

Samper, D. A. (2010). "Africa is still our mama": Kenyan rappers, youth identity, and the revitalization of traditional values. *African Identities 2*(1), 37–51.

Sastimdur, L. Y., 2023. *Breaking down heteronormativity: The power of queer narratives on social media.* https://ddd.uab.cat/pub/trerecpro/2023/285212/TFM_Sastimdur_Lina_Yasmine.pdf

Ssewakiryanga, R. (2004). "Bringing the global home": Locating agency in the reconfiguration of western music by Ugandan youth. In S. Thorsén (Ed.), *Sounds of change – Social and political features of music in Africa* (pp. 135–151). Sida Studies.

Strinati, D. (2004). *An introduction to theories of popular culture*. Routledge

Taylor, A. S. (2022). *Authenticity as performativity on social media*. Springer Nature.

Thumim, N. (2012). *Self-representation and digital culture*. Palgrave Macmillan.

Tucker, J. A., Guess, A., Barberá, P., Vaccari, C., Siegel, A., Sanovich, S., Stukal, D., & Nyhan, B. (2018). Social media, political polarization, and political disinformation: A review of the scientific literature. *Political polarization, and political disinformation: a review of the scientific literature*.

Udoinwang, D. E. (2022). The 'digital natives' and the crossroads of indigenous languages, literatures, and identities. *AKSU Journal of English*, *4*(1), 175–188

Ugor, P. (Ed.). (2021). *Youth and Popular Culture in Africa: Media, Music, and Politics*. Boydell & Brewer.

Uzuegbunam, C. E. (2017). Between media celebrities and the youth: Exploring the impact of emerging celebrity culture on the lifestyle of young Nigerians', *Mgbakoigba: Journal of African Studies*, *6*(2), 130–141.

Uzuegbunam, C. E. (2020). Toward hybridized and glocalized youth identities in Africa? Revisiting old concerns and reimagining new possibilities for media education. In D. Frau Meigs, et al. (Eds.), *Handbook of media education research* (pp. 97–104). Wiley-Blackwell & IAMCR.

Uzuegbunam, C. E. (2024). *Children and young people's digital lifeworlds: Domestication, mediation, and agency*. Palgrave Macmillan.

Wasko, J. (2008). The commodification of youth culture. In K. Drotner & S. Livingstone (Eds.), *The international handbook of children, media, and culture* (pp. 460–474). Sage.

Yeku, J. (2022). *Cultural netizenship: Social media, popular culture, and performance in Nigeria*. Indiana University Press

CHAPTER SEVEN

Black Women's Self-Representation on Social Media: A Discourse Analysis of the Ladies House Facebook Group

MAUD BLOSE

INTRODUCTION

Black women are among the largest consumer groups of social media in South Africa (Statista, 2022). These women have curated spaces such as the *Ladies House* Facebook group to converse about their womanhood and resist gendered and biased mainstream media content that does not promote their empowerment. This attests to what Matsuzaka et al. (2023) state about women and their use of social media in their study investigating Black American women's social media use integration in relation to social media addiction. According to these scholars (Matsuzaka et al., 2023, p. 1) "women are shown to use social media for social interaction, information access, and entertainment … social media can hold emotional significance for and become deeply integrated into a person's life." They explore both how much social media is used, and the subjective importance social media holds for people. Black women across the world use social media and effects of such platforms are global. Facebook is the most used social media platform in South Africa and due to its massive growth, it is imperative to understand the role played by social media in a user's life and its influence on the user's online decision-making and behaviour (Budree et al., 2019). The research problem this study investigates are the habitual behaviors of Black women's social media usage, engagement, self-representation and identities in South Africa focusing on content and reactions on the *Ladies House* Facebook group.

LADIES HOUSE FACEBOOK GROUP

The *Ladies House* on Facebook is a closed group that embraces different social and cultural identities and provides a space for Black women to discuss issues that uniquely affect them. The group was created 16 October 2014 by a Chriss Bhoni and it consists of 802 501 members recorded as of April 17, 2024 at 13:46.

Women are either invited by existing group members, or new members send an invite request. The group has two administrators who vet the gender of members through their profile pictures and account names. A potential member is then requested to read rules of engagement in the group as shown below:

> **Hi ladies akuthukwana lana.* [there should be no swearing]
> **Akekho ongcono kunomunye.* [no one is better than the other]
> **Akushelwa lana. [no romantic proposals here]*
> **Akucwasanwa.* [there is no discrimination]
> **Unga undermayni ezinye izinkolo.* [there is no religious discrimination]
> **Don't advertise amanye amagroups lana.* [do not advertise other groups here]
> *Any problems 07442*****.*

The invitation is accepted by group administrators upon the invitee's agreement to the rules. The invitee can then participate in the group through posting and reacting to content, or simply by commenting on other members' posts. Group members can participate as much or as little as they wish through this non-hierarchal space that affords members an equal opportunity for their voices to be heard.

The *Ladies House* Facebook group consists of a non-hierarchal agenda in practice and shows that all members can speak as loudly as they want to, whenever they want, using their choice of words without being ignored or their voices and opinions validated. Administrators at times can be viewed as being gatekeepers of the group with authority to vet membership, remove members or delete posts inciting profanity. There have been some posts that broke the rules of the group which have slipped through the administrators. It is debatable whether this has been done deliberately or not as such posts tend to attract more user-interaction and engagement and have popularized the group even outside of its digital borders. There have also been cases where some posts originating from the group have been shared on other people's social media walls and even discussed on some mainstream media platforms, such as radio shows. Such cases have not deterred group members from participating in the group as they still feel that *Ladies House* affords them a space where everybody is equally heard to a point where women unite for individual and collective development. Some members have shared on the group information about their businesses with the hopes of attracting more clients and customers, and some have shared their experiences about using certain products with the hopes of spreading information that can assist other women in their walk of life.

The *Ladies House* group enables women to facilitate information and mobilize themselves according to their common goals. Other applications of mobilizations include but are not limited to skills transfer, information sharing, awareness tips, and acknowledgement of success. Such groups are havens for mobilizations as they enable participants to easily express their concerns, become aware of common problems, and begin to question hierarchal social institutions that inhibit their growth and abilities to explore their identities and potential. The *Ladies House* group provides such a haven for its members. This results in strengthened online collective identities which also result in offline networks and community. There have been instances where some of the women, who only know each other through their posts and comments, have organised and participated in social gatherings offline to share information and build friendships. Online groups establish a sense of solidarity, shared identities, and culture.

The *Ladies House* group has not only created online friendship networks, but it has now also shifted to being a social movement where women empower each other through skills transfer, information sharing, awareness tips, and acknowledgement of success. Platforms like Facebook, as seen through *Ladies House*, "nurture individual and collective identities" and provide users with "interpersonal relationships" (Crossley, 2015, p. 253), "facilitate the construction of politicized collective identities" (Taylor, 2013, p. 46) and provide an area of "social interaction in which holders of specific world views reinforce mutual solidarity and experiment with alternative lifestyles" (Diani, 1995, p. 348). This creates communities of solidarity through the simplification of content that is shared online.

The group, through its content, gives members a sense of purpose and belonging. *Ladies House* can be referred to as a consciousness-raising group because it is a space separated from men where women discuss their shared personal experiences and how these experiences intersect with larger socio-economic and socio-political issues of their lives. There is a sense of social justice embedded in the group. Pruchniewska (2020, p. 4) lists core features of a consciousness-raising group as a "group without men, non-hierarchal membership where women could discuss everyday experiences and build communities that laid the foundation for actions that challenges the gendered status quo both in their personal lives and collectively." *Ladies House* incorporates these features making it a non-hierarchal online conscious-raising group where Black women members can comment, post, react and interact with other members in the group. At a glance, *Ladies House* supports feminist practices but not "wider feminist project by the exclusion of some women across lines of difference such as race, class, and gender" (Pruchniewska, 2020, p. 1).

BACKGROUND AND RATIONALE

Using the *Ladies House* Facebook page as a case study, the researcher seeks to find out how Black women represent their identities through shared content and engagement on digital platforms, how they negotiate gender cultural norms and how they navigate female-dominated digital platforms. The focus of this study is Black women because their ability to represent themselves seems liberating because this group has endured structural gendered atrocities for centuries (Owens & Fett, 2019). Centuries later, news reports and social media platforms are showing how Black women are being dehumanized and commodified because of their gender, race and class. South Africa with its history of exclusion and discrimination, is no exception (StatisticsSA, 2023). Black women as a vulnerable group continue to be victimized because of their gender as seen in the increasing cases of gender-based violence and intimate partner violence. According to a crime statistics report in the year 2022, more than 11 855 cases of gender-based violence against women were reported in that year alone. Digital social media platforms are disrupting this narrative by providing platforms for Black women to empower themselves by engaging in digital storytelling through recounting their histories, celebrating their cultures, religions, achievements, and engaging in dialogues about the injustices they face through lived experiences. They engage in self-representation, narrate their stories, and negotiate their identities. Through digital media spaces, such as posts shared on *Ladies House*, Black women "re-envision an emancipatory logic whereby gender, race, class hierarchies, and sexual violence are no longer viable threats to liberation" (Conley, 2019, p. 256).

Black women are not immune from gender, class and racial inequalities. Media reports depict Black women as victims, uneducated, superficial, emotionally unstable and financially dependent. Such objectification promotes negative stereotypes and false narratives against women who continue to suffer from effects of historical atrocities. Some Black women as media consumers, have been influenced by such images. For example, this can be seen during their encounter with media texts whereas viewers, they temporarily lose their own reality and live through their idolised media character(s) (Blose, 2020, p. 40). A clear indication of this is found in soap operas. This happens through viewers' parasocial interaction and relationships with media characters, identification, imitation and transportation processes. Viewers lack knowledge and ability to decipher between fantasy and reality as they easily emulate, either consciously or unconsciously, characteristics and scenes of media content, for example, in soap operas. These characteristics can be witnessed in society through the behaviour and attitudes of and about Black women.

Social networking sites, through the growth of digitisation, have enabled Black women to be active media participants and creators of their own self-represented identities. Through social media platforms such as Facebook, Black women are championing their narratives, creating their own identities, and taking ownership of their stories. This presents opportunities for Black women to actively engage and participate in social justice through social media as such platforms present power and opportunities to communicate constructive information for social development. The hypothesis raised by this study is that closed Facebook groups, such as the *Ladies House*, provide a platform for Black women to represent themselves, negotiate their identities and own their narratives through content that they decide to share and engage with in public.

Black African women are faced with many socio-economic issues that inhibit their development and media content packaged through stereotypes on mainstream media adds to already existing social issues faced by this group. Using virtual autoethnography, the researcher explores self-representative content posted by this demographic focusing on what this group posts; how they engage with posts and what environment and identities they create. I explore what contributes to the construction of the users' gender identities and how they in turn represent and negotiate those identities through the content they create and publish on the *Ladies House* closed group on Facebook.

AFRICA IN THE GLOBAL CONVERSATION

When the rapid spread of mobile phones occurred in the developed world during the 1990s, few thought of Africa as a potential marketplace (Essoungou, 2010). However, subscribers have surpassed those in North America. According to Essoungou (2010, p. 3–4) Africans' use of mobile phones is now coupled with their "massive interest in social media … Africans are leading what may be the next global trend: a major shift to mobile Internet use, with social media as its main drivers." Bosch (2020, p. 11) defines social media as "internet-based websites and applications that allow users to create and share content, and that connect them and allow them to interact with each other". Bosch (2020, p. 9) further states that social networking sites are used by South Africans to "document life, preserve memories and as a curated stream of self-reflection and self-creation." In Africa, online reflects offline realities. Mobile phones and Internet usage are not accessible to all citizens thereby increasing the socio-economic divide between those who are affluent and those who are not. Online and offline illiteracy is a lived reality for many. However, social media spaces have afforded users platforms to expand their social groups by building new communities (Nyabola, 2018), transform political engagement (Dwyer & Molony, 2019), close gender divides (Bosch, 2020) and reinforce power dynamics (Mano & Ndlela, 2020). Of all the various social media platforms, Facebook remains the most visited social media platform in Africa (Essoungou, 2010). Facebook requires less data usage compared to other social media platforms, and it was the first social media platform to enable users to create and share pictures, videos, audio, and engage with each other by reacting to and sharing posts.

FACEBOOK IN SOUTH AFRICA

Although there is a digital divide between the Global North and South, social media usage continues to grow in South Africa (World Wide Worx, 2016). Social networking platforms such as Facebook provide "communicatory utility, convenience utility, expression of opinion, information sharing, and surveillance/knowledge about others" (Budree et al., 2019, p. 315). South Africa is one of the leading countries in the African continent with most mobile social networking users (UNICEF, 2012) overcoming the age barrier and urban-rural divide (World Wide Worx, 2012). According to Bosch (2020) this growth can be credited to the country's use of mobile internet outside of fixed line broadband access. In her book titled *Social Media and Everyday Life in South Africa*, Bosch (2020, p. 11) states that there are over "31.18 million active users, representing 54% penetration; 85% use a mobile phone and 60% have smartphones; and there are 23 million active social media users (22 million mobile social media users) and the majority of Facebook and Twitter users access these sites via mobile." Most users access social media through their smartphones, juggling multiple online personas on various social media platforms for various human social needs such as internal satisfaction, the ability to influence and be influenced by others. The key component is the social aspect in social media "which still mirrors basic social norms and human social needs" (Budree et al., 2019, p. 316). Social media has undoubtedly enlarged the social network of Black women by providing a platform to express themselves, explore and negotiate their identities, represent and own their narratives.

BLACK WOMEN AND SOCIAL NETWORKING SITES

History is filled with evidence of discrimination against Black women as this group found itself at the periphery of the social structure having to navigate through the triple oppression of race, gender, and class (Burden-Stelly, 2020). But technology has afforded Black women different platforms to not only express themselves, but also form and explore their identities. Social media platforms do not only introduce the world to who Black women are, but they also introduce Black women to who Black women are. Some research relates the use of social networking sites to self-representation, and contact building and maintaining among users (Lee, 2012; Perkov & Saric, 2020; Schlosser, 2020; Mertz et al., 2020). This is also known as social capital or resources available to users due to their interactions. The more diverse a user's social network contacts are, the more social capital a user has, giving that user an advantage over other users with less diverse networks. Kalpidou et al. (2011) suggest that spending too much time on Facebook is an indication of low self-esteem even if one has too many friends. Analysis of content provided in the later passages contradicts this notion. Underwood et al. (2015, p. 5) distinguish between social communicators and social broadcasters stating that communicators "have anchored relationships and focus more on maintenance of close-knit social friendships, while broadcasters engage in self-promotion and self-orientation." They concluded that high interaction users are seldom into "quality interaction" yet have "greater comfort in lying." However, we cannot deny the positive social adjustment that comes with using the social networking sites due to the emotional stability of users' extroversion and openness. Some scholars (Vasalou et al., 2010) have found that Facebook does come with user benefits due to diverse cultures that each user is exposed to online. For example, Facebook is also an informative tool teaching users about other cultures through posts shared and behaviours displayed online. Culture is broadcasted and communicated through high-interaction users.

According to Gipson (2019), portrayal of Blackness and Black womanhood are constantly being challenged, redefined, and creatively used through public voices. Gipson further argues that online communities of Black women separately and collectively serve as diaries that impact popular culture by influencing the producers, while simultaneously contributing and reshaping the content. Conley (2019, p. 256) agrees in that "women of colour have been leveraging digital spaces to tell their own stories while necessarily resisting white supremacy, misogynoir, anti-blackness, and white feminism." Social media platforms are enabling Black women to reclaim their space by placing themselves in their stories and theories no longer as victims, but as victors of their stories. It is through these spaces that Black women remember the self and community amid gender-based violence, classism, racism, and other social factors that hinder their development. Digital spaces are testament to how Black women's lived experiences are catalysts for theories of self and community as Black women forge ahead to be perceived as shapeshifters and movement builders.

Noble and Tynes (2016, p. 2) highlight the internet as not being a neutral space because it is "a system that *reflects*, and a site that *structures*, power and values." Although Daniels (2013) is of the belief that digital technologies limit the experiences of underrepresented groups, this notion has changed over the years. Digital spaces provide different and unique environments for users. Nagy and Neff (2015) highlight that online platforms such as Facebook allow users to interact with technologies based on their imaginations on the purpose and functionalities of the technology. This means that users carry either a sense of belonging or rejection, depending on the technology's user-interface or features. The number of the group members in the Ladies House Facebook group attests to how this application is popular among Black women because it is perceived as a safe space where they can share who they are, their previous and current experiences, and aspirations. According to Pruchniewska (2020, p. 4), "the way people perceive a technology impact how they use it."

The theoretical model on Online Entertainment in Figure 7.1 shows that a user's intention, such as content production, may lead to their entertainment experience of relief, which in turn provides the user with a sense of self-representation and identity engagement. Spinner (2022, p. 1) states that closed social media groups provide a spirit of collectiveness alongside the central role of family and friends which are "prevalent core values in Black culture". When a person feels like they belong to a group, they are bound to reach out for help and make better decisions. The opposite is also true where external triggers such as social media perceptions could be detrimental to how a user values or devalues themself. Although the *Ladies House* administrators warn against foul language and toxic comments, however some posts by the nature of their content attract foul language and dislikes. Such posts dismantle the notion of community and collectivity and create a toxic environment and sense of attack. This attests to how a social media environment can influence Black women positively or negatively.

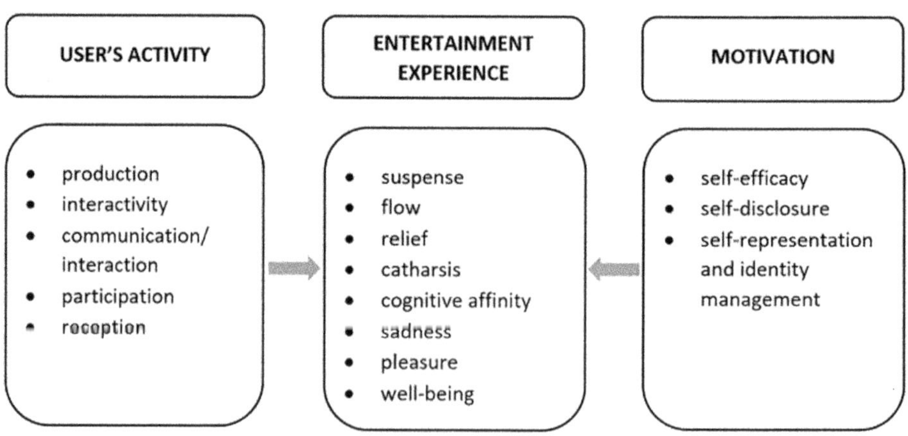

Figure 7.1. A theoretical model on Online Entertainment by Trepte and Reinecke (2019) displaying the online user's activity, entertainment experience and motivation or self-representation.

THEORIZING THE PERSONAL

This study draws on Gloria Anzaldua's notion of Autohistoria as a personal essay that theorizes and describes "the genre of writing about one's personal and collective history using fictive elements, a sort of fictionalized autobiography or memoir" (Conley, 2019, p. 231). Autohistoria is evident in personal posts of lived experiences that women share in *Ladies House*, and it is amplified through their critical mass which transcends beyond time and space. The group provides a rich site for analysis and exploration into women's self-representation and identity construction. It can be determined through posts shared on the group that women communicate "eventful, traumatic, tragic, and beautiful stranger-than-fiction stories" and these can be used as theoretical resource for examining communicative practices and cultural phenomena generated online. According to Conley (2019, p. 232) "the message relayed throughout popular culture suggests that Black women and girls are trendsetters; the ideas, talents, traditions, practices, and cultural attitudes are indeed infectious." The infectivity derived from posts shared in the *Ladies House* group is evident. It transcends the boundaries of the group and can be found discussed in various other mediums such as radio, newspapers and television. This is what Conley (2019, p. 235) refers to as transmedia storytelling which is characterized by "a practice by which individuals and communities employ various forms of writing and mediamaking to (re)tell stories." The difference, however, between transmedia storytelling and autohistoria is that the former does not rely on the storyteller to include themselves in their story whereas the latter relies on the self to produce knowledge about the world around them even if it's fiction. When radio personalities discuss content posted in the *Ladies House* group, they do so to create public opinion that seldom empowers but rather disempowers. The opinions are formulated by radio hosts who have thousands of followers that believe in what they say. The content creator is not given a chance to elaborate on their post and defend themselves. This perpetuates the one-sidedness of perceptions about Black women by mainstream media.

What is visible in *Ladies House* is autohistoria where Black women as content creators produce their own knowledge of the world around them, personalize their experiences, and interpret content from others based on their own meaning-making extra-textual resources, such as their race, gender, culture, class, religious beliefs, childhood experiences and traumas, and generic life experiences. In autohistoria, Black women as content creators are not producing content for fandom although their content can be influential and shape other people's perceptions. One of the key features of autohistoria witnessed in *Ladies House* is that it brings forth personal and community testimonies. It is evident through the hundreds and thousands of comments and reactions on some posts that experiences are shared, and a sense of community support is developed among group members. *Ladies House* provides a space which shows Black women no longer in a space of marginalisation as this space helps to transform a personal experience initially shared by one member on the group's wall, to a community-shared experiences based on comments and reactions by other members who attest to having experienced similar encounters in their own lives. From one post, the group endures a transformation of community. Therefore, autohistoria enhances the tradition of transmedia by centering the critical imaginations of Black women who have for years struggled with a history that has failed them.

RE-PRESENTATION OF IDENTITIES AND CULTURE

Black women's identities have in the past been defined by the color of their skin, their literacy levels, class, and beauty. Toxic culture has suppressed Black women and inhibited their empowerment. It presents them as dependent and voiceless beings who are subordinates of the male gender. However, digital media spaces are affording Black women spaces to define and negotiate their own identities, and to negotiate their culture. The growth of the *Ladies House* group is not only found in the number of members it has but how it continues to challenge other people's narratives about Black women in society. Struggles and challenges faced by Black women because of how their identities and culture are represented in mainstream media are not only found in the physical world but they are now even more dominant in the virtual world. As Conley (2019, p. 232) posits "online, algorithms and Google searches represent Black women and girls as one-dimensional caricatures of contemporary life" where "even the most accomplished are mocked in memes for their public visibility" which indicates that "there is a cost of being contained within these cultural spaces." The advantages of online spaces far outweigh the disadvantages as online communication technologies highlight Black women's experiences of exploitation, discrimination and brutal dehumanization acts. Closed Facebook groups provide a platform for communal support for women by women. It is in such spaces that Black women own their narratives, reclaim their personhood and emerge as shapeshifters and movement builders of society in their own public user accounts and offline. Black women are not now seen and heard in public life. Closed groups carve out a new public space for Black women's voices that is not limited to the virtual world, reactivating the power of Black women's existence online and offline, and evoking their spirit of emancipation.

BORDERED AND BORDERLESS

Closed Facebook groups such as the *Ladies House* position Black women "as being part of a global and digitally connected Black experience, albeit one that is not monolithic or accessible to all Black people" (Sobande & Brownlie, 2020, p. 2). Sobande and Browlie (2020, p. 14) define the concept of glocalization as "the synthesis of both local and global qualities, including in ways that can result in a degree of international and regional appeal." They further state that "online technologies liberate individuals from the restrictions of geographical borders and create a perceived borderless virtual place, where [users] can feel connected to people much further afield". Content in the *Ladies House* is produced by, about, and for Black women. The fact that it is a closed group made up of only Black women provides members with a sense of being part of a safety net and community that is carving out their own narratives and are not shy to share information, engage in agreements and disagreements, and ultimately uplift each other. Members display re-embodied solidarity as they self-represent their identities in ways where they have control over their own stories. Such digital spaces enable Black women opportunities to identify, negotiate and create alternatives identities to those presented by mainstream media.

Social media affords its users experiences that "transcend geo-cultural borders" (Sobande, 2022, p. 137). Sobande further speaks about Black-geographies referring to the "histories of places, politics, and violence which affect the daily lives of Black people." In her study on the burgeoning nature of Black digital studies in Britain, she points out that social media is both bordered and borderless when zooming in to the geo-cultural and sociopolitical contexts, and thinking the opposite being true would be naïve. She further defies the thought of social networking sites floating in the air and elaborates that (in)access to social media is determined by where the user is located and whether their sociopolitical environment permits. This is true for South African users especially in the backdrop of daily scheduled power outages referred to as loadshedding where a social media user's access depends on whether the mobile device has enough battery power, data or Wi-Fi access. In some parts of the world with strict state-controlled cyberspaces and harsh sociopolitical environments, social networking sites are either temporarily or permanently banned. These are examples of how social media (in) access is linked to geo-cultural and sociopolitical environments. According to Sobande (2022, p. 138) "the relationship between social media and geographies includes online experiences and expressions of identity and the self which are influenced by locations (social, geographical, cultural, political, assumed, imagined)." She further states that social media experiences are located, dislocated and relocated. When looking at the number of members in the *Ladies House* group, that is over 700 000, one can see that some users' experiences are indeed located as they identify with certain posts and react to them, dislocated when they do not identify or react to some posts, and relocated when others state in their comments how a post is personal to them and their experiences. Sobande (2022) concludes in her study that locations and forms of locatedness are thus both tangible and imagined as fluid and constantly in flux. When writing this chapter, I did so specifically with an interest in trying to link negotiated identities of Black women, how they represent themselves in the *Ladies House* Facebook group and their engagement with the content. I realize that locations and locatedness are not fixed just as Black women's identities are constantly changing depending on their sociopolitical, socioeconomic, and geo-cultures. Ultimately, social networking sites provide users with moments of enjoyment, escapism, and online entertainment. Social networking sites provide spaces where Black women's identities are being negotiated as they self-represent their own narratives.

METHODOLOGY

This qualitative research explored the phenomenon of self-representation of identities by Black women on digital social media platforms such as the *Ladies House* group on Facebook through shared content and their engagement on published posts. Through autoethnography, I studied the posts closely to ascertain those which are most popular determined by the number of reactions such as 'likes' and 'comments' using the method of content analysis. This methodology was suitable for this study because it employed "an array of interpretative techniques which seek to describe, decode, translate, and otherwise come to terms with the meaning, not the frequency, of certain more or less naturally occurring phenomena in the social world" (Van Maanen, 1979, p. 520). Since qualitative research focuses on the process of research rather than the outcome, I analysed content posted over a period of three months from January to March 2023. In my observation of the group, I have realised that members are most active in the duration of these first three months of the year. This could be because this period is symbolic of the beginning of the year in South Africa where people welcome personal change, possible progress and hope for things to come.

I observed the online engagement of members in the *Ladies House* group to see what topics were popular among members, how they received and decoded messages, and in turn how they engaged with each post. Data consisted of written texts, photographs, symbols, signs and sentences. Using discourse analysis which according to Gee (2011, p. ix) is "the study of language at use by the world, not just to say things, but to do things", I focused less on *what* the data was saying but more on *how* ladies said what they were saying, that is, "how meanings were constructed and how they shaped and constructed the subjects' perception of the world" (Blose, 2020, p. 127).

An inductive analysis was used for this study to engage with the data by mining for popular phrases, establishing emerging themes, and then grouping those themes. Popular themes that emerged from the data are discussed in the next section.

FINDINGS

Findings show that lack of representation and misrepresentation of Black women in mainstream media is still visible (Kendall, 2022). Whether this refers to various body types, races, gender, and class, media are still selective in who they represent and how they represent what they represent. Social media platforms such as Facebook on the other hand, have provided platforms for users to own their narratives by self-presenting and representing their identities and offer ways for Black women to negotiate their culture. These platforms enable users to push for diverse and inclusive representation. Kendall (2022, p. 3) states that social media is designed to showcase a "highlight reel" of the user's life as users previously refrained from posting "discouraging moments, the unflattering images, or the boring days online for the whole world to see." *Ladies House* group members are challenging this notion as members have minimal limitations to which parts of their lives they choose to share. They are not selective in what they post with the hopes of empowering other group members. Group members not only post a highlight reel of their lives, but they also post about discouraging moments and unflattering images. In addition to positive posts, members share content about their failed relationships, abuse, depression, sexual experiences, to name a few. This goes to show that growth in digitisation platforms has given more Black women voices to own their experiences, both good and bad, and to take control of the shape and direction of their narratives. They have the power to present themselves differently on social media platforms compared to how they have always been represented and misrepresented by mainstream media.

The *Ladies House* members are classified as an under-represented group however this platform offers members an opportunity for their voices to be heard. The support of women by women is evident in the reactions and comments on posts. Although closed Facebook groups provide bordered virtual spaces for online communities (Pruchniewska, 2020), like any other community, certain communal issues may arise, some neighbours might not get along, there will be pockets of excellence and that of chaos. Some reactions and comments when closely analysed, reveal that there does exist a level of exclusion of other women based on their race, class and gender. Some comments are borderline online harassment and hate speech. Some users find it easy to bully others using their fingers behind their screens. This shows that some women project their own emotions onto others.

When taking a closer look at the posts and interactions between members in the group, differences between women and the concomitant exclusionary practices become magnified. This is due to what Pruchniewska (2020, p. 9) points out as amplified "woman to woman problem that the patriarchy has handed to us." In the *Ladies House* group, there are divisions around class, culture and sometimes gender. Women who can afford a certain lifestyle will be seen posting about material valuables. Some posts may contain culture and language discrimination. And at times, there is visible woman-on-woman hatred. However, such incidences are few compared to the camaraderie among group members. There have been instances where women support each other financially, socially, and most of the time emotionally. Overall, harmony supersedes discrimination. Positive posts and content far outweigh negative posts and comments displayed in shared values and practices of this community.

POPULAR THEMES EMANATING FROM CONTENT

Humor

Humor is a source of entertainment and a means of coping with difficult or awkward situations intended to derive a smile or laughter from the message encoder or decoder. According to the Cambridge Dictionary, humor is "the ability to be amused by something seen, heard, or thought about, sometimes causing you to smile or laugh, or the quality in something that causes such amusement" (Cambridge Dictionary, 2023). There was at least one humorous post uploaded every other day on the *Ladies House* group. This was in the form of affiliative humor with the aim of making others laugh, or self-enhancing humor to make the post's creator feel better about themselves. Such posts were popular among group members and gained many reactions and comments.

For example, there was a post about a lady who attempted to make steamed bread, but the endeavor was unsuccessful. Within 5 hours of the post being uploaded, it attracted over 10 000 reactions and close to 3 000 comments. Comments indicated that members found humor in the post and some shared pictures and recipes of their own home-made steamed bread. This post also shows solidarity of women coming together to help each other learn how to make steamed bread. The number of reactions and comments are an indication that group members gravitate towards humor.

Entrepreneurship

Entrepreneurship is the activity or process of starting up a business while taking some risks to make a profit. Some of the ladies in the group mentioned that they are unemployed, seeking business or work opportunity ideas and others utilize the group to advertise their own entrepreneurship skills.

In a study conducted by the Global Entrepreneurship Monitor (GEM, 2021) the results showed that "millions of women across the globe have started businesses over the last five years alone. Tellingly, the highest percentage of these women reside in Africa." According to Aida Diarra, Senior Vice President and Head of Sub-Saharan Africa at Visa, "women still own and manage significantly fewer businesses than the opposite sex" citing complex and multifaceted reasons such as "female behavioral traits, motivations, and success rates, and their gender-related distinctiveness" (GEM, 2020).

During the three months period under observation of content posted on the group, there were at least 30 posts by women advertising their businesses on the group. Businesses ranged from making and selling products, house chore services, hair braiding, and make-up artists, to name a few. All posts contained comments where women encouraged each other and shared how they started their businesses.

Appreciation

The assumption surrounding the attitudes of women towards each other is that they seldom celebrate each other. This is due to historical challenges women have faced ranging from gender inequalities, a patriarchal system, negative stereotypes, and socio-economic factors that hindered their self-development in life.

Another assumption is that women exhibit the "pull her down syndrome" towards one another where they struggle to celebrate each other's successes and instead, are jealous of each other and want to see each other fail. What I observed in the content posted was that women seldom spoke badly about one another but instead they were quick to encourage each other. There were several examples of appreciation posts where women recognized good qualities in others and expressed feelings of gratitude and admiration. Appreciation posts ranged from physical appearances and dress-codes to professions and academic qualifications.

Support

During the period under observation, there were several posts that displayed various types of support: be it emotional, financial, psychological, spiritual, and physical. The women support each other from issues of depression and anxiety, feedback on the usage of certain products, and shared advice on family and relationship issues, to name but a few.

Some women send money using electronic wallets, also known as e-wallets, to assist other with groceries, tuition fees, and self-run businesses. There were posts which showed grocery items bought by one of the group members with donated money she received from other members. Such posts display the spirit of Ubuntu, humanitarianism and communism where society shares resources for the benefit of those who have little to nothing at all. This post attracted close to five thousand reactions and close to four hundred comments, mostly which were hearts indicating how members loved such a display of camaraderie.

Inspiration

There was a post where one of the ladies showed several of her certificates and degrees and she elaborated on how she pursued her studies against the odds. She did not let her financial circumstances and childhood background deter her ambitions.

The post received over nine thousand reactions and over one thousand comments all commending her for the good work she had done. Other ladies even asked how she managed to tune her positive mentality to acquire her accolades. This post attests to how members in this group vary in their academic qualifications ranging from those who are barely literate to those who have reached the last level of the national qualifications' framework, that is the Doctor of Philosophy. Despite what others call the "pull her down syndrome" where women discriminate against each other, the Ladies House group shows camaraderie and unity among women helping develop one another in various aspects of their lives.

Challenge

There was a challenge posed on the group where members were encouraged to upload a *before* and *after* of something that they had worked on improving. The challenge was open to all members to participate. Some posted pictures of how they looked years ago to how they now look. Frame one on the top left corner shows a picture of three rondavels in one yard. The rest of the pictures show the renovated homestead. One of the aims of the challenge was to show the spirits of resilience and hard work that women possess. The post garnered close to seven thousand reactions and over two hundred comments all praising the original uploader for the work she has done to her homestead.

Activism and Solidarity

In the *Ladies House Facebook* group, members also share acts of activism and solidarity against gender-based crimes. Pictures of missing women are shared so they circulate far and wide with the hopes of victims still being found alive. Unfortunately, there have been instances where some of the victims' stories end in tragedy. For example, there was a post of a missing lady which group members were encouraged to circulate it in their social media networks. Unfortunately, the victim's body was discovered mutilated three days after she had gone missing.

Her circulating poster of a missing person turned into a story that attracted media attention, forcing law enforcement to search for her until she was found. This picture attests to the many violent acts of gender-based violent towards women in South Africa. There have been many other posts where women posted pictures of bruised bodies following domestic abuse and others posts where women have written texts detailing traumatic experiences they endure in their abusive relationships. In such instances, women display solidarity and activism against abuse and oppression. They further offer tips and guidelines for reporting abuse displaying acts of activism towards the attainment of social transformation and social justice.

Social Justice

The group to an extent also provides transformative justice described by Philly Stands Up in Bailey and Cole (2021, p. 857) as "a way of practicing alternative justice which acknowledges individual experiences and identities and works to actively resist the state's criminal injustice system … incorporating transformative justice into a social media platform means getting the community of users to start thinking about its application in this digital space but also in their real lives". This attests to how social media are both bordered and borderless as transformation does not only happen online in the digital spaces, but it also transcends offline to the user's physical world.

An example of transformative justice from a physical space into a social media space could be seen in a post which originated from a lady allegedly in an abusive relationship. She posted pictures of bruises she had allegedly endured from that relationship, and she also shared a picture of her perpetrator. One of her friends decided to share her post with the *Ladies House* group seeking advice on behalf of the friend and to raise awareness of other ladies about the alleged perpetrator. Women share advice, give emotional support, financial support, raise awareness and share appreciation posts that extend beyond the group's borders.

Rettberg (2017, p. 432) defines representation as "an object, a sign that is seen as constricted in some way, and that stands instead of an object to which it refers.

Talking about representations let us analyse the selfie, the tweet or the graph of a run. A presentation is an act, something that a person does, so talking about presentations allows us to analyse the way that the person acts to present themselves." Black women have previously been represented as submissive, dark, loud, gold-diggers, dependent, and illiterate beings. Social media platforms such as Facebook continue to enable this previously marginalised group to negotiate and own their identities and self-represent as successful, beautiful, educated, fashionable, and compassionate beings. According to Kendall (2021, p. 4) "presentation and self-representation in social media is less about the truth of the population and more about the identified ideal … to be the best of the best of an individual's lives." This statement presupposes that all social media users are selective in what they share because they must appear as "the best of the best". But we have seen through this study that closed groups such as the *Ladies House* on Facebook allows its members to not be afraid to share where they lack and that not all is well. We have also seen the irony of such posts getting more reactions and comments from other users compared to polished posts of perfection and perfect lives. The former is deemed to be more realistic, relatable, and show real life experiences. This defies societal expectations of what the identities of Black women ought to be, their standards of beauty, success, literacy, and class. These have in the past all been very exclusive and not representative of the general Black women population. Kendall (2021, p. 4) further suggests that "this idea of the "ideal" is perpetuated by people striving to accomplish what is presented for them, as well as encouragement from those sources that you are not enough unless you meet the criteria of the ideal." Mainstream media such as magazines, television and radio have in the past insinuated to the audience, especially Black women, that they are not enough as they are and have driven them to an elusive better version of themselves, they should strive towards. Burnette (2017) states that "mass media are powerful transmitters of societal values and standards, especially those regarding ideal beauty, weight, food, fashion, and gender roles." However, social media platforms have shifted this power relation by affording Black women the power to self-represent their identities and negotiate their culture. *Ladies House* group members are representative of the many identities of Black women. Content in the group shows how Black women are smart, educated, entrepreneurs, beautiful, resilient, supportive, ambitious, nurturing, humorous, role models and persevere in life. Posts in *Ladies House* show Black women as being successful, hard workers, fighters, builders, and people who do not easily give up in life regardless of the odds mounted against them. Black women are constantly exploring their identities and negotiating their freedom through a patriarchal cultural sphere that historically sought to suppress their capabilities and empowerment.

CONCLUSION

It has been determined that the *Ladies House* Facebook group affords its members the ability to interact with one another using words, videos, and links and this creates a space for discussions and sharing of personal experiences. This group links geographically distanced members based on their similar interests, networking, and shared resources that one would ordinarily get offline. Friendships and connections are developed displacing women from a point of under-representation to that of privilege and empowerment to self-represent their identities and own their narratives. This affords Black women access to opportunities and communities that were historically not available to women. However, it is also true that this group "retains ideologies born of physical, temporal, and social beliefs" (Noble & Tynes, 2016, p. 7) thereby prioritizing the opinions and experiences of those who are beautiful, are economically well-off and those whose social beliefs are more socially acceptable and popular to public belief. Therefore, Pruchniewska (2020) advises towards the acknowledgement of the benefits of private Facebook groups not being equally available to all. She further warns against the popularism of such groups stating that they contribute to the upholding of capitalist structures by generating income for those companies who own these platforms. She says that by women engaging in such groups and sharing experiences against patriarchy and the capitalist system, they are invariably feeding that same beast they are trying to kill which hinders their development abilities. However, there is no denying that such platforms and groups do contribute towards the empowerment of Black women, affording them spaces to interact with a wider audience, share experiences, self-represent their identities and negotiate cultural ideologies that suppress and oppress Black women. Closed Facebook groups such as the *Ladies House* display a different and new yet growing type of feminism where women hold each other accountable for their actions, promote activism and solidarity against things that oppress and suppress their capabilities. Closed Facebook groups for women empower them and offer safe spaces where they can be their authentic selves without fear of judgement from the male gender and classist discrimination from those who have more.

Ladies House captures Black women's aspiration to exist beyond the confines of their skin, situations, and conditions. It shows how Black women are aware of themselves and their surroundings and helps them re-imagine their lives, rewrite their stories, and control their own narratives. They are no longer speaking from a marginalised social standpoint but are erasing oppressive historical accounts by occupying a contentious digital space, using their fingers to engage in the online world, fighting to be heard and recognised amidst oppressive systematic environments of their uncomfortable realities, both in their private and public lives. *Ladies House* helps its members create new stories of healing, self-growth, cultural critique, and individual plus collective transformation. It is a platform that enables Black women to celebrate their self and collective identities by connecting their experiences across time and space. It affords people to see the bridging work done by Black women across social, gender, class, and cultural divides and across generational lines. This is a classic case depicting a change and negotiation in identities and histories of Black women over time. Black women's experiences in a digitized world are not the same as experiences of Black women who lived during non-technological times. Digitization has created spaces for the former to be more vocal about who they are, what they are, and who they potentially could be. The future has become the present based on the essential foundations of resistance experienced by Black women. Their identities are no longer imagined but are explored and shared by them on social media platforms. Digital spaces such as the *Ladies House* group have given Black women methods of re-imagining blackness and womanhood and curate their identities through self-representation content.

REFERENCES

Aniefuna, L. I., Aniefuna, M. A., & Williams, J. M. (2020). Creating and undoing legacies of resilience: Black women as martyrs in the black community under oppressive social control. *Women & Criminal Justice*, *30*(5), 356–373

Bailey, M., & Cole, D. (2021). New tools, new house: building a black feminist social (justice) media platform. *Feminist Media Studies*, *21*(5), 857–859. https://doi.org/10.1080.14680777.2021.1954970

Blose, M. (2020). Exploring Gender Identities of Females from Townships in Durban as Represented and Negotiated through Stereotypes by South African Soap Operas: Generations: The Legacy and Isidingo: The Need. PhD diss, University of Kwazulu-Natal.

Bosch, T. E. (2020). Social media and everyday life in South Africa. Routledge.

Budree, A., Fietkiewicz, K. J., & Lins, E. (2019). Investigating the use of social media platforms in South Africa. *The African Journal of Information Systems*, *11*(4), 314–336.

Burden-Stelly, C. (2020). Modern US racial capitalism. *Monthly Review*, *72*(3), 8–20.

Burnette, B. C., Kwitowski, M., & Mazzeo, S. E. (2017). "I don't need people to tell me I'm pretty on social media:" a qualitative study of social media and body image in early adolescent girls. *Body Image*, *23*, 114–125.

Cambridge Dictionary (2023, March 22). Retrieved December 20, 2024, from https://dictionary.cambridge.org/dictionary/english/humor

Conley, T. L. (2019). *Black women and girls trending: A new(er) Autohistoria-Teoria* (pp. 231–256). Columbia University.

Crossley, A. D. (2015). Facebook feminism: Social media, blogs, and new technologies of contemporary U.S. feminism. *An International Quarterly*, *20*(2), 253–264.

Daniels, J. (2013). Race and racism in internet studies: a review and critique. *New Media & Society*, *15*(5), 695–719.

Diani, M. (1995). "Networks and participation." In D. A. Snow, S. A. Soule, & K. Hanspeter (Eds.) *The Blackwell companion to social movements*. (pp. 339–359). Blackwell.

Dwyer, M., & Molony, T. (2019). Mapping the study of politics and social media use in Africa. Social Media and Politics in Africa: Democracy, Censorship and Security, pp1-18.

Essoungou, A. M (2010). A social media boom begins in Africa. *Africa Renewal*, *24*(4), 3–4.

Global Entrepreneurship Monitor (2021). Viewed 10 March 2025: https://www.gemconsortium.org/economy-profiles/south-africa/policy

Gee, J. P. (2011). Reflections on empirical evidence on games and learning. Computer games and instruction, 223232.

Kalpidou, M., Costin, D., & Morris, L. (2011). The relationship between Facebook and the well-being of undergraduate college students. *CyberPsychology, Behaviour, and Social Networking*, *14*(4), 183–189.

Kendall, Z. (2022). Representations and analysis of the effect of media and interaction with social media on its consumers. *Chancellor's Honors Program Project*. Retrieved December 18, 2024, from https://trace.tennessee.edu/utk_chanhonoproj/2494

Lee, B. E. (2012). Young, black, and connected: Facebook usage among African American college students. *Journal of Black Studies*, *43*(3), 336–354. SAGE Publications.

Matsuzaka, S., Avery, L. R., & Stanton, G. (2023). Black women's social media use integration and social media addiction. *Social Media and Society* (pp. 1–10). SAGE Publications.

Mano, W., & Ndlela, M. (2020). *Social media and elections in Africa*. Palgrave Macmillan, Cham.

Metz, M., Kruikemeier, S., & Lecheler, S. (2020). Personalization of politics on Facebook: Examining the content and effects of professional, emotional and private self-personalization. *Information, Communication & Society*, *23*(10), 1481–1498.

Nagy, P., & Neff, G. (2015). Imagined affordance: reconstructing a keyword for communication theory. *Social Media & Society*, *1*(2), https://doi.org/10.1177/2056305115603385

Noble, S. U., & Tynes, B. (2016). Introduction. In: S. U. Noble & B. Tynes(Eds.). *The intersectional internet: Race, sex, class and culture online*. (pp. 1–21). Peter Lang.

Nyabola, N. (2018). *Digital democracy, analogue politics: How the internet is transforming Kenya*. London.

Owens, D. C., & Fett, S. M. (2019). Black maternal and infant health: Historical legacies of slavery. *American Journal of Public Health, 109:10,* pp1342–1345. https://doi.org/10.2105/AJPH.2019.305243

Pruchniewska, U. (2020). *"A group that's just women for women": Feminist affordances of private Facebook groups for professionals*. Klein College of Media and Communication, Temple University.

Rettberg, W. J. (2017). Self-representation in social media. *The SAGE handbook of social media* (pp. 429–443). Sage.

Schlosser, A. E. (2020). Self-disclosure versus self-presentation on social media. *Current Opinion in Psychology*, *31*, 1–6.

Sobande, F. (2022). Locating social media in black digital studies. In D. Rosen (Ed.) *The social media debate: Unpacking the social, psychological, and cultural effects of social media* (pp. 137–151). Routledge.

Sobande, F., Fearful, A., & Brownlie, D. (2020). Resisting media marginalization: Black women's digital content and collectivity. *Consumption, Markets and Culture (CMC)*, *23*(5), 413–428. https://doi.org/10.1080/10253866.2019.1571491

Spiner, J. R. (2022). An examination of the impact of social and cultural traditions contributing to overweight and obesity among black women. *Journal of Primary Care and Community Health*, *13*, 1–8.

Statistics South Africa (2023, February 26). https://www.statssa.gov.za/?page_id=737&id=6=6

Stemmet, I. (2023). Critical challenges impeding women's ascendancy to positions of leadership in South Africa. *Gender, Race, and Politics in South Africa, 101.*

Taylor, V. (2013). Social movement participation in the global society: Identity, networks and emotions. The future of social movement research: Dynamics, mechanisms, and processes, pp37-57.

Underwood, J. D., Kerlin, L., & Farrington-Flint, L. (2011). The lies we tell and what they say about us: Using behavioural characteristics to explain Facebook activity. Computers in Human Behavior, 27:5, pp1621-1626.

UNICEF (2012). *South African mobile generation, s.l.*, UNICEF.

Van Maanen, L. (1979), Reclaiming Qualitative Methods For Organisational Research: A Preface, Administrative Science Quarterly, 24, Dec.,pp 520-26.

Vasalou, A., Joinson, A. N., & Courvoisier, D. (2010). Cultural differences, experience with social networks and the nature if "true commitment" in Facebook. *International Journal of Human-Computer Studies, 68*(10), 719–728.

World Wide Worx., (2012). World Wide Worx, viewed 10 March 2025, from Social Media Breaks Barriers in SA: https://www.worldwideworx.com/socialmedia 2012

World Wide Worx., (2016). World Wide Worx, viewed 10 March 2025, from Social Media Breaks Barriers in SA: https://www.worldwideworx.com/socialmedia 2016

CHAPTER EIGHT

Acting With Algorithms: Feminists' Daily Encounters With Algorithmic Cultures

SIHLE NYATHI

INTRODUCTION

The aim of this chapter is to discuss the content creation strategies of Pusheka Girl with the view of establishing how they inspire their members to create content based on several hashtags. We were also interested in the neoliberal discourses that are constructed by the organization. Dewa (2019) established that the discursive construction of Zimbabwean women's femininities is necessarily a weaving of different discourses that tap into wider social formations and intersect in powerful ways. Their constitution ranges from traditional, liberal feminist to postfeminist. A neoliberal position that emphasises the power associated with access to money and power over men is discernible on Pusheka Girl's platforms. The platforms engage with neoliberal ideals and consumer culture that embodies notions of choice, freedom, and personal responsibility hence the name Pusheka Girl which means that' Girl be pushed' into presumably becoming a businesswoman.

In researching the use of social media by women in Zimbabwe, Dewa (2019), says that women occupy an agonistic space in which their enunciation shows that they are subjects of different discourses because of the complex knotting of Christianity and tradition whereby biblical truths are represented as tradition thereby legitimating these discourses as unquestionable in most instances. The ultimate conclusion was that Zimbabwean femininities performed on social media platforms are in a state of uncertainty and unresolved tension as they move from one discursive realm to another (Dewa, 2019; Talbot, 2010; Prinsloo, 2009).

Women have historically been associated with media consumption, but user-friendly interfaces of smartphones have simplified the means for content creation and this has allowed women easier access to media production and distribution (Kanai & Dobson, 2016; Viviene & Burgess, 2012). We see social media platforms as Technologies of Gender (De lauretis, 1987) because this allowed us to see the construction of gender both as representation and self-representation on the social media platforms that we studied. In this sense, gender is seen as the outcome of various social technologies which include social media platforms that depict and create gender norms (De Lauretis, 1987). The representations on social media platforms reproduce gender conceptions and show the pre-existing gender expressions of the photographed individual through their clothing and mannerisms (Doring et al., 2016; Dinsmore, 2014). The content production by *Pusheka Girl* happens within this framework.

BACKGROUND TO THE STUDY

Pusheka Girl was founded by Makaita Tekere and Tatenda Tekere because of the desire to build a community for young women, to uplift each other (Pusheka Girl interview). Makaita and Tatenda are Bulawayo-based entrepreneurs and influencers who run beauty spas and salons.

"Our main goal is to create a community where women are successful in their businesses, in any venture that they try to pursue. We were motivated to empower the girl child because we have a lot of programmes that are directed towards empowering the girl" (Pusheka Girl interview).

Pusheka Girl hosts quarterly business showers which are open to registered members and non-Pusheka Girl members for advertising purposes and the sale of various products. The business showers have enlarged the client bases of their members. The organization runs a skills training Centre in Bellevue in Bulawayo, Zimbabwe and members volunteer in the teaching of skills such as Nail art, Digital marketing, Makeup training, Basic Cookery, and Baking. The Bellevue Training Centre is located in the Bellevue Suburb in Bulawayo Province of Zimbabwe, South West of Harare, the country's capital city. The majority of those coming for training are the unemployed and in need of skills to start their businesses. The alumni have started catering businesses and some are working as make-up artists. Pusheka Girl seeks to encourage economic development and growth. The Pusheka Girl founder, Makaita Tekere was nominated for the African influencer awards in 2021. The award is for game changers that have been influencing trends and inspiring change in 2021 in the top female social media influencer category (www.affluencer.com). Pusheka Girl has 2200 followers and 2000 likes on Facebook as of February 2023. The page was created in November 2020. The organization has 1878 followers on Instagram and 91 followers on TikTok. Pusheka Girls joined Instagram in August 2021. The *Pusheka Girl* pages are managed by administrators who are the founders and the Public Relations Officer respectively.

Zimbabwe is a sub-Saharan African country with an estimated population of 15 million (https://zimstat.co.zw/). The country has been plagued by the 'Zimbabwean crisis' as it has come to be popularly known among a host of other euphemisms that have been employed to describe the socio-economic and political situation in the country since the early 2000s. The economic crisis in Zimbabwe was a result of the widely publicized Economic Structural Adjustment Programme (ESAP), which was introduced as an economic revitalizing programme in the 1990s (Brett, 2005). The introduction of ESAP resulted in mass retrenchments and the collapse of indigenous businesses (Makina, 2010; Simpson *& Hawkins*, 2018). The economic crisis resulted in an informal economy which is punctuated by small and medium scale enterprises.

LITERATURE REVIEW

The chapter considers how social network sites are used in content creation for ideological purposes. Social network sites are defined as web-based services that allow users to build public profiles for the purposes of making connections (Boyd *& Ellison* 2008). According to data portal, Zimbabwe's internet penetration stands at over 30% of the population while there are over a million social media users. The internet in Zimbabwe has been used for a variety of purposes and women have gained critical acclaim by monetizing their content (Mungwari & Kembo, 2022).

Social media platforms gave rise to audiences who produce and consume content (Bruns, 2008) because they have both a creative and interactive nature. Pusheka Girl members can therefore be described as producers and consumers of social media content. Social media supports activism because most of the communication takes place between friends and activists who exist within a network (Fuchs, 2014). Harcourt (2011) argues that the internet emerged as a tool that can be used by global women's movements around the world in their struggles for rights, justice and social change. The use of the internet for organizing within the women's movement has birthed new strategies for feminist transformation while respecting global cultural differences (Harcourt, 2011). While the internet has been lauded for its democratic potential, other scholars are of the view that it empowers dominant capitalist interests (Morozov, 2011). A critical political economy approach to the interests affirms that corporate businesses operate according to the logic of capital accumulation because they turned personal data into commodities and sold to advertising companies (Zuboff, 2019). This has arguably given rise to micro celebrities who produce content within the framework of the attention economy. Pusheka Girl activists work within this framework where they use platform affordances to drive engagement while the platforms mine personal data.

THEORETICAL FRAMEWORK: FEMINIST NEOLIBERALISM AND TRANSHUMANISM

Feminist neoliberalism and Transhumanism underpin this work as we try to understand content creation by feminists. Feminist neoliberalism is predicated on the notion of affording freedoms to women to be what they desire to become, and this is in line with the notion of transhumanism and in particular Giovanni Pico della Mirandola's Oration on the Dignity of Man (1948). Mirandola stated that man can proudly and freely shape himself in the manner that he wishes. Human agency as well as the creative will of the individual are facets that are considered to be very important. Mirandola's oration on the dignity of man ascribes agency to man because man can fashion himself in the way in which he desires as long as he wills. This has close affinities to Neoliberal Feminist theory. Nietzsche (1999) and Transhumanists in particular see science as a means for overcoming nature and even death. Transhumanists are of the view that man overcomes nature and so we sought to examine the aspects of nature that Pusheka Girl members would like to overcome through the responsible use of technology. One of the central questions of the study is on the affordances availed by technology so that women can become better and achieve 'perfection' which has come to be associated with Neoliberal Feminism. Technology is an important part of the transformation of human beings and so it can be argued that social media platforms can assist in this transformation. In light of this, we sought to unravel the role social media platforms play in the transformation discourse. One of transhumanism's most important contributions is the metaphor of the child's metamorphosis (Nietzche, 1999). This metaphor speaks to the creation of a new being, so we analyzed how this discourse pans out in the articulations of the Pusheka Girl members. The ultimate goal of transhumanism is the use of bio-transformative technologies in a bid to enhance human beings with the ultimate aim of modifying them and overcoming human limitations so that human beings become 'posthuman' (Nietzche,1999). In this vein, Glover (1984) argues that technology can be used to enhance features of human nature that contribute to self-development.

Neoliberal Feminism has been touted as a new brand of feminism that has the express aim of controlling women to maintain existing power relations and to hide male dominance. This feminism takes the form of feminine self-regulation, and the notion of 'perfection' is introduced as part of the 'individualizing project' and the creation of competition among women (McRobbie, 2015). Harris (2004) argues that the idea of perfection refers to a girl who can do anything and this can be dangerous because it can result in self-harm. She further contends that the idea of perfection is disseminated according to the socio-economic and ethnic backgrounds of female subjects. The notion of the perfect speaks to a heightened form of self-regulation based on aspiring to a good life. This involves self-assessment against an elevated and rarely described benchmark. Various influencers then come in to help women to measure themselves daily and this becomes the neoliberal spreadsheet which results in a deluge of images that seek to prove how well one did each day. This spreadsheet becomes a form of self-management and self-government (Skeggs, 1997). Various technologies are availed which help one to measure how well they did daily. The Neoliberal era is punctuated by "heightened demands on bodily capacity" (Jasbir Puar, 2012:149). Women are forced to seek validation in terms of their looks (Yeatman, 2014). Contemporary power works through policing of bodies while offering the illusion of control for those who undertake the required amount of self-control (Foucault, 2008). In the attention economy content creators use infrastructural affordances and this has seen the penetration of economics because they have to develop publishing strategies that are aligned with the business models of platforms (Nieborg & Poell, 2018). The concept of neoliberalism is relevant to this study on feminist content production on Facebook and Instagram because of its recognition of the effects of consumer capitalism on feminist identity. Neoliberal feminism provides powerful media images showing deep satisfaction with this popular feminism that holds no threat to patriarchy (McRobbie, 2008). For this study, I identify Zimbabwe as a patriarchal nation in a neoliberal world economic order.

METHODOLOGY

The methodological approach for this study was qualitative. Qualitative research produces descriptive data through the study of attitudes and behaviours best understood within their natural settings (Babbie & Mouton, 2001). I employed purposive sampling in selecting texts on Facebook, Instagram and TikTok for analysis (Hansen 1998; Deacon et al., 2007). I chose posts and media articles that contributed to the social problem under investigation (Wodak & Meyer, 2009). Our aim was to investigate how Pusheka Girl members were interpellated into producing content using various hashtags that were peddled by the organization.

A total of 10 posts were considered for analysis from all platforms – Facebook, Instagram and TikTok.

Ethnography has been traditionally applied in physical settings but in recent years it has come to be applied to the internet while maintaining its epistemological foundations (Hine, 2000; Murthy, 2008). Ethnography of the internet allowed us to examine how technology was experienced and negotiated by people and in this case how feminists experience social media platforms (Boellstorff, 2012; Hine, 2009). Online ethnography captures the essence of "an adaptive self-reflexive 'lived experience' between the researcher (who constitutes the primary research instrument) and the context of the research" (Mabweazara, 2013, p. 100). Our role as primary research instruments involved long-term participation in the research context (Jankowski & Webster, 1991). To this end, we 'lived' online from June 2022 to February 2023. I also used in-depth interviews because it is a "valuable adjunct to observation" and "interviews also have the potential to offer balance and corroboration where observed phenomena are complex or involve several factors," (Gorman et al., 2005, p. 41).

Qualitative content analysis was used to analyze the content of texts and how they are combined (Deacon et al., 1999). It adopts an interpretive approach that seeks to explore how language and images are used in a complimentary fashion. This involves exploring the meanings that are embedded in the representations (Mayring, 2001). The posts that were analyzed were those posted during the period that the ethnography was carried out (June 2022 -February 2023).

THE INVENTION OF THE BUSINESS SHOWER

Pusheka Girl came up with the business shower concept in a bid to encourage and promote women's empowerment in Bulawayo (Bhebe, 2021 personal communication). The showers are meant to give businesswomen a platform to network and learn from each other. The showers are held quarterly, and they take the form of exhibitions. Various influencers come in as speakers to converse about women's empowerment and growing businesses. Tekere said that empowering women was essential to the development of communities.

The transformative ideology is apparent in their discourse because the founder says that "Empowering women is essential to the health and social development of families, communities, and countries. When women are living safe, fulfilled, and productive lives, they can reach their full potential. Empowering girls is the key to economic growth, political stability, and social transformation" (Chronicle interview, December 2, 2021). The page administrators uploaded flyers for the December 2022 business shower, and they motivated other people to participate by offering a free stall at the business shower to a vibrant entrepreneur with a business page that has 200 or more followers. Those who wanted a free stall were asked to tag five friends so that they would like and follow the Pusheka Girl page. This shows that they believe that social media platforms play a meaningful role in growing businesses, and this was corroborated in an interview with the Pusheka Girl, Public Relations Officer. Pusheka Girl members have moved from having 'baby showers' to business showers, the diction shows contradictions when one considers the history of 'baby showers' and this could be a condition of women living within the contradictions of Feminism and Patriarchy in Zimbabwe. A baby shower is a party thrown to celebrate the impending birth of a child. This concept has been changed by Pusheka Girl members and now they have business showers in order to support the businesses of their members. They link their members to new clients and also support their membership through entrepreneurial development.

SOCIAL RESPONSIBILITY PROGRAMS

Social Responsibility Programs are an integral part of the work that the Pusheka Girl movement does. They use the programs to invite people to participate in content creation. In February 2023, Pusheka Girl in partnership with Nurses24 and Green Earth held a clean-up campaign at Mpilo hospital, and they invited volunteers to help with the clean-up. They invited different stakeholders to participate by making donations. Nurses24 is an academy that offers health care courses that are designed to help the community. Green Earth is an environment company based in Bulawayo. The social responsibility programs are part of social marketing programs. Pusheka Girl has done several of these programs and these include donations of sanitary pads for the girl child under *The Period is not a punishment* campaign. They created content by making a Facebook post and then they live-streamed the event on Instagram thereby producing content. Several of their members live-streamed the event and had the following hashtags #bulawayo#bulawayogirls#pusheka_girl#pusheka#zimgirlskillingit#byocelebs#togetherwecanmakeadifference#zimnews#chroniclezimbabwe#. Social media hashtags are used to categorize specific themes or content (Ott, 2018). Pusheka Girl, therefore, uses hashtags in a bid to show the categories of content that they are producing.

Several ideologies can be gleaned from their hashtags. The hashtag #zimgirlskillingit# has resonances with Neoliberal Feminism and the concept that girls can do anything. Their brand of feminism has become popular hence they can tag the *Chronicle*, a Bulawayo-based newspaper. The organization is already getting a lot of media coverage hence they were also interviewed by the national broadcaster, The Zimbabwe Broadcasting Corporation (ZBC) on their clean-up campaign. Pusheka Girl also collaborated with a gynaecologist in offering free breast cancer checks. During the cancer checks, the women were asked to shoot pictures with Pusheka Girl placards, and these were posted on Facebook and Instagram. The posting of glamorous images on social media pages is one of the ways in which competition is created in neoliberal feminism because the images give the impression that Pushes Girls are successful because of the media coverage that they get. Other women are then led to join Pusheka Girl because media visibility is equated with success. This success is then measured through the number of 'likes' that the images receive on online platforms. The media success is measured through platform matrices and so they have to create content frequently so as to improve engagement. While Pusheka Girl identifies as a feminist movement, their primary aim is wealth creation because they believe that the emancipation of women is predicated on financial freedom. Pusheka Girl members therefore create content that is strongly aligned with corporate interests because they desire to make money from their corporate alliances. They use platform affordances that help them to increase engagement and content visibility because that helps them to market their goods and services.

THE PERFECTION TROPE

The women in Pusheka Girl strive to achieve perfection because they have the pressure of overcoming themselves in several ways. The desire to overcome their physical limitations is in line with the idea of perfection. They do this in several ways such as using makeup and exercise regimes. This is in line with transhumanism and the concept of the Over human (Nietzsche, 1999). Nietzsche's influence can be gleaned from a newspaper interview that the organisation gave. The newspaper article which was uploaded on Instagram ran under the headline 'It will no longer be a man's world'. In this case, they seem to see the world as a place that has to be overcome and so they are circumventing the limitations which women have been subjected to. A conclusion can be drawn that Pusheka Girl members embark on businesses that are intertwined, and the industries require meager qualifications and focus on the body. Pusheka Girl members construct themselves as micro celebrities, firstly because they have followers and so they believe that their bodies must be slim and that they have to be adorned in the latest fashion. They enjoy micro celebrity status within spaces that are business oriented and that celebrate female entrepreneurship. The body is a site of business due to individualization, which is a facet of the neoliberal economy. Makaita Tekere, one of the Pusheka Girl founders posted on TikTok a video where her grandmother was giving her advice. The grandmother stated that the reason why she was still single was that she was not filtering the pictures that she was posting on social media platforms. Filtering is one of the TikTok affordances which allows users to appear better-looking. The women believe that technology can help them to overcome physical limitations and help them to have better relationships. Part of Maxy Tekere's content involves images where she is in the gym, with background audio encouraging people to achieve their goals. Maxy Tekere also posts content from hairdressers who are part of the *Pusheka Girl* collective. The videos are composed of weaves which are a method of overcoming limitations perceived to be deriving from having ethnic hair. The hashtags allow the content to be discoverable by people who use the search function and are part of identifying people in the hair community. She has the hashtags #bulawayotiktok #, #bulawayo#, #bulawayohairdresser#, and #zimbabwe#maxytekere. One notices that they use several hashtags so that their content can be discovered by a lot of people who might be searching for several things like hairdressers, Bulawayo and Zimbabwe.

THE PROMISE AND THE POWER IN COLLECTIVISM

In recruiting its members, the organization promises the power of collectivism because the members can grow their businesses as they share their business contacts. The founders are of the view that women can accumulate wealth if they work together as a collective by acknowledging that all women are denied opportunities. They believe that they can overcome their financial limitations by working as a community of like-minded women. Pusheka Girl uses various media platforms such as Facebook, Instagram, and TikTok for the recruitment of members. They post messages in picture format on Facebook and Instagram using the affordance of posting stories to their timelines to recruit members. Part of their recruitment drive states that they are a community of female business owners working together to build each other up toward growth and success. Part of their recruitment drive states: "We want you. Take your business to greater heights by becoming a Pusheka_girl member. Registration is now open".

They promise members that they can take their businesses to greater heights because of the power of their collective synergies. The collective stimulates business which is said to be necessary for the Zimbabwean economy. Pusheka Girl creates synergies by posting business adverts on the 'status update' function on the Whatsapp Platform. They do this during 'business Wednesday'. All the registered members post business advertisements in the hope of stimulating business for the members and so all members create content in the form of advertisements for uploading during business Wednesday. They encourage their members to increase platform visibility though using the "Like" button on Facebook and Instagram on all posts. This is because followers see the content that is liked by the people that they follow. This is in line with neoliberal feminism which encourages young women to take advantage of all opportunities availed to them (McRobbie, 2009).

THE USE OF OTHER PLATFORMS TO CREATE CONTENT

Pusheka Girl members use various media in the creation of content. Sharon Lindelwa Dube, a Pusheka_ Girl member who runs a financial advisory consultancy called the *Financial Grind* conducted an interview on the Bulawayo-based radio station *Khulumani FM* on Valentine's day. She live-streamed the interview on her Instagram page (Interview with Sharon Dube) thereby creating content for her page by live-streaming the *Khulumani FM* program. Pusheka Girl founders were interviewed by the *Chronicle* newspaper, and they converted the print article into a picture to make it suitable for Instagram given that the application is dominated by pictures and videos. Different media houses actively cover Pusheka Girl events because of the mainstreaming and popularization of their brand of feminism. This dovetails with Dewa's (2019) findings that the media is filled with glamorous images of feminists who conform to a non-confrontational brand of feminism. This brand of feminism has become associated with commercial success and thereby attractive. This lures young women to produce content under the Pusheka Girl brand.

USE OF HEAVYWEIGHT INFLUENCERS

In chronicling the rise of neoliberal feminism Rottenberg (2014) stated that celebrities have been claiming to be feminists making feminism lose its critical edge. Pusheka Girl has been making use of celebrities in their programming. An example is South African-based actress, Nombulelo Mhlongo who was the celebrity guest at the launch of the *Grace Anne Talk* show in 2022. The use of the celebrity was meant to attract women to the event and improve engagement on social media platforms. The talk show is about finding solutions for community and business matters. The show chronicles the journey of people in business. Another example is the use of a Zimbabwean influencer Lorraine Guyo who has 298 000 followers on Facebook and 125 000 likes on the platform. Guyo, who has 359 000 followers on Instagram was used as a speaker during an event on finances. According to Pusheka Girl, the turnout for both events was good, and they received extensive media coverage. The type of feminism peddled by Pusheka Girl has been rendered desirable because of the use of celebrities. The *Chronicle* (19 November 2022) published an article about Pusheka _Girl, which stated that "Bulawayo women are fighting back. Not against men, no. They are fighting against poverty and economic disempowerment and their fight is now 'televised' thanks to Pusheka Girl, a woman-focused empowerment movement that "was founded by two women". The introduction provides ample evidence that the feminist foundations of the organization are based on consumer capitalism, and this is attractive in a country that has experienced a severe economic meltdown (Brett, 2005).

THE ALLURE OF METAMORPHOSIS

Nietzsche's (1999) child metamorphoses speak to the creation of a new being because everyone can have a new beginning and this is seen in the creation of new selves on TikTok and Instagram as societal values transform. There are various testimonials on Instagram from Pusheka Girl members on how their lives have been transformed since assuming membership in the organization. This is in line with the founding ethos of the organization.

In line with the discourse of transformation, Pusheka Girl members uploaded their pictures with testimonials on Instagram and Facebook. The members were pictured clad in jeans and pink Pusheka Girl t-shirts and one of the testimonials read that "The Pusheka _girl movement has provided tremendous opportunities for young women in the network. There is a lot I have learned, and the most important thing is to be self-driven. We move, we work, we push"@lungiesn. The post is accompanied by hashtags #togetherwecan#bethechange#pusheka_girl.

The discourse that Pusheka Girl is a movement reverberates in the testimonials of the members.

THE INVENTION OF THE PHOTO SHOOT

The photo shoot is an important part of giving the impression of perfection and also stimulates content creation. The photoshoot is one of the widely used tools in the attention economy. The photo shoot creates customers for makeup artists and boutique industries because the women engage the services of make-up artists and boutiques for the photoshoots. Photoshop is one of the technologies of gender that enable self-representation and the construction of conventional femininities.

Platform filters can be viewed as 'cultural filters' (Rettberg, 2014, p. 22) and one finds that cultural filters show the societal norms and expectations which govern photoshoots. In line with this concept our analysis shows that photoshoots that have been done by Pusheka Girl members show certain conventions. The photoshoots show women that are wearing heavy make-up, and artificial hair in a studio setting. The mannerisms of the women are choreographed, and the clothes are part of popular fashion. In a sense, women have been taught to have a particular aesthetic appeal so that they can get 'likes' in the attention economy. Social media platforms and in this case, the photoshoot function as technologies of gender that serve to define culturally accepted gender norms (Krijnen & Van Bauwel, 2015).

CONCLUSION

The proliferation of the beauty industry aided by social media platforms is organizing women into hegemonic womanhood. This happens through manufacturing discontent, thereby creating the desire to improve themselves physically and economically. The physical and economic transformations are packaged as content which is posted on social media platforms so that followers can approve of their transformation. The mainstream media is also colluding in this endeavour by celebrating neoliberal feminism as that is part of Zimbabwe's blueprint. We therefore conclude that the promise of economic emancipation is the major driving force in terms of content creation for Pusheka Girl members. This is because the country has been going through an economic crisis. Notions of equality and fight against discrimination become subordinated because of the economic crisis.

REFERENCES

Amakoh, K., Krijnen, T & Van Bauwel, S. (2015). Gender and media: Representing, producing, consuming. *MedieKultur: Journal of media and communication research, 36*(67), 141–143.

Babbie, E., & Mouton, J. (2001). *The practice of social science research.* Wadsworth.

Boyd, D., & Ellison, N. B. (2008). Social network sites: Definition, history, and scholarship. Journal of Computer-Mediated Communication, 13(1), pp210-230.

Boellstorff, T., Nardi, B., Pearce, C., & Taylor, T. L. (2012). *Ethnography and virtual worlds: A handbook of method.* Princeton University Press

Brett, E. A. (2005). From corporatism to liberalization in Zimbabwe: Economic policy regimes and political crisis, 1980–97. *International Political Science Review, 26*(1), 91–106.

Bruns, A. (2008). *Blogs, Wikipedia, Second Life, and beyond: From production to produsage (Vol. 45).* Peter Lang.

De Lauretis, T. (1987). *Technologies of gender: Essays on theory, film, and fiction.* Indiana University Press

Deacon, A., & Mann, K. (1999). Agency, modernity and social policy. *Journal of Social Policy, 28*(3), 413–435.

Deacon, D., Pickering, M., Golding, P., & Murdock, G. (2007). Researching communications: A practical guide to methods in media and cultural analysis. Arnold.

Dewa, N. (2019). *Zimbabwean women online: An investigation of how gendered identities are negotiated in Zimbabwean women's online spaces.* Rhodes University

Döring, N. (2016). How gender-stereotypical are selfies? A content analysis and comparison with magazine adverts. *Computers in Human Behavior, 55*(2016), 955–962

Dinsmore, B. (2014). "Chicks Be Like": Masculinity, Femininity, and Gendered Double Standards in Youth Peer Cultures on Social Media. *Sociology Honours Paper. 3.* http://digitalcommons.conncoll.edu/sociologyhp/3?utm_source=digitalcommons.conncoll.edu%2Fsociologyhp%2F3&utm_medium=PDF&utm_campaign=PDFCoverPages

Foucault, M. (2008). Panopticism" from" discipline & punish: The birth of the prison. *Race/Ethnicity: Multidisciplinary Global Contexts, 2*(1), 1–12.

Fuchs, C. (2014). Social media and the public sphere. *TripleC: Communication, Capitalism & Critique*, *12*(1), 57–101.
Glover, D. J. (1984). Contract farming and smallholder outgrower schemes in less-developed countries. *World Development*, *12*(11–12), 1143–1157.
Gorman, G. E., Clayton, P. R., Shep, S. J., & Clayton, A. (2005). *Qualitative research for the information professional: A practical handbook*. Facet Publishing.
Hansen, A. (1998). Mass communication research methods. NYU Press.
Harcourt, W. (2011). Using the master's tools: Women's movements and social media. *Media Development*, *58*(1), 19–22
Harris, A. (2004). *Future girl: Young women in the twenty-first century*. Routledge.
Hine, C. (2000). *The virtual objects of ethnography. Virtual ethnography*. Sage Publications
Hine, C. (2009). How can qualitative internet researchers define the boundaries of their projects?. In Internet inquiry: Conversations about method (pp. 1-20). SAGE Publications, Inc.
Jankowski, N. W., & Webster, J. G. (1991). Researching the Internet: A guide for students and scholars. In J. K. Burgoon, J. K. Burgoon, & N. W. Jankowski (Eds.), Researching the audience (pp. 135-156). Sage Publications.
Kanai, A., & Dobson, A. (2016). *Digital media and gender*. Communications & Media Studies. Wiley-Blackwell
Mabweazara, H. M (2013). Normative dilemmas and issues for Zimbabwean print journalism in the "information society" era. Digital Journalism, 1:1, pp135-151.
Makina, D. (2010). Historical perspective on Zimbabwe's economic performance. *Journal of Developing Societies*, *26*(1), 99–123.
Mayring, P. (2001). Combination and integration of qualitative and quantitative analysis. In Forum Qualitative Sozialforschung/Forum: Qualitative Social Research 2:1. 967
McRobbie, A. (2008). *The aftermath of feminism: Gender, culture and social change*. Sage Publications
McRobbie, A. (2009). Reflections on precarious work in the cultural sector. Governance der Kreativwirtschaft: Diagnosen und Handlungsoptionen, 123, pp123-38.
McRobbie, A. (2015). Notes on the perfect: Competitive femininity in neoliberal times. *Australian Feminist Studies*, *30*(83), 3–20.
Morozov, E. (2011). *The net delusion: How not to liberate the world*. Penguin.
Mungwari, T., Mapuranga, S., & Kembo, S. (2022). Reorganisation of news production in Zimbabwe during COVID-19. *International Journal od Advanced Mass Communication and Journalism*, *3*(1), 8–15
Murthy, D. (2008). Digital ethnography: An examination of the use of new technologies for social research. *Sociology*, *42*(5), 837–855.
Nieborg, D. B., & Poell, T. (2018). The platformization of cultural production: Theorizing the contingent cultural commodity. *New Media & Society*, *20*(11), 4275–4292.
Nietzsche, F., & Friedrich, N. (1999). *Nietzsche: The birth of tragedy and other writings*. Cambridge University Press.
Ott, K. (2018). Social media and feminist values: aligned or maligned? *Frontiers: A Journal of Women Studies*, *39*(1), 93–111.
Pico della Mirandola, G. (1948). Oration on the dignity of man. E. Cassirer, PO Kristeller, JH Randall, Jr.(Eds.), *The renaissance philosophy of man* (pp. 223–255). The University of Chicago Press.
Prinsloo, J. (2009). Theorising news mediations of the Zuma rape trial–citizens and subjects in collision. Critical Discourse Studies, 6(2), 81-96.

Puar, J. K. (2012). Coda: The cost of getting better: Suicide, sensation, switchpoints. *GLQ: A Journal of Lesbian and Gay Studies*, *18*(1), 149–158.

Rettberg, J. (2014). *Seeing ourselves through technology: How we use selfies, blogs and wearable devices to see and shape ourselves*. Springer Nature.

Rottenberg, C. (2014). The rise of neoliberal feminism. *Cultural Studies*, *28*(3), 418–437.

Simpson, M., & Hawkins, T. (2018). *The primacy of regime survival: State fragility and economic destruction in Zimbabwe*. Springer Link

Skeggs, B. (1997). *Formations of class & gender: Becoming respectable*. Sage Publications

Talbot, M. (2010). *Language and gender*. 2nd edition. Polity press

Vivienne, S., & Burgess, J. (2012). The digital storyteller's stage: Queer everyday activists. Negotiating privacy and publicness. *Journal of Broadcasting & Electronic Media*, *56*(3), 362–377.

Wodak, R., & Meyer, M. (2009). Critical discourse analysis: History, agenda, theory and methodology. Methods of critical discourse analysis, 2:1, pp1-33.

Yeatman, A. (2014). *Postmodern revisionings of the political*. Routledge.

Zuboff, S. (2019). January. Surveillance capitalism and the challenge of collective action. *New Labor Forum*, *28*(1), 10–29.

SECTION THREE

PLATFORMED VOICES, PROTESTS, AND RESISTANCE CULTURES

CHAPTER NINE

Dominance, Resistance, Affect: Whatsapp Use in Bungoma County, Kenya

JOB ALLAN WEFWAFWA

INTRODUCTION

AThis chapter is about the use of WhatsApp space and the role of social media influencers in Bungoma County in Kenya during the 2017 electoral deliberations. It leverages the Social Construction of Technology theory (SCOT) with a qualitative approach. I conceptualize WhatsApp space as the texting component, the video clips, audio clips, and voice notes used to participate in electoral deliberations (Jamie et al., 2019). The Kenyan electoral process refers to the activities and deliberations around elections. It includes the period between three months to the polling day, up to 48 hours before elections are held. The process involves political party nomination of the candidates who would contest in the countrywide elections at the levels of the county assembly, National Assembly, women county representative, senate, gubernatorial, and presidency (The Election Act, 2011). Article 196 of Kenya's 2010 Constitution allows those who win the party tickets to campaign for three months. The electoral campaigns enable them to sell their agendas to the people before the countrywide elections. During the electoral campaigns, WhatsApp among other social media is used for communication by the people, political class, the electoral body, and other stakeholders. For instance, the people use WhatsApp space to participate in the electoral deliberations by commenting on the processes; engaging with the issues around the electoral processes in groups; and mobilizing for public rallies in support of preferred candidates;

among others (Diepeveen, 2021). The WhatsApp space is the most used social media platform during electoral deliberations in Kenya (Wamuyu, 2020). Using the case of Bungoma County I examine the use of WhatsApp space in electioneering process deliberations. The County has 9 parliamentary slots called constituencies. They include Kanduyi Constituency, Bumula Constituency, Kabuchai Constituency, Sirisia Constituency, Kimilili Constituency, Mt Elgon Constituency, Tongaren Constituency, Webuye East Constituency, and Webuye West Constituency. The predominant ethnic group in the County is Luhya of Bukusu speaking dialect, from the larger Bantu people (KNBS, 2019). Other Luhya dialect occupants include the Tachoni people. The non-Luhya ethnic groups occupying the County include Teso and Sabaot speakers, from the larger Nilotic people (County Government of Bungoma, 2020).

I chose Bungoma County as the research site because it is the fourth most populous in Kenya (KNBS, 2019). It is also the host to the third most vibrant WhatsApp groups after Nairobi and Nakuru counties respectively (Wamuyu, 2020). Besides the relatively sufficient social media infrastructure, in the county, the vibrancy can be attributed to the people's engaging culture. Overall, Kenyans are among the highest networked communities in Africa (Internet World, 2020 p. 2); which allows massive (mis)use of social media by both the government and the people. During the 2013, 2017, and 2022 elections, the incumbents, and the opposition parties' use of social media and ICT in general rose to an all-time high in the country (Wamuyu, 2020). According to the Kenya National Commission on Human Rights (KNCHR, 2017) the (mis)use led to historical electoral milestones such as election results nullification in 2017. Social media was used to gather evidence of election malpractice for presentation to the Supreme Court of Kenya (KNCHR, 2017). The (mis)use motivated me to analyze how people use WhatsApp space, and the role of influencers. The chapter uses face-to-face in-depth interviews, observation, and content analysis, to analyze how people's cultural interaction with WhatsApp technology allows them to shape how and why they use the space for electoral deliberations, in a way that relegates the influencers to the peripheries of the discourses.

EMERGENCE OF INFLUENCERS, STRUCTURES, AND RELEVANCE OF SOCIAL MEDIA

This subsection examines the emergence of social media influencers in Bungoma County and Kenya at large. The emergence was because the private media failed to meet the people's informational needs (Oriare et al., 2010). The Kenyan media is aware that news reporting that is critical of the government would increase their ratings but comes at the price of government clampdown (Oriare et al., 2010). Thus, the kind of journalism that would strike a balance became difficult to attain. For instance, the media houses find it too expensive to hire competent journalists who are not easily swayed by government threats. Over time, this has led to over-reliance on interns, and untrained and less experienced journalists (MCK, 2020), with no spine to stand the threats. Furthermore, commercial pressure leads some private media houses to hire celebrity figures with little or no journalism skills, to increase ratings (MCK, 2020). These lower the journalistic standards and result in defamation cases where the media houses are forced to pay fines in damages as was the case with Royal Media Services in 2018 when the media house was found guilty of defaming a politician. Observably, the commercial and government pressure resulted in private media's inability to fully articulate public interest issues, especially candid electoral deliberations. As a result, a brand of citizen journalism emerged, where individuals with powerful online presence such as Robert Alai, Denis Itumbi, Boniface Mwangi, and Cyprian Nyakundi, amassed a massive following, larger than some media houses (Ogola, 2015). Budzinski and Gaenssle (2018) discuss this concept as social media influencers. It involves combining content creation and one's personality as a brand for sale. We can observe that the citizenry is now opting to seek information from social media influencers instead of traditional media. The influencers provide space to the massive followers for deliberate electoral issues, thereby attracting the political class seeking to reach out to voters, to sell their ideologies. This national-level influencers' ability to bring together the people, enables them to attract advertisers too. The traditional media has also adapted the social media, by owning social media handles, websites, and WhatsApp numbers, among others.

MEDIA INFRASTRUCTURE IN BUNGOMA COUNTY

The internet availability in Bungoma County is constant and strong; allowing for 2G, 3G, 4G, and 5G internet coverage, aimed at enabling people's economic activities; to open up economic potential in rural areas (Mandela, 2016). This is attributable to the 1990s fiber cable infrastructural layout across the country during media liberalization (Kenya Information Communication Act – KIC Act, 2012). By 2016, the county was leading countrywide with a 2G internet coverage penetration of 97.2%, and a 3G internet coverage penetration of 95.2%. Internet availability enables people to engage in vibrant social media electoral deliberations across the country (Wamuyu, 2020). The deliberations are historical and culturally inclined, often seeking to exclude perceived political opponents. According to Article 23 of the KIC Act (2012), the function of regulating the mass media is at the national level. Among the big communication infrastructures in Bungoma county are the Kenya News Agency – KNA and Kenya Broadcasting Corporation – KBC equipment, and offices managed and maintained by the central government (Oriare, 2010). Under the Kenya Corporation Act (2012), private individuals, and county governments, among others, may access the equipment for use with permission. Section 2(h) of the Act allows for the Corporation to offer internship positions to media students countrywide. As a result, the infrastructures are used to offer quality internship training to students from Bungoma's numerous middle-level colleges offering media-related courses.

STRUCTURE OF WHATSAPP GROUPS IN BUNGOMA COUNTY

WhatsApp groups in Bungoma County operate at many levels, including international, national, regional, county, constituency, ward, clan, and family. I was concerned with county, constituency, and ward-level groups because most electoral deliberations in the county take place at these three levels. A member could belong to all three group levels at the same time. For instance, individuals could join ward-level groups, constituency-level groups, and county-level groups. This enables them to update themselves about the ward, constituency, and county development news. I established that some members take part in the WhatsApp electoral deliberations while outside Bungoma County, say in other cities within and outside Kenya, from where they engage in gainful employment and other economic activities. However, the admission of such members into the groups is ethnically inclined. The group administrators only admit people based on their ethnicity. The ethnic majority in the county are the Bukusu dialect speakers, and the administrators are reluctant to admit those who do not speak the dialect into the groups because they are perceived as political traitors. This prompts ethnic minority people to infiltrate into the groups through misrepresentation to access electoral information perceived as critical. This implies that the WhatsApp voice is considered as among the most important sources of information during electoral deliberations.

Jamie et al. (2019) indirectly attribute WhatsApp's increased use to its potential to manipulate the public, especially through misinformation and disinformation. The two concepts are political and ideologically inclined (Curran et al., 2016; Wasserman,2017). As a result, the impact of misinformation and disinformation on WhatsApp users remains contested; with scholars arguing that the concepts are over emphasized; because all news either misinforms or disinforms depending on the ideological leanings of the media houses (Curran, 2016; Wasserman, 2017). The monopoly of ideologies and opinions about news, which was enjoyed by the traditional media houses has been disrupted by social media, prompting the thinking that traditional media does not disinform and misinform. The efficacy of fact-checking is hindered by financial constraints associated with setting up a new department or hiring more editors to check the facts (Cheruiyot & Ferrer-Conill, 2018 p. 967).

STATISTICS OF SOCIAL MEDIA USE IN KENYA

In Kenya, social media use is gaining more acceptance in electoral deliberations than in the rest of the countries in the region. Social Media Lab Africa – SIMElab, 2019, an African center for research in big data and social media analytics, documents WhatsApp as the most used social media in Kenya at 88.6%, Facebook at 88.5%, YouTube at 51.2%, Instagram at 39.0%, Twitter at 27.9%, Yahoo at 18.6%, LinkedIn at 9.3% and Snapchat at 9.0% (p. 3). As seen in the table below, there is a general increase in social media use including the adoption of new ones such as TikTok. There is a network linkage between WhatsApp and other social media as well as traditional media such as T.V. and radio. The messages 'jump' from one platform to another, eliciting different deliberations and emotions. According to interview responses, Kenyans mainly use social media for online citizenship, political debates, news acquisition, resource mobilization, entertainment, and staying in touch with others. This is because the traditional media lacks sufficient capacity to effectively enable them to actualize these uses above. For example, the structure of traditional media does not allow people to generate the content that they wish to consume (SIMELab, 2019). Urban users predominantly access social media by mobile phones and laptops, while most rural inhabitants use mobile phones and cyber cafés. By the end of 2020, there were over 46.9 million internet subscribers in Kenya, in a population of about 56 million people (CA, 2021; Internet World Stats, 2020). The majority of users are aged between 21 and 35 years, spending an average of three hours on the platform daily (Wamuyu, 2020). More than 66% of this age group participate in public debates using the platforms, often through WhatsApp groups (p. 20). People aged above 46 years least use social media, only visiting the platform for 'interesting' 'viral' news (SIMElab, 2019, p. 13). Viral news refers to the 'spreadability' of news made popular through rapid sharing among individuals via the internet, based on the perception that the news is interesting (Papacharissi, 2016 p. 28). Techno-optimists regard social media activists and other influencers as credible public figures (Budzinski & Gaenssle, 2018), and trust them for information (Wamuyu, 2020 p. 21; SIMElab, 2019, p. 11). The techno-optimists believe the public figures help to keep the government in check, by highlighting to people the vices in government. Besides contributing to the nullification of the presidential election in 2017, there are incidences where corruption cases in the central and county governments have been brought into the public limelight through social media, and public accountability demanded. For

Table 9.1. Social media usage – Adapted from SIMELab (2018) and Statista (2023).

Social Media	**2017**	2022
WhatsApp	88.6	93.5
Facebook	88.5	89.6
YouTube	51.2	71
Instagram	39	69.4
TikTok	–	60.8
Twitter	27	60
LinkedIn	9.3	57.7
Facebook Messenger	–	55.8
Telegram	–	50.5
Pinterest	–	35
SnapChat	9.0	33.1
Skype	–	23.3

example, in Bungoma County, a fraudulent tendering process popularly known as the 'non-carcinogenic wheelbarrows' was unearthed through social media. In the fraud, the cost of wheelbarrows purchased by the county government had been super-inflated, raising the price of a single wheelbarrow to over ten times higher than the market price. The country's justice system took over the case for prosecution. Such revelation of corruption scandals through social media in the county informed this study's quest to establish how and why the people use the WhatsApp space, and the role of the influencers therein. There are techno-pessimists who regard WhatsApp use as unethical because of allegations that individuals use ghost accounts to influence electoral deliberations, employ Artificial Intelligence (AI) for online presence, and command undue surveillance on perceived opposition, among others (CIPESA, 2019 p. 35).

THEORETICAL FRAMEWORK: SOCIAL CONSTRUCTION OF TECHNOLOGY (SCOT)

I particularized the notion of Social Construction of Technology (SCOT) to Bungoma County people, to explain their use of the WhatsApp space in electoral deliberations. The theorization of SCOT came up in the 1970s and 80s to provide a critique of McLuhan's Technological determinism theory (Bijker, 2015). The term 'social construction of technology can be broadly used to denote two different things: First, it is a methodology for studying technological change in society, both in historical and in contemporaneous ways. Second, it is a theory about the relations between society and technology (Bijker, 2015). The main methodological tenet of the theory holds that there must be a symmetry principle whereby sociological elements seem equally applicable to technology. Centrally, the symmetry principle argues that there should be a similar explanatory approach to scientific knowledge, regardless of whether it is held to be true or false. In other words, sociological interests and group processes would be used to explain the development and acceptance of 'true' as well as 'false' knowledge. In studying technology, this would mean that working and nonworking machines can be analyzed symmetrically and in the same terms.

The key concepts of SCOT theory include 'relevant social group,' which refers to a society/social group that shares information about a technology, 'interpretive flexibility,' which refers to the users' radical and subjective interpretation of a technology such as artifacts, 'stabilization,' meaning the level of disruption a technology brings in society, 'inclusion' meaning the involvement of the people in determining how a technology is designed. The phrase 'seamless web of society and technology' is often used to elaborate on some of the methodological issues, including the 'principle of symmetry'. The SCOT theory conceptualizes the hardness and obduracy of technology, thus offering a new interpretation of technological determinism and the politics of technology. The theory is broadened to include such issues as the politicization and democratization of technological culture, gender and technology, technology assessment, and reflections on the information society.

The Autonomous Marxists' re-reading of Marx leads to the argument that people in society shape available technology for (mis)use to solve their problems (Mithun et al., 2016). They also drew from Foucault (1978) reflection that, '[w]here there is power, there is resistance'; to argue that (mis)use of technology is a form of resistance to technological power relations, thus a reactive force (Mithun et al., 2016 p. 95). Feenberg (2013) agrees that technologies are not neutral but embody specific values used by dominant groups to perpetuate ideologies.

We can link SCOT to the technological determinism theory of the 1960s, in which McLuhan (1994), popularized the notion of the 'medium theory'. He romanticized the idea that channels are a dominant force that must be understood to know how the media influence society and culture. His infamous metaphorical statement 'the medium is the message' holds that technology is very powerful and influences society. SCOT criticizes the concept for focusing on characteristics of the medium rather than how it is designed, or how a technology is received by the people. McLuhan emphasizes that media, other than the content it transmits, powerfully influences individuals and society. SCOT theory refutes the notion, arguing that people are powerful enough to decide how their technology should be designed.

METHODOLOGY

The chapter used a qualitative approach with both traditional and digital ethnography (Hine, 2019). I joined five WhatsApp groups as a covert participant observer for three months. I obtained permission from the group members. I first explained to the group administrators the objective of the research, and they clarified to the members my intention. The members then agreed that I join the groups. The WhatsApp groups were among the most active and popular in the county. I then proceeded to fieldwork where I contacted respondents identified and selected based on their articulate and activeness on WhatsApp group participation. I conducted in-depth face-to-face interviews with the respondents I had selected. The interviews took place with two categories of respondents: The WhatsApp citizenry users and the WhatsApp group administrators from the five WhatsApp groups selected. The interviews were "semi-structured" in nature to allow for the adaption of the research instrument to the level of comprehension and articulacy of respondents (Fielding, 2012, p. 124).

The interview questions mainly sought to understand the people's detailed information on how often they engage in WhatsApp group deliberations; the challenges and opportunities offered by the deliberations; their understanding of the Kenyan electoral process; and the support systems they rely on from the administrators. I went to informal places such as the open-air informal gatherings, the waiting bays for short-distance travel motorbike and tri-cycle service providers locally called *bodaboda* and *tuk-tuk* respectively, the bus stops, with taxi drives, the marketplaces, recreational places, local universities' public lecture days, the 'jobless corners' – where people temporarily unemployed gather to pass time discussing current affairs. Observations were collected as field notes and used to in/validate interview responses. While presenting the citizenry interview responses, the researchers conceptualized them as important in the electoral deliberations, to set forth the way respondents perceived themselves – as important actors who resisted dominance. Among the challenges experienced is the respondents' fatigue because in the past, many researchers had asked them to participate as interviewees. I engaged them to build a relationship that obliged them to take part, again.

During data collection, I retrieved viral WhatsApp voice messages on electoral deliberations and observed the WhatsApp group electoral deliberations. I was born and raised in Bungoma County, which helped me to interpret behaviors among the people under study; including subtle but decisive gestures/actions informed by respondents' cultural practices expressed through emojis, GFIs, and textual symbols, among others. I was interested in respondents who were 18 years and above during the 2017 elections. This is because the legal voting age in Kenya is 18 years of age. However, in the analysis, I included the responses from participants who claimed to have been 18 years old but did not have the required documentation for voting. I considered their lack of documentation as a form of electoral dominance. I acknowledged that this category of respondents has some 2017 electoral lived experiences that are not readily observable. The issuance of electoral documentation in the perceived oppositional regions within Bungoma County was deliberately delayed, to keep the number of registered voters low. The county government social actors aligned themselves to benefit from the form of electoral dominance.

I used a thematic analysis, with the starting themes of 'electoral dominance' and 'social media influencers'. I then analytically coded in full, the extracts from the interview audio transcripts. This was done manually to retain as many of the qualitative values as possible, including interview quotes. The identities of the respondents were concealed during analysis due to security reasons, as discussed and agreed with them. Immediately I embarked on the coding process, many additional themes began to emerge from the data. I adopted a hierarchical method of coding to allow for relationships between codes to be established and worked with (see Kelle, 2000 p. 287–289). I realized the core themes of 'electoral dominance' and 'social media influencers' were soon respectively positioned under the much larger analytical umbrella themes of 'mis/use and misrepresentation on WhatsApp space', 'oversimplification of social relations', 'infra politics of the minority', 'economic deprivation' and 'in/security/affect'.

SOCIAL MEDIA INFLUENCERS AND AVOIDANCE

I established that the Bungoma County influencers have shaped WhatsApp space to enable them to avoid engaging in WhatsApp electoral deliberations for fear of the citizenry's criticism. Such criticism would negatively affect their online reputations. On the other hand, the people have shaped the WhatsApp space to enable them to deliberate controversial and emotive deliberations. I observed that the influencers avoid the controversial debates and maintain publicity in the groups, by preoccupying themselves with endorsing commercials that are less controversial and emotive. However, the national-level influencers have shaped the WhatsApp space to allow for engagement in national-level electoral deliberations, even as they risk criticism from sections of their followers who do not share similar political opinions. Some respondents said they unfollow the influencers whose political stance they do not share. I also observed that in case some influencers are perceived by incumbents as too critical of their government, they risk constant harassment, closure of their social media accounts, and arbitrary arrests, among others (KNCHR, 2017). Thus, the government has also shaped the space for harassing critics. Although the influencers have a massive following, it is not clear whether they really sway the followers to vote for the candidates of their choice. This is because I observed that people have shaped the WhatsApp space for emotive, ethnic, and irrational engagements. Voting patterns are largely along ethnic lines, with the people more interested in knowing the opinions of the influencers, to criticize them than seek guidance on who to vote. Overall, the majority and minority people engage in dominance and resistance in what I call 'infra-politics' (Scott, 1990).

Namisi (Not her real name) narrates that:

> These people [non-Bukusu/minority tribes] need to know that we do not go to their ancestral homes to influence their county politics … Therefore, *mababuu zetu hawawatambui hapa* (our ancestors do not recognize them here in Bungoma County). *Tumewasoma tangu kitambo … hawaezi pigia mtu sio wao kura …* (we have observed them for a long time, and we know they can never vote for anyone who is not of their tribe in this County).

From the narration above, Namisi confesses that her majority ethnic people deny WhatsApp space for the minority people in Bungoma County, to limit their electoral freedom for deliberation. As we shall see in the narration from Wairimu (not her real name) below, minority ethnic speakers in Kanduyi Constituency acquire multiple ghost WhatsApp accounts with names that suggest they share an ancestral origin with the majority ethnic speakers – Bukusu. This is usually to enable the minority speakers to infiltrate the WhatsApp groups, and stay unnoticed, to allow them to acquire political information about possible impending attacks, virtual or physical, discussed on the platform by the majority ethnic speakers. We can draw from Scott (1990) conception of infra-politics of the poor, to explain the minority speakers' misrepresentations. The ethnic minority people misrepresent themselves as a way of shaping the WhatsApp space to resist the majority speakers' dominance. Wairimu narrates that in Bungoma County, WhatsApp deliberations are used to plan physical attacks. Therefore, the minority speakers need to be in the majority-speaking groups to stay informed about the discussions, just in case of impending attacks. The attacks are informed by the ethnic majority people's perception that the ethnic minority people unfairly own comparatively more economic resources in Bungoma County, despite their minority status (KNCHR, 2017). In Wairimu's narration below, she explains that she attempted to stay in the WhatsApp groups during the 2017 electoral deliberations, by acquiring several SIM cards with different WhatsApp usernames that suggest her ancestral origin is Western Kenya, even though she originates from Nyandarua, in Central Kenya. Wairimu says:

> I use these WhatsApp usernames because I need to masquerade as a (majoritarian) Bukusu person without suspicion. The usernames included: *Jumbe, Soteri, Tindi, and Tolomet.* This way I will stay informed about the politics of the County. But most important, *nijue*

kama kuna msako inakuja nijipange (to keep me aware of impending politically motivated physical attacks so that I may escape in time).

Autonomous Marxist View of WhatsApp use in Bungoma County

We see that both the majority and minority ethnic people in Bungoma County have shaped the WhatsApp space for (mis)use during electoral deliberations. From Wairimu's narration above, Bungoma people use the space to undermine each other during electoral deliberations in the County. We can analyze Wairimu's narrative above by reflecting on the Autonomous Marxists' re-reading of Marx. In Marxian wording, both the majority people – Bukusu and the minority people Kikuyu in Bungoma County have shaped the WhatsApp technology for (mis)use in electoral deliberations to maintain their social and political positions Thus, the WhatsApp space enables the Bukusu people to perpetuate dominance, which the influencers are reluctant to (re)address. The minority Kikuyu people reactively shape how they (mis)use WhatsApp space, by faking usernames during electoral deliberations to resist the Bukusu people's dominance. Therefore, the WhatsApp space enables the politics of misrepresentation which robs electoral deliberations of the authenticity needed.

As previously seen in Namisi's, and Wairimu's narrations, there is a common thread of affect during WhatsApp use in electoral deliberations. The affect denies the people of the sobriety needed for deliberation. We can locate affect in Foucault's (1978) conception of surveillance and punishment, in which he discusses the use of technology for surveillance – though he does not mention the word technology. Mbembe (2017) decries that abdication of the fight for social justice including electoral deliberations, to technology is fundamentally undemocratic. Besides robbing the people of sobriety, it removes human relations in the electoral deliberations (Mbembe, 2017). The WhatsApp space enables the re-ignition of the emotive deliberations about Bungoma County's economic deprivation, which were denied platforms by the mainstream media in Kenya during the 1990s and early 2000s (KNCHR, 2017). These deliberations coupled with the people's emotive culture (see Mbembe, 2001) resulted in more physical violence than ever witnessed in the history of Bungoma County and Kenya at large. This is because the WhatsApp platform provides a 'gathering point' for the majority of people from where they dominate and exclude the minority (see Papacharissi, 2016 p. 17). From Wairimu's narration above, we see that the dominance enables the majority of people to execute their virtual will in physical terms with ease. This means the majority people easily carry out physical attacks on the minority people because of the lack of dissenting voices in the groups. Part of the evidence adduced to the International Court of Crimes against Humanity during Kenya's 2007 Post Election Violence prosecutions indicated that media, including social media, was used to mobilize and coordinate the attacks (KNCHR, 2017; Ushahidi, 2021).

There is also a correlation between physical attacks and social media/WhatsApp-mediated electoral deliberations within ethnic groupings in Kenya (Fahamu, 2021; KNCHR, 2017; Ushahidi, 2021). Currently, there is no documentation on the emotional violence caused by the virtual attacks during electoral deliberations in Bungoma County and Kenya due to the challenges associated with quantifying emotions (KNCHR, 2017). Perceptibly, although the highest recorded election-related violence in Bungoma County and Kenya was in 2007, the highest emotional violence was arguably during the 2013 and 2017 elections, when both the incumbent and opposition parties deployed the highest level of social media and ICT technologies into their electoral campaigns. This is ironic, owing to the fact that the 2013 and 2017 elections in Kenya were cited as relatively peaceful periods that allegedly provided stability (Lynch et al., 2019 p. 1). It is the emotive nature of the electoral deliberations in Bungoma County and Kenya that makes it difficult for the influencers to actively engage in shaping opinion or assuming an unpopular side on matters electoral. Boniface Mwangi, an influencer known to oppose government stances on many issues is regularly harassed by dominant social actors, arbitrarily arrested and his social media accounts closed.

OVERSIMPLIFICATION OF SOCIAL RELATIONS

I established that the majority and minority people (mis)use WhatsApp space to dominate and resist the dominance, respectively, during electoral deliberations. From Namisi and Wairimu's previous narrations, we learn that there are complex minority/majority relations that involve ancestry, economic wealth, and emotions, among others, which the WhatsApp space overlooks; thereby increasing chances of dominance and resistance. In other words, the people have shaped the technology to meet their needs. We can borrow from Mouffe's (2019) analysis of social problems, in which she questions the depiction of social problems as solvable by simplistic singular logic; to argue that the designers of WhatsApp space oversimplified Bungoma County social relations leading to people's reshaping of the technology during electoral deliberations. Laclau and Mouffe (1985) perceive people's social problems in terms of complex power and oppressive relationships, which the people seek to liberate themselves from. Wiredu (1997 p. 310) uses an Afrocentric concept of 'super consensus' democracy to discuss the complex societal problems involving power and oppressive relations. Wiredu (1997) argues that the relationship between the majority and minority in indigenous Africa was that, even when the minority felt like losers in the decision-making process of the day, they knew they would find themselves as the majority in the next decision-making process, and their preferences and desires would be favored. We can transpose this onto the WhatsApp space in Bungoma County electoral deliberations to mean that, the space enables for dominance and resistance, where the majority people/whose desires are favored dominate the minority people, who believe their turn to dominate shall come and their desires favored.

We can pursue further, WhatsApp's exceptional oversimplification of relations in Bungoma County by drawing from Wairimu's narration; that the minority people in Bungoma County are willing to stay as minorities in the majoritarian WhatsApp groups. We see that at face value, the WhatsApp space implies that the relationships in the WhatsApp groups are unjust. However, upon analysis from the Afrocentric point of view, we can see that the complexities and perceived injustice provide for the 'binding glue' between the majority and minority groups in Bungoma County during electoral deliberation (Wiredu, 1997 p. 310). For instance, the minority Kikuyu people of Bungoma County simultaneously pride themselves as a majority people in other Counties within Kenya. This enables them to make a physical minority in Bungoma County and a psychological majority in other counties within Kenya. As a result, they stay contented as a minority in Bungoma County knowing they form a majority elsewhere. For example, Wairimu's ancestral origin is in Nyandarua County in central Kenya where her ethnic people form a majority. Therefore, she simultaneously holds a minority status on the Bungoma County WhatsApp groups, and a majority status in the Nyandarua County WhatsApp groups. This makes her so comfortable with her minority status in Bungoma County that she resists rather than fight for dominance. These relational complexities that bind the minority and majority people are overly simplified and almost invisible on the WhatsApp space. The social media influencers' role in shaping the WhatsApp electoral deliberations at the county level is overshadowed by the complexities. The deliberations are instantaneous, controversial, and emotive, often initiated and driven by the people themselves.

CONCLUSION

In conclusion to the chapter, the role of the influencers in Bungoma County people's WhatsApp use during electoral deliberation is marginal. The major factors that inform the people's use of the space include ethnicity, insecurity/affect, and dominance/resistance. The factors are intertwined, running through the chapter in an interrelated manner. The factors, discussed under terminologies as Infrapolitics of the poor, and Autonomous Marxism, among others, demonstrate how the Bungoma County people subtly but decisively use the WhatsApp space. The people engage in ethnic-inclined controversial debates, in which the majority of people seek to dominate and exclude the minority from the WhatsApp space. The debates relegate the local social media influencers to peripheral positions during electoral deliberations because they are reluctant to engage in ethnic debates for fear of losing some of their fans. At the national level, the influences who engage in shaping electoral issues face the danger of harassment by the political class, social media account closure, arbitrary arrests, and criticism from followers, among others. The local level influencers engage in online advertisements of products and services, popularly known as endorsements, to enable them to stay noticeable in the groups without being attacked or losing their fanbase.

REFERENCES

Aldardasawi, A. F. (2017), McLuhanian perspective of Facebook, *Research in Social Sciences and Technology*, *2*(2), 59–75

Bijker, W. (2015). *International Encyclopedia of the social & behavioral sciences (second edition)*, Elsevieer Ltd. https://www.sciencedirect.com/topics/social-sciences/social-construction-of-technology

Budzinski, O., & Gaenssle, S. (2018). The economics of social media (super-)stars: an empirical investigation of stardom and success on YouTube. *Journal of MediaEconomics*, *31*(3–4), 75–95.

Cheruiyot, D., & Ferrer-Conill, R. (2018). "Fact-checking Africa": Epistemologies, data and the expansion of journalistic discourse. *Digital Journalism*, *6*(8), 964–975.

Communication Authority of Kenya - CA (2021). Annual-Report-for-Financial-Year-2020-2021. https://www.ca.go.ke/sites/default/files/2023-05/Annual-Report-for-Financial-Year-2020-2021.pdf

County Government of Bungoma. (2020). Integrated development plan 2018–2022. Retrieved October 12, 2023, from https://www.cog.go.ke/downloads/category/106-county-integrated-development-plans-2018-2022?download=303:bungoma-county-integrated-development-plan-2018-2027 https://bungoma.go.ke/wp-content/uploads/2022/06/BUNGOMA-COUNTY-CIDP-2018-2022.pdf

Curran, J., Fenton, N., & Freedman, D. (2016). Misunderstanding the internet. *Pedagogies, 11*(3), 270–273.

Diepeveen, S. (2021). *Searching for a New Kenya: Politics and social media on the streets of Mombasa.* University of Cambridge.

Fahamu, A. (2021). A Fahamu fellow organises a SMS peace campaign during Kenya's elections. Retrieved February 12, 2024, from http://www.fahamu.org/blog/a-fahamu-fellow-organises-a-sms-peace-campaign-during-kenyas-elections/

Feenberg, A. (2013). What I said and what I should have said: On critical theory of technology *Techné: Research in Philosophy and Technology*, *17*(1), 163–178.

Fielding, G. N. (2012). Triangulation and mixed methods designs: Data integration with new research technologies. *Journal of Mixed Methods Research*, *6*(2), 124–136.

Foucault, M. (1978). *The history of sexuality: An introduction*. Penguin.

Hine, C. (2019). Ethnographies in Online Environments. In P. Atkinson, S. Delamont, A. Cernat, J. W. Sakshaug, & R. A. Williams (Eds.), *SAGE research methods foundations*. Sage Publications.

Internet World Stats. (2020). Number of internet users in African countries. Retrieved October 17, 2023, from https://www.statista.com/statistics/505883/number-of-internet-users-in-african-countries/

Jamie, H., Jonathan, F., Idayat, H., & Cheeseman, N. (2019). *WhatsApp and Nigeria's 2019 elections: Mobilising the people, protecting the vote*. Abuja, Centre for Democracy Development.

Kelle, U. (2000). Computer-assisted analysis: coding and indexing. In M. Bauer & G. Gaskell, G. (Eds.), *Qualitative researching with text, image and sound* (pp. 283–298). Sage Publications.

Kenya Broadcasting Corporation Act, 2012. Retrieved September 10, 2023, from http://www.kenyalaw.org/kl/fileadmin/pdfdownloads/Acts/KenyaBroadcastingCorporationAct_Cap221.pdf

Kenya Information and Communications – KIC Act, 2012, https://eregulations.invest.go.ke/media/Kenya%20Information%20and%20Communications%20Act%201998.pdf.

Kenya National Commission on Human Rights – KNCHR (2017), *A Human Rights Monitoring Report on the 2017 Repeat Presidential Elections*, KNCHR publishers.

Kenya Population and Housing Census-KPHC. (2019). *Population by County and Sub-County*. Retrieved September 10, 2024, from https://tech-ish.com/wp-content/uploads/2019/11/VOLUME-1-KPHC-2019.pdf

Laclau, E., & Mouffe, C. (1985). *Hegemony and socialist strategy: Towards a radical democratic politics*, Verso.

Lynch, G., Cheeseman, N., & Willis, J. (2019). From peace campaigns to peaceocracy: elections, order and authority in Africa, *African Affairs*, *118*(473), 603–627.

Mbembe, A. (2001). *Post colony*, University of California Press.

Mbembe, A. (2017). December 5th, rethinking democracy beyond the human. Retrieved November 28, 2019, from https://www.youtube.com/watch?v=A_k3YIupGok

McLuhan, M. (1994). *Understanding media: The extensions of man*. MIT Press.

Media Council of Kenya - MCK (2020), 2020 Status of the Media report,https://mediacouncil.or.ke/sites/default/files/downloads/2020-STATUS%20OF%20THE%20MEDIA%20REPORT%20%281%29.pdf

Mithun, B., Joost, J., Pieter, L., & Guido, R. (2016). Technological mediation and power: Postphenomenology, critical theory, and autonomist Marxism. *Philosophy & Technology*, *28*(3), 449–474.

Mouffe, C. (2019). May 12th, politics, and the dynamic of affect. Retrieved November 2023, 2019, from https://www.youtube.com/watch?v=0HMi6_F6mvk

Ogola, G. (2015). Social media as a heloroglossic discursive space and Kenya's emergent alternative/citizen experiment. *African Journalism Studies*, *36*(4), 66–81

Oriare, P. Okello-Orlale, R., & Ugangu, W. (2010). *The media we want. The Kenya media vulnerability study*. Friedrich Ebert Stiftung (FES).

Papacharissi, Z. (2016). *Affective publics sentiment, technology, and politics*. Oxford University Press.

Scott, J C. (1990). *Domination and the arts of resistance: Hidden transcripts*. Yale University Press.

Social Media Lab Africa (SIMElab) (2019). *Social media consumption in Kenya report, Nairobi, USIU*. Retrieved December 2, 2019, from https://www.usiu.ac.ke/1346/simelab-launches-social-media-consumption-in-kenya-report/

Mandela, N. (2016). Bungoma County tops in 2G and 3G use, Wangusi, the standard. Retrieved May 19, 2021, from https://www.standardmedia.co.ke/ureport/article/2000224894/n-a

Statista. (2023). *Most used social media platforms in Kenya as of Q3 2021* https://www.statista.com/statistics/1229091/most-popular-social-networks-in-kenya/

The Constitution of Kenya (2010). National Council for Law Reporting with the Authority of the Attorney-General. Retrieved May 19, 2021, from http://www.kenyalaw.org/

The Election Act (2011) Qualifications and requirements for nomination of candidates for the different elective positions. Retrieved May 19, 2021, from https://www.iebc.or.ke/uploads/resources/D2CtRkduPk.pdf

Ushahidi, (2018). How the Ushahidi platform works, and what comes next, https://www.ushahidi.com/blog/2018/11/05/how-the-ushahidi-platform-works-and-what-comes-next

Wamuyu, P. K. (2020) *The Kenyan social media landscape: Trends and emerging narratives.* Nairobi, SIMElab.

Wasserman, H. (2017). Fake news from Africa: Panics, politics and paradigms, *Journalism*, *21*(1), 3–16, Sage Publications.

Wiredu, K. (1997). Democracy and consensus in African traditional politics: A plea for a non-party polity. In E. C. Eze (Ed.), *Postcolonial African philosophy. A critical reader* (pp. 303–312). Blackwell.

CHAPTER TEN

Political Satire and Performance Activism on Social Media Platforms in Zimbabwe: The Case of *Magamba T.V.* and *Bustop T.V.*

MBONGENI JONNY MSIMANGA AND
CONSTANCE KASIYAMHURU

INTRODUCTION

Zimbabwe has since the turn of the millennium continued to face socio-economic and socio-political crisis, resulting in what scholars have termed a multi-faceted/or a multi-dimensional crisis (Mhiripiri and Ureke, 2019). This multi-dimensional crisis has spanned from the Mugabe era to the "Second Republic". There are various causes of this multi-dimensional crisis, and these range from human rights abuses, social injustices, electoral fraud, international isolation, and intimidation of journalists amongst others (Zamponi, 2005). Thus, scholars have acknowledged that there has been no rupture between Mugabeism and the so-called "Second Republic" under Mnangagwa. Mugabeism, according to Ndlovu-Gatsheni (2009:1141) "articulated issues of liberation and oppression; peace and war; reconciliation and retribution; empowerment and dispossession; victimhood and heroism; social justice and injustice; social harmony and violence." This has prompted the questioning of the "newness" of the "New Dispensation". Ndlovu-Gatsheni and Ruhanya (2020:4) have argued that that the "The Mnangagwa regime is a direct child of Mugabeism." This also seems to be the view of Tagwirei (2021:19) who regards the "New Dispensation" as the patriotic present which "carries traces of the old, including the motivation to monopolize narratives about Zimbabwe and entrench Z.A.N.U-P.F. dominance". It is within this context that we approach this study considering how both regimes under erstwhile leader Robert Mugabe and Emmerson Mnangagwa have not only perpetuated the Zimbabwean multi-dimensional crisis but has contributed to social injustices and human rights abuses.

Given this background, the chapter considers how, amidst this crisis, social media platforms, mainly YouTube, have been appropriated by satirists to reflect on Zimbabwe's multi-dimensional crisis and comment on the human rights and social injustices perpetrated by erstwhile leaders. The two case studies that this chapter draws from, that is *Magamba T.V.* and *Bustop T.V.* are a metonymy of virtual spaces that speak truth to power. These case studies are used in this study as we consider them to have a subversive function as well as act as a "social barometer/moral watchdog". The chapter broadly seeks to achieve the following two objectives: to understand the dominant social justice and human rights issues that Zimbabwe social media users under study tackle on YouTube and to explore the various performative aspects adopted by both *Magamba T.V.* and *Bustop T.V.* to challenge the incumbent Zanu-PF government.

SOCIAL MEDIA ACTIVISM, DISSIDENCE, AND POLITICAL SATIRE IN ZIMBABWE

Social media platforms in Zimbabwe function as sites for political activism (Mutsvairo and Ronning, 2020). The reasons are varied and mainly point to the compressed media landscape in Zimbabwe that is tightly controlled by the Zanu-PF government and the intimidation of journalists. Thus, social media activism has been used as an arena of not only commenting on the socio-political and socio-economic issues in Zimbabwe, but an attempt to bring change to Zimbabwe's multi-dimensional crisis. There are multiple case studies that one could point to in Zimbabwe such as *#ShutdownZimbabwe*, *Pachedu*, *Baba Jukwa*, *Zimbabwe Yadzoka*, *Her Zimbabwe*, *Magamba T.V.* and *Bustop T.V.*, *#ThisFlag*, *#Tajumuka Sesijikile*, *#ThisGown*, and *@ProfJMMoyo* amongst others that have emerged over the years. These platforms have played a pivotal role in attempting to democratize communication, expose Zanu-PF misdeeds, appeal for gender mainstreaming and the active participation of women in mainstream politics. Related to this, Gukurume (2017) for example, in his exploration of *#ThisFlag* and *#ThisGown* shows how social media activism has been used to mobilize people both on and offline. He further explores how social media platforms act as counter-power platforms that "created a virtual community of dissent that actively fostered counter-hegemonic discourses, hence affording the hitherto suppressed voices an audible voice against the authoritarian Mugabe government" (Gukurume, 2017:49). However, Matsilele (2019) regards these hashtags and social media accounts as promoting what he terms "social media dissidence" in Zimbabwe's tightly controlled media spaces. Matsilele (2019) defines social media dissidence as platforms that allow ordinary citizens to question, critique, challenge, resist and speak truth to those with "ultimate" power. It is within this paradigm that we think political satire on social media platforms such as *Magamba T.V.* and *Bustop T.V.* as they exhibit elements of social media activism and dissidence.

However, although political satire exhibits elements of both social media activism and dissidence, we are also interested in the performative aspects that define its "communication ethics" on social media. That is, parody, irony, paradox, antithesis, colloquialisms, topicality, pastiche, obscenity, vividness, and exaggeration (Highet, 1962) that are frequently utilized to convey and achieve satiric intent. These aesthetic instruments of satire bring out intended – and at times unintended – meaning and are prevalent under both *Magamba T.V.* and *Bustop T.V.* As highlighted by Highet (1962: 5), satire is "topical; it claims to be realistic (although it is usually exaggerated or distorted); it is shocking; it is informal; (and although often in a grotesque and painful manner) it is funny". Related to this definition, there is consensus in the scholarship on satire that one of its main functions is to speak back, or speak truth, to power (Gray et al., 2009; Neale and Krutnick, 2006).

However, from a Zimbabwean perspective, Willems (2011) characterizes aesthetic satire as everyday forms of resistance during the Robert Mugabe era, implying that cartoons published by, for instance, the *Daily News*, played a critical subversive reporting role. Privately owned media such as *The Standard*, *The Zimbabwe Independent* and their online versions provided conventional platforms for cartoonists and satirists to deride Robert Mugabe and Zanu-PF during the Zimbabwe crisis era (Kuhlman, 2012). Related to this aspect, Nyamanhindi (2009) assesses how polarization in Zimbabwean media has a bearing on satiric content in newspapers. Thus, cartoons from private press mostly criticized Murambatsvina, policy contradiction, flawed elections and international isolation by the Zanu-PF led government (Nyamanhindi, 2009) while state owned media portrayed Operation Murambatsvina in positive light and praised the policy. However, recent scholarship on satire shows how it mediates politics in the "New Dispensation", responds to the incumbent Presidents speeches and oratory skills, is used to understand complex economic policies, and how it is used to oppose narratives of the establishment on the cyberspace (Msimanga et al., 2021; Tshuma et al., 2021; Matsilele and Mututwa, 2021). Research has also examined how, humor, particularly memes is used as a means of silent resistance in Zimbabwe (Kasiyamhuru, 2020; Siziba and Ncube, 2015), as a coping mechanism during the Covid-19 pandemic and as an advertising tool (Msimanga et al., 2022). While all these studies are meant to assess the subversive or critical nature of satire, this paper aims to look at the performative aspects of both *Magamba* and *Bustop T.V.* and the themes emerging from this.

THE CASE OF *MAGAMBA T.V.* AND *BUSTOP T.V.*

Magamba T.V. is a YouTube platform or metonymy of virtual spaces that uses political satire skits to speak truth to power in Zimbabwe (Msimanga et al., 2021; Zirugo, 2021). *Magamba T.V.* produces skits that are shared on social media platforms Facebook, YouTube, and Instagram. Ureke (2021:219) classifies *Magamba T.V.* as a form of artivism. Artivism, he states, is "activism through art" including videos that reveal the factors influencing their content and how these factors reflect their broad radical agenda of "speaking truth to power." The name *Magamba* is a Shona word that means "liberation war heroes" and the television station uses youth activism to open democratic space in Zimbabwe (Msimanga, 2022). *Magamba T.V.* was originally founded by Samm Farai Monroe known as Cde. Fatso and Tongai Makawa known as "Outspoken" in 2007 at the height of the Zimbabwean Crisis when the country was going through hyperinflation, political violence, and the fast-track land reform program. One of the key actors for *Magamba T.V.* is Cde. Fatso who presents the show The Week. The use of the moniker "Comrade" by Cde. Fatso is used to denote a common struggle against a common enemy, and it is historical, dating back to the liberation struggle.

Bustop T.V., formerly *P.O. Box T.V.*, is a popular Zimbabwean social media channel that produces news, skits and documentaries that speak to socio-economic and socio-political issues affecting citizens (Nyaungwa, 2021). *P.O. Box T.V.* was begun by Lucky Aaroni, Rolland Lunga and Admire Kuzhangaira in 2014 but split in 2015 over contractual and financial disagreements linked to corporate sponsorship (Zimoyo, 2016). Aaroni then partnered with Mufakose Film Society and Totally Second Animation Studio, rebranding to *Bustop T.V.* (Ureke, 2021). *Bustop T.V.* draws its name from the concept of a bus stop where people meet on their way to different destinations. The bus stop is framed not only as a strategic meeting place for citizens but as a democratic site and space for the discussion of pertinent socio political and socio-economic issues that are affecting communities and the country (Msimanga, 2022). In this chapter, we interpret the bustop as an iteration of the Habermasian coffee shop. The skits on *Bustop T.V.* are dominated by three actors: Maggie (Sharon Chideu), Gonyeti (Samantha Kureya) and Dereck Nzwiyakwi (DRC) although they occasionally invite guest actors. Both *Magamba T.V.* and *Bustop T.V.* use the suffix "T.V.", which could be an indication of yearning for the opening of the public space to more creatives or alternative broadcasters that are not affiliated to the Z.A.N.U-P.F. government (Ureke, 2021).

THEORETICAL FRAMEWORK: SATIRE AS OR DISSENT/ DISSIDENCE

The chapter makes use of Amber Day's (2011) seminal study of satire and dissent that considers the contemporary turn within the satiric register of genres such as parodic news shows (for instance, *The Daily Show*, *The Colbert Report* in the United States and *This Hour Has 22 Minutes* and *The Rick Mercer Report* in Canada), satiric documentary (for instance, the films of Michael Moore and Morgan Spurlock) and ironic activism (for instance, Billionaires for Bush, the Yes Men, and Reverend Billy). These genres as explained by Amber Day, incorporate "deconstructions of real news events, improvisational pranks (which) share a uniquely performative form of parody and satire that injects the satirist's body into the traditional political world" (Day, 2011:2). Day examines the contemporary relationship between satire and dissent that is threaded through readings of spectacle, irony, authenticity ("ironic authenticity"), truth ("truthiness"), and activism, among other themes. For Day (2011), parodic news shows, ironic activism, and satiric documentary facilitate a form of viable circumvention of inauthentic (even stage-managed, scripted and choreographed) political discourse and, in so doing, provides audiences with a sense of community. Day (2011) however views digital technologies as the heart of contemporary digital dissidence. Thus, Day regards the space of contemporary satiric register as, if not counterhegemonic, certainly operating on the margins of organized politics. These margins are sources of a more productive, dialogic, and authentic political praxis compared to the sterile, scripted fare of mainstream discourse.

However, *Bustop T.V.* and *Magamba T.V.* appear to fit fairly and squarely what Day calls "oppositional counter publics,". The Zimbabwean digital platforms also incorporate several "satiric devices" that Day has compellingly identified as central in the satiric register. For example, she talks of the aspect of "identity nabbing" a practice where "participants pretend to be people they are not, appear in public as exaggerated caricatures of their opponents, or ambiguously co-opt some of their power" (Day, 2011: 146). A further "satiric device" within the register identified by Day (2011) is what she terms "culture jamming". Culture jamming is "a catchall term for … ironic activism" (Day, 2011: 149), which involves "creative, easily replicable, mediagenic style designed to capture attention". Finally, Day (2011) emphasizes the sheer importance of irony – the "language of dissent" – not only within the satiric register but in the all-important aspect of digitality as well.

She argues that "There is something synergistic about the relationship between new technologies and the emergent forms of irony, satire, and parody. The way in which contemporary irony has developed is intimately tied to the creation of digital technologies (Day, 2011: 24)".

METHODOLOGICAL CONSIDERATIONS

This chapter adopts a multiple case study approach precisely in the sense that it "includes more than one single case" (Baxter and Jack, 2008: 550), that is *Magamba T.V.* and *Bustop T.V.* Our research questions in this study called for this approach that included actual viewing of the skits produced by *Magamba T.V.* and *Bustop T.V.* YouTube channels. It was not possible to do a study of this nature without repeatedly and closely watching the content to familiarize with the satiric register barb. The data for analysis was purposively sampled from both *Magamba T.V.* and *Bustop T.V.'s* YouTube channels. We selected YouTube because the material was systematically organized, convenient to sample, and up to date. The skits sampled for analysis from both *Magamba T.V.*, and *Bustop T.V.* were organized under the heading "playlists" on their YouTube channels and dated back to the time when the social media platforms started posting skits in 2015. In total, there were 240 videos uploaded on both *Magamba T.V.* and *Bustop T.V.* channels. However, a total of 150 were interviews with political actors, civil society leaders and student leaders, which were not relevant to this chapter. We purposively sampled skits that made use of performative strategies such as identity nabbing, satiric barb, culture jamming, parody and irony and narrowed down to eight skits from both *Magamba T.V.* and *Bustop T.V.* The skits were drawn from both Mugabe and Mnangagwa era. We made use of a multi-modal approach in analyzing the skits as it makes use "of multiple semiotic resources; ... language, visual images, space and architecture" (Çoşkun, 2015:41). The following themes formed a basis for analysis: Questioning Z.A.N.U-P.F.'s legitimacy of the "Second Republic", electoral violence and propaganda in Zimbabwe and satire, gender equality and sexual harassment.

QUESTIONING Z.A.N.U-P.F.'S LEGITIMACY DURING THE "SECOND REPUBLIC"

The question of the legitimacy of Zanu-PF's governance record has been a source of historical contention which was the original source of the Gukurahundi genocide itself. The genocide began because Zanu-PF felt its legitimacy to be under existential challenge. Because the spirit of democratic contestation is weak, this unleashes violence (Mawowa, 2017). The satire platforms continue the dangerous work of questioning Zanu-PF's legitimacy, walking the delicate path between just enough critical commentary and what Zanu-PF might perceive as dangerous. However, the satirists use self-censorship to walk that delicate line. Often, they get it right, until one day they are visited by the "C10"[1], as happened to Samantha Kureya when she was abducted in August 2019[2].

We saw the work of questioning Zanu-PF's legitimacy, for instance, in *Magamba T.V.*'s skit titled "Coupbinet"[3]. The skit had two parts. The first part showed a deposed cabinet minister from the pro-Mnangagwa Lacoste faction (one of the two main Zanu-PF intra-party factions, along with the pro-Mugabe G40 faction), finally walking into Munhumutapa offices after the Operation Restore Legacy in 2017. The Munhumutapa offices, located in Zimbabwe's capital city, Harare, houses Zanu-PF government cabinet Ministers and are symbolic of the Zanu-PF state's power base.

The first part of the skit begins with a cabinet minister walking into Munhumutapa offices. As he enters his ministerial office, he confidently kicks the main door and walks in, with a victorious bounce in his step. The politician shouts at the secretary and CIO agents present, saying:

> Yes, I am back now. This is my Ministerial post, now we can work. You better be prepared to start working now because I am back. Catch my bag and put it where it belongs. This time, there is nothing that you can do to me. This is now my Ministry again!

It becomes apparent that that the minister is a former member of the Lacoste faction that had been involved in a fierce tussle with the G-40 faction to succeed Robert Mugabe and eventually have control of the Z.A.N.U-P.F. government[4]. His body language and deliberate swagger as he moves into the Munhumutapa building signifies how much control the Lacoste faction has newly gained following so-called "Operation Restore Legacy". The kicking of the door at the beginning of the skit and the throwing of the bag to the secretary in the office and

1 C10 is the street lingo used to refer to the Central Intelligence Organisation (CIO) in Zimbabwe
2 https://mg.co.za/article/2019-12-04-00-you-are-too-young-to-mock-the-government-zimbabwean-comedian-relives-her-abduction/
3 https://www.youtube.com/watch?v=UnRqyJA9V7g
4 The battle to succeed Mugabe saw two rival factions, the G-40 and Lacoste in Zimbabwe fighting for power. Jonathan Moyo was regarded as the brains behind the G40 (Generation 40), whose name denoted the group's philosophy that Zimbabwe should be led by a younger generation of politicians (who will replace the old guard in Z.A.N.U-P.F.). The 'Lacoste' faction is so-called because its leader, Emmerson Mnangagwa is nicknamed Ngwena(crocodile in the Shona language), the emblem used by the French cosmetic company Lacoste. Lacoste triumphed as Mnangagwa replaced Mugabe in the November 2017 coup. Most leaders of the G40 fled into exile while some were arrested and face different restrictions within Zimbabwe.

the CIO agents in the Munhumutapa building signifies the arrogance of power, of saying "we are not going away – this power thing is ours forever". The "New Dispensation", and therefore the Lacoste faction, shaped in Mnangagwa's image, has taken over. Power, in the hands of the Lacoste faction, still means what it meant to the Mugabeists. This imagery, symbolism, and tussle is important in the context of the contentiousness of political succession and politics of succession in Zanu-PF.

The cabinet minister in the skit announces that "Ndechangu ChiMinistry ichi" (This is my Ministry), a statement that signified how politicians in Zanu-PF have "personalized" the state to belong to them, as indicated in the phrase "Chinhu chedu" (Our thing), drawn from the putschist code phrase "chinhu ichi chine vene vacho" (this thing has owners), first made by former Mugabe spokesperson, George Charamba, in January 2017 when he said "Chinhu ichi chine vene vacho" (this thing – power, or the presidency – has its undisputed owners) as a way of indicating that the army and Mnangagwa were the undisputed successors of Mugabe. *Chinhu chavo* echoes harmful "commandism, authoritarianism, violence, impunity, and personality cults" (Ndlovu-Gatsheni, 2009: 53). More importantly, the phrase "*Chinhu chedu*" has been used by Zanu-PF politicians and supporters to refer to power in Zimbabwe and to Zimbabwe itself. Zimbabwe, in the framing, is Zanu-PF property. It is this entitlement to power that the satirical irony of *Magamba T.V.* and *Bustop T.V.* attacks. This form of irony ridicules the Z.A.N.U-P.F. government and the Lacoste faction manifesting as a form of "challenging".

The second part of the skit is "Coupbinet" presented by Cde Fatso who narrates the *illegitimacy* of the Operation Restore Legacy that ushered in the "New Dispensation" in 2017. It further highlights how Mnangagwa's government attempts to create legitimacy by moving political chess pieces, buying and coercing loyalty, and shuffling perceived opponents around, and rewarding loyal cadres. Even some cabinet ministers and military personnel who were previously loyal to Robert Mugabe, but had now changed sides, were appointed as part of the "new", signaling a continuation of Mugabeism given how these military men and cabinet Ministers had persistently failed in the old dispensation.

Cde. Fatso connects the dots, showing how most of the cabinet ministers in the "New Dispensation" government are former members of the army or pro-military coup and thus how there is a new *military dynamic* in Zimbabwe's body politic – but without a change of the politics. This is highlighted when he uses a sarcastic tone throughout the skit and states:

> Zimbabwe had a record where we had a coup that was not a coup, and a cabinet that was not a cabinet. The whole country has been waiting impatiently for the new cabinet. Yes, it's a new lean cabinet – Air Marshal Perence Shiri got the lands Ministry. Does it make

> sense for a guy with air and bird in his name to get land? Meanwhile General Sibusiso Moyo aka General Bae of the ZBC takeover fame got the Foreign Affairs Ministry. We thought he would get the Broadcasting Services. There is a lot of new blood in the cabinet, well, military blood of course. Meanwhile, the biggest winner was Patrick Chinamasa who went from being the Minister of WhatsApp and data bundles to being the Minister of Bond notes and Ecocash.

The mere reference to the "coup" shows courage because officially this was not allowed in Zimbabwe. This is seen in the title of the skit, a portmanteau of the words "coup" and "cabinet". Instead, it was called a "special military operation" or a "military assisted transition". The skit satirizes this Orwellian news-speak.

Cde Fatso argues how there is no change in the government, and instead a replacement of the same Ministers who will not bring change to the economic or political hopes and aspirations of Zimbabweans. Instead, corruption and mismanagement will continue. That is, the skit in highlighting continuities rather than discontinuities between the "New Dispensation" and the *ancient regime*, deprives the "new" of much sought after political legitimacy that it needed to bring around most Zimbabweans to believe in the new project of a new Zimbabweanness. As pointed out by Ndlovu-Gatsheni and Ruhanya (2020: 4), "The Mnangagwa regime is a direct child of Mugabeism; indeed, Mugabeism is its recurrent theme". Just like the military under the tutelage of Robert Mugabe, Mnangagwa's government assumes the same. Tagwirei (2021: 19) coins this as the "patriotic present", arguing that the patriotic present "carries traces of the old, including the motivation to monopolize narratives about Zimbabwe and entrench ZANU PF dominance" (Tagwirei, 2021:19).

The legitimacy of the purported sovereigns in Zimbabwe is further questioned in *Bustop T.V.*'s *Kududunura Scarf* ("Undoing/unravelling/taking apart the Scarf")[5]. After the coup, Mnangagwa began to wear a scarf with Zimbabwean flag colors around his neck. He would not go out in public without it. Inevitably, the skit raises notions of what it means to be a Zimbabwean, especially during the era of the "New Dispensation". We view the skit raising questions such as "Was it external shows of 'belonging' and identity or was it the outcomes of one's actions?" This question follows election promises by Zanu-PF about delivering "a Zimbabwe everyone wants", provision of "affordable accessible quality healthcare", zero tolerance for corruption, "*kujekesa nyika yese nemagetsi*" (adequate electricity in the whole country) modernizing the economy, and ensuring "real, jobs, jobs, jobs"[6] by solving the high unemployment figures[7]. When none of this transpired, all

5 https://www.youtube.com/watch?v=ysTrZkt2w_g

6 The pointers made here are some of the promises made the "New Dispensation" government during the elections. These were promises made during election campaigns.

7 In 2018, Z.A.N.U P.F. used banners with these tags and promised to offer "Visionary and Mature" leadership.

that was left was the patriotic flag around the president's neck. It is this scarf (the fake Zimbabweanness) the skit was seeking to undo and unravel. The notion of *kududunura* ("Undoing/unravelling/taking apart the Scarf") is fully performative, since one can only take apart something *transitively*, by doing. This deeply performative skit is one of the clearest (and most brazen) statements about the dissidence of the contemporary satirical platforms and of what they see as their purpose: undoing the "patriotic present" and replacing it with a "patriotic future" without Z.A.N.U-P.F. at its center. This calls for a complete overturning of the social and political order.

Maggie and Gonyeti, in conversation about "undoing the scarf", reflect on the complexities of this task. Maggie, showing concern, questions why Gonyeti is "undoing" the scarf. Gonyeti replies thus:

> Was this scarf so much of a cost to you or it was me who paid for it? The scarf is mine and I do anything that I want with it. I had expectations when I got this scarf, only to discover that it is useless! There is nothing it has done for me, not even to protect me in any way. I have travelled internationally, thinking it will protect me, even from the cold. But there is nothing it is doing for me. Instead, I am coming back with a flue! It is useless. For 38 years I thought this scarf will keep me warm. But it has not. It is a useless scarf. It's best I undo the scarf.

By "undoing" the scarf, Gonyeti openly questions the legitimacy of the "New Dispensation" government, and the governments performance and track record of upholding promises made. This government cannot be trusted to deliver, and it is a waste of time to vest one's hopes and aspirations in it. Gonyeti subtly ridicules Emmerson Mnangagwa's foreign trips that have not improved the livelihoods of Zimbabweans or the country's economy when she states, "I have travelled internationally thinking it will protect me from the cold". The "cold", in this case, signifies poverty and economic turmoil that Zimbabweans have had to endure for years. That the scarf has not "kept her warm for 38 years" is a rather unsubtle way of pointing out Zanu-PF's failure since independence.

A larger point of the "Undoing the Scarf" skit, however, is essentially that *Z.A.N.U-P.F. must go*. There is no way Zanu-PF can remain after the scarf is undone. This, in a way, is calling for what Zanu-PF itself would regard as "regime change". Thus, it raises the question that "Is Zanu-PF. therefore correct to allege that civil society and the "pro-democracy" forces are after regime change?" This is not a question that seems to bother the activists, since they argue that Zanu-PF is illegitimate and must be legally removed from power. Zanu-PF however counters that its opponents seek to remove it illegally. The question that remains is still: *how will the scarf be undone?* The setting of the scarf skit is telling: poverty, dilapidation, bare life and survival on selling old items such as old tire. The question becomes how long, or if, Zimbabwe can survive its illegitimate sovereigns.

The undoing of the scarf becomes urgent. It seems that the primary aim of satire in this instance after all is not only to ridicule but also to go all the way: *to destroy the established order.* Skits such as "Undoing the Scarf" is not merely subversive – rather, it offers a new outlook of the world (Day, 2011). What this completely new order of things would look like in Zimbabwe is not patently clear. However, the framing is already being put in place by the sorts of questions being asked by *Bustop T.V.* and *Magamba T.V.*

ELECTORAL VIOLENCE AND PROPAGANDA

The skits dealing with electoral violence and propaganda are titled "How to rig an election"[8] and "The Big Announcement"[9]. What is interesting here is the cross-cutting production that shows the themes have remained salient, bestraddling the Mugabe and Mnangagwa eras. Both skits show a counter-narrative on elections and legitimacy of the Zanu-PF government that is in contradistinction to what is presented on Zimbabwe's state media. The skit "How to rig an election" targets the 2018 Zimbabwe elections that saw Mugabe's long-time henchman, Emmerson Mnangagwa, contest presidential elections for the first time after the 2017 military coup. In the episode, one of the actor's identity nabs a political editor at state controlled ZBC who is at a "diary session", brainstorming story ideas with newscasters and reporters. The diary session is centered on adverts, stories, and tactics that the state broadcaster seeks to use to set the electoral agenda in favor of Zanu-PF.

One of the conspiratorial "newscasters" in the skit rehearses what could be a "suitable" advert to use during election time, parodying adverts from the Zimbabwe Electoral Commission (ZEC). This "rehearsal" represents a mode of presentation that we would call a skit in a skit, whereby the mode of address of the skit is utilized self-referentially within a skit. This allows for the skit to not take itself too seriously while self-announcing itself as a skit. The self-announcement in skits is important in notifying the authorities that "this is just satire", thus pre-empting any attempts at censorship. It is akin to a form of aestheticized voluntary self-censorship. In the "rehearsal", the newscaster says:

> The joint election rigging group (J E R G) wishes to advice the nation that the voting season is now open. Those who are deceased and still registered are advised to go and vote within their area of registration. All political parties are advised to desist from violence. However, if you are to beat up someone, make sure it is away from the media or from

8 https://www.youtube.com/watch?v=hF0BqF gR08
9 https://www.youtube.com/watch?v=flWBOuu2MxY&t=303s

> smart phones which can film and record. To all Zimbabweans, go and vote – dead or alive. We might count your vote, we might not. But your vote still matters to us.

The skit parodies the ZEC adverts often carried by ZBC "encouraging" the electorate to vote in a process that critics see as a shameless attempt to legitimize sham elections. ZEC is not seen, in oppositional circles, but also by many ordinary Zimbabweans, as an impartial player. It is viewed, rather, as a Zanu-PF enabler organization.

The skit "How to rig an election" further casts light on how the voters roll is alleged to have been manipulated such that non-existent voters could vote for Zanu-PF., how Zanu-PF deliberately delayed election results to facilitate rigging, and how Zanu-PF systematically perpetrated and glorified violence. The episode also raises the issue of polarization of the media, with state media being pro-Zanu-PF and anti-MDC and private media being anti-Zanu-PF and pro-MDC. Finally, the episode highlights the importance of the media and, lately, citizen journalism, in holding power to account and exposing impunity.

JERC, the organization referred to in the skit is in fact ZEC. JERC is also meant to rhyme with "jerk", showing the strategy of *ukuthethisa/ kutukirira* (insulting) (cf. Matsilele, 2019) employed in some of the skits. *Magamba T.V.* uses satire to provoke awareness and trigger discussion of potential vote rigging by Zanu-PF and collusion by state institutions such as the ZEC. The perception amplified by *Magamba T.V.* is that ZEC colludes with Zanu-PF that state institutions are not to be trusted, and that the establishment is full of hypocrites and, even, corrupt liars. During the Mugabe era, for example, accusations of vote rigging, and manipulation of the voters roll by Zanu-PF were rife. The idea that there is a vast conspiracy denying Zimbabweans their electoral and democratic rights is promoted and amplified. Interestingly, state media and functionaries allege a conspiracy against Zanu-PF by private media and civic organizations.

In the skit, Cde. Fatso, dressed in a suit, parodies sham election promises by mimicking Zanu-PF politicians. Cde. Fatso presents a campaign manifesto for the position of a Member of Parliament (M.P.) for Uzumba-Maramba-Pfungwe (U.M.P.) district, a die-hard Zanu-PF stronghold, which often tips the scale in general elections when its huge numbers help the ruling party to win disputed elections. In the background is an inscription in the top right corner with the words, "Be the *Futseke* you want". As already noted, "*pfutseke*" is an insulting term, like "fuck off". Cde. Fatso outlines his election manifesto to the electorate thus:

> Hello Cde.'s and friends. My name is Cde. Fatso, and I would very much like to represent the province of Uzumba-Maramba-Pfungwe in Parliament. Uzumba-Maramba-Pfungwe is not really my home you know, but *ine ka that thing* (it has this special thing). I did not go to primary school or university or anything in the district, but I have heard about it on the news. It is very much well known for violence around election time and not much

development too. My plan for Uzumba-Maramba-Pfungwe is to bring development for the constituency.

Uzumba-Maramba-Pfungwe, a district in Mashonaland East Province, is one of the poorest districts in Zimbabwe, prone to dry spells, flooding, and hunger, yet also highly politicized in the national imagination. The district is also infamous as an opposition no-go-area, with recorded incidents of state sponsored abductions and intimidation by chiefs, intelligence, and state security agents. By using U.M.P. as a background, Cde. Fatso is symbolically wading into a no-go-area, which broadly signifies how the satirists routinely touch taboo topics. In this skit, there is not much subtext, however. Instead, all the meanings are on the surface: corruption, election lies, violence, underdevelopment, poverty, and so on. None of these issues require special subtext to convey. Rather, they are known by most Zimbabweans, and it takes little effort for an audience to get the message conveyed. When meanings are on the surface like this, the satire becomes not so much lost as plain. Plain or surface-level satire (that is, without subtext) means that the satirists do not struggle to make a satirical point. The satire is produced with minimum set up and little theatrical improvisation. The audience is already primed to appreciate the surface text at face value. Thus, any mention of Uzumba- Maramba-Pfungwe already signals, in counterhegemonic terms, Zanu-PF backwardness. The downside of such surface satire is that it comes across almost like news reading. normative talking points – amplifying issues of human rights during elections, raising awareness, and promoting civic action, and so on – are tacked onto the satirical piece in a mechanical way. Satire becomes just an instrument for delivering standard "N.G.O" talking points, making the skits feel promotional and one-sided.

SATIRE, GENDER EQUALITY AND SEXUAL HARASSMENT

Satirical dialogue mostly by *Bustop T.V.* is used to highlight gender inequalities and the place of women in Zimbabwean society. *Bustop T.V.* satire to empower women politically, question public policies and structures that infringe women in Zimbabwean society. They highlight issues of sexuality that are often taboo to be talked about in Zimbabwe considering that it is male dominated. Skits by *Bustop T.V.* have generated public interactions that advocate for the fight for equal treatment of women in the workplace and social institutions particularly the family structure that is hub of patriarchy. Academics advocating for the equality of women in Zimbabwean society have highlighted how women shape political and social issues that situate them to belong in Zimbabwe.

One of the skits titled *Her and Him*[10] by *Bustop T.V.* explores the dimensions and realities of equality in Zimbabwean society. The skit shows Gonyeti and Maggie discussing the topic of equality between men and women in Zimbabwean society. As the discussion progresses, Gonyeti and Maggie talk about how some women are subservient to man, while other women view man as their equals. Gonyeti, however insists that man have more power in society than women. For Gonyeti, politics and workspaces should be dominated by male figures. Gonyeti's view is informed by the Zimbabwean patriarchal family structure that socializes women to be subservient to man-reinforcing patriarchy. Maggie, on the other hand denies that men are more powerful than women and insists that both are equal. For her, women deserve the same treatment that man are given in the Zimbabwean society set up. They deserve better work positions and should actively participate in politics and make decisions, particularly what affects the girl child.

The conversation between Gonyeti and Maggie reflects the different representations of women in Zimbabwean society. Gonyeti, portrays women who are meant to subservient and should always respect male figures as the head of the house. Such women can contextually be read as those who stay at home taking care of the family while waiting for the man to provide for the family. *Bustop T.V.* use satire to show how primary socialization institutions such as the family structure in Zimbabwe play a role in socializing women to be secondary class citizens. Gonyeti shows this by stating in the conversation that her grandmother and aunt advised her to be subservient to a man when since he would have paid for the bride price. This is so that her marriage is successful. I view her aunts, in this case as extensions of patriarchy who socialize other women to remain in the comfort zone of being oppressed by man. This is complemented by using religion that socializes women to view themselves as inferior to man. As mentioned above, women in Zimbabwe then find the patriarchal space as a haven and a place to belong.

A different view can be ascribed to Maggie, who in the skit advocates for the equality of women in political and workspaces. Using satire and irony, she disrupts patriarchal institutions and beliefs that are firmly embedded in Zimbabwe's social fabric. She challenges views that are widely held by women and society that views them as subservient. For her, women are incapable of doing the same work that man can do and can equally be the same in political spaces. She views both and man as equal and advocates the same to be applied within the family structure that is viewed as the "hub" of patriarchy. Maggie challenges traditional structures and other extensions of patriarchy that oppress women and treat them as second-class citizens. In relation to the above conversation, Maggie represents women in Zimbabwean society who challenge extensions of patriarchy

10 https://www.youtube.com/watch?v=0iEekx3DpY0

that oppress women. Her radical nature towards the treatment of women in society shows how satire is a space for challenging misconceptions about women who are equally capable like man.

Closely related to the above conversation are two skits titled *Mukadzi Chaiye* (A true Woman indeed) and *Kuvaka Nyika 50/50* (Building the country 50/50). In both skits, Gonyeti and Maggie discuss the need to teach young children, particularly young males the importance and significance of gender equality. Again, the Zimbabwean family system is critiqued as a hub that is responsible for extending patriarchy. In both skits, Gonyeti believes that women should be subservient to man in marriage and in a family set up. For her, teaching the young males about the need for gender equality only destroys the cultural values and systems that have been passed on from older generations. Gonyeti believes that respecting a man should be emulated so that marriages are successful. Maggie using irony fights the patriarchal system and how it socializes men to infringe women in society. She blames the system in Zimbabwe that does not enable the young to recognize that both young boys and girls are equal. For Maggie, recognizing that both young girls are equal is the beginning of gender equality in society.

Bustop T.V. also tackles how women are sexually harassed and treated as sex objects at the workplace. This is highlighted in a skit titled *Tembo muHardy* that pokes fun and parodies Zimbabwe's former Vice President, Kembo Mohadi. The skit is supported by the United Nations and has a caption at the end titled *Zero Tolerance for Sexual exploitation and Abuse*. Tembo Mohadi was forced to resign from his political office after a string of stories and recorded voice notes were published by *Zimlive*. The conversations revealed the former vice president having improper sexual liaisons with married women, including his subordinates (Ndebele, 2021). In the skit, one of the *Bustop T.V.* satirists, DRC playing the role of Tembo Mohadi makes several phone calls to his subordinates asking for sexual favors in exchange for tenders, promotion and money. The phone calls he makes are similar to the audios leaked to the public.[11] In the skit, DRC, clad in scarf similar to the one worn by the president that represents the "New Dispensation" he states:

> Can I fuck you today? Does your brother still want that tender? So, can I fuck you today? I mean right now. *Ngiyakurata* (I love you) you know that right? Come on please I need to fuck you today. I am in a fucking mood right now. From January to December, I am always in a fucking mood. So, you don't have a car? Such a beautiful lady? You can come to my office even with a bicycle or anything. Even if you get pregnant, I will fuck that pregnancy. So, you can't come, and we fuck today? Come on! (Bangs the phone).

11 https://www.zimlive.com/2021/02/19/mohadis-phone-was-cloned-aide-claims-after-call-leaks-reveal-sex-scandal/

The skit highlights the abuse and treatment of women not only by a senior government officer, in this case the Vice President. *Bustop T.V.* speak to how public officials offer favors in exchange for sex with women in lower positions.

CONCLUSION

The chapter has assessed how political satire deployed by *Magamba T.V.* and *Bustop T.V.* can be characterized as a form of performative activism. Although there are various themes that the two YouTube channels focus on, this chapter has focused mainly on three themes: questioning Z.A.N.U-P.F.'s legitimacy of the "Second Republic", electoral violence and propaganda and satire, gender equality and sexual harassment. The chapter has shown how the two YouTube channels use performative activism and satiric register such as identity nabbing, satiric barb, culture jamming, parody, and irony. These satiric registers, however, are important as they make issues that pertain to Zimbabwean crisis and society more pronounced. Thus, political satire is one of the tools of the ordinary citizens used to speak truth to power. The findings of the chapter further show that there is continual contestation on the question of the Zimbabwe that must emerge, for whom it must emerge, and how. For the satirists, creative performance points to a Zimbabwe that must emerge should be broadly and more fully democratic. *Magamba T.V.* skits are directly counter hegemonic, speaking to "targeted" counter publics while those of *Bustop T.V.* seek out more generalized counter publics. Either way, counter publics deprive illegitimate regimes of valuable sources of legitimacy. Satire here functions as a "privileged arm of the weak". Reparation is thus an important part of the work of performative activism as they contest the Z.A.N.U-P.F. project. That is, performative activism is not just diagnosis and analysis, but also intervention, solution, and repair.

REFERENCES

Baxter, P., & Jack, S. (2008). Qualitative case study methodology: Study design and implementation for novice researchers. *The qualitative report*, *13*(4), 544–559. https://nsuworks.nova.edu/tqr/vol13/iss4/2/

Çoşkun, G. E. (2015). Use of multimodal critical discouse analysis in media studies. *The Online Journal of Communication and Media*, *1*(3), 40–43.

Day, A. (2011). *Satire and dissent: Interventions in contemporary political debate.* Indiana University Press.

Gray, J., Jones, J. P., & Thompson, E. (2009). The state of satire, the satire of state. *Satire TV: Politics and comedy in the post-network era* (pp. 3–36).

Gukurume, S. (2017). # ThisFlag and# This Gown cyber protests in Zimbabwe: Reclaiming political space. *African Journalism Studies*, *38*(2), 49–70. https://doi.org/10.1080/23743670.2017.1354052

Highet, G. 1962. The Anatomy of Satire. Princeton, New Jersey: Prince Town University Press

Kuhlmann, J. (2012). Zimbabwean diaspora politics and the power of laughter: Humor as a tool for political communication, criticism and protest. *Journal of African Media Studies*, *4*(3), 295–314. https://intellectdiscover.com/content/journals/10.1386/jams.4.3.295_1

Matsilele, T. (2019). *Social media dissidence in Zimbabwe* [Doctoral dissertation, University of Johannesburg].

Matsilele, T., & Mututwa, W. T. (2021). The aesthetics of 'laughing at power' in an African cybersphere. In Mpofu, S. *The politics of laughter in the social media age: Perspectives from the global South*. 23–41. https://link.springer.com/chapter/10.1007/978-3-030-81969-9_2

Mawowa, S. (2017). Zimbabwe's quest for legitimacy. *Daily Maverick*. Retrieved June 4, 2024, from https://www.dailymaverick.co.za/opinionista/2017-12-20-zimbabwes-quest-for-legitimacy/

Mhiripiri, N. A., & Ureke, O. (2019). Mobile journalism, cellphilms, and the use of the Storymaker multimedia software at a Zimbabwean media training university. In L. Briz-Ponce, J. A. Juanes-Ménde & F. J. García-Peñalvo. *Handbook of research on mobile devices and applications in higher education settings*. (pp. 318–343). IGI Global

Msimanga, M. J., Ncube, G., & Mkwananzi, P. (2021). Political satire and the mediation of the Zimbabwean crisis in the era of the "new dispensation": The case of Magamba TV. In S. Mpofu.. *The politics of laughter in the social media age: Perspectives from the global south* (pp. 43–66). Springer. https://link.springer.com/chapter/10.1007/978-3-030-81969-9_3

Msimanga, M.J., 2022. Satire and the discursive construction of National Identity on online media platforms in Zimbabwe: a case study of Magamba and Bus Stop TV (Doctoral dissertation, University of Johannesburg)

Mutsvairo, B., & Rønning, H. (2020). The Janus face of social media and democracy? Reflections on Africa. *Media, Culture & Society*, *42*(3), 317–328. https://journals.sagepub.com/doi/abs/10.1177/0163443719899615

Ndlovu-Gatsheni, S. J. (2009). *Do 'Zimbabweans' exist?: trajectories of nationalism, national identity formation and crisis in a postcolonial state* (Vol 3). Peter Lang.

Ndlovu-Gatsheni, S. J., & Ruhanya, P. (2020). *The history and political transition of Zimbabwe*. Springer International Publishing.

Neale, S., & Krutnick, F. 2006. *Popular film and television comedy*. Routledge.

Nyamanhindi R [illegible].2009. Cartooning Murambatsvina: Representation of Operation Murambatsvina in Zimbabwe. In Vambe, M (ed): The hidden dimensions of Operation Murambatsvina in Zimbabwe. Weaver Press, Harare

Nyaungwa, M. (2021). Laughing at trouble: A multimodal analysis of online economic satire in Zimbabwe. In S. Mpofu. *The politics of laughter in the social media age: Perspectives from the global south*. (pp. 137–153). Springer. https://link.springer.com/chapter/10.1007/978-3-030-81969-9_7

Siziba, G., & Ncube, G. (2015). Mugabe's fall from grace: Satire and fictional narratives as silent forms of resistance in/on Zimbabwe. *Social Dynamics*, *41*(3), 516–539. https://www.tandfonline.com/doi/abs/10.1080/02533952.2015.1106124

Tagwirei, C. (2021) The patriotic present: The urgency of now in Zimbabwe's "New Dispensation". In O Nyambi, T Mangena & G Ncube (Eds.). *Cultures of change in contemporary Zimbabwe* (pp. 19–37). Routledge.

Tshuma, B. B., Tshuma, L.A., and Ndlovu, N. 2021. Humour, Politics and Mnangagwa's Presidency: An Analysis of Readers' Comments in Online News Websites. In Mpofu, S (ed. s). The Politics of Laughter in the Social Media Age: Perspectives from the Global South. Palgrave MacMillan: New York. 93-111

Ureke, O. (2021). Aesthetic norms and motivations of Subaltern Video-Filmmaking: comic skits and mobile journalism of the everyday in Zimbabwe. In A. Vailati & G. Z. Villareal (Eds.). *Ethnographies of 'On Demand' films: Anthropological explorations of commissioned audiovisual productions* (pp. 219–241). Springer

Willems, W. (2011). Comic strips and "the crisis": Postcolonial laughter and coping with everyday life in Zimbabwe. *Popular Communication*, *9*(2), 126–145. https://www.tandfonline.com/doi/abs/10.1080/15405702.2011.562099

Zamponi, M. (2005). From social justice, to neo-liberalism, to authoritarianian nationalism: Where is the Zimbabwe state going?, In D. Suzanne, M. Zamponi & M. Henning (Eds.) *Zimbabwe: The political economy of decline* (pp. 27–43). Nordiska Afrikainstitutet.

Zimoyo, T. (2016). Busstop in breakthrough productions. *The Herald*, 7. https://www.herald.co.zw/bus-stop-T.V.-in-breakthrough-productions/

Zirugo, D. (2021). Audiences as agents of collective memory–Implications for press criticism and journalism boundaries. *Journal of Broadcasting & Electronic Media*, *65*(2), 270–288.

CHAPTER ELEVEN

Humor and Digital Media as a Tool for Social Intervention in Mozambique

DÉRCIO TSANDZANA

INTRODUCTION

Humour can be considered as one of the most common human qualities. From a psychological perspective, humour is a rather broad, multifaceted, and complex phenomenon (Martin & Ford, 2018). According to Bourgeois (2006), '*l'humour*' (humour) is to the thymic sphere, which encompasses all affections, what consciousness is to the noetic sphere, which consists of all representations. It is both the most elementary and general manifestation of them. The basis of the affective life is made up of a scale of moods, just as the basis of the representative life is made up of a scale of consciousnesses" (Bourgeois, 2006: 7). It can be noted that the definition of humour is complex and polysemic, especially when applied to the health or political context.

In that sense, politics can be done in different ways, humour being one such strategy. In countries where traditional spaces for civic participation are blocked, finding 'new escapisms' using humour for participation can be an alternative (Hoffmann et al., 2017). Similarly, in some contexts, music has offered tools for political participation, especially through what might be termed 'artivism' (Kennerley, 2021). In Mozambique, recent research has shown that a field of social intervention is flourishing through culture, such as rap, poetry, and music (Bussotti & Chinguai, 2020; Tsandzana, 2022). This reality is part of what the political science literature has long referenced as informal, non-conventional or non-institutional political participation (Dalton, 2008; de Rooij & Reeskens, 2014; Kaim, 2021).

Most of these alternative forms of participation are happening through social media platforms. In this case, citizens are frequently exposed to political news posts embedded in humorous context, such as funny videos or pictures. Thus, social media has become an important source of political information, especially for younger generations (Heiss & Matthes, 2016). Although research on humour's effects has focused on traditional media contexts, especially ones presenting commercial advertising – culture industry (Adorno, 1991), "social media constitute a new context in which political and non-political content often occur separately from, but in juxtaposition with each other" (Heiss, 2022: 17). There are many different contexts in the Global South where humour has been used by ordinary citizens targeted at exposing the follies of those in power and the consequences have been devastating (Mpofu, 2021). It is in this context that this chapter intends to use the Mozambican case studies to examine ways in which humours content is used to engage in social and political debates.

Like in other countries (Burkley, 2022), with the outbreak of COVID-19, the media landscape in Mozambique was transformed, giving opportunity to actors who used the digital space as a new form of social and political intervention. These social media performers and influencers adopted strategies that included disseminating third-party content and producing videos posted on platforms such as Instagram and TikTok. According to Heiss (2022), social media constitute a new context in which political and non-political content often occur separately from but in juxtaposition with each other. In such cases, the humorous content is not only unrelated to the political content, but also distinct in storyline and topic.

In the vast repertoire of discourses and representations of power, satire unquestionably occupies a privileged place (Shelton, 2014). Before becoming a genre, historically suitable, it is a critical discourse, through which the speaker denounces morals, a policy, a society, or personalities, by making fun of them or by mocking them (Devars, 2015). Etymologically, the word satire comes from the Latin *satura* – a popular term applied to all sorts of 'mixtures' and designating, more specifically, a literary or dramatic medley (Lichtenstein & Nitsch, 2023). By imposing on reality, the laughing mask of indiscipline and detachment, it undermines the symbolic springs of authority.

Satire reminds the plurality of voices that make up the social body and the right of citizens to scrutinise the public officials to whom they have freely given their votes (Holbert, 2013). Traditionally linked to the denunciation of the exercise of political power, satirical statements are part of the symbolic register of the struggle – that of the weak against the powerful, that of words against reality (Davis, 2017). Satire opposes the management of public affairs and its staging by political actors with the critical gaze of derision. Whether it takes the form of a speech, a photograph, a drawing, or a video, it intends to turn representation into a weapon, to assign it a power, that of changing the world or influencing the course of things (Brock, 2018). It is important to highlight that this research is important because it makes an analysis concentrated on the Lusophone context, which is a unique contribution, to the extent that there are few studies on this aspect (Tsandzana, 2023), most of them being on Anglophone-speaking or Francophone countries in Africa.

This chapter is divided into five parts, each one interconnected with the other. It is structured as follows: the next section deals with literature on the role of humour and other creative forms as tools for social and political participation, including in the Global South. It proceeds to present a brief presentation of the digital space in Mozambique. It then presents the methodological route that this chapter has adopted. It then presents findings based on the three case studies in Mozambique. The last section analyses the data, before ending with a brief conclusion.

HUMOUR AS SOCIAL AND POLITICAL PARTICIPATION

In general, political participation can be loosely defined as citizens' activities affecting politics (van Deth, 2021). Much previous work has centered on participation in the arenas of electoral politics and has regarded participation as varying along a single dimension of costliness or difficulty (Norris et al., 2005). However, participation is understood to involve several quite different types of activity and of activists, and to vary according to the institutional setting in which it occurs (Lamprianou, 2013). The wide variety of definitions of political participation has led to divergent research outcomes, including those that count non-political civic engagements as political participation. In addition, numerous additional research studies (Wajzer, 2015; Goroshit, 2016) consider social activities to be political participation (Sairambay, 2020).

There is no single definition of what can be understood by political participation (Verba & Kim, 1978). Some authors (Verba & Kim, 1978) distinguish four main types of political participation: 'voting, campaign activity, citizen initiated contacts, and cooperative activities' (Verba & Kim, 1978: 52). Both formal and informal involvement can be considered as part of political participation. Such a reality can be explained by the research around political participation which has changed over the past decades. In fact, various fields of research have contributed to broadening our understanding of political participation. However, because of the complexity of the definition itself, it has become less clear to understand what the central assumptions and criteria are related to the concept of political participation (Ekman, 2012). In this chapter, I conceptualise political participation as a combination of formal and informal, from elections, demonstrations, occupations, boycotts or writing political petitions.

When linked to the field of digital technologies, we observe that political participation has always been at the forefront. In fact, the Internet has clearly allowed for an extension of exchanges, but these have essentially been deployed outside the spaces of 'institutionalised digital participation' (Duran & Truong, 2013). As demonstrated by some scholars (Vaccari & Valeriani, 2021), the efforts of the public authorities to promote consultation and deliberation mechanisms have not been very effective. Research suggests that there is a marked enthusiasm for horizontal exchanges outside the traditional circuits and their historical structures (parties, unions). Recent advances in the development of social media platforms have led to a renewed interest in political participation and the construction of two distinct forms – "online" and "offline" political participation.

Salovaara (2015: 164) asserts that digital media technologies are causing significant changes "not only in political communication, but also in the social, political, and participatory experiences of communities". In his research, Matthes (2013) found that in political speeches, using humour can distract individuals from engaging in political learning processes, while humour that is related to politics may increase the elaboration of the political content among individuals with high needs for humour. In that sense, especially for today's younger generations, social media have become important sources of political information (Heiss & Matthes, 2016). Some literature (Street et al., 2013; LaMarre, 2015) discusses the role of entertainment in citizens' political engagement (Heiss, 2022), but also in relation to political actors.

As noted by Mendiburo-Seguel et al. (2022: 1), "politicians have long been aware of the power of humour to endear themselves with their constituents, to communicate their messages in a persuasive and memorable way, and to mock their opponents." Humour is viewed as a socially desirable and positive characteristic (Martin and Ford, 2018). Research also suggests that humour benefits the persuasiveness of a message through several mechanisms: by drawing attention to the message (Hansen et al., 2009), improving message recall (Cline & Kellaris, 2007), biasing thoughts in favour of the persuasive arguments of the message and perceptions of the communicator's credibility (Eisend, 2011), and mobilising emotions effectively (Wodak, 2015). Most of this literature has little background in the context of countries referred to from the South.

HUMOUR AND POLITICS IN THE GLOBAL SOUTH

There is not much research that has accurately addressed the topic of humour in politics from a Southern perspective, or more precisely in Africa (Filani, 2016;

Iwata, 2020). Some works in this sense focus in Asia (Perera & Pathak, 2022) or still largely focused on European countries and especially the United States (Tsakona & Popa, 2011). For instance, Perera & Pathak (2022) have discussed and the humour and the performance of power in South Asia in unstable times. Their study has opened novel avenues for research in our efforts to unpack a troubled world disrupted by political instability, violence, anxiety, and trauma in Asia (Perera & Pathak, 2022).

Focusing in Africa, Chukwumah (2018) edited a volume titled *"Joke-Performance in Africa: Mode, Media and Meaning"*. It focused on countries such as Egypt, Kenya, Malawi, Morocco, Nigeria, and Zambia. The book analyses jokes from various perspectives, ranging from critical discourse analysis, interviews, humour theories, psychoanalysis, the postcolony and technauriture, to the interactive dramaturgy of joke, irrespective of media and modes of performance. Chukwumah and his colleagues also consider the pervasive phenomenon of jokes and their performance across Africa in such forms as local jests, street jokes, cartoons, mchongoano, ewhe-eje, stand-up comedy, internet sex jokes, and 'comicast' transmitted via modern technology media such as the T.V., CDs, DVDs, the internet platforms of YouTube, Facebook, and other social arenas, as well as live performances.

Discussing case studies from Benin, Togo, and Burkina Faso, Iwata (2020) has demonstrated that it is significant that politics and laughter have kept close relation in African countries. Iwata (*ibid*) argues that political transitions from one-party or military regimes to multi-party regimes characteristics of laughter were affected significantly, because laughter has an important meaning in the political transformation in African countries. In this context, the failure of democratization often provides laughter with a fertile ground to germinate. Focusing on the case of Nigeria, Filani (2016) has shown that mimicry is conceived as a strategy in the routines of Nigerian stand-up comedians, who adopt two kinds of mimicry acts: verbal and nonverbal. For comedians to use mimicry, they draw from collective beliefs to share with their audience.

In his edited book, Mpofu (2021) explores social media and humour to better understand how ordinary people make sense of their lived conditions. This book is one of the few to meticulously look at the politics of laughter on social media in the Global South. It brings together a broad range of scholars to explore how laughter is used to define, critique, resist and mock power (Nkoala, 2021; Matsilele and Mututwa, 2021; Osiebe, 2021). Mpofu (2021) demonstrates that digital media could be powerful platforms for the marginalised, spaces to share humorous moments of life and politics. These platforms can be used as weapons of the weak in complex relationships between politics, politicians, challenges, and citizens.

Particularly, drawing connections between laughter in folklore and laughter on the cybersphere, Matsilele & Mututwa (2021) establishes that online comedy allows ordinary Zimbabweans to laugh at their own socio-economic challenges while at the same time, exposing the vices and follies of those in power. Osiebe (2021) presents a critical-theoretical chronicling of activism as performed by celebrities in show business through postcolonial Nigerian history. The studies also highlight the changes that occurred as Nigerian celebrities came in contact with digital and social media, but also how humour on social media, in the form of vlogs by satirist, Coconut Kelz, serves as a useful tool for critiquing the kind of race-thinking prevalent in South Africa (Osiebe, 2021; Nkoala, 2021).

THE DIGITAL LANDSCAPE IN MOZAMBIQUE

The use of the internet in Mozambique proves to be a challenge, as shown by data from Hootsuite (2024). It represents Mozambique had 7.96 million internet users at the beginning of 2024, with an internet penetration rate of 23.2%. Data published in Meta's advertising resources indicates that Facebook had 3.20 million users in Mozambique in early 2024 – the same source (Hootsuite, 2024) also indicated that the numbers published in X's advertising resources indicate that X had 68.7 thousand users in Mozambique in early 2024.

According to A4AI (2017), though the government and regulator have introduced much needed reforms, further efforts to reduce the price of broadband for all — especially for the significant number of citizens living under the poverty line — are needed. This figure means that X's ad reach in Mozambique was equivalent to 0.2% of the total population at the time. These modest figures suggest a reflection to question: what extent social media networks can be considered as a place for social and political humour in the country?

Internet access remains a challenge in Mozambique (23%), which partly limits our own analysis. In many countries, mainly in Western, X has become a useful tool for politicians to show interest and personally connect to people, thereby influencing their audience's general evaluation of their credibility and image. However, in the case of Mozambique figures demonstrates that Facebook is the most used tool in the country with around 3 million users, compared to X (Hootsuite, 2024).

The selected social media network for our analysis is Instagram. According to data from Meta's planning tools, Instagram's potential ad reach in Mozambique increased by 201 thousand (+51.1%) between January 2023 and January 2024. The company's quarterly figures also show that the number of Instagram's ad audience in Mozambique fell by 16 thousand (-2.6 percent) between October 2023 and January 2024 (Hootsuite, 2024).

HUMOR, HEALTH, AND DIGITAL COMMUNICATION

The pandemic of COVID-19 caused dramatic shifts in the delivery of comedy as an entertainment commodity, not only in Africa, but all over the world. As demonstrated by some literature (Bennett & Lengacher, 2006; Savage et al., 2017), in relation to health, evidence shows that humour can relieve stress and improve quality of life. Precisely, it may transform fears and other negative emotions into positive emotions expressed through laughter (Baumeister & Fischer, 2021). Humour has been shown to improve the persuasiveness of preventive messages (Blanc & Brigaud, 2014). Some of the research on humour in health communication has focused mainly on the implications of mass media like television and radio (Penney, 2020), less on digital media particularly focused on Africa, which is why this chapter is of particular importance.

Some authors (Reizer at al., 2022) observed that the interest in coronavirus memes was positively correlated with interest in mortality due to COVID-19 on a global scale, and positively associated with the real number of deaths and cases reported in different countries (Skórka et al., 2022). It has already been proven that users of social media (Facebook, Instagram, Snapchat, X, or TikTok) have spread and commented on different information about the pandemic (Krittanawong et al., 2020). scholars have discussed the role of humour in times of a pandemic in the different countries (Andrew & Hempelmann, 2021). Chlopicki & Brzozowska (2021) explored COVID-19 memes in Poland and identified humorous mechanisms behind the sophistication of such memes and the cultural memories of absurd socialist times that they embody in comparison to absurdity of COVID-19 times. Sebba-Elran (2021) reported on the Israeli meme responses to the pandemic, mainly as culturally specific but also as instances of the worldwide reaction, i.e., as global phenomena.

Burkley (2022) notes that humour has become a prevalent response by the public to a multitude of events. Internet memes[1] have been found to be used for political participation. Little research has been undertaken to investigate the role of memes during health crisis situations. Memes transmit information with a humorous tone with generally a short statement or none. Combining the short digital humour with a serious situation such as a health crisis was a unique experience at the height of the COVID-19 pandemic, which requires systematic investigation. Despite the tragic consequences of the COVID-19 pandemic, it offers us a window to investigate the role of digital humour in health communication. This is the gap that this chapter seeks to fill.

1 This refers to "a piece of culture, typically a joke, which gains influence through online transmission" (Penney, 2020: 793).

Scholars such as Ridanpää (2019: 23) defends that "... humour contains an emancipatory power and healing effect, and thus in events of crisis it can be used to help with handling sensitive and delicate issues". According to Burkley (2022), in health care situations, the patient may feel as though they are in a crisis – life or death. This explains why it can be used effectively to relieve the tension of health situations. Humour can also be used outside of inter-personal communication for other reasons (Yeo et al., 2022). Beyond inter-personal communication, humour has also been found in text health advertising communication, as happened in the case of Mozambique during the recent coronavirus pandemic. In fact, the communication of public health information about COVID-19, in contrast to the politicisation of the virus, was vital to people's ability to make life and death decisions (Andrew & Hempelmann, 2021).

Although few, there is research done on the contribution of humour in everyday life in countries outside the Global North. Looking to the African context, Mpofu (2021) focuses on the politics of ridicule, humour, and laughter in the Global South. The author explains that there are many different contexts in the Global South where humour has been used by ordinary citizens targeted at exposing the follies of those in power and the consequences have been devastating. To demonstrate his argument, Mpofu (2021) suggests that Global South scholars should be given a chance to tap from the intellectual traditions and cultures of their region and bring forth understandings and analyses of people's lived experiences.

In Mozambique, prior to COVID-19, information about health crises and general health were usually spread through MISAU – the Ministry of Health in Mozambique using press releases. There was little use of social media networks. These announcements were on television primarily, and hence the public did not provide more room for audience engagement and feedback because there were limited ways for them to do so. Social media provided new opportunities for health organisations to communicate quickly through interactive means.

Thus, we have observed that with the dissemination of daily formal messages about the pandemic of COVID-19 by the local authorities, some creators of art and humour have found in the digital space an escape tool to diffuse their contents in a virtual way. This was massively done through Instagram and closed dialogue platforms like WhatsApp. As illustrated in the previous figures, Facebook is widely used in Mozambique and was also used as a platform for interaction and communication about the pandemic.

MATERIAL AND METHODS

This chapter is a qualitative research, based on digital ethnography and interview with key informants that are part of our case studies. Of the three, in one of them I have privileged Instagram publications, while in the other two the procedure was through semi-structured interviews. In fact, in my fieldwork, I faced some limitations to engage with one of the content creators, while two others were open to answering the main question on how and why they used the digital space and humour to promote pandemic awareness? The responses were obtained via virtual contact (WhatsApp) – the discussions were not recorded as an initial agreement.

Specifically, data for analysis comprised three routines of three Mozambican stand-up comedians purposively selected because of the comics' extensive use of mimicry. Based on case studies of three young users: @maxh258, @txiobullet_madlipz and @alcy_caluamba, who are considered the country's leading digital humour content producers, this study sought to examine the humorous content they produced on the pandemic and how ordinary reacted to it. Combined, all three have more than one million of followers and can be considered digital influencers during COVID-19 pandemic and afterwards.

This chapter adopted a nethnography or 'digital ethnography' (Kozinets, 2016) to analyse posts and online engagement from 20 March 2020 to 20 March 2021. Ethnography of the Internet is used to describe the use of ethnographic tools, techniques, methods, and insight to collect and analyse data from online sources (blogs, vlogs, discussion forums and boards, chat rooms and social media) – is sometimes used to describe online ethnography, although this is better understood as an umbrella term that encompasses all forms of digital ethnography involving digitalisation (Dawson, 2019).

First, I have researched and then downloaded their content for qualitative content analysis. Considering the multiplicity of Alcy Caluamba's publications, I did not adopt a thematic-content research or analysis, but rather through the hashtags that this user used during his publications. Strategically, I made an open search for terms like #parodia, #mozmemes, #mozweon #alcycaluamba. The two interviewees gave oral consent to the interviews and did not object to being quoted in this chapter.

The period analysed is one year, given that March 2020 is the month in which the first case of COVID-19 was publicly declared in Mozambique. The choice of March 2021 was made with the intention of limiting the number of the scope, as it is not possible to carry out a study that could encompass such a long period of time. The number of followers was collected until 10th March 2024.

All publications shared by the digital creators were used in this chapter because they are public/open on Instagram. Prior the use, there was oral consent for the content to be analysed, as long as it did not distort the real meaning of

Table 11.1. Influences and social media engagement (by the author, March 2024)

Influencer	Followers
txiobullet_madlipz	526 000
alcy_caluamba	532 000
maxh258	319 000

what was being posted. Under a formal consent, the name of the creator of the publication is publicly shown, but the name of the users who made comments was censored, as we did not receive authorization to do so, out of respect for ethics and confidentiality of the research. The analysis of the comments follows a qualitative approach (textual analysis) by selecting specific comments. The following section describes three case studies on how humour has transformed the space for debate and civic participation in times of healthy crisis.

POPULAR INSTAGRAM INFLUENCERS IN MOZAMBIQUE

In this section, each case is presented separately, based on the interviews and the virtual ethnography of what the Instagram pages of the three influencers show as publicly accessible data. In each case, an interpretation is made based on the context in which the data was collected, including the implications *vis-a-vis* the literature review and theories of humour.

@alcy_caluamba

Born in Cuamba in Niassa Province, Alcides Caluamba, better known as 'Alcy', is one of the standout content producers in terms of parody in the country. He is generally known amongst the Mozambican diaspora through social networks. Apart from parody, Alcy has skills in other areas such as dance, production and editing of videos. He studied Computer Engineering in India. He has ambitions to the United States of America to learn about filmmaking. He has dreams of being an actor. Through his Instagram page Alcy has become one of the most followed young Instagram users in Mozambique. His reach and influence increased exponentially during the pandemic. In 2021, he was judged to be one of the most influential personalities in Lusophone Africa.

In the case of Alcy's content production, I managed to analyse four (4) videos that focused on the COVID-19 pandemic. In these videos, the influencer and actor appeared doing parody journalistic pieces that highlighted the dangers of COVID-19. He also spoke about resistance against government and World

Health Organisation (WHO) public health restriction measures. In almost all the videos, Alcy appeared with hashtags #stayhome and #coronavirus that were written in Portuguese.

In one of the videos, Alcy appeared reporting an error that virally spread in Mozambique about the correct name of the virus. Instead of the coronavirus, most people were referring to the virus as '*coronavil*'. This video showed in part how humour can be used not only to laugh, but also to teach, in this specific case the correct pronunciation of the name of the pandemic. In fact, humour was one of the most frequent and widely used strategies in an attempt to deal with the seriousness of the situation and make the day-to-day more bearable. During the COVID-19 crisis, the main means or channels of communication were social media platforms. These spaces became the venues where a common and familiar situation was shared thereby bringing people together. In this regard, memes were some of the pieces of information which were shared via social media (Cancelas-Ouviña, 2021).

In another video, Alcy described a tactic that he considered to be the solution for Mozambicans to circumvent police harassment that became popular at the peak of the hard lockdowns. In this video, one can notice that the content producer used his computer science skills to perfection. As a trained graphic designer and image editor, he was able to use a humorous language to convey important information at that time.

This video also gives an idea that the lockdown could be somehow violated by the people. In this video, Alcy used the hashtags called #mahindra, which is the brand of the car used by the Mozambican police. Mahindra is an Indian car manufacturing company that established itself in Mozambique for local assembly of vehicles.

Alcy described in his video a tactic that he considered to be the solution for Mozambicans to circumvent police harassment that became popular at the peak of the hard lockdowns. In this video, one can notice that the content producer used his computer science skills to perfection. As a trained graphic designer and image editor, he was able to use a humorous language to convey important information at that time. This video also gives an idea that the lockdown could be somehow violated by the people. In this video, Alcy used the hashtags called #mahindra, which is the brand of the car used by the Mozambican police. Mahindra is an Indian car manufacturing company that established itself in Mozambique for local assembly of vehicles.

In that video it is possible to see a reaction of one of the users who even says that certainly the solution suggested by Alcy would be a great option and that she/he would buy it. We are facing a situation where humour seems to constitute a link between what is illustrated and seems to be reality. This reality is part of what the literature has analysed to illustrate the contribution of optimism and humour styles to well-being during the COVID-19 lockdown period (Reizer at al., 2022). This is in line with what has been demonstrated in Zimbabwe, where findings show that memes were used to comment on lockdown regulations and speak against public authorities, to raise awareness of COVID-19 and expose poor health delivery systems (Msimanga et al., 2022). In another video, Alcy can be seen doing an imitation in the form of humour of some news reports that were recorded at that time. This was meant to test the capacity of Mozambicans to understand the seriousness of the disease. Alcy parodied the speech of a lady trying to differentiate between Influenza A and cough.

In another video, Alcy focused on the problematic issue of dis/misinformation which became a pandemic on its own during the health crisis. In this video, Alcy used humour to convey a news report that the disease could not affect black people because they are poor. The statement referenced in the video was from a lady who was distressed by the privileges that white people had during the pandemic compared to black people. It is important to note in that video the reference by Instagram that it is related to COVID-19. The speech said (in Portuguese):

> The corona is for the rich people …
> Those are in restaurants … white people.
>
> When you are black and get sick with coronavirus, they will quarantine you, because you don't have money.
>
> When you are poor, they give you a vaccine and you die.

This kind of discourse can be seen as an attempt by the content producer to conscientize Mozambicans on the dangers of spreading of dis/misinformation about the pandemic. Some literature (Krittanawong, 2020; Cancelas-Ouviña, 2021; Skórka, 2022) had already shown that several tweets contained misinformation regarding the relationship between influenza infection and COVID-19. In addition to that, it was found misinformation regarding the possible mislabelling of influenza or allergy-related deaths or cases as a COVID-19 death or case is relatively common among non-academic tweets.

Finally in this case, it is important to highlight some similarity in the reactions of the users, which produced more of a scenario of laughter and not necessarily of practical action. In other words, the sharing of memes is dominant, which demonstrates that as Alcy was transmitting his message, he was also provoking emotions through laughter.

@txiobullet_madlipz

Ângelo Machaia, is popularly known as Txiobullet. He has already worked as a security guard for a private company. He has also done almost any kind of work in order to survive. He even said that he was an informal salesman for some time. He claimed that when you are in these situations and you are young, it is easy to fall into shady deals.

In the interview we had with the influencer, Txiobullet talked about how he described his own profile and what drove him to adopt new ways of making content during the COVID-19 period:

> I see myself as a low-class influencer, because I am of the masses – population, and I transmit to young people the message that it is possible to dream even if we have so much difficulty. During COVID-19, the use of digital tools was fundamental because I thought of guiding citizens to take preventive measures against COVID-19, because everything with good humour can bring solutions to the everyday problems of the population (Txiobullet, 15 November 2022).

In the interview extract above, Txiobullet reveals a multiplicity of factors that lead him to start producing health information on Instagram during the pandemic. By classifying his profile as a 'low-class influencer', he is trying to distance himself from the representations which influencers try to project online which sometimes does not correspond with the lived realities. He also believes in the power of humour as a tool for communication and social impact in times of crisis. Txiobullet also explained that what forced him to record videos was his belief in the power of activism and social intervention. In short, he believed humour is an easy way to transmit the message:

> I used social media during the pandemic because early on I noticed that people don't like to be too focused or concentrated, so by using humour they get the message or advertisement better. My work had a positive impact and inspired several colleagues to do the same (Txiobullet, 15 November 2022).

This speech leads us to what the literature has tried to classify as 'artivism'[2] (Weij et al., 2022). It illustrates that the Internet has a significant effect on the way we access information and has provided us with a platform for public opinion on social issues (Cohen, 2017). It can be used as a creative space as well as a social space to discuss and to view art and the connectivity is a starting point for new ways of collaborating and socialising. This practice tends to amplify in

2 Thus, the expansion of Web 2.0 interactive spaces presents opportunities and challenges to artistic communities.

Mozambique, especially with the use of rap and hip-hop as alternatives to youth political participation in the virtual space (Tsandzana, 2022).

Txiobullet was also known for the way he dubbed different realities to express social problems or draw attention to a particular reality. He also organised laughter and comedian sessions to entertain people stayed at home. On the poster are young influential artists and T.V. presenters, who have thousands of followers on social media. The event was entitled 'open presidency', an analogy of the government initiative of the current President of Mozambique, which consists in informal discussion with the citizens on different issues. The most interesting thing about this event is the time it was held. It was hosted in May 2020, one month after the first case was reported in Mozambique. Txiobullet said he organised these events as a way of entertaining people who were confined in their homes. He used catchy and trendy hashtags such as #FicaEmCasa (Stay at Home).

In other case, we bring an example of union between the two comedians in case 1 and 2, Alcy and Txiobullet, respectively. In that same video (published on 7th April 2021), one of the comedians reproduce an interview. The fact that the same video was published on a public holiday in Mozambique, April 7th, 2021, Mozambican Women's Day, can demonstrate the way the comedians found to commemorate that date. In the video, the speech said (in Portuguese):

> As a woman we should celebrate the 7th of April …
> We Mozambican women should buy the masks …
> We should play Mozambican music …
> We should be at home with our husbands or boyfriends.

In other words, we believe that this reality demonstrates how humour found a solution to encourage Mozambicans even on public holidays when they were not allowed to celebrate collectively. This demonstrates, as the literature has already pointed out (Heiss, 2022), that in moments of health crisis humour and laughter are a good solution. In fact, Savage (2017: 341) explains that "Laughter is part of a universal language of basic emotions that all humans recognize. Health care providers and educators may utilize the power of laughter to improve health and enhance teaching and learning".

@maxh258

Angelo Machelewe also known as Maxh revealed that he started making content in 2019.This was soon after he graduated with a technical degree. The reason he started producing content was because he found himself unemployed despite completing his university studies. He revealed that started working with art through the production of musical instrumentals a long time ago. Despite attempting to curve a name for himself in the music sphere, he didn't manage to succeed as he had hoped. It was only during the COVID-19 pandemic that he decided to record videos and share it with people on social media networks. He mentioned that he inspired by a lot of United States of America and United Kingdom creatives and social media influencers. Maxh further revealed that he always writes the script first before recording the video. His are hopes that the people are able to understand the content he produces, even if it started by accident.

> When I started making my content, I didn't understand anything, but today I consider humour as a way of bringing a different view of things. If I make a joke about November 11, many people may laugh … but if we have a painter drawing what happened on that date it becomes art. Humour does not have a pilot; it is a form of expression. I have been recording humour on issues of bribery, corruption … it is a vehicle I use to express any message I want. If I am in hospital and have a bad experience with public servants, when I get home, I take the moment to share that experience, because I think that videos and humour are forms of liberation (Maxh, 11 November 2022).
>
> When the pandemic started, I was already making content, but COVID-19 made me who I am today and doing something that no one else was doing. However, I was scared because it became difficult to know if my content was good or people was watching because everyone was at home that time. In fact, I didn't know if people followed me because it was good or maybe because everyone was connected on social media networks. Even if I say all of that, I confess that pandemic born Maxh and I seized the opportunity (Maxh, 11 November 2022).

Maxh's interview extracts illustrate how the pandemic allowed for the emergence of talent through digital culture. It allowed creatives that were mostly unknown to come to the surface. Most of these creatives used humour to educate the masses about the pandemic. It was notable with the sudden emergence of different people in the Mozambican digital space. Most of these were producing tons of diverse content. It is partly due the fact that more virtual interactions were happening than ever before. Consequentially, more humour is now being delivered virtually, just as in general the joke no longer dominates as much as, for example, memes (Olah & Hempelmann, 2021).

CONCLUSION

Throughout this chapter the aim was to discuss how during the COVID-19 pandemic digital humour was used to educate the masses about the dangers of the virus. It also explored the ways in which three Mozambican content creators emerged during the pandemic as social media influencers with a significant online following. It has shown that humour and cultural creativity serve in various contexts to promote and disseminate invaluable health communication and support government interventions such as mandatory wearing of masks and staying at home during hard lockdowns. It has been concluded that humour illuminates the way in which social problems are conveyed.

The chapter has demonstrated that although the Internet is only available to 23% of Mozambicans, digital humour has transformed the civic and political culture in Mozambique. Although it is still centred in the large urban centres (especially Maputo), dominated by social media influencers, there is evidence that digital cultures associated with memes and humour are taking shape through the production of parody, satirical skits, and humorous videos. Interestingly, this study found that there are a few female content creators and social media influencers in Mozambique. This can be attributed to the gendered nature of the Mozambican society and the digital divide, where males have access to more stable, reliable, and faster Internet when compared to their female counterparts. This chapter has shown that laughter is a mirror that reflects a social and political situation. However, this mirror reflects images much differently within different times, cultures, political positions, and other elements.

REFERENCES

A4AI (2017). Mozambique affordability report highlights. Retrieved December 20, 2024, from A4AI_2017_AR_Mozam_Screen_AW.pdf

Adorno, T. W. (1941). On Popular Music. Zeitschrift für Sozialforschung, 9, pp17-48.

Andrew, R., & Hempelmann, C. (2021). Humor in the age of coronavirus: a recapitulation and a call to action. *Humor: International Journal of Humor Research*, *34*(2), 329–338.

Baumeister, R., & Fischer, F. (2021). Effects of humor in health communication: Experimental evidence for video sequences aiming to increase the willingness to donate organs. *Frontiers Public Health*, *24*(9), 1–12.

Bennett, M & Lengacher, C. (2006). Humor and laughter may influence health. I. History and background. *Evidence-based Complementary and Alternative Medicine*, *3*(1), 1–3.

Bourgeois, M. L. (2006). Qu'est-ce que l'humeur?. In M. Bourgeois (Ed.), *Les troubles de l'humeur* (pp. 7–16). Presses Universitaires de France.

Blanc, N., & Brigaud, E., (2014). Humor in print health advertisements: Enhanced attention, privileged recognition, and persuasiveness of preventive messages. Health Communication, 29, pp669–677

Brock, M. (2018). Political satire, and its disruptive potential: irony and cynicism in Russia and the US, *Culture. Theory and Critique*, *59*(3), 281–298.

Burkley, S. (2022). Social media, humor, and crisis health communication: Humor used to inform over social media during COVID-19. *Student Research Submissions*, *4*(18), 1–18.

Bussotti, L., & Chinguai, J. (2020). O rap de intervenção social em Maputo, Moçambique. *Estudos de Sociologia*, *26*(1), 75–109.

Cancelas-Ouviña, L. (2021). Humor in times of COVID-19 in Spain: Viewing Coronavirus through memes disseminated via WhatsApp. *Frontiers in Psychology*, *12*(611788), 1–12.

Chlopicki, W. et al. (2021). Sophisticated humor against Covid – the Polish case. *Humor: International Journal of Humor Research*, *34*(2), 201–227.

Chukwumah, I. (2018), *Joke-performance in Africa: Mode, media and meaning*. Routledge.

Cline, T. W., & Kellaris, J. (2007), The influence of humor strength and humor—message relatedness on ad memorability: a dual process model. *Journal of Advertising*, *36*(1), 55–67.

Cohen, A. (2017). Communicating graphically: Mimesis, visual language, and commodification as culture. *Cultural Politics*, *13*(1), 81–100.

Dalton, R. (2008). Citizenship norms and the expansion of political participation. *Political Studies*, *56*(1), 76–98.

Davis, J. (2017). *Satire and politics: The interplay of heritage and practice*. Palgrave Macmillan.

Dawson, C. (2019). *A-Z of digital research methods*. Routledge.

de Rooij, E., & Reeskens, T. (2014). Conventional and unconventional political participation. In Wil Arts & Loek Halman, *Value contrasts and consensus in present-day europe* (pp. 185–212). Brill.

Devars, T. (2015). Les vertus démocratiques du rire. *Effeuillage*, *4*(1), 76–81.

Duran, P., & Truong, F. (2013). La participation politique: nouvelles dimensions, nouveaux problèmes. *Idées économiques et sociales*, *173*(3), 4–7.

Eisend, M. (2011). How humor in advertising works: a meta-analytic test of alternative models. Marketing *Letters*, *22*(2011), 115–132.

Ekman, J., & Emňa, E. (2012). Political participation and civic engagement: Towards a new typology. *Human Affairs*, *22*(3), 283–300.

Filani, I. (2016). The use of mimicry in Nigerian stand-up comedy. *Comedy Studies*, 7(1), 89–102.

Goroshit, M. (2016). Political participation: A latent variable approach. Testing measurement equivalence of political participation using ESS data. *Eurasian Journal of Social Sciences*, *4*(1), 26–38.

Hansen, J., M. Strick., van Baaren, R. B., Hooghuis, M. & Wigboldus, D. H. J. (2009). Exploring memory for product names advertised with humour. *Journal Consumer Behaviour*, *8*(2–3), 135–148.

Heiss, R., & Matthes, J. (2016). Mobilizing for some: The effects of politicians' participatory Facebook posts on young people's political efficacy. *Journal of Media Psychology*, *28*(3), 123–135.

Heiss, R. (2022). How humorous posts influence engagement with political posts on social media: The role of political involvement. Theories, *Methods, and Applications*, *34*(1), 16–29.

Hoffmann, C., Lutz, C., Müller, S., & Meckel, M. (2017). *Facebook escapism and online political participation*. #SMSociety17: Proceedings of the 8th International Conference on Social Media & Society, Estonia.

Holbert, R. (2013). Developing a normative approach to political satire: An empirical Perspective. *International Journal of Communication*, 7(1), 305–323.

Hootsuite 2024 (online source): Hootsuite/Data Reportal (2024). Digital in Mozambique. Retrieved 7 November. 2024, from HYPERLINK "https://zaf01.safelinks.protection.outlook.com/?url=https%3A%2F%2Fdatareportal.com%2Freports%2Fdigital-2024-mozambique&-data=05%7C02%7Coswelledu%40uj.ac.za%7C403e59c09b104aa6ae3308dd761db7c9%7Cfa785acd36ef11bc8a9489841327e045%7C0%7C0%7C638796592217317830%7CUnknown%7CTWFpbGZsb-3d8eyJFbXB0eU1hcGkiOnRydWUsIlYiOiIwLjAuMDAwMCIsIlAiOiJXaW4zMiIsIk-FOIjoiTWFpbCIsIldUIjoyfQ%3D%3D%7C0%7C%7C%7C&sdata=WWlzpwMeZqwuif-CzT9DusY3WGIj1zEOmsLZJEv92UV4%3D&reserved=0"https://datareportal.com/reports/digital-2024-mozambique

Iwata, T. (2020). Political satire and laughter in Africa, In Y. Ofosu-Kusi & M. Matsuda (Eds.), *The challenge of African potentials: Conviviality, informality and futurity* (pp. 143–168). Langaa Research and Publishing Common Initiative Group.

Kaim, M. (2021). Rethinking modes of political participation: The conventional, unconventional, and alternative. *Democratic Theory, 8*(1), 50–70.

Kennerley, D. (2021). Music, politics, and history: An introduction. *Journal of British Studies, 60*(2), 362–374.

Kozinets, R. (2016). *Netnography: Redefined.* Sage publications.

Krittanawong, C., Narasimhan, B., Virk, H. U. H., Narasimhan, H., Hahn, J., Wang, Z., & Tang, W. H. W. (2020). *Misinformation dissemination in Twitter in the COVID-19 era. The American Journal of Medicine, 133*(12), 1367–1369.

Lamprianou, I. (2013). Contemporary political participation research: A critical assessment. In K. N. Demetriou (Ed.). *Democracy in transition* (pp. 21–42). Springer.

Lichtenstein, D., Nitsch, C. (2023). Content analysis in the research field of satire. In F. Oehmer-Pedrazzi, et al. (Ed.), *Standardisierte Inhaltsanalyse in der Kommunikationswissenschaft – Standardized Content Analysis in Communication Research* (pp. 277–286). Springer VS.

Martin, R., & Ford, T. (2018). *The psychology of humor: An integrative approach.* Elsevier Academic Press.

Matsilele, T., & Mututwa, W. (2021). The aesthetics of 'laughing at power' in an African cybersphere. In: Mpofu, S. (Ed.) *The politics of laughter in the social media age* (pp. 23–41). Palgrave Macmillan.

Matthes, J. (2013). Elaboration or distraction? Knowledge acquisition from thematically related and unrelated humor in political speeches. *International Journal of Public Opinion Research, 25*(3), 291–302.

Mendiburo-Seguel, A., Alenda, S., Ford, T. E., Olah, A. R., Navia, P. D., Argüello-Gutiérrez, C. (2022). #funnypoliticians: How do political figures use humor on Twitter?. *Journal Frontiers in Sociology, 7*(788742), 788–742.

Mpofu, S. (2021). Social Media and COVID-19: Taking Humour During Pandemics Seriously. In: Mpofu, S. (eds) Digital Humour in the Covid-19 Pandemic. Palgrave Macmillan, Cham

Msimanga, M., Tshuma, L., & Matsilele (2022). The why of humour during a crisis: An exploration of COVID-19 memes in South Africa and Zimbabwe. *Journal of African Media Studies, 14*(2), 189–207.

Nkoala, S. (2021). The curious case of "Coconut Kelz": Satire as a critique of race-thinking in South Africa. In: S. Mpofu (Ed.) *The politics of laughter in the social media age* (pp. 233–247). Palgrave Macmillan.

Norris, P., Walgrave, S., & Van Aelst, P. (2005). Who demonstrates? Antistate rebels, conventional participants or everyone? *Comparative Politics, 37*(2), 189–205.

Olah, A. & Hempelmann, C. (2021). Humor in the age of coronavirus: a recapitulation and a call to action. *HUMOR, 34(2),* 329-338

Osiebe, G. (2021). The prank of celebrity activism through postcolonial Nigeria. In S. Mpofu (Ed.), *The politics of laughter in the social media age* (pp. 175–196). Palgrave Macmillan.

Penney, J. (2020). It's so hard not to be funny in this situation: Memes and humor in U.S. youth online political expression. *Television & New Media, 21*(8), 791–806.

Perera, S., & Pathak, D. (2022). *Humour and the performance of power in South Asia anxiety, laughter and politics in unstable times.* Routledge India.

Reizer, A., Munk, Y., & Frankfurter, L. K. (2022). Laughing all the way to the lockdown: On humor, optimism, and well-being during COVID-19. *Personality and Individual Differences, 184*(111164), 1–5.

Ridanpää, J. (2019). Crisis events and the inter-scalar politics of humor. *GeoJournal, 84*(4), 901–915.

Sairambay, Y. (2020). Reconceptualising political participation. *Human Affairs, 30*(1), 120–127.

Salovaara, I. (2015) Digital democracies and networked publics. In J. Zielonka (Ed.), *Media and politics in new democracies: Europe in a comparative perspective* (pp. 154–64). Oxford Academic.

Savage, B., Lujan, H. L., Thipparthi, R. R., & DiCarlo, S. E. (2017). Humor, laughter, learning, and health! A brief review. *Advances in Physiology Education, 41*(3), 341–347.

Sebba-Elran, T. (2021). A pandemic of jokes? The Israeli Covid meme and the construction of a collective response to risk. *Humor: International Journal of Humor Research, 34*(2), 229–257.

Shelton, A. (2014). The power of parody and satire in the 21st century English classroom. *Honors Projects, 131*, 1–20. Retrieved December 20, 2024, from https://scholarworks.bgsu.edu/honorsprojects/131

Skórka, P., Grzywacz, B., Moroń, D., & Lenda, M. (2022). COVID-19 in memes: The adaptive response of societies to the pandemic?. *International Journal of Environmental Research and Public Health, 19*(19), 1–24.

Street, J. (2013). *From entertainment to citizenship: Politics and popular culture*. Manchester University Press.

Tsakona, V., & Popa, D. (2011). *Studies in Political Humour: In between political critique and public entertainment*. John Benjamins Publishing Company.

Tsandzana, D. (2023). Political parties and social media: Between screenshots, memes and hashtags during municipal elections in Mozambique. In D. Omanga, A. Mare & P. Mainye (Eds.), *Digital Technologies, Elections and Campaigns in Africa* (pp. 75–90). Routledge.

Tsandzana, D. (2022). Entre a poesia, o rap e a Internet: práticas e experiências de participação política urbano-juvenil em Moçambique. In. A. Sarrouy, J. A. V Simoes, & R. Campos. (Eds.), *A Arte de Construir Cidadania: Juventude, práticas criativas e ativismo* (pp. 301–322). Tinta da China.

Vaccari, C., & Valeriani, A. (2021). *Political participation in the digital age, outside the bubble: social media and political participation in Western democracies*. Oxford Academic.

van Deth, J. (2021). *What is political participation?*. Oxford University Press.

Verba, N., & Kim, J. (1978). *Participation and political equality: A seven nation comparison*. Cambridge University Press.

Wajzer, M. (2015). Political participation: Some problems of conceptualization. Unpublished working paper.

Weij, F., & Berkers, P. (2022). Artivist reception on Twitter: art, politics and social media, *Information. Communication & Society, 26*(8), 1–20.

Wodak, R. (2015). *The politics of fear: What right-wing populist discourses mean*. Sage.

Yeo, S., Becker, A. B., Patel, K., Anderson, A. A., & Patel, K. (2022). Humor can increase perceived communicator effectiveness regardless of race, gender, and expertise — if you are funny enough. *Science Communication, 44*(5), 593–620.

CHAPTER TWELVE

"I had to Speak Truth to Power!": How Kenyan Active Digital Citizens Tag, Crowdsource, Name and Shame Their Way Past Structural Governance Hierarchies

WAMBUI WAMUNYU

INTRODUCTION

Citizen participation and engagement are essential aspects of democracy, widely perceived as a model form of national governance expressed in guarantees such as freedoms of association, expression and movement, free and fair elections, an independent media system, and governmental institutions accountable to the citizenry (Nasong'o & Murunga, 2007). But these presumptions are often rhetorically espoused by a powerful political elite rather than experienced or participated in by the average citizen (Melber, Bjarnesen, Lanzano & Mususa, 2023; Taylor, 2018).

There is a conceptualization spectrum of who may be considered a citizen, including the individual with certain membership, rights and privileges within a nation-state, to individuals who may engage in practices and performances — alone or in collaboration with others — in an effort to better their day-to-day lives while promoting their rights and dignity (Bijl & van Klingen, 2019; Hoskins, 2014). This chapter uses the former definition when referencing the notion of 'citizenship' in general, while the latter definition is applied to the concept of the 'active citizen' discussed later in this chapter.

The nation-state is "a territorially bounded sovereign polity … that is ruled in the name of a community of citizens who identify themselves as a nation" (Feinstein, 2024). The emergence of the contemporary nation-state over the past 200 years occurred by the overthrow, subsummation or other disruption of pre-existing groupings held together by common interests and governance structures. It is therefore difficult to establish a consistent language related to citizenship because of the historical, cultural and governance heterogeneities that underpin the formation of the different nation-states (Wimmer & Feinstein, 2010).

For modern African states, the challenge of defining citizenship is exacerbated by the colonial past where European nations carved up the continent and their administrative, political and bureaucratic structures filtered into the colonies, and into the post-colonial governments that emerged after Independence. Thus the (unspoken) presumptions in much of the discourse related to democratic governance are founded on Max Weber's conceptualization of the centralized bureaucratic state and parliamentary representation, with all citizens having equal ability to elect their representative leaders (Aiyede, 2023; Whimster, 2019).

Nyamnjoh (2006), as cited in Melber et al. (2023), stated the following: "… hierarchies of citizenship and belonging are encoded in contemporary governance structures. This exclusionary legacy has created narrow definitions of citizenship that pit 'insiders' against supposed 'outsiders'" (Melber et al., 2023, p. 6). In Kenya, the harrowing post-election violence of 2007–2008 served as a brutal reminder that the average citizen was the most vulnerable and excluded entity within those hierarchies, and that Kenya was a 'democracy at risk' (Kagwanja & Southall, 2009). More recent opinion refers to Kenyan political leaders who reject the post-constitutional order, a weakened parliament that hardly holds the executive accountable, and rampant elitist entitlement that has weakened state institutions (Shilaho, 2023).

But from colonial times to the present day, Kenyans have expressed their angst against even the most autocratic of regimes through various platforms, including street protests, theatrical or comedic productions, religious institutions, and mediated spaces such as newspapers and television. The tools of choice have included coded language, caricatures and satire, music, poetry and street marches that ridicule or hold accountable self-serving political systems and personalities, protest against government excesses and brutalities, and expose absurdities in government policy (Imbuga, 1976; Mwaura, 2009; Mwangola, 2007; Shilaho, 2023).

This agency has made its way online where individuals expose injustices, and express on digital platforms their frustration and anger with poor stewardship of public resources. They use hashtags, social media posts, and tagging of leaders, organizations and fellow citizens. In focusing on these actions, as exhibited by three purposively selected social media users with accounts on X (formerly Twitter), Tik Tok, Facebook or Instagram, this chapter considers the actions to be forms of active digital citizenship. The chapter draws from content posted by the three individuals on different platforms, as the three individuals frequently post the same/similar content across their social media platforms, which extends the reach of the post.

Scholarship has established the exclusion of citizens in African governance structures but is not as comprehensive on notions of active citizenship on the continent, and much less so in digital spaces. This chapter seeks to address this by way of interrogating the nature of digital engagement from Kenyans who exhibit 'active citizenship' using platforms such as Tik Tok, X and Facebook. The next section provides conceptualizations of citizenship and an overview of political protests in Kenya, followed by an overview of the methodological approach, findings and discussion.

CONCEPTUALIZING CITIZENSHIP IN KENYAN POLITICAL LIFE

For many countries in sub-Saharan Africa, the contemporary discourse on democracy begins in the early 1990s. Citizen dissatisfaction with poor governance from autocratic, long-serving leaders, a push from legacy media, civil society and global financial institutions, and the fall of the Soviet Union variously contributed to a wave of democratization sweeping over large swathes of the continent and the ushering in of multi-party states (Makinda, 1996). Kenya underwent a similar political transformation, which coincided with the beginning of Internet use and the liberalization of the mass media (Mureithi, 2017).

Democratic processes globally have received extensive discussion with electoral participation being among the more widely studied aspects (Birch, 2018). In the African context, recent scholarly engagement with democratic processes includes a focus on elections, constitutionalism and judicial affairs, political leadership, and philosophical contributions to democratic theory (Arriola, Rakner, & van de Walle, 2023; Branch & Cheeseman, 2009; Fombad, 2021; Masabo, 2023). Citizen participation in democratic engagement has received scholarly attention from various contexts such as Negretto's (2020) study of the role of citizens in constitution making, and the engendering of democratic citizenship through education policy in Singapore (Thaiyalan, 2020) and Australia (Whitington, Sisson, & Shin, 2023).

There are various scholars who have addressed citizen agency in African democracies such as Ngunjiri (2023) who addresses citizen participation through the institutions of local governance, and Mbithi, Ndambuki and Juma (2019) who established that among the limitations of the citizenry in engaging in public affairs were difficulty in accessing information related to budgets both its legislation and operationalization in projects, unresponsive legislators, corruption in the executive, and citizens' inability to influence decision making. The presumptions in many of these studies are of the individuals with collective membership, rights and privileges within a nation-state. Additionally, in a range of literature, the citizen's contribution to democratic governance is as a voter who actively exercises that role by showing up to cast their ballot and who needs quality information to keep leaders accountable (Banda, Mudhai & Tettey, 2009; Lieberman, Posner & Tsai, 2013). Civic education programmes and the involvement of the mass media have been studied as ways in which citizens learn how to engage in democratic processes (Finkel & Smith, 2011) but these approaches do not always translate into enabling a more engaged citizenry (Lieberman et al., 2013).

The study of 'active citizenry' is relatively young, dating to the 1990s. For instance, Kearns (1995) and Marinetto (2003), who situated their studies in the United Kingdom, established that geographical location and government policies influenced by contrasting ideological positions on the concept of citizenship respectively were contributing factors in whether active citizenship was practiced. Thaiyalan (2020) proposes ways to improve the inculcation of active citizenship through the education system. Hoskins (2014) defines 'active citizenship' as a term that has practical and normative components, where the former refers to citizens participating in a wide range of activities that promote and contribute to the engendering of democratic practice. The latter component presumes a recognition of the value of individuals in a given society or community, who deserve respect and dignity.

The scholarship on citizen participation in African democracies — particularly that of 'active citizens' — is also relatively limited. Contributors to this scholarship include Chando (2021) who indicates that active citizenry is a concept lacking in African democracies. He suggests its achievement through the building of a self-confident, economically strong citizen, and the deployment of a governance model that starts at the village/community level. By focusing on the concept of 'active citizenship' as a broader engagement beyond electoral practice or collectively holding leaders accountable, this chapter addresses the gap in extensive knowledge about active citizenship in African democratic norms and practice. The chapter notes that while 'active citizenship' may not get as much attention as other components of democratic process, it is not new and has migrated to virtual spaces.

PROTEST IN KENYAN POLITICAL LIFE

From colonial times, there were individuals and institutions within the geo-political entity known as Kenya who sought the betterment of others they recognized as members of their community or as fellow citizens. Mass media institutions have played a visible role since the colonial era in documenting and registering protest against the political status quo. Henry Muoria, a newspaper publisher in the 1940s and 1950s, used his publication *Mûmenyereri* (a word that means *The Guardian* in Gîkûyû, a language spoken in Kenya) to promote the interests and improvement of his fellow *Agîkûyû* people through his writings, and his support of African political rule over colonial rule (Lonsdale, 2009). The publishers or editors of the magazines *Society*, *Beyond*, and *Finance* faced imprisonment, banning of their publications, financial woes and exile for exposing the excesses of President Daniel Arap Moi's regime in the 1980s and 1990s (Reporters Without Borders, 2016; The Media Observer, 2021).

Beyond the mediated expressions of citizen discontent, there have been instances of citizens speaking directly against authoritarianism or "the ludicrousness and the intemperance of the national polity" (Mwaura, 2009, p. 218) through theatre, art, nudity, hunger strikes, and creative street protests (Halliday, 2019; Mwaura, 2009). Abonga, Kerali, Porter and Tapscott (2020) observed that for the protestor who has little to no political power, actions of protest provide a moral and symbolic power. But such efforts can be stifled (Gathigi, 2018) and citizen protests have been co-opted on occasion, becoming a tool that is mobilized by the powerful elite, to become "insular, sectarian, tribal, unashamedly personality driven and elitist" (Shilaho, 2023).

With the emergence of the Internet, protest would move online. Kipkoech (2023) has also established a positive relationship between social media use and political participation in Kenya. Internet use was launched in Kenya in the early 1990s. Initially, it was expensive and accessible only to those with the incentive and funding to pay for it (Mureithi, 2017). It has since become much more available and pervasively used across the country, particularly on mobile devices. *A report from the Communications Authority of Kenya (2024) indicated that in the July–September 2024 quarter, 55% of more than 68 million mobile devices.* in use nationwide were smartphones. DataReportal (2024) recorded the country's Internet rate at 40.8% with 23.5% of the population being social media users. The access the average citizen has to digital platforms has allowed an independence from the control of powerful gatekeepers such as the political elite or legacy news media outlets. Examples include hashtags such as #UtuNaUzalendoKE ['#HumanityAndPatriotismKE], and social media contributions from @GabrielOguda, @MutemiwaKiama and a host of other netizens across various social media platforms. This has emboldened the active citizenship typified by the individuals

Table 12.1. Followers of Mwangi, Seii & Tarus on select social media accounts

	X.com*	Instagram*	TikTok*	Facebook*
Boniface Mwangi**	2 million	289,100	125,500	623,000
Jerotich Seii	196,800	Private	Private	961
Mercy Tarus***	82,500	16,000	118,600	11,000

* approximate number in March 2025
** He also has a separate Youtube channel titled Sema Ukweli (Speak the Truth) which had 6,100 Its slogan is 'an independent platform to expose the truth: injustices and human rights issues faced by ordinary Kenyans.
*** has multiple handles on social media. Only @thisafricangirl were studied for this chapter.

discussed in this chapter, enabling them to use their digital platforms to disdain the political elite's misuse of public resources and to raise awareness among Kenyans of their right to dignified lives.

METHODOLOGY

There are three individuals' social media platforms studied in this chapter: Jerotich Seii, a self-described 'active citizen' on X; Boniface Mwangi, an award-winning photojournalist-turned-activist who has mobilized street protests and has a large following on several social media platforms including Instagram, X, TikTok, and Facebook; and Mercy Tarus, a university student whose bold exposure of an education scam on X and Tik Tok has drawn censure and praise alike. The three individuals – Jerotich Seii, Boniface Mwangi and Mercy Tarus – were purposively selected because of the public declarations of why they engage as active citizens, their active engagement on digital spaces, and bold nature of their social media posts. The number of followers or reactions they had generated by the writing of this chapter (and that could be ascertained) speaks to their reach on their digital platforms as shown in Table 12.1.

For each individual, the study assesses purposively selected social media posts and responses for the type of content shared and evidence of action or reaction in response to the posts. Seii and Mwangi have also worked together on an initiative formed in 2020 dubbed *Linda Katiba* [Protect the Constitution]. The three individuals are referred to as 'active digital citizens' for the rest of the chapter. The two following sections present the findings and discussion.

CONTENT FROM AND REACTIONS TO ACTIVE DIGITAL CITIZENS

@JerotichSeii is a self-described 'active citizen' (Kipkemoi, 2022) who discusses socio-political issues in the country. She has a private Instagram account and a public X account. Her tagline on X reads: "*More than a little bit fed up. Doing something about it. Justice for Wakenya. Liberation: third time's a charm.*" Her posts may reference the hashtags #LindaKatiba (Kiswahili for #Protect the Constitution), and #SwitchOffKPLC (a rallying cry against high electricity costs from the state-run Kenya Power and Lighting Company which has a monopoly on supplying electrical power nationwide). At the time of this writing, she had about 171,000 followers on X. In 2024, she began inviting those who read her tweets to share evidence of building violations with the hashtags *#NairobiCrimeScene* and *#ConstructionCartelsWillFall*[1]. She linked the post to a clip of her speaking on a radio station talk show about a Chinese Property Developers Association[2] formed by Chinese building contractors. The invitation yielded replies in the form of pictures, names of violators, and an invitation to participate in resident association meetings[3].

Boniface Mwangi (@bonifacemwangi) is a socio-political activist who speaks out publicly and often about societal problems and injustices including corruption, abuse of power, and the failure of government to provide services. He has an extensive digital presence that includes personal social media accounts and website as well as *Sema Ukweli*, a stable of social media accounts and website that shares crowdsourced stories of corruption and malfeasance in Kenyan public life. The slogans on his personal and *Sema Ukweli* platforms provide insight into what drives him to engage as an active citizen, by making a difference and exposing truth. His slogan on X and Instagram is *Husband. Dad. You can never achieve anything without COURAGE. Living my life to make a difference.* In clips shared on X and Instagram accounts, ds@bonifacemwangi showed the July 13, 2023 arrest of a protestor chained to a street sign, protesting the high cost of living. Part of the caption alongside the Instagram version of the clip stated:

> Julius Kamau is assaulted, and arrested in every protest. His only crime is exercising Article 37 of the constitution which gives him the right to protest … He was today charged for taking part in "illegal assembly" and denied bail … [Kamau's lawyer] says after the police arrested him, they drilled a screwdriver in his ear. His lawyer told the court about

1 https://twitter.com/JerotichSeii/status/1751527697560256613
2 https://twitter.com/i/status/1750793954612625486
3 https://twitter.com/JerotichSeii/status/1751527697560256613

> the assault. The court denied him cash bail for a simple misdemeanour offence. Tomorrow at 9 am we meet at Milimani Law Courts to demand #ReleaseJuliusKamau[4].

The post generated more than 113 thousand views on X On July 14, 2023, @ bonifacemwangi posted a videoclip of his family and him waiting in an empty courtroom for the arraignment of Julius Kamau. He also posted a tweet the same day, indicating that Kamau had been freed and the charges dropped[5]. Later that year, Kamau would be arrested again for staging a street protest alone, and social media pressure from @bonifacemwangi again contributed towards his release[6]. @ bonifacemwangi is also a defender of the police service, reviled by many citizens for documented corruption and brutality against citizens. However, even as @ bonifacemwangi decries those practices, he speaks of the inhuman conditions in which the police operate and calls for reform within the service. In a video clip on *Sema Ukweli*[7], a police officer narrates the struggles they face within the force including being shamed for being corrupt, yet no one asks them about the conditions in which they work. @bonifacemwangi shares the clip with the following (edited) caption:

> Police officers have sent me this video and asked me to forward it to President [William] Ruto. Does Ruto know police officers buy their uniforms? The officers have explained not justified why they go looking for bribes. It's worth a listen. #PolisiNiRafiki #bonifacemwangi

Mercy Tarus (@thisafricangirl) has a smaller social media presence compared to Seii and Mwangi. At the time of writing, she had slightly more than 4,600 followers on X and 1,290 on TikTok. Her Tik Tok slogan is *Pursuit for Justice. Stand with us. 1.1 billion KSh.*, alluding to the amount of money that had been siphoned in an education scam that was meant to have helped her and about 200 other students to receive scholarships to study in Finland and Canada (Kirui, 2023). Tarus gained notoriety from August 7, 2023, when a video clip of her was shared on multiple social media platforms. The Kenyan university graduate had attended a meeting called by leaders from a section of the country known as Uasin Gishu County, to discuss the botched education scholarship scheme. The programme had been rolled out during the leadership of the former governor of the county, Jackson Mandago, who now represents the county as a legislator in the national assembly.

In the clip, Tarus castigated the leaders for arriving late for the meeting, for the botched scheme, and for the mental, emotional and financial anguish it had

4 https://www.instagram.com/reel/CupktEAtwxi/?utm_source=ig_web_copy_link
5 https://twitter.com/bonifacemwangi/status/1679823213327425536
6 https://twitter.com/bonifacemwangi/status/1720700394190303659
7 https://www.tiktok.com/@thebonifacemwangi/video/7291936298896559366

caused among the students and their families. It was a powerful expression of citizen frustration at outright corruption and a lack of accountability in political leadership. The video clip went viral, receiving news media attention and reactions from other social media users. Tarus followed it up with social media posts such as one shared on August 9, 2023. In it, Tarus posted on her X account that there would be citizen protests: "Leo tunaenda maandamano [today there will be protests]. There will be no rest for the wicked!! All we want is what is RIGHTFULLY OURS!! REFUND IS THE SONG"

The original video clip was also shared by citizens and prominent personalities alike, and generated chatter on WhatsApp groups, and other social media platforms. In one tweet, Martha Karua, a leading member of the political opposition, shared on her X account a section of the clip as it had been broadcast on a news media station. The tweet generated more than 500 reposts and nearly 195 thousand views[8]. Karua tagged the Directorate of Criminal Investigations – Kenya and the National Police Service as she called for the matter to be addressed. Tarus then responded to Karua's tweet by stating the following: "*I HAD TO SPEAK TRUTH TO POWER!!!*"

In December 2023, Mandago and three other individuals were arrested and charged with, among other offences, conspiracy to commit economic crime, abuse of office, and fraudulent use of public property (Kirui, 2023). The case, as at the time of this writing, remained ongoing though Mandago continues to serve as legislator of his county. Seii, Mwangi and Tarus share particular characteristics that expose the challenges and potential of citizen agency in young democracies. While their individual audience reach differs, they are similar in their ability to boldly present allegations and evidence of government/political corruption and culpability. Their context is particular, be it a place (e.g. Nairobi), topic (building violations), and individuals (an identified prominent politician). They name and shame leaders and government officers who have failed in service delivery. They tag public authorities and interested parties (such as resident associations, politicians, and news media) when highlighting an issue. Through tools of social media discourse such as hashtags and tagging of interested parties, they rally calls to action and create public records and updates of the issues they highlight. They provide spirited responses to their critics, who accuse them of being anti-government, unnecessarily negative, and in the service of external interests, among other allegations. In the reactions to the posts of the active digital citizens, other social media users expand the discourse and are challenged to see or consider their own agency.

8 https://twitter.com/i/status/1688622222246547456

DISCUSSION: DISRUPTION OF PRESUMPTIONS

Citizen agency in 'young democracies' such as Kenya's has received some scholarly scrutiny, though it is relatively limited compared to institutional aspects of governance, such as election processes and constitutionalism. The study of citizen agency leans towards the focus on the citizen as an entity that belongs to a larger collective with prescribed rights and privileges. The presumption that citizen agency is a homogenous concept, enacted as in democracies from other cultures and geo-political contexts, informs the presumptions that access to information, a free press, credible electoral processes, adherence to constitutionalism and strong institutions work alongside an informed citizenry. But this Weberian application of democracy and citizen agency is an awkward fit for young democracies in other contexts. Autocratic executive governments, inefficient bureaucratic systems, weakened legislative and other institutions, the co-opting of street protests by the political elite, and a marginalized, down-trodden citizenry are among the hallmarks of 'democratic governance' in countries like Kenya.

It is in this politically dysfunctional context that social media has become a place to counter government/official narratives. Active digital citizens use their posts and responses to posts to express displeasure with the status quo, submit evidence that counters official narratives, engage in keeping leaders accountable openly, re-post news from legacy media outlets, share protests that are not carried on legacy media platforms, and begin citizen-to-citizen discourse that provides explanations for the socio-economic and political contexts in which individuals find themselves, and makes demands for better stewardship of public resources. The number of views the posts of the three individuals receive are another telling indicator that their posts resonate with fellow citizens, even when the latter do not respond or react. The three individuals have participated in street protests, but their use of digital platforms serves as a potent illustration that 'active citizenry' can be deployed and engendered in digital spaces, thus rendering irrelevant geographical limits. This section posits three premises around which 'active digital citizenry' disrupts accepted presumptions.

The first presumption is that in many young democracies such as Kenya's, democracy occurs and is enacted primarily at national level by institutions, not individuals. Dominici (2022) notes that democracy is becoming more technical and ritualistic, rather than focused on the human beings affected by and enacting it. This has certainly been the experience in Kenya, which ritually holds elections every five years, has an elaborate constitutional framework, and executive and legislative structures that theoretically provide representation for citizen interests and the public good. The active digital citizen chooses to engage in democratic practices at local level, be it by speaking openly and boldly in public such as to individuals alleged to have stolen from students in Uasin Gishu County (Tarus), crowdsourcing evidence of building and zoning violations in Nairobi suburbs (Seii), or exposing constitutional violations experienced by citizens and civil servants alike (Mwangi). The three individuals deliberately create alternative voices of protest on digital platforms, using terms that show their engagement and the catalyzing forces behind their actions such as: 'COURAGE;' 'living life to make a difference;' 'more than a little bit fed up. Doing something about it;' and stand with us.'

The second presumption is that the political elite are the lead actors and controllers of narrative in democratic governance, and despite documented incompetence and corruption, remain at the helm (Goin, 2024). In legacy media, the corrupt are often unnamed, and frequently get away with crimes against the public (Wasuna, 2024). But not so with the active digital citizen who names individuals and disrupts hierarchies of power, be they cultural or institutional. Tarus, the university student who spoke against the education scam, was censured online for being disrespectful to her elders. This was an allusion to culture, where her youth and gender would make it taboo to censure older men. especially in public. The release of serial street protestor Kamau from police custody and the dropping of charges against him occurred after Mwangi's social media posts that created public pressure. Seii also breaks hierarchies by calling out the Nairobi County governor for allowing building violations and refusing to respond to questions about the high-profile, favorable treatment a group of Chinese building investors have been perceived to receive from his government.

The third presumption is that the average citizen is helpless against the powerful, disengaged, and cannot successfully counter the status quo. The three individuals studied showed that exposing wrong-doing and malfeasance among public officials can lead to some action being taken, and to generating discourse among fellow citizens who respond to their posts and calls to action, positively or negatively. The three individuals discussed in this chapter have deliberately chosen to engage in practices that contribute to a betterment of the lives of Kenyans, with an emphasis on human dignity and rights. Seii responded to an online critic who claimed her #SwithOffKPLC campaign was sponsored by a political figure. She responded, indicating that even the critic would gain from her choice to speak up:

> *@JerotichSeii:* Lack of research seems to be an occupational hazard for tribalist trolls. We are in the Court of Appeal. #SwitchOffKPLC is alive and well and even as you try to be insulting, our victory one day, will benefit you too.

Just under a quarter of the Kenyan population is on social media (DataReportal, 2024), and those engaged in active digital citizenship as exemplified by the three individuals discussed in this chapter, remain few in number. But the reactions among fellow social media users to the posts from these three individuals – and others among them – show a resonance among even those citizens who may not be active digital citizens *per se*.

The interaction between the active digital citizens and those who respond to them further upends the top-down approach to democratic governance practiced by political and governing authorities. Instead the interaction creates a conversation among peers, where the discourse on governance is led or controlled by the citizens. This in turn extends the moral and symbolic power appropriated by active citizens against personalities and institutions – such as members of the political elite – that deem themselves higher in the political hierarchy (Melber et al., 2023).

CONCLUSION

Kenya holds elections every five years and its citizens are courted during the campaign season for their votes. But they are not treated as significant players in other aspects of the democratic process and have remained marginalized in the active building of the democratic state. Digital spaces, however, have afforded citizens a virtual place where they can choose practices and performances that seek communal, rather than individual, good. The uptake of Internet use in Kenya, the growing numbers of social media users, and the responses they provide to the active digital citizens give credence to Radoli and Langmia's (2023) observation that "the [contemporary] political consciousness of a country depends on social media" (p. 8). Given the active digital citizenry described in this chapter, the contributions of individuals who deliberately choose to speak up against injustice and poor stewardship of public resources may not lead to instantaneous change. But in crowdsourcing for evidence of public wrongdoing, naming and shaming individuals who do wrong, and mobilizing discourse through hashtags, the active digital citizens have shown that long-standing governance hierarchies can be disrupted, perhaps even dismantled, one post at a time. Melber et al. (2023) call for a change in how African countries relate with their citizens. This chapter extends this call by proposing that the active digital citizen is contributing to a more human expression of democratic governance.

Post scriptum: This chapter was written before the June 2024 protests that Kenya experienced, where demonstrators took to the streets to successfully challenge the passage of a contentious law. The demonstrators evolved to address wider ranging concerns, including rampant graft and mediocre governance, leading to an even greater number of 'active digital citizens' pushing for political and socio-economic change. The three individuals highlighted in this chapter retained their vocality and advocacy during this period.

REFERENCES

Abonga, F., Kerali, R., Porter, H., & Tapscott, R. (2020). Naked bodies and collective action: Repertoires of protest in Uganda's militarised, authoritarian regime. *Civil Wars*, *22*(2–3), 198–223. https://doi.org/10.1080/13698249.2020.1680018

Aiyede, E. R. (2023). Governance and politics of public policy in Africa. In E. R. Aiyede & B. Muganda (Eds.), *Public Policy and Research in Africa*. (pp. 87–121). Palgrave Macmillan. https://doi.org/10.1007/978-3-030-99724-3_5

Arriola, L. R., Rakner, L., & van de Walle, N. (2023). Democratic backsliding in Africa? Autocratization, resilience, and contention. In L. R. Arriola, L. Rakner, L., & N. van de Walle (Eds.), *Democratic Backsliding in Africa? Autocratization, Resilience, and Contention*, Oxford Academic. https://doi.org/10.1093/oso/9780192867322.003.0001

Banda, F., Mudhai, O. F., & Tettey, W. J. (2009). Introduction: New media and democracy in Africa – A critical interjection. In O. F. Mudhai, W. J. Tettey, & F. Banda (Eds.)., *African media and the digital public sphere. Palgrave Macmillan Series in International Political Communication* (pp. 1–20). Palgrave Macmillan. https://doi.org/10.1057/9780230621756_1

Bijl, P., & van Klingen, G. (2019). Citizenship in Asian history. *Citizenship Studies*, *23*(3), 189–205. https://doi.org/10.1080/13621025.2019.1603268

Birch, S. (2018). Democratic norms, empirical realities and approaches to improving voter turnout. *Res Publica 24*, 9–30. https://doi.org/10.1007/s11158-017-9380-3

Branch, D., & Cheeseman, N. (2009). Democratization, sequencing, and state failure in Africa: Lessons from Kenya. *African Affairs*, *108*(430), 1–26. https://doi.org/10.1093/afraf/adn065

Chando, T. (2021). Active citizenship in contemporary democratic practice in Africa: Challenges and prospects. *South African Journal of Philosophy*, *40*(1), 75–92. https://doi.org/10.1080/02580136.2021.1885908

Communications Authority of Kenya. (2024). First quarter sector statistics report Financial Year 2024/2025 (July 1st – September 30th, 2024). https://www.ca.go.ke/sites/default/files/2025-01/Sector%20Statistics%20Report%20Q1%202024-2025.pdf

Communications Authority of Kenya. (2024). Second quarter sector statistics report Financial Year 2023/2024 (October – December 2023). *Communications Authority of Kenya*. Retrieved December 20, 2024, from https://repository.ca.go.ke/bitstream/handle/123456789/1369/Sector%20Statistics%20Report%20Q2%202023-2024.pdf?sequence=1&isAllowed=y

DataReportal. (2024, February 23). Digital 2024: Kenya. *DataReportal*. Retrieved December 20, 2024, from https://datareportal.com/reports/digital-2024-kenya

Dominici, P. (2022). The weak link of democracy and the challenges of educating toward global citizenship. *Prospects*, *53*, 265–285. https://doi.org/10.1007/s11125-022-09607-8.

Feinstein, Y. (2024, January 5). *Nation-state. Encyclopedia Britannica*. https://www.britannica.com/topic/nation-state

Finkel, S. E., & Smith, A. E. (2011). Civic education, political discussion, and the social transmission of democratic knowledge and values in a new democracy: Kenya 2002. *American Journal of Political Science*, *55*(2), 417–435. https://doi.org/10.1111/j.1540-5907.2010.00493.x.

Fombad, C. M. (2021). Democracy, elections, and constitutionalism in Africa: Setting the scene. In C. Fombad & N. Stytler, N. (Eds.). *Democracy, elections, and constitutionalism in Africa* (pp. 19–35) Oxford Academic.. https://doi.org/10.1093/oso/9780192894779.003.0002.

Gathigi, G. (2018, May 6). How artistic expression is being stifled in East Africa. *The Conversation*. Retrieved December 20, 2024, from https://theconversation.com/how-artistic-expression-is-being-stifled-in-east-africa-96028

Goin, C. (2024, January 21). 20,000 ghost workers found in gov't payroll as PSC unmasks departments with excess staff. *Citizen Digital*. Retrieved December 20, 2024, from https://www.citizen.digital/news/20000-ghost-workers-found-in-govt-payroll-as-psc-unmasks-departments-with-excess-staff-n335222

Halliday, C. (2019). Animating political protests through artivism in 21st century Nairobi, Kenya. *The Journal of Law, Social Justice and Global Development, 24*, 100–113. https://doi.org/10.31273/LGD.2019.2406.

Hoskins, B. (2014). Active citizen. In A. C. Michalos (Ed.). *Encyclopedia of quality of life and well-being research* (pp. 14–16) Springer, Dordrect. https://doi.org/10.1007/978-94-007-0753-5_16

Imbuga, F. (1976). *Betrayal in the city*. East African Educational Publishers.

Kagwanja, P., & Southall, R. (2009). Introduction: Kenya – a democracy in retreat? *Journal of Contemporary African Studies*, *27*(3), 259–277. https://doi.org/10.1080/02589000903216930

Kearns, A. (1995). Active citizenship and local governance: Political and geographical dimensions. *Political Geography*, *14*(2), 155–175. https://doi.org/10.1016/0962-6298(95)91662-N

Kipkoech, G. (2023). Connections between Internet, social media news use, and political participation in Kenya. *Social Science Computer Review*, *41*(3), 871–885. https://doi.org/10.1177/08944393211058702

Kipkemoi, A. (2022). Jerotich Seii: I'm not an activist but an active citizen who means well for our country. *The Standard*. Retrieved December 20, 2024, from https://www.standardmedia.co.ke/health/national/article/2001431687/jerotich-seii-im-not-an-activist-but-an-active-citizen-who-means-well-for-our-country

Kirui, B. (2023, December 9). DPP allows EACC to arrest Senator Mandago over KSh. 1.1B Uasin Gishu scholarship scam. *Citizen Digital*. Retrieved December 20, 2024, from https://www.citizen.digital/news/dpp-allows-eacc-to-arrest-senator-mandago-over-ksh11b-uasin-gishu-scholarship-scam-n332846

Lieberman, E. S., Posner, D. N., & Tsai, L. (2013). Does information lead to more active citizenship? Evidence from an education intervention in rural Kenya. *MIT Political Science Department* Research Paper No. 2013–2. https://ssrn.com/abstract=2228900.

Lonsdale, J. (2009). Henry Muoria, public moralist. In W. Muoria-Sal, B. F. Frederiksen, J. Lonsdale, & Peterson, D. (Eds.), *Writing for Kenya: The life and works of Henry Muoria* (pp. 3–58). Brill

Makinda, S. M. (1996). Democracy and multi-party politics in Africa. *The Journal of Modern African Studies*, *34*(4), 555–573. https://doi.org/10.1017/S0022278X00055762

Marinetto, M. (2003). Who wants to be an active citizen? The politics and practice of community involvement. *Sociology*, *37*(1), 103–120. https://doi.org/10.1177/00380385030370013 90

Masabo, C. J. (2023). Nyerere and the African theory of democracy. *Democratic Theory*, *10*(1), 36–51. https://doi.org/10.3167/dt.2023.100104

Mbithi, A., Ndambuki, D., & Juma, F. O. (2019). Determinants of public participation in Kenya county governments. *Journal of Asian and African Studies*, *54*(1), 52–69. https://doi.org/10.1177/0021909618794028

Melber, H., Bjarnesen, J., Lanzano, C. & Mususa, P. (2023). Citizenship matters: Explorations into the citizen-state relationship in Africa, *Forum for Development Studies*, 50(1), 35-58. DOI: HYPERLINK "https://doi.org/10.1080/08039410.2022.2145992"10.1080/08039410.2022.2145992

Mureithi, M. (2017). The Internet journey for Kenya: The interplay of disruptive innovation and entrepreneurship in fueling rapid growth. In: B. Ndemo & T. Weiss, T. (Eds.). *Digital Kenya* . Palgrave Studies of Entrepreneurship in Africa (pp. 27–53). Palgrave Macmillan. https://doi.org/10.1057/978-1-137-57878-5_2

Mwangola, M. S. (2007). Leaders of tomorrow? The youth and democratisation in Kenya. In G. R. Murunga & S. W. Nasong'o (Eds.), *Kenya: The struggle for democracy* (pp. 129–163). Zed Books & CODESRIA

Mwaura, B. (2009). Political ridicule: Medialized notions of 'transparent concealment'. In K. Njogu & J. Middleton (Eds.), *Media and Identity in Africa* (pp. 218–225). Edinburgh University Press Ltd.

Nasong'o, S. W., & Murunga, G. R. (2007). Prospects for democracy in Kenya. In G. R. Murunga, & S. W. Nasong'o (Eds.), *Kenya: The struggle for democracy* (pp. 3–16). Zed Books & CODESRIA.

Negretto, G. (2020). Constitution-making and liberal democracy: The role of citizens and representative elites. *International Journal of Constitutional Law, 18*(1), 206–232, https://doi.org/10.1093/icon/moaa003

Ngunjiri, M. (Ed.). (2023). *Citizen participation in local governance in Africa: A selection of case studies*. International Institute for Democracy and Electoral Assistance.

Nyamnjoh, F. B. (2006). Insiders and Outsiders: *Citizenship and Xenophobia in Contemporary Southern Africa*, London: Zed Books

Radoli, L., & Langmia, K. (2023). Of deep fakes, misinfomation, and disinformation. In K. Langmia (Ed.)., *Black communication in the age of disinformation: Deepfakes and synthetic media*. (pp. 1–14). Palgrave Macmillan.

Reporters Without Borders. (2016, January 20). Magazine editor sentenced to six months in prison. *Reporters Without Borders*. Retrieved December 20, 2024, from https://rsf.org/en/magazine-editor-sentenced-six-months-prison

Shilaho, W. K. (2023, April 3). Mass protests in Kenya have a long and rich history – but have been hijacked by the elites. *The Conversation*. Retrieved December 20, 2024, from https://theconversation.com/mass-protests-in-kenya-have-a-long-and-rich-history-but-have-been-hijacked-by-the-elites-202979

Taylor, I. (2018). 'Democracy in Africa'. African Politics: A Very Short Introduction (Oxford, 2018; online edn, Oxford Academic, 27 Sept. 2018). Retrieved October 24, 2024, from https://doi.org/10.1093/actrade/9780198806578.003.0008

Taylor, Ian, 'Democracy in Africa'. *African Politics: A Very Short Introduction* (Oxford, 2018; online edn, Oxford Academic, 27 Sept. 2018). Retrieved October 24, 2024, from https://doi.org/10.1093/actrade/9780198806578.003.0008

Thaiyalan, S. G. (2020.) Towards an education for active citizenship in Singapore. In A. Peterson, G. Shahl, & H. Soong (Eds.), *The Palgrave Handbook of Citizenship and Education* Palgrave Macmillan, pp. 497–519. https://doi.org/10.1007/978-3-319-67828-3_78

The Media Observer. (2021, October 18). Mashujaa Day: Nyamora, unsung Second Liberation hero why first cartooned Moi. *The Media Observer*. Retrieved October 24, 2024, from https://mediaobserver.co.ke/index.php/2021/10/18/mashujaa-day-nyamora-unsung-second-liberation-hero-who-first-cartooned-moi/

Wasuna, B. (2024, February 14). Why ghost workers may get away with Sh35bn illegal pay: Judge said any audit at a public entity must be done with Auditor-General's authority. *Daily*

Nation. Retrieved October 24, 2024, from https://nation.africa/kenya/news/why-ghost-workers-may-get-away-with-sh35bn-illegal-pay-4524422#story

Whitington, V., Sisson, J. & Shin, AM. (2023). Enacting everyday democratic pedagogies in a birth-five early years setting. The Australian Educational Researcher. https://doi.org/10.1007/s13384-023-00664-2

Whitington, V., Sisson, J., & Shin, AM. (2024). Enacting everyday democratic pedagogies in a birth-five early years setting. *The Australian Educational Researcher*, *51*, 1795–1811. https://doi.org/10.1007/s13384-023-00664-2

Whimster, S. (2019). Max Weber and federal democracy. *Journal of Classical Sociology*, *19*(4), 346–360. https://doi.org/10.1177/1468795X19851344

Wimmer, A., & Feinstein, Y. (2010). The rise of the nation-state across the world, 1816 to 2001. *American Sociological Review*, *75*(5), 764–790. http://www.jstor.org/stable/20799488

CHAPTER THIRTEEN

Digital Repression and National Dialogue: Understanding the Elephant in Ethiopia's Dialogue Room

HENOK ASHAGREY KREMTE

INTRODUCTION

Ethiopia kicked off a dialogue initiative by enacting the Ethiopian National Dialogue Commission Establishment Proclamation 1265/2021 (ENDC Proclamation). This Proclamation establishes the Ethiopian National Dialogue Commission (ENDC), the body responsible for leading the dialogue process (Art 6). The main reason cited for launching the dialogue is the presence of "difference of opinions and disagreements among various political and opinion leaders, as well as segments of society in Ethiopia, on the most fundamental national issues" (ENDC Proclamation, Preamble, para 1). To address and resolve these differences, the ENDC Proclamation emphasizes the importance of a broad-based, inclusive public dialogue aimed at fostering a national consensus (Preamble, para 1). It also underlines the role of a dialogue in cultivating a culture of trust and collaboration (Preamble, para 2).

The ENDC Proclamation stipulates that the ENDC, composed of eleven Commissioners, must be appointed by the Parliament (Art 11), which accordingly appointed the Commissioners on February 21, 2022 (Harter, 2022; Sahlu, 2022). The ENDC has officially begun working on the preparatory phases of the dialogue since July 2022 (Fana Broadcasting Corporate, 2022). However, from the outset, doubts have clouded the trustworthiness of the process. Chief among these concerns is the doubt surrounding the government's commitment to credible, and inclusive dialogue. Critics aver that the government's continued military operations against insurgent groups nationwide indicates a lack of sincere political will for engaging in credible and inclusive dialogue (Gemechu, 2022, Tura, 2023, pp. 653–664), suggesting that the regime initiated the dialogue merely as a tactic to buy time until opposition, including armed groups, is subdued (Edjeta, 2022). The government's genuineness in initiating the dialogue has also faced scrutiny in light of the entrenched mistrust and polarization among ethnic elites. For instance, a joint statement issued by over 35 Amhara civil society organizations denounced the process as a charade orchestrated by the Oromo dominated regime, which they contended seeks to further reinforce and entrench the 'Amharaphobic' status quo stemming from similar illegitimate processes in the 1990s that did not include Amhara representation (Amhara Civic Organizations, 2024).

The other major contention revolves around the perceived lack of transparency, hurried decision-making, and non-inclusivity in the adoption of the ENDC Proclamation and the appointment of ENDC members (Tsegaye, 2022; Addis Standard, 2022b). For instance, the Ethiopian Political Parties Joint Council criticized the rushed approval of the ENDC Proclamation and deemed the process for appointing ENDC members as non-consultative and flawed, even by the standards set by the ENDC Proclamation (February 17, 2022). It also expressed its concern that the regime is approaching the dialogue process more as an arbiter than as an equal stakeholder (Harter, 2022). These concerns are echoed by various opposition parties including the Caucus of Opposition Parties, which denounced the process as unilateral and not-inclusive (Addis Standard, 2023; 2022b). The Balderas for True Democracy Party has stated that the ENDC 'failed before its formation' (February 21, 2022), while the Afar People's Party has announced its non-participation in the process, citing 'exclusiveness, lack of transparency, and the substantial, direct influence and involvement of the federal government' (*Ethiopian Political Parties Joint Council* February 26, 2022). Likewise, influential parties in Oromia and Somali regions, Oromo Federalist Congress, Oromo Liberation Front, and Ogaden National Liberation Front, dismiss the process altogether, citing *inter alia* a lack of trust in the process (Addis Standard, 2022a). A further dimension of scepticism surrounds the impartiality of the ENDC members, which are accused of bias towards the regime, leading some to characterize the process as an 'intra party negotiation' (Wight, 2022). Further still, the trust deficit ingrained in Ethiopian politics is highlighted as another challenge to the dialogue's transformative potential (Yared, 2022, p. 18).[1] These concerns,

1 The criticism from the two leading religious institutions in the country deals a further blow to the process's chances of success: the Ethiopian Orthodox Church Holy Synod condemns the

whether valid or not, cast a shadow over the process's genuineness, inclusiveness, and legitimacy.

This chapter examines whether and how the government's use of digital repression tactics further damages the transformative potential of the dialogue. The subsequent sections of the chapter are structured as follows: Part two explores the nexus between digitalization and national dialogue. Section three delves into the various digital repression tactics in Ethiopia, examining whether and how they pose a threat to the success of the dialogue. The chapter ends with a section summarizing key takeaways.

NATIONAL DIALOGUES AND DIGITAL TECHNOLOGY: AN OVERVIEW OF THE CONCEPT OF NATIONAL DIALOGUE

National dialogue can be defined in various ways depending on the context, but it is generally understood as a nationally owned process aimed at generating consensus among different social and political groups 'in times of deep political crisis, in post-war situations or during far-reaching political transitions' (Berghof Foundation and Swisspeace, 2017, p. 21). Its transformative potential, however, relies on its insulation from governmental manipulation, preventing its instrumentalization as a facade to consolidate power or recapture waning legitimacy (Paffenholz, Zachariassen, & Helfer, 2017, p. 8). The success or failure of the process hinges on various critical factors (Stigant & Murray, 2015, p. 1). These factors relate to both the political context and the design or process of the dialogue (Haider, 2019, p. 2; Stigant & Murray, 2015, pp. 2–3). Beginning with the design or process dimension, critical factors include inclusion, transparency and public participation, credible convener, agenda-setting, decision-making procedures, mechanism for implementation of outcomes, and confidence-building measures (Haider, 2019, pp. 2–3; Stigant & Murray, 2015, pp. 2–3). In the political context dimension, additional factors come into play including political will and public buy-in. Political will, especially on the government's part, influences the legitimacy of the process significantly (Haider, 2019, pp. 2–3). Public buy-in, which hinges on factors such as the availability of public information, media engagement, and trust in the government's sincerity in initiating the process, also holds paramount importance (Haider, 2019, pp. 2–3).

Commission for failing to invite the church to select participants and set the agenda (Yared, 2024), while the Ethiopian Islamic Affairs Supreme Council denounces the insufficient representation of the Muslim community (**Invalid source specified.**). This adds another layer of doubt that seems to dim any remaining hope for the dialogue's success.

THE INTERPLAY BETWEEN DIGITAL TECHNOLOGY AND NATIONAL DIALOGUES

National dialogues unfold in an increasingly digitalized world, resulting in growing, yet understudied interplays in three different dimensions. The role of digital technologies in facilitating the conduct of national dialogue constitutes the first dimension. Digital technologies are now integral to the conduct of national dialogues. They are used in the preparation, and coordination of dialogues even in contexts where most or all actual dialogue activities occur "in person or offline" (Hirblinger, 2023, p. 15). For instance, the Berghof Foundation's capacity development for Ethiopia's ongoing process incorporates a blend of digital, remote, and in-person elements (ibid.). This use of online coordination mechanisms, like messaging groups, ensures efficient and flexible communication. However, reliance on digital tools presents its own set of challenges like surveillance and infrastructure issues (ibid.).

Digital tools also aid in informing the public about the dialogue process and fostering trust and momentum (ibid). Those leading dialogues may, for example, utilize digital tools to disseminate information to the public, and invite them to participate in the process (Hirblinger, 2020a, p. 24). This is exemplified by instances in Ethiopia, South Sudan, and Libya (Hirblinger, 2023, p. 16; Wittig & Ghosheh, 2020, p. 82; UNDP, 2017). Notably, in Ethiopia, the ENDC utilizes social media platforms like Facebook and X, where it issues weekly activity reports to the public and encourages participation (ENDC, 2024a; ENDC 2024b). This not only increases transparency, but also helps to establish trust in the process (Hirblinger, 2023, p. 16). Nonetheless, public communication is not a cure-all for trust issues (ibid.), especially when broader concerns exist regarding the independence of convening bodies, and if there is perceived lack of genuineness on the part of government to the process, as evidenced by the ongoing dialogue in Ethiopia. Despite the ENDC's two year-long existence and attempts to leverage social media, only about 10,000 people follow its Facebook and less than 3,000 its X (formerly Twitter) (out of 6.4 million social media users nationwide) (Galal, 2023). Even then, most posts draw less than 100 likes and a few comments, often critical (ENDC, 2024a, ENDC 2024b). This lukewarm response does not appear to stem from lack of awareness about the ENDC or its work. Rather, it seems to reflect either indifference towards the ENDC's work or distrust in the dialogue process itself. Public faith and interest in the ongoing process may be undermined by several factors, as briefly discussed in the introductory section of this chapter, like the perceived lack of transparency in the appointment of ENDC members (Yared, 2022, p. 18), and the government's perceived lack of commitment to an inclusive dialogue, as evidenced by its intensification of military crackdowns amid the continuing political crisis rather than exploring reconciliation or de-escalation (Yared, 2022, pp. 19–20).

Furthermore, digital tools can be utilized by dialogue conveners and support actors to map stakeholder interests and narratives on social media (Hirblinger, 2023, pp. 17–18). Support organizations like Build Up, for example, used social media platforms like WhatsApp to conduct surveys and focus group talks to assure women's participation in the Yemeni peace process (Hirblinger, 2023, pp. 17–18). The use of automated data- and text-mining tools also aids in mapping different stakeholder positions through systematic analysis of social media data, including tweets, to generate insights into specific population groups' narratives, beliefs, or positions (Hirblinger, Morrison, & Larrauri, 2020, pp. 83–87; Hirblinger, 2023, p. 18). While, in this digital age where opinions and narratives are increasingly shaped through online interaction, analyzing social media data may provide valuable additional insights, the challenge lies in obtaining a representative sample due to varying user demographics (Hirblinger, 2023, p. 18), potential biases in algorithms, and individuals' reluctance to express diverse perspectives. To address these challenges, triangulating data from online, in-person dialogues, and alternative sources is thus critical (Hirblinger, 2023, p. 18).

Moreover, digital tools play a role in facilitating remote consultations. In Libya in 2012, the Prime Minister-elect employed Facebook to poll citizens on the preferred method of constituting the constitution making body (Grant, 2012; Gluck & Ballou, 2014, p. 3), and in 2018, the Centre for Humanitarian Dialogue, during local consultations held in preparation for the Libya National Dialogue, which were part of the UN Action Plan for Libya and designed in collaboration with the UN Special Representative of the Secretary-General in Libya, utilized digital tools such as online questionnaires, social media platforms, websites, and facilitated direct virtual discussions to engage different sections of Libyan society (Hirblinger, 2020b, p. 26). Similarly, in Ghana in 2010, the Constitutional Review Committee solicited public submissions through online forms, text message, email, and social media to amend the 1992 Constitution (Constitutional Review Commission, 2011). While these remote consultations enhance inclusiveness, challenges arise in ensuring representativeness (Hirblinger, 2023, p. 18), particularly in countries with limited digital access, and in tackling data misuse and privacy issues, as seen in a 2022 online consultation by the Tunisian presidency with only a 3% turnout (ANSA English, 2022) (Hirblinger, 2023, p. 19).

Using digital tools also facilitate remote direct participation of groups who are unable to participate in person (Beierle, 2002, p. 10; Hirblinger, 2023, p. 20). For example, during the South Sudan dialogue process in 2017, digital tools facilitated virtual connectivity for South Sudanese refugees abroad, with the assistance of UNCHR (UNHCR South Sudan, 2020). Moreover, digital tools extend the opportunity for involvement to other actors, such as political exiles and diaspora groups (Hirblinger, 2023, p. 20).

The second dimension in the nexus between national dialogues and digitalisation concerns the role dialogues can play in addressing digital issues. (Hirblinger, 2023, pp. 26–27). This occurs during both the pre-dialogue and during-dialogue phases (Hirblinger, 2023, pp. 26–27). Pre-dialogue accords increasingly embed commitments to curb problematic social media conduct given its violence-enabling effects (Hirblinger, 2023, p. 26). For instance, local ceasefires in South Sudan and municipal deals in Libya illustrate pledges to counter hate speech and inflammatory propaganda (Hirblinger, 2023, p. 26). While it is not social media-specific, Ethiopia's 2022 Pretoria "Peace Accord" also mandates parties to cease destructive rhetoric (African Union, 2022). These pre-dialogue accords, as one aspect of confidence-building measures, create a favorable atmosphere when national talks commence. Digital issues can also become themes within the national dialogue itself (Hirblinger, 2023, p. 27). For instance, the outcome of the Kenyan, 2008 dialogue called for reforms such as finalizing hate speech legislation and reviewing media/communications policy in light of digitalization concerns (Kenya National Dialogue and Reconciliation (Mediated by HR Kofi Annan, 2008, p. 8). Likewise, Yemen's National Dialogue Conference Outcomes upheld digital rights checks against state surveillance (2013, paras 16(b), 50 & 51). It remains uncertain, at the time of writing, whether digital issues are included in the agendas of the ongoing dialogue in Ethiopia.

The third dimension, the key subject of this chapter, is the implication of digital repression by governments on the success of ongoing dialogues. The next section of the chapter investigates this dimension by utilizing case studies of the Ethiopian government's digital repression tactics in the post-initiation of the dialogue project.

UNRAVELLING THE IMPLICATIONS OF DIGITAL REPRESSION ON ETHIOPIA'S NATIONAL DIALOGUE

The Ethiopian government continues to utilize digital repression to stifle critical voices online after the launch of the dialogue process on December 29, 2021. For the purposes of this chapter, digital repression is defined as 'the use of information and communications technology to surveil, coerce, or manipulate individuals or groups in order to deter specific activities or beliefs that challenge the state' (Feldstein, 2021, 25), which enhances a state's ability to carry out "traditional" modes of repression. These include deprivation of liberty, internet shutdown, surveillance, and other tactics. The purpose of this section is to investigate some of the digital repression tactics deployed by the Ethiopian government and to assess how they affect the country's ongoing dialogue.

DEPRIVATION OF LIBERTY OF DIGITAL DISSENTERS

The civic space in Ethiopia exhibits a pronounced limitation on critical voices, exemplified by Ethiopia's consistent categorization as 'not free' by Freedom House since 2011 (Freedom House, 2018) (Freedom House, 2022). Furthermore, the Committee to Protect Journalists (CPJ)'s recurrent ranking, placing Ethiopia in the top three for worst journalists' incarceration rates in Africa, underscores an authoritarian clampdown on critical voices that, traditionally confined to offline platforms, has now permeated the digital domain (CPJ, 2024) (CPJ, December 9, 2021c) (CPJ, December 15, 2020). This expansion, manifesting in deprivation of liberty of digital dissenters signals a troubling trend. Since the launch of the dialogue, thousands of critical voices have been deprived of their liberty, including dozens who were targeted specifically for their online criticism (Amnesty International, February 19, 2024; Freedom House, 2023).

Public watchdogs, who engage in digital journalism and activism, are particularly susceptible to these silencing measures. According to reports from CPJ, prominent online voices targeted include Journalists Abay Zewdu (chief editor of the digital media, *Amara Media Center*), Gobeze Sisay (Editor, and founder of YouTube-based broadcaster, *Voice of Amhara*), Genet Asmamaw (YouTube-based broadcaster *Yeneta Media*), and Meskerem Abera, the founder and editor of the YouTube-based media *Ethio Nikat* (CPJ, 2023b). These targeted figures, engaging in community journalism with distinct focuses, some on specific communities and others on nationwide issues, are widely known for their critics against the government.

CPJ notes that many of the abovementioned targets primarily report and commentate on political and social issues affecting the Amhara people (CPJ, 2023b), Ethiopia's second-largest community, which harbors serious skepticism against the regime, as evidenced by frequent and widespread anti-government protests (Houreld, 2023; Zelalem, 2022; Endeshaw, 2020; Crisis2024, 2019) and the recent insurgency against the government (Crisis Group, November 16, 2023). Abay Zewdu, for instance, renowned for reporting on ethnically motivated massacres against the Amhara people in the Oromia region and government complicity, has faced arrest over three times just since the initiation of the dialogue including his ongoing imprisonment since August 10th, 2023, as documented by the Ethiopian Human Rights Defenders Center (EHRDC) (EHRDC (a), 2023); (EHRDC (b), August 2023); CPJ, 2023b). The arrest of Abay is emblematic of a broader crackdown on journalists amplifying the voices of the Amhara people, which has become particularly pronounced subsequent to the intensification of armed conflict between the Government and the Amhara militia known as Fano since April 2023. Journalist Gobeze Sisay similarly encountered the specter of unlawful detention and repeated abductions. Gobeze has been arrested or abducted four times since the launch of the dialogue, including his current arrest as of May 6, 2023 (EHRDC (b), August 2023) (EHRDC (a), 2023). The latest arrest of the journalist followed his reporting on unrest unfolding in the Amhara region after April 2023 (CPJ, 2023c). In another crackdown on critical voices amplifying Amhara cause, Journalist Genet Asmamaw, was arrested on April 6, 2023 and remains in prison after interviewing the former Commander of the Amhara Special Force (The Coalition for Women in Journalism, 2023). Likewise, Journalist Meskerem Abera has been arrested at least three times since the launch of the dialogue, including her ongoing arrest (EHRDC (a), 2023) (EHRDC (b), August 2023). Known for her critical commentary against the government, her arrest has drawn condemnation as a perceived 'silencing of critical voices' (The Coalition For Women in Journalism, April 10, 2023). Other online human rights defenders and activists who were detained or abducted for reporting on issues regarding the Amhara people since the launch of the dialogue include: Journalists Dawit Begashaw (CPJ, 2023a), Woman of Courage awardee Journalist Meaza Mohammed (CPJ, 2023e), and Journalist Belay Manaye (CPJ, 2023g).

This clampdown on digital dissenters is not limited to voices advocating for the Amhara community but extends to those speaking out against injustices faced by other ethnicities or addressing nationwide concerns. For instance, those who reported on rights violations in Tigray Region during the two-year war between the Ethiopian government and the Tigray Liberation Front (TPLF), and those advocating for the cessation of the war became targets for arrests and abductions. Digital journalists like Yayesew Shimeles and Abebe Bayu from the YouTube-based media outlet *Ethio Forum*, and Bekalu Alamrew from *Alpha T.V.* serve as prime examples, facing repression, including arrest and abduction for their critiques against the government in relation to the war (EHRDC, 2023a; CPJ, 2022d; Ethiopian Civil Societies, 2022, p. 16; CPJ, 2022d; CPJ, 2023e).

Many other digital dissenters, like Journalist Tamerat Negera and poet Belay Bekele Weya, also face prosecution for their critiques on various public issues; for instance, Tamerat Negera was detained without charge for 128 days until April 2022 (Freedom House (Freedom on the net report), 2023). Likewise, Poet Belay Bekele, known for politically provocative poems and humorous expressions criticizing the government on social media platforms has faced arrest and enforced disappearance multiple times since the launch of the dialogue (EHRDC, 2023a), with his latest deprivation of liberty on August 17, 2023 (ibid.).

The government's crackdown has not also spared peoples' representatives. Since the launch of the dialogue, there have been instances of parliament members being deprived of their liberty, with some singled out due to their online criticism. For instance, Christian Tadele, an opposition member of the Federal parliament, has been imprisoned since August 4, 2023 (Amnesty International, 2024), after publicly criticizing Abiy's administration on social media and urging condemnation of civilian massacres in the Amhara Region (Tadele, 2023). Likewise, Taye Dendea, State Minister of Peace and a member of the Oromia Council, was sacked from his position and subsequently arrested after his successive critical comments on social media, where he criticized the government's inability to maintain peace (Aredo, 2023a), and referred to the Prime Minister as a 'barbarian who plays with human blood' (Aredo, 2023b; Amnesty International, 2024).

Such vindictive attacks on peoples representatives for simple online dissent raises real doubt whether the regime tolerates any dissenting perspectives at all. This is especially true given that other MPs critical of the government, such as Desalegne Chanie, a Federal Parliamentarian, Kassa Teshager, a member of the Addis Abeba City Council, and Yohannes Buayalew, a member of the Amhara Council, have been arrested by the regime though not necessarily because of their online criticism (Amnesty International, 2024).

THE IMPLICATIONS OF DEPRIVATION OF LIBERTY OF ONLINE DISSENTERS ON THE NATIONAL DIALOGUE

The deprivation of liberty of online dissenters throws a wrench into the ongoing dialogue, especially when viewed alongside other simmering issues within the country. It not only raises doubts about the government's political will to commit itself to a credible and inclusive dialogue but also undermines the necessary confidence-building measures crucial for the success of the process. To begin with, even if the Abiy leadership has relented to opposition appeals and international pressure by finally initiating a dialogue process, its continued use of deprivation of liberty against online dissenters exposes a stark dissonance between the proclaimed commitment to dialogue and the concrete actions taken. Such repressive tactics also represent a monumental failure in confidence-building measures, which are the cornerstones of any successful dialogue (Haider, 2019, pp. 2–3). Building confidence among various stakeholders requires concrete actions, such as releasing political prisoners, easing restrictions on free speech and assembly, and ceasing military operation (Berghof Foundation and Swisspeace, 2017, p. 61). However, the government's current actions, including the arrest of online voices, are diametrically opposed to these essential steps.

The deprivation of liberty of online critics also undermines the inclusiveness of the dialogue, which is critical to its success (Berghof Foundation and

Swisspeace, 2017, p. 63). The impact on the inclusiveness of the process manifests in several ways. First and foremost, some of the targets are high-level politicians and people's representatives who should be at the table when the dialogue begins. For example, the arrest of Christian Tadele and Desalegne Chane, Federal Parliamentarians with significant backing in the Amhara region, calls into question whether all major perspectives will have seats at the table. If political figures like Chrstian and Desalegne, who have significant support base, are excluded from participating due to continued arrest or chooses to boycott the process, the inclusivity of the dialogue is seriously called into question, compounding existing factors that hinder inclusiveness.

Second, the clampdown signals limited tolerance for dissent, potentially chilling participation or self-censorship among those present. If people feel unsafe when expressing themselves digitally, it is unlikely they will feel comfortable sharing their perspectives freely during face-to-face dialogues. Third, the clampdown, by creating a chilling effect on free speech and other legal activities online, impedes the opportunity to inculcate the perspectives of the broader population, beyond the delegates present at the negotiation table, using automated data- and text-mining tools to extract information through systematic analysis of social media data (Hirblinger, 2023, pp. 17–18).

Fourthly, the government's suppression of online dissent through the deprivation of liberty, coupled with its militaristic approach to addressing insurgent factions across various regions, has the potential to exacerbate the tensions that the dialogue aimed to alleviate. For example, in the case of the Amhara people, the government's heightened military campaigns against the Fano, a group closely associated with the Amhara community, together with the suppression of peaceful dissenting voices advocating for the Amhara cause both online and offline, undermine confidence in the dialogue process. This simultaneous suppression of armed and peaceful dissent may alienate the Amhara people from trusting the process. In this regard, it is important to note that the repression of critical voices during the dialogue could have a detrimental impact in two ways. Firstly, it dissuades insurgent groups from participating in the dialogue when they witness the suppression of their peaceful counterparts. Secondly, individuals who were previously part of peaceful movements and endured persecution for their dissent may be driven towards armed opposition due to the lack of avenues for peaceful struggle. This shift is evident in the case of former Journalist and political leader Eskindir Nega, who received several international acclaims for his journalistic work but eventually joined armed struggle in 2023 after facing multiple arrests for expressing peaceful yet critical views (Amnesty International, 2018).

Finally, the chilling effect of depriving online critics of their liberty undermines public participation and transparency, critical factors in the success of national dialogue, as well as hinders public buy-in, which is equally vital for the dialogue process to thrive (Haider, 2019, pp. 2–3). To ensure transparency and participation of the dialogue, frequent media outreach and coverage are vital (Stigant & Murray, 2015, p. 2). The chilling effect, coupled with other issues clouding the ongoing dialogue in Ethiopia, further erode trust in the process and deprive the necessary public buy-in for the dialogue to effectively move forward (Haider, 2019, p. 2).

INTERNET SHUTDOWNS AND THEIR IMPLICATIONS ON THE DIALOGUE

The other digital repression tactic employed by the government, which has implications on the success of the ongoing dialogue, is internet shutdowns, which affect factors critical for successful dialogue such as confidence building, inclusiveness, and public participation. Internet shutdowns are implemented with concerning frequency in Ethiopia (Ayalew, 2019, pp. 212–214), with figures indicating at least twenty-six such incidents since 2016 (Access Now, 2023c). This figure positions Ethiopia as a major perpetrator of shutdowns in sub-Saharan Africa (ibid.). The blackouts measures are taken 'without a clear legal basis, which are disproportionate in their range and duration' (Human Rights Committee, 2022), and with little transparency (Freedom House, 2023). Post ENDC alone, the government has imposed internet blackouts several times, ranging from complete (total blackout) to partial (targeting specific networks/services; for example, social media and messaging applications). The internet outages in the Afar, Amhara, and Tigray Regions following the onset of the two-year-long civil war in late 2020 persisted for several months, extending even after the launch of the dialogue (Access Now, 2023a). In 2023, the country witnessed three significant internet shutdowns. The first occurred in February, following nationwide protests called by the Ethiopian Orthodox church, sparked by tensions over an attempt to split the Church (Netblocks, 2023; Freedom House, 2023). The government-imposed restrictions on social media platforms like Facebook, Telegram, and YouTube from August 9 to July 19, 2023 (Access Now, 2023c). The second shutdown, implemented on April 6, 2023, blocked mobile internet services in the Amhara region after protests erupted against the Government's decision to dismantle the region's special force (Access Now, 2023b). The third shutdown, again targeting the Amhara region, began on August 3 and continues to date, triggered by clashes between the Government and Fano (Access Now, 2023c). In addition to these major shutdowns, internet outages are prevalent in the western part of the Oromia Region, marked by armed conflict and ethnically-motivated massacres (Freedom House, 2023).

While this does not mean that all blackout measures are illegitimate, its repeated uses indicate nothing, but the government is afraid of information flow or critical voices. This trend undermines the dialogue in different ways. It erodes public confidence in the process by putting in question the government's sincerity in launching the dialogue. It may be difficult for the public, particularly the opposition voices, to take the dialogue seriously, as it is the same government, which is known for suppressing dissent through internet shutdowns, is claiming to facilitate a dialogue, which is meant to encompass critical perspectives, conflicting claims, and uncomfortable truths. This perceived lack of genuity means people, who would otherwise constructively participate in the process, may now doubt the motives behind the initiative. So they may outright refuse to participate, as some have already done, or be disinterested and unlikely to seriously debate the issues in good faith.

The internet blackouts also hamper inclusive and informed debate. People in blackout areas may get the opportunity to physically participate in the dialogue but lack enough information for meaningful input. The shutdowns prevent them from accessing information needed to effectively contribute. This holds especially true given that in the current political landscape in Ethiopia, opposition leaders and activists use social media platforms to mobilize their support base to either take action or refrain from doing so in specific ways. In addition, internet shutdowns measures, by hindering people in affected areas from sharing their views online, also limit the ENDC's ability to incorporate a perspectives of the broader population by utilizing automated data- and text-mining tools to extract information from social media data (Hirblinger, 2023, pp. 17–18).

In summary, the frequent shutdowns call into question the government's sincerity and undermine the inclusiveness and credibility of the process-crippling key pillars of a constructive dialogue. For example, much of the Amhara region in Ethiopia has faced shutdowns since August 2023 amidst conflict. With continuing violence and no internet, the Amhara people cannot safely shape the dialogue agenda, nor access information to meaningfully contribute their views if they could attend. Thus, their voices will go unheard in determining key issues for discussion.

THE IMPLICATION OF UNWARRANTED STATE SURVEILLANCE ON THE DIALOGUE

There is also evidence that the Ethiopia government employs surveillance as another tactic of digital repression, both before and after the launch of the dialogue. It has been documented that the various governments in Ethiopia, including the incumbent government, use surveillance of online and mobile phone communications as a tool against dissenting voices both home and abroad (Marczak,

Alexander, McKune, & Scott-Rai, December 6, 2017), and the relevant laws and practices have not been reformed since the establishment of the ENDC. Government officials employ a combination of manual and digital surveillance tactics to crack down on online dissenters (Freedom House, 2023). They surveil opposition voices through wire-tapping (ibid.). They also use individual informants to spy on people (ibid.). Furthermore, they use coercive measures like detaining individuals and forcing them to hand over passwords to their digital devices and social media accounts, enabling extensive searches of digital content (ibid.). In addition, government security agencies leverage technological tools for backend surveillance activities to monitor the phone and online communications of those critical of the regime (ibid.). In the year 2023 alone, there are various indications that reveal government is involving in surveillance of critical voices. For instance, in April 2023, the circulation, by pro-government bloggers, of an alleged phone call recording between Journalist Meskerem Abera and a prominent opposition physician Wondwosen Assefa criticizing the government highlights concerns that the Ethiopian government is conducting communication surveillance on dissident voices (ibid.).

The threat of surveillance against dissidents in Ethiopia is fuelled by factors such as legislation fraught with loopholes like the 2016 Computer Crime Proclamation (which permits real-time monitoring or interception of communications and obliges service providers to store records of all communications and metadata for at least a year). Technological capacities supported by surveillance-savvy states like China further contribute to this threat. Ethio-Telecom, a state-owned telecom service provider that held a monopoly on the country's telecommunications services until recently, uses comprehensive ZSmart customer-management database, which Chinese company ZTE installed at the Ethiopian government's behest in 2009 (Grinberg, 2017, pp. 432–438). The government, through its higher-level authorities like the National Intelligence and Security Service (NISS), has almost unrestricted access to the database (ibid.), allowing it to monitor mobile networks and the internet. The database, ZSmart, provides the government with full access to user information, allows it to intercept SMS text messages and record phone conversations, as well as to locate targeted individuals through real-time geolocation tracking of mobile phones (Freedom House (Freedom on the net report), 2023). It is believed that the government has employed ZTE's advanced surveillance system, as law enforcement officials often present intercepted emails, social media communications and phone calls as trial evidence against dissenting voices (ibid.). The government is also allegedly working with other Chinese companies such as Huawei and Hengbao, which are known for their involvement in surveillance activities in countries like Uganda and Zambia (Parkinson, Bariyo, & Chin, 2019) (Gravett, 2022, p. 8).

There are also reports that the Ethiopian government, under Abiy's leadership, is utilizing a surveillance system from Israel, purchased from the company

Cellebrite, to hack into detainees' mobile phones since 2021 (Freedom House, 2023). Likewise, in the pre-Abiy regime, spyware use against dissenting voices was documented by the Toronto-based Citizen Lab in 2015 and 2018, but it is uncertain if the Abiy regime employs similar surveillance techniques (Marczak, Alexander, McKune & Scott-Rai, 2017; Deibert, 2019).

Ethiopia's lack of a comprehensive privacy and data protection law until recently, coupled with loopholes in national security laws in the country, may have contributed to unwarranted surveillance. However, the culture of disregarding existing protections, including the Constitution, which protects the right to privacy (FDRE Constitution, art 26), has also played a role. This is evident, for instance, in the neglect of procedural protections available in Ethiopia's former and current anti-terrorism laws. The laws dictate surveillance of terrorism suspects (including social media surveillance) may only happen with judicial approval through court warrants.[2] In actual practice though, there is widespread warrantless interceptions, and even more alarming is the failure of courts, such as the High Court, to verify warrant issuance before admitting intercepted materials as evidence in counterterrorism prosecutions (Kassa, 2022, pp. 197–208).

The unwarranted surveillance of online dissenters, like other repression tactics, erodes the trust between political groups and between the state and citizens – trust the ongoing dialogue seeks to build. It transgresses privacy rights and public faith in the authorities, especially in their commitment to a democratic system that respects dissent -- a prerequisite for a genuine and credible dialogue. It raises doubts about the government's sincerity in the dialogue project, potentially seen as a facade to consolidate power. Such skepticism, especially among opposition factions, may lead to disengagement from the process; indeed, some opposition groups have already boycotted the process. Furthermore, surveillance and resulting self-censorship hinder open discourse critical to the dialogue, as groups and individuals fear their communications will be monitored should they voice dissent.

ADDITIONAL THREATS TO THE DIGITAL LANDSCAPE AND THEIR IMPLICATIONS ON THE NATIONAL DIALOGUE

There are also other documented digital rights challenges in Ethiopia, both before and after the launch of the dialogue. These challenges range from confiscation to burglaries of media equipment, revocation of media licenses, and bullying and harassment of online dissenters. Documented cases of equipment confiscation

2 Prevention and Suppression of Terrorism Crimes Proclamation No 1176/2020 art 42. The Anti-Terrorism Proclamation No 652/2009 art 14.

from online media outlets include an incident in October 2021, two months before the ENDC's establishment, where the government confiscated the equipment of an online media outlet called *Awlo Media Centre*, which was known for its criticism of the government (Freedom House (Freedom on the net report), 2023). In another incident happened on May 19, 2022, government security officials raided the studio of *Ashara Media* (YouTube channel), confiscating office equipment and arresting five employees (CPJ, 2022b). *Nisir International Broadcasting Corporation* (NIBC), another YouTube channel, also experienced a raid on the same day, involving arrests and the confiscation of computers, memory cards, and external hard drives (ibid.). The raids on *Ashara,* and *NIBIC* were conducted in response to their reporting on the worsening security conditions in the Amhara region (ibid.).

Beyond equipment confiscation, a series of seemingly orchestrated burglaries and lootings have targeted independent digital medias in Ethiopia (CPJ, 2023d). In the first six months of 2023 alone, at least four online media outlets, namely *Arat Kilo Media*, *Ethio-251*, *Yeneta Tube*, and *Ethiopia Insider*, were victims of targeted robberies, characterized by the Ethiopian Media Council (EMC) as 'targeted attacks on digital media' (ibid.). Though no clear evidence yet ties these robberies to state orders, the message of intimidation is unambiguous. Reports reveal that burglars and looters particularly target valuable equipment, such as digital cameras, Neck-mic, Zoomer, laptops, and smartphones, crucial for journalistic work (EHRDC, 2023b, p. 16; Haq Media and Communication, 2023). This hampers the immediate operations of the media and instill a sense of vulnerability that may discourage them from addressing sensitive issues in the feature (ibid.). These repercussions seem to be the reason that prompted the Ethiopia Media Council (EMC) and CPJ to condemn the targeted robberies. The EMC said the robberies are not random incidents, noting that they seem coordinated and show signs of premeditation (Ethiopia Media Council, 2023). The leadership of the Council expressed concern that the robberies come as officials crack down on independent media through arrests (EHRDC, 2023, p. 16). Likewise, the CPJ described the robberies of media outlets as threat and reminder of risks to journalistic works in Ethiopia (ibid.).

The fact that these acts of robbery extend beyond media outlets, to human rights organizations as well, raises suspicions that governmental actors may be complicit in or connected to these activities in some capacity. For instance, it was reported that the Ethiopian Human Rights Council, and the Centre for Advancement of Rights and Democracy, local NGOs known for documenting rights violations, have previously fallen victim to robbery (ibid.).

The suppression of online voices extends its reach to foreign media outlets and journalists as well. In May 2022, the Ethiopian Media Authority revoked the press accreditation of Economist journalist Tom Gardner, subsequently expelling him from the country (CPJ, 2022a). This action followed a public warning issued two months earlier, accusing Gardner of tweeting information that was not 'properly sourced or supported by appropriate authorities' (Ethiopia Media Authority, 2022). Similar measures had been taken against international press outlets and journalists even before the establishment of the ENDC (CPJ, 2021b).

In addition to these instances, other documented cases against digital voices involve physical harassment (CPJ, 2021a) and coordinated online smear campaigns (Ethiopia Mass Media Action, 2024; Mulugeta, 2023).These issues contribute to a hostile environment for open discourse. Some online journalists have also been compelled to leave their countries under the threat of persecution. According to documentation by EHRDC, at least three journalists were forced to flee from Ethiopia after the launch of the dialogue (EHRDC, 2023b, p. 17). These include Tewodros Asfaw, the owner of the online media outlet Ethio-Selam, who was forced to depart the country following his arrest in mid-April 2023, and journalists Yayesew Shimelis and Abebe Bayu, editors at another online media platform called *Ethio-Forum*, who departed for Europe after experiencing repeated arrests and abductions (Freedom House, 2023).

There are many ways in which these digital repression tactics undermine the ongoing dialogue. Firstly, they not only obstruct the immediate operations of digital outlets or pose threat to dissenters but also send profound messages to a broad spectrum of potential participants in the dialogue that dissenting opinions may not be tolerated. They may lead to an atmosphere in which potential participants, be they citizens, opposition politicians, or civil society actors, feel constrained and discouraged from freely expressing their opinions. This, in turn, undermines the very essence of a dialogue – a platform designed to encourage open, diverse, and meaningful discourse. The digital repression tactics send a message that expressing dissent or engaging critically in the dialogue may result in reprisals, thereby discouraging people from actively participating or expressing their genuine concerns. They, therefore, have impacts on the principle of inclusivity and diversity of perspectives, which lies at the heart of genuine dialogue. The dialogue thus risks becoming a platform dominated by a singular narrative, devoid of the diversity of thought necessary for robust problem-solving.

Secondly, the repression tactics casts doubt on the government's sincerity in initiating the dialogue, eroding public trust in the process, which compromises both the inclusivity of the dialogue and the feasibility of implementing any resulting outcomes. In light of the consistent suppression of dissenters, the launch of the dialogue suggests a more cynical objective than a commitment to open dialogue. It implies that the dialogue may be a calculated move to consolidate political power, rather than a genuine effort to foster collaborative solutions to the country's challenges.

Thirdly, when media outlets come under siege due to repression, the public pays the ultimate price as their access to vital information is curtailed, which undermines what constitutes a constructive dialogue, that which is informed and participative. For instance, the confiscation of equipment from media outlets, such as the raids on *Awlo Media Centre*, *Ashara*, and *NIBC*, disrupts the normal functioning of these outlets. This disruption has a cascading effect on the public's right to receive diverse and unbiased information. In an era where online media plays a crucial role in shaping public opinion, limiting the operational capacity of critical media outlets restricts the flow of information that is essential for an engaged and informed citizenry. Increasing burglaries and looting of independent media outlets adds to the problem. Beyond the immediate loss of equipment, these acts create an environment where media organizations, including those critical of the government, may struggle to operate effectively. The public, in turn, is deprived of the diverse perspectives and critical analysis that independent media outlets often provide. Likewise, the broader pattern of harassment, persecution, and forced exodus of journalists not only stifles individual voices but contributes to an atmosphere of self-censorship within the media industry, denying the public of access to the full spectrum of viewpoints necessary for a robust and participatory national dialogue. The digital repression tactics have also several additional implications for the effectiveness of the ongoing dialogue. For instance, the forced exodus of journalists implies a potential brain drain of individuals who could contribute valuable insights and expertise to the dialogue.

CONCLUSION

The chapter has examined the crippling impact of digital repression on Ethiopia's ongoing dialogue. While Ethiopians widely agree on the necessity of an inclusive dialogue to tackle deep-rooted issues threatening Ethiopia, the current initiative appears to be on shaky ground, with a cloud of uncertainty surrounding its success. From the beginning, doubts have shrouded the transformative potential of process, fueled by lack of transparency in the establishment of the ENDC, and concerns over the independence of Commissioners, leading some political parties to boycott the process. This chapter further challenged the transformative potential of the process, asserting that the government's recurrent resort to digital repressions, even post the launch of the dialogue, reveals an absence of sincere political will to a credible and inclusive dialogue, and suggests that the government might initiated the process to bolster its faltering legitimacy to solidify its grip on power. It is also argued that the digital repression represents a monumental failure in the expected confidence-building measures, a critical prerequisite for fostering trust in the dialogue process and stand in stark contradiction to the principles of inclusiveness, public participation and transparency, and public buy-in—all essential factors for the success of a dialogue. The chapter also noted how the suppression of peaceful dissenters exacerbates the issues the dialogue seeks to address by: first, discouraging armed groups from laying down their arms and participating in the dialogue because they see even peaceful voices, including those in the online sphere, being silenced, and second, pushing peaceful dissidents towards more radical forms of protest, seeing no space for nonviolent dissent.

It is, therefore, recommended that the Ethiopian government should immediately change course and demonstrate a true commitment to inclusive dialogue. This includes not only addressing the original deficits of the process, but also ending all types of repression, restoring confidence, and demonstrating a genuine willingness to engage with its fiercest opponents.

REFERENCES

Addis Standard. (August 23, 2023). News: Opposition groups urge end to forceful measures, call for 'meaningful dialogue' to resolve nationwide instability'.

Addis Standard. (June 6, 2022). News: Newly formed caucus sets conditions for restructuring, reforming planned national dialogue. *Addis Standard.*

Addis Standard. (February 4, 2022b). *NewsAlert: OFC,* ONLF say Dialogue Commission process unrepresentative, not impartial; decline Parliament invitation today.

Access Now. (March 17, 2023a). After years in the dark, Tigray is slowly coming back online. Retrieved November 18, 2024, from https://www.accessnow.org/tigray-shutdown-slowly-coming-back-online/

Access Now. (April 27, 2023b). Open letter to the Ethiopian Government: urgently end ongoing internet shutdowns in all regions across the country. Retrieved November 18, 2024, from https://www.accessnow.org/press-release/open-letter-to-the-ethiopian-government/

Access Now. (September 12, 2023c). Preserving freedom in crisis: Ethiopia's internet shutdowns must not become the norm. Retrieved December 20, 2024, from https://www.accessnow.org/press-release/open-statement-internet-shutdown-amhara/

African Union. (2022, November 2). Agreement for Lasting Peace through the Permanent Cessation of Hostilities (COHA) between the Government of Ethiopia and the Tigray People's Liberation Front (TPLF). Retrieved December 20, 2024, from https://www.peaceau.org/en/article/cessation-of-hostilities-agreement-between-the-government-of-the-federal-democra tic-republic-of-ethiopia-and-the-tigray-peoples-liberation-front-tplf

Amhara Civic Organizations. (2024, April 30). Joint Statement From Amhara Civic Organizations on the Abiy Regime's Sham National Dialogue Process. Retrieved December 20, 2024, from https://www.amharaamerica.org/post/joint-statement-amhara-civic-organizations-abiy-reg ime-sham-national-dialogue-process

Amnesty International . (August 3, 2018). Eskinder Nega: Defending human rights is the right thing to do.

Amnesty International. (February 19, 2024). Ethiopia: Authorities must stop using state of emergency law to silence peaceful dissent. Retrieved December 20, 2024, from https://www.amnesty.org/en/latest/news/2024/02/ethiopia-authorities-must-stop-using-state-of-emerge ncy-law-to-silence-peaceful-dissent/

Aredo, T. D. (2023 (b), December 11). ለክቡር ጠቅላይ ሚኒስትር ዐቢይ. Facebook page. Retrieved December 19, 2024, from https://www.facebook.com/tayedendea.StateMinisteratMoP/posts/pfbid022APWpqp5nTZB2SzY1GhXwQvbR2qJciC9JpKqu7xnNDnoYBC7kbPtDBVvpU1uN8qT1

Aredo, T. D. (2023 December 10). ጦርነትን መቃወም አትችሉም …? ለምን?. *Facebook*. Retrieved December 20, 2024, from https://www.facebook.com/tayedendea.StateMinisteratMoP/posts/pfbid0B-7jMNy89ZX4MrCL2Kr2S54ByBexbZBfQaX9E8NFgH73oBfpn5335Lbnqt6uZ6BG1l

Ayalew, Y. E. (2019). The internet shutdown muzzle(s) freedom of expression in Ethiopia: Competing narratives. *Journal of Information & Communications Technology Law*, *28*(2), 208–224.

Beierle, T. C. (2002). Democracy on-line: An evaluation of the national dialogue on public involvement in EPA decisions. Washington D.C.: Resources for the Future. https://archive.epa.gov/publicinvolvement/web/pdf/rff-rpt-demonline.pdf.

Berghof Foundation and Swisspeace. (2017). National dialogue handbook: A guide for practitioners. Berghof Foundation Operations GmbH.

Constitutional Review Commission. (2011). From a political to a developmental constitution: a report of the Constitutional Review Commission of Ghana 2011. https://constitutionnet.org/vl/item/political-developmental-constitution-report-constitutional-review-commission-ghana-2011

CPJ. (April 14, 2023b). At least 8 journalists detained amid renewed unrest in Ethiopia. Retrieved December 20, 2024, from https://cpj.org/africa/ethiopia/page/2/

CPJ. (September 6, 2023f). Three more journalists arrested under Ethiopia's state of emergency. Retrieved December 20, 2024, from https://cpj.org/2023/09/three-more-journalists-arrested-under-ethiopias-state-of-emergency/

CPJ. (May 12, 2023c). Journalist Gobeze Sisay facing terrorism investigation in Ethiopia after arrest in Djibouti. Retrieved December 20, 2024, from https://cpj.org/2023/05/journalist-gobeze-sisay-facing-terrorism-investigation-in-ethiopia-after-arrest-in-djibouti/

CPJ. (April 12, 2023a). *Dawit Begashaw: Imprisoned.* Retrieved December 20, 2024, from https://cpj.org/tags/dawit-begashaw/

CPJ. (September 12, 2022e). Ethiopian authorities detain journalists Gobeze Sisay and Meaza Mohammed. Retrieved December 20, 2024, from https://cpj.org/2022/09/ethiopian-authorities-detain-journalists-gobeze-sisay-and-meaza-mohammed/

CPJ. (December 4, 2023g). Ethiopian authorities detain Ethio News chief editor Belay Manaye without charge. Retrieved December 20, 2024, from https://cpj.org/2023/12/ethiopian-authorities-detain-ethio-news-chief-editor-belay-manaye-without-charge/

CPJ. (June 29, 2022c). Ethiopian authorities re-arrest journalist Yayesew Shimelis 1 week after release on bail. Retrieved December 20, 2024, from https://cpj.org/2022/06/ethiopian-authorities-re-arrest-journalist-yayesew-shimelis-1-week-after-release-on-bail/#:~:text=At%20about%207%20a.m.%20on,CPJ%20on%20condition%20of%20anonymity%2C

CPJ. (July 6, 2022). Ethiopian journalist Abebe Bayu detained 1 day after colleague Yayesew Shimelis arrested. Retrieved December 20, 2024, from https://cpj.org/2022/07/ethiopian-journalist-abebe-bayu-detained-1-day-after-colleague-yayesew-shimelis-arrested/

CPJ. (August 10, 2023e). Ethiopian authorities detain Alpha Media founder Bekalu Alamrew. Retrieved December 20, 2024, from https://cpj.org/2023/08/ethiopian-authorities-detain-alpha-media-founder-bekalu-alamrew/

CPJ. (May 24, 2022b). Ethiopian authorities arrest 11 employees of 4 independent media outlets. Retrieved December 20, 2024, from https://cpj.org/2022/05/ethiopian-authorities-arr

est-11-employees-of-4-independent-media-outlets/#:~:text=Authorities%20have%20arrested%20at%20least,people%20for%20allegedly%20illegal%20activity

CPJ. (July 20, 2023d). CPJ calls for swift and credible investigation into burglary of Ethiopia Insider office. Retrieved December 20, 2024, from https://cpj.org/2023/07/cpj-calls-for-swift-and-credible-investigation-into-burglary-of-ethiopia-insider-office/

CPJ. (May 16, 2022a). Ethiopia expels Economist correspondent Tom Gardner. Retrieved December 20, 2024, from https://cpj.org/2022/05/ethiopia-expels-economist-correspondent-tom-gardner/

CPJ. (May 21, 2021b). CPJ condemns Ethiopia's expulsion of New York Times reporter Simon Marks. Retrieved December 20, 2024, from https://cpj.org/2021/05/cpj-condemns-ethiopias-expulsion-of-new-york-times-reporter-simon-marks/

CPJ. (February 24, 2021a). Unidentified armed men ransack home of Ethiopian journalist Lucy Kassa, question her about conflict coverage. Retrieved December 20, 2024, from https://cpj.org/2021/02/unidentified-armed-men-ransack-home-of-ethiopian-journalist-lucy-kassa-question-her-about-conflict-coverage/

CPJ. (2024). 2023 prison census: Jailed journalist numbers near record high; Israel imprisonments spike. Retrieved December 20, 2024, from https://cpj.org/reports/2024/01/2023-prison-census-jailed-journalist-numbers-near-record-high-israel-imprisonments-spike/

CPJ. (December 15, 2020). Record number of journalists jailed worldwide. Retrieved December 20, 2024, from https://cpj.org/reports/2020/12/record-number-journalists-jailed-imprisoned/

CPJ. (December 9, 2021c). Number of journalists behind bars reaches global high. Retrieved December 20, 2024, from https://cpj.org/reports/2021/12/number-of-journalists-behind-bars-reaches-global-high/

Crisis24. (April 8, 2019). Ethiopia: Violence and protests reported in Amhara region April 6–8 further likely. Retrieved December 12, 2024, from https://crisis24.garda.com/alerts/2019/04/ethiopia-violence-and-protests-reported-in-amhara-region-april-6-8-further-likely

Crisis24. (April 8, 2019). Ethiopia: Violence and protests reported in Amhara region April 6–8 further likely. Retrieved December 12, 2024, from https://crisis24.garda.com/alerts/2019/04/ethiopia-violence-and-protests-reported-in-amhara-region-april-6-8-further-likely

Crisis Group. (November 16, 2023). Crisis Group Africa briefing: Ethiopia's Ominous New War in Amhara. Retrieved November 18, 2024, from https://www.crisisgroup.org/africa/horn-africa/ethiopia/b194-ethiopias-ominous-new-war-amhara

Deibert, R. (2019, December 6). Evidence that Ethiopia is spying on journalists shows commercial spyware is out of control. *Wired.*

Dejene, A. (2024, May 30). በሀገራዊ ምክክር ኮሚሽን ሂደት ላይ የሙስሊሞች ውክልና አነስተኛ ነው ሲል የኢትዮጵያ እስልምና ጉዳዮች ጠቅላይ ምክር ቤት ቅሬታውን አሰማ።. Addis Ababa: Ethio Fm. Retrieved December 19, 2024, from https://ethiofm107.com/2024/05/30/%E1%89%A0%E1%88%80%E1%8C%88%E1%88%AB%E1%8B%8A-%E1%88%9D%E1%8A%AD%E1%8A%AD%E1%88%AD-%E1%8A%AE%E1%88%9A%E1%88%BD%E1%8A%95-%E1%88%82%E1%8B%B0%E1%89%B5-%E1%88%8B%E1%8B%AD-%E1%8B%A8%E1%88%99%E1%88%B5/

Edjeta, B. (2022, March 12). Ethiopia's stillborn National Dialogue. *Ethiopia Insight.* Retrieved October 19, 2024, from https://www.ethiopia-insight.com/2022/03/12/ethiopias-stillborn-national-dialogue/

EHRDC (a). (2023). Censorship by detention: A look at the detention of human rights defenders in Ethiopia since 2020. Addis Ababa.

EHRDC (b). (August 2023). The second 2023 periodic assessments on the situation of human rights defenders in Ethiopia. Addis Ababa.

ENDC (Web Site). (2024, February 26*)*. Ethiopian National Dialogue Commission. Retrieved December 19, 2024, from https://ethiondc.org.et/

ENDC (Facebook). (2024, 1 10). Facebook. Ethiopian National Dilaogue Commission. Retrieved December 19, 2024, from https://www.facebook.com/EthioNDC

ENDC (X). (2024a, 1 2). *X (formerly Twitter).* Ethiopian National Dilogue Commisison. Retrieved December 20, 2024, from https://twitter.com/ethiondc?lang=en

Endeshaw, D. (2020, February 2). Kidnapping of students sparks anti-government protests in Ethiopia. *Reuters*. Retrieved December 19, 2024, from https://www.aol.com/news/kidnapping-students-sparks-anti-government-123339509.html

Ethiopian Civil Societies (joint submission to Human Rights Committee). (October 2022). *Civil society report on the implementation of the International Covenant on Civil and Political Rights in Ethiopia*. Report to the 136th session of the Human Rights Committee. Retrieved December 18, 2024, from https://ccprcentre.org/files/documents/ICCPR_report_FINAL.pdf

Ethiopia Media Council. (July 21, 2023). *ለሁሉም መገናኛ ብዙሀን አስቸኳይ.*

Ethiopian Media Authority. (March 23, 2022). Ethiopian Media Authority issued a letter of warning to Mr. Tom Gardner, who is a correspondent of The Economist.

Fana Broadcasting Corporate. (2022, July 4). Dialogue Commission to start discussing national issues from July. *Fana Broadcasting Corporate*. Retrieved December 20, 2024, from https://www.fanabc.com/english/dialogue-commission-to-start-discussing-national-issues-from-july/

Feldstein, S. (2021). The Rise of Digital Repression How Technology Is Reshaping Power, Politics, and Resistance. New York: Oxford University Press.

Freedom House. (2018). Reform in Ethiopia: Turning promise into progress. Washington: Freedom House.

Freedom House. (2022). Freedom in the world: Ethiopia. Washington: Freedom House.

Freedom House . (2023). *Freedom in the world 2023: Ethiopia*. Washington: Freedom House

Freedom House (Freedom on the net report). (2023). *Freedom on the net 2023: Ethiopia.* Retrieved November 18, 2024, from https://freedomhouse.org/country/ethiopia/freedom-net/2023

Galal, S. (2023, August 15). Number of active social media users in Ethiopia 2014–2024. *Statista*. Retrieved December 20, 2024, from https://www.statista.com/statistics/1307184/number-of-social-media-users-ethiopia/#:~:text=The%20number%20of%20active%20social,6.4%20million%20as%20of%202023

Gemechu, M. M. (2022, January 27). Ethiopia's new 'national dialogue' cannot deliver inclusive peace. *Aljazeera*. Retrieved October 21, 2024, from https://www.aljazeera.com/opinions/2022/1/27/can-ethiopias-national-dialogue-deliver-inclusive-peace

Gluck, J., & Ballou, B. (2014). New technologies in constitution making. United States Institute of Peace. United States Institute of Peace.

Grant, G. (2012, November 24). Four-fifths of Libyans support electing Constitution-drafting committee: poll. Libya Herald. Retrieved October 20, 2024, from https://libyaherald.com/2012/11/four fifths of libyans support electing constitution drafting committee poll/

Gravett, W. H. (2022). Digital neocolonialism: The Chinese surveillance state in Africa. Retrieved October 12, 2024, from https://repository.up.ac.za/bitstream/handle/2263/89872/Gravett_Digital_2022.pdf?sequence=1

Grinberg, D. (2017). Chilling developments: Digital access, surveillance, and the authoritarian dilemma in Ethiopia. *Surveillance & Society*, *15*(3–4), 432–438.

Haider, H. (2019). National dialogues: lessons learned and success factors. K4D Helpdesk Report. Institute of Development Studies.

Haq Media and Communication. (2023, July 17). A statement from Haq Media and Communication regarding the robbery in 'Ethiopia Insider' office. *Ethiopia Insider.*

Harter, F. (2022, April 18). Ethiopia launches a national dialogue, but divisions run deep. *The New Humanitarian*. Retrieved December 20, 2024, from https://www.thenewhumanitarian.org/news-feature/2022/04/18/ethiopia-launches-national-dialogue-divisions-run-deep

Hirblinger, A. (2023). National dialogues at crossroads: National dialogues x digitalisation. Berghof Foundation.

Hirblinger, A. (2020a). Digital inclusion in mediated peace processes: How technology can enhance participation. United States Institute of Peace.

Hirblinger, A., Morrison, M., & Larrauri, H. P. (2020). Digital analysis: Peacemaking potential and promise. In C. Buchanan, *Pioneering peace pathways: Making connections to end violent conflict* (pp. 83–87). Concilation Resources.

Hirblinger, A. (2020b). Digital inclusion in peacemaking: A strategic perspective. *CCDP Working Paper*, *14*, 1–41.

Houreld, K. (2023, April 10). Ethiopian plan to disarm regional forces sparks protests in Amhara. *The Washington Post*. Retrieved November 18, 2024, from https://www.washingtonpost.com/world/2023/04/10/ethiopia-disarm-amhara-tigray/

Kassa, W. D. (2022). Comment: Court's reluctance to safeguard rights of the accused in the Ethiopian counter-terrorism prosecutions and its broader implication. *Mizan Law Review*, *16*(1), 197–208.

Kenya National Dialogue and Reconciliation (Mediated by HR Kofi Annan). (2008, July 30). Statement of principles on long-term issues and solutions. Retrieved December 19, 2024, from https://peacemaker.un.org/sites/default/files/document/files/2024/05/ke080523kenya20national20dialogue20and20reconciliation2c20statement20of20principles20on20long.pdf

Marczak, B., Alexander, G., McKune, S., & Scott-Rai, J. (December 6, 2017). Champing at the Cyberbit: Ethiopian Dissidents Targeted with New Commercial Spyware. The Citizen Lab.

Mulugeta, E. (2023, December 7). Technology's sour blessing: technology facilitated gender based violence in Ethiopia. *GenderIt.Org*.

Netblocks. (February 9, 2023). Social media and messaging apps restricted in Ethiopia amid religious tensions. Retrieved November 18, 2024, from https://netblocks.org/reports/social-media-and-messaging-apps-restricted-in-ethiopia-amid-religious-tensions-DA3RJz8W

Paffenholz, T., Zachariassen, A., & Helfer, C. (2017). *What Makes or Breaks National Dialogues?* Inclusive Peace & Transition Initiative.

Parkinson, J., Bariyo, N., & Chin, J. (2019, August 15). Huawei technicians helped African governments spy on political opponents. The Wall Street Journal. Retrieved November 18, 2024, from https://www.wsj.com/articles/huawei-technicians-helped-african-governments-spy-on-political-opponents-11565793017

Political Settlements Research Programme (University of Edinburgh). (2013). The National Dialogue Conference outcomes document 2013–2014. (2013).

Stigant, S., & Murray, E. (2015). National dialogues: A tool for conflict transformation? *United States Institute of Peace, Peace Brief*, *94*, 1–5. https://www.peaceagreements.org/masterdocument/1400

Sahlu, S. (2022, February 26). Oppositions disgruntled over "rushed" appointments of commissioners. *The Reporter.*

Tadele, C. (2023, August 3). *Facebook page*. Retrieved December 20, 2024, from https://www.facebook.com/MARHEIRGEBRYE/posts/pfbid036AqNgav5YhzXJFAAjstYNp8g1K-w3qz74yVRENLdZrcG2FJSjhQNFVpWdsXY2z71Bl

The Coalition For Women in Journalism . (April 10, 2023). Ethiopia: Police violently arrest two Amhara women journalists – CFWIJ demands immediate and unconditional release. Women Press Freedom. Retrieved November 18, 2024, from https://www.womeninjournalism.org/threats-all/ethiopia-police-violently-arrest-two-amhara-women-journalists

The Ethiopian Political Parties Joint Council. (2022, February 17). ከየኢትዮጵያ ፖለቲካ ፓርቲዎች የጋራ ምክር ቤት የሀገራዊ ምክክር የዝግጅት ሂደትን በተመለከተ የተሰጠ መግለጫ. Retrieved December 20, 2024, from https://www.facebook.com/EthiopianPoliticalPartiesJointCouncil/posts/244670637857247

Tsegaye, G. (2022, February 14). News: Ethiopian Political Parties Joint Council request Parliament to temporarily halt National Dialogue commissioners' selection, resume process in inclusive, trustworthy manner. *Addis Standard*. Retrieved December 19, 2024, from https://www.facebook.com/AddisstandardEng/posts/4867717236609566/?_rdr

Tura, J. S. (2023). Critical Appraissal of Challenges and Prospects of Ethiopia's National Dialogue. *European Scientific Journal, ESJ*, *19*, 653–664.

UNDP. (2017). Guide on the National Dialogue Process in South Sudan. UNDP. Retrieved December 19, 2024, from https://www.undp.org/south-sudan/publications/guide-national-dialogue-process-south-sudan

UNHCR South Sudan. (2020). UNHCR welcomes the participation of refugee and internally displaced persons in South Sudan's national dialogue conference. Juba: UNCHR. https://data.unhcr.org/ar/documents/details/82675

Wight, P. (2022, March 28). Ethiopia: Why PM Abiy's National Dialogue is dead on arrival. *African Arguments*. Retrieved December 19, 2024, from https://africanarguments.org/2022/03/ethiopia-why-pm-abiys-national-dialogue-is-dead-on-arrival/

Wittig, K., & Ghosheh, S (2020). The role of social media in early peacemaking: Help or hinderance. In C. Buchanan, *Pioneering peace pathways: Making connections to end violent conflict* (pp. 78–82). Conciliation Resources.

Yared, T. (2022). Ethiopia's national dialogue: Reconciling competing approaches. *Institute for Security Studies*. Retrieved October 20, 2024, from https://issafrica.org/research/east-africa-report/ethiopias-national-dialogue-reconciling-competing-approaches

Yared, T. (2024, July 11). Ethiopia's national dialogue needs a reset. *ISS Today*, 1–2.

Zelalem, Z. (2022, July 6). Death sentence: Massacres fuel protests, resentment in Ethiopia. *Al Jazeera*. Retrieved December 2, 2024, from https://www.aljazeera.com/news/2022/7/6/massacre-of-hundreds-fuels-protests-resentment-in-ethiopia

CHAPTER FOURTEEN

Africanizing Digital Cultures, Digitalizing African Cultures

ADMIRE MARE AND OSWELLED UREKE

INTRODUCTION

This book, which is the first of its kind to empirically, methodologically and theoretically look at African digital cultures, has gone beyond mainstream literature, which often relies on anecdotal evidence, and parachute researchers from the global North, who spend a few weeks and months before producing articles, book chapters and manuscripts on Africa. As Teschner (2022, p. 1) has aptly observed, "in parachute research, global North … researchers collect samples [or data] from another country, return directly home and analyze them without consulting the people …" Given the unequal power relationships between researchers from the global North and South, digital cultures in Africa have tended to be treated as part of what Willems (2020) calls "digital universalism". This universalization of African digital cultures has unintentionally reproduced stereotypes and has been equated as trying to fit round plugs in square holes. There are exceptions to these conclusions. A number of digital anthropologists from the global North have spent an extended period of time trying to understand how Africans are integrating technology into their everyday lives (cf. Archambault, 2013; Pype, 2016; Pype and Bernal, 2023; Bernal, 2004, 2014; 2020; Burrell, 2012; Willems, 2020). In order to rectify this scholarly misnomer, this volume presents fresh empirical data from Africans based on the content who are at the cutting edge of studying the adoption, adaptation and integration of digital technologies.

While acknowledging the undeniable social shaping of technologies, this book views the "digital" as socio-technical systems designed, deployed, used, governed, and regulated within specific socio-cultural and political contexts. This should be seen as a first attempt to contribute towards a much more nuanced understanding of "*pluriversal digitalitie*s" in the global South. It has also focused on textual, audio-visual and multi-media digital platforms as 'simulacrum theatres' where the front and backstages as theorised by Goffman are collapsing in complex ways thereby creating avenues for unique social, political and economic performances. These performances often defy traditional approaches to identity construction, political action, political communication, and satire. It has highlighted the varied ways in which the digital has been deeply embedded in the daily lives of millions of African people. This social embeddedness of the digital in the everyday lives of connected and unconnected Africans foregrounds the ambivalent dual processes of *digitization* and *Africanization* of sociotechnical systems and artefacts. These global digital platforms' interactive and creative affordances "have augmented and altered our cultures, practices, politics, and power dynamics of engaging with publics for various beliefs and social agendas" (Lee and Abidin, 2023, p. 1).

The current global platform and app studies scholarship has often missed the lens of locality in the discussion. This volume has shown that although the history of the digital and indeed the internet can be located within the Anglo-American tradition (Poell et al., 2024), there is need to shift the empirical and theoretical cloth in order to make sense of digital cultures in other contexts. Building on Nemmani and Rodriguez's (2023, p. 258) insightful call that there is an urgent need for "… a shift in how we conceptualize technology adoption in the Global South", we argue that *African digitalities or digital cultures* must be understood on their own terms without imposing normative standards and expectations from other regions of the world. Whilst we agree that there are similarities and differences in ways in which the digital is adopted and adapted in various contexts, in this volume, we have demonstrated through illustrative examples how African netizens have appropriated digital technologies to address specific social, political, and economic objectives. This approach toward the study of the *flow and contraflows* of digital technologies in the Global South, dovetails with Nemmani and Rodriguez's (2023, p. 258) observation that "… prioritizes specific historical, cultural, and epistemological contexts in … [Africa] and acknowledges the fragmentation left behind by colonization and divergent economic policies". In line with this observation, contributors in this volume methodically demonstrate that Africans, like their counterparts across the world, appropriate digital communication technologies in complex ways and weave them into their existing ancestral epistemologies. This is partly because "digital media anywhere in the world [Africa included] are caught up in a world-historical process in which social, cultural, and economic exchanges are transnational, multidirectional, and driven by a multipolar and predominantly capitalist media system" (Punathambekar and Mohan, 2019, p. 3). These socio-historical processes and temporalities have shaped emerging African digital cultures in diverse ways. Analogue and digital temporalities have merged and converged in synchronous and asynchronous ways paving way for the establishment of hybrid digital cultures.

While this book does not uncritically celebrate positioning Africa as a site of *digital difference*, it acknowledges that the continent is part of an ongoing global transformations which has significantly reconfigured the state and processes of *being African* and *being digital yet African*. As a post-colony, Africa has been shaped by historical colonial ties with Western countries and ongoing globalization and digitization winds. These headwinds have geopolitically and geoeconomically inserted the continent into a parasitic global capitalistic system. By extension, the continent has also been plugged into the "surveillance capitalistic system" (Zuboff, 2019), where platforms exploit free digital labor, harvest tons of free data and engage in what Mejias and Couldry (2023) call "data grab". In this system, digitization and platformization are celebrated as part of technology transfers. As Hjorth (2018, n.p.) aptly puts it, "digital culture requires us to acknowledge that datafication and algorithmic cultures are now commonplace—that is, where data penetrate, invade, and analyze our daily lives, causing anxiety and seen as potentially inaccurate statistical captures". These processes are reified as part of technological solutionism discourses meant to bring efficiency and effectiveness in public service delivery and good governance. The net effects of these processes like digital surveillance and disinformation campaigns are generally ignored when such grandiose claims are made. Sandwiched in-between the machinations of global superpowers, the continent's digital cultures are increasingly "… shaped by transnational circulations of ideas, people, technologies, and capital, and are caught up in deeper histories than popular or academic discourses care to admit" (Punathambekar and Mohan, 2019: 3).

On the one hand, the continent has relied heavily on Western designed and operated platforms like Facebook, X, WhatsApp, YouTube, Instagram, Pinterest, Spotify, Google, Amazon, Apple, Uber, and Microsoft. On the other hand, Africa has had to look to the East. This Look East Policy has seen the continent relying on Asian platform and telecommunication companies like TikTok, Huawei, ZTE, Samsung and Alibaba. This overreliance on foreign-owned and operated companies and apps has adversely affected the development of the technology sector in Africa. Cognizant of the fact that data has always been an instrument of colonialism, Benyera (2021) has advanced the concept of 'coloniality of data' to explain insidious forms of Big data extraction associated with Big Tech operations in the global South. In the past two decades, several apps have suffered stiff births because of the lack of protection from giant tech companies from the West and East. These include MXIT, Viber and 2go. Attempts to jumpstart the tech ecosystem in Africa have not received significant government support despite the fact that there are universal service funds which are collected from telecommunication operators yearly. This means that African content creators are vulnerable to the algorithmic tweaks, business model changes and community standards updates from Western and Eastern-based platform owners. There is no protection of local tech start-ups by national governments from unfair competition exerted by Big tech corporations in the global South.

On another level, this volume contributes to what Guobin Yang (2015) describes as "deep internet studies". This is partly because it unpacks the black box of digital infrastructures, platforms, and users/publics in Africa. Although this volume does not go deep in terms of studying the institutions, policies, and market activities of the African digital ecosystem, it sheds light on the multiplicity of digital cultures thereby circumventing the taken-for-granted "universalizing tendencies of Anglo-American discourse" (Parks and Kumar, 2003). This allows us to run away from falling into the trap of what scholars call "global *digital* cultures" (Kraidy, 2017; Punathambekar and Mohan, 2019) or "global perspectives on platforms and cultural production" (Poell et al., 2024). This trap often leads to the cultural homogenization thesis associated with early globalization writings. Instead, we prefer to use 'African digital cultures' to underscore our locus of enunciation, nuances associated with uniquely 'African' cultural productions, circulation and consumption. In doing so, we are cognizant of the fact that the word *culture* "has taken on new infections . . . many of which embody its association with digital computational tools" (Striphas, 2016, p. 78). This enjoins us to foreground digital cultures as a lens through which to understand African netizens' practical, perceptual, and moral experiences as well as in the contexts of use. As already shown, some of the chapters in this book have shown the multiple ways of *doing politics* and *being political* in Africa.

This book has demonstrated the varied ways in which African netizens are performing roles as users and producers in the burgeoning do-it-yourself (DIY) maker culture movement which has taken the digital public sphere by storm. For instance, chapters by Henok Kremte; Mbongeni Msimanga and Constance Kasiyamhuru; Wambui Wamunyu, and Allan Wefwafwa show how Africans adeptly negotiate the divide between online and offline spaces. The result is a new form of associational life and citizen activism, one that aims to promote alternative forms of political participation in a context of shrinking offline civic spaces. This dovetails with Mare's (2016) observation that marginalized populations with no visibility in the mainstream media often find horizontal, vertical and oblique voices online. Focusing on oblique voice through memes and humour in Mozambique, Dercio Tsandzana argues that production and circulation of these cultural artefacts vary according to their cultural and social contexts. Shrinking spaces of voice articulation have led to digital contestations. These contestations are evident in the Kenyan, Zimbabwean, Ghanian, South African, Nigerian, Ethiopian and Malawian digital public sphere. For instance, chapters in this volume have shown how Zimbabweans, Mozambicans, Kenyans and Nigerians "have endeavoured to make their voices heard through online civic engagement, activism, and protest" (Yang, 2014: 139). Given that inequalities in terms of participation, voice and representation are reproduced and reconfigured in the digital sphere, celebrities and online opinion leaders use their social and cultural capital to build large followings and gain influential voices. While there are cases of 'nobodies' like Mai Tt, Madam Boss, Shadaya, Musa Kawula, and many more who have risen to stardom from nothing, most of the people with a lot of followers, likes, downloads, shares and tweets are political, cultural and economic elites.

MAKING SENSE OF THE CENTS: HOW DIGITAL AFRICANS MONETIZE CONTENT

The "dominant capital accumulation model of contemporary corporate internet platforms is based on the exploitation of users' [and content creators'] unpaid labour" as these users/creators "engage in the creation of content and the use of blogs, social networking sites, wikis, microblogs, content sharing sites for fun and in these activities create value that is at the heart of profit generation" (Fuchs & Sevignani, 2013: p. 237). Based on this surveillance capitalism business model, digital media platforms have harvested huge profits. However, this profit has not been shared equitably with the content creators who are responsible for creating surplus value. Instead, these platforms stand accused of exploiting free labour. The situation is worse in the global South where these platforms operate without any regulations and policies. This state of affairs has been described as follows by Kopf (2020, p. 1) "the ones who make platform companies what they have not shared in the financial gains for the most part" (Kopf, 2020, p. 1). Social media users and content creators, the individuals who either just use the site or even produce the content that motivates site visits, have, predominantly, not received financial compensation for their work and the resulting product, that is, in the case of content creators compensation for their producing/uploading content and the content itself as a digital product. Research has shown that platform companies have found ways to commodify users/creators to generate revenue (Fuchs, 2014). This consists of selling user data to third parties, selling audience attention to advertisers, and commodifying creators' social media content. Most platform companies have figured out ways to insert paid advertising into uploaded videos. Because these companies know the front and back-end of their operations, they have managed to dribble past content creators especially in the global South. Although in theory, social media creators "are economically powerful because they create economic value" for the company that operates the SM platform (Fuchs, 2015, p. 199), they earn little or nothing from their labour. Cases in Ghana, Kenya and Namibia have shown that social media influencers are still struggling to monetize their content. Despite this state of affairs, there are no collective bargaining platforms for African content creators. This means that although African content creators "... have the power to bring corporate social media to a standstill" (Fuchs, 2015, p. 39) if they refuse to upload their content, the situation remains dire until there is collective bargaining in the digital creative economy. Alienation of content creators from their labour and surplus value remains the elephant room in the Africa digital economy. However, efforts to bring about platform accountability are emerging. In Kenya, strategic litigation cases against Meta and other Big Techs have been brought before the courts. Other countries have resorted to internet and social media shutdowns as alternative ways of reigning in on Big techs (Mare, 2020).

While digital media provides entertainment for networked users, many have taken advantage of its commercial rewards. They have discovered ways of getting paid while playing. Many chapters in this volume try to make sense of how social media users make their dollars and cents. These vary from brand promotion to product endorsement and from gifting to paid sponsorships and promoting influencers' own entrepreneurial activities as shown in the chapters by Ndavula; Nyathi; Appiah, Asiamah, Sackey and Osei-Mensah. As Uzuegbunam, Mwaura and Ononiwu show, the constraints and rewards of digital technologies influence all aspects of daily life, just as conventional media and old technologies like electricity did in earlier years. However, Ndavula's chapter calls into question the sustainability of cultural content online, showing that some TikTok users, for instance did not have any knowledge on how to monetize their content. This raises questions about digital exploitation and age-old economic inequalities replicated online. All digital content creators provide labor for platform companies that earn revenue from traffic and attention associated with the content posted by these creators. On platforms with audio-visual affordances, creators also indirectly market the music that they use as soundtracks as well as the fashion they wear for their performances. Thus, the concept of *playbor* (Ferril-Conill 2018) is amply demonstrated in all the submissions on content monetization and is latent in other chapters that explore performative affordances of digital platforms.

FROM TEXT TO AUDIO-VISUAL CONTENT

This volume acknowledges that digital content is in a state of flux. Digital technologies are also constantly mutating into new things. The process of becoming has no prescribed destination. At the time of writing this volume, X (formerly Twitter) was in the process of rolling out new features, whilst Meta had launched Threads aimed at competing with X. Because of the fierce competition in the tech and apps sector, vertical and horizontal integration of companies has become one of the survival strategies. Whilst most of the chapters focused on traditional Western platforms like Facebook, WhatsApp, X and Instagram and YouTube, there is a significant shift in the apps' ecosystem from text and pictures to videos. The popularity of TikTok and YouTube bears testimony to this digital shift. This shift, which is associated with the roll out of 4G and 5G capabilities has made digital platforms more interactive. Unlike in the late 1990s, where internet video content was mainly held in a few media organizations that owned content copyrights, nowadays, video production tools have become popular. This has also been enabled by the growth of the network bandwidth. The growth of network bandwidth has allowed users to produce, upload and share video content on the internet. Founded by Chad Hurley, Jawed Karim, and Steve Chen in 2005, YouTube changed the way videos were hosted on the Web. The technology YouTube adopted allows users to upload various video coding formats and then transcode them into a form that could be quickly loaded on the internet. The release of the iPhone 4s in October 2011 allowed the world to accelerate its entry into the era of mobile Internet. Relying on mobile smart terminals, the threshold for users to produce videos has become lower. The trend of video sharing has evolved from long videos that are shot by VCR to short videos that are shot by mobile phones. Short videos are mainly less than five minutes and can be shared in real-time on social networking platforms. Since the early 2000s, many short videosharing apps have entered the market. These include Vine, Keek, and Mixbit. It was TikTok which achieved unparalleled success in the video-sharing ecosystem. This TikTok popularity is captured in the three chapters in this volume. There is no doubt that other platforms are now copying the audio-visual first strategy. Examples include Facebook, X, and Instagram, which are pushing a lot of video content. The future of African digital cultures is highly likely to be interspersed with audio-visual content.

BEING DIGITAL AFRICANS: AGENCY AND REWARDS IN ONLINE CULTURE

As reflected in this volume digital content creators produce and share material on just about anything. This varies from the trivial to the critical, the dramatic to the didactic, the bizarre to the banal, the past to the present, the traditional to the modern and the funny to the sad. Sometimes there are distinct differences depending on the geolocation, age range, talent and other demographic characteristics of the creatives. The concept of 'being' lies at the centre of the corpus of digital content examined by submissions in this volume. The various expositions contained in the book are about Africans *being digital* as well as the *digital beings* inhabiting African digital spaces. As stated before, the 'African' appellation is deployed with caution, conscious of the deterritorialization of digital spaces as well as fluidity of digital identities. It has been shown in this volume how digital Africans in different locations and platforms make sense of their being and express it to connected others online. All of the chapters in the volume broadly respond to the overarching questions: Who/what are Africans online? What do they do when they are online?

Culture, being an expression of the everyday, is reflected online in many ways. The submissions in this volume extend the understanding of culture as a way of life to *digital culture as a digital way of life* as well as *ways of life expressed digitally*. Whether this is about artistic exhibition, showcasing fashion and beauty, humor, traditional practices, gender activism, political activism, or youth activism the chapters suggest what one might expect on African digital spaces. The communities and performances foregrounded in this book are often times regarded as *marginalized* and *trivial,* but it is within this ordinary and quotidian that we can unravel ordinary people's ways of life.

The empirical data presented in most chapters in the volume epitomize McLuhan's (1964) idea of technology as an extension of man. We can think of digital media as some virtual canvass upon which we scribble ephemeral moments of our lives. Essentially, our digital inscriptions on digital media platforms such as X, Instagram, Facebook and TikTok constitute bodies of meaning that represent us individually and (sometimes) collectively. As shown in this volume, most of the time, such acts of representation are neither spontaneous nor accidental but well calculated and intended. Chikezie Uzuegbunam, Job Mwaura and Richard Ononiwu as well as Oswelled Ureke deploy Erving Goffman's theorization to demonstrate this, arguing that when individuals present themselves before millions of online gazes, they engage in performances, in the same manner that television or stage actors do. Digital platforms in this case become the stages upon which these performances take place. While the term 'perform' might suggest that what we see online are completely enacted spectacles, it is also true that these performers are influenced by lived experiences as well as the expectations of other interconnected users and the associated reward system. The performers are in most cases aware of the numerous ways in which their acts may be perceived whether positive or negative. Performance becomes a veil behind which content creators can tackle serious subjects, speaking truth to power against the excesses of political power and patriarchy, for instance. By packaging content as performances, creators are able to circumvent reprisals and pre-empt possible backlash.

This innovation may be informed by history in conflict prone societies. Wambui Wamunyu as well as Mbongeni Msimanga and Constance Kasiyamhuru, for example, show how Kenyans and Zimbabweans have historically dealt with autocratic regimes by way of street protests, theatrical or comedic productions, religious institutions, and mediated spaces such as newspapers and television. In both chapters, it is shown how this agency has shifted onto online spaces where individuals expose injustices and express their dissatisfaction and frustrations with political leaders. These chapters interlink with Ndavula's submission which shows how Kenyan content creators satirize local governments, corruption, religion, and unemployment. Wamunyu characterizes such cybergladiators as active digital citizens who use their visibility to question the status quo by submitting evidence that counters official narratives, re-posting news from legacy media outlets, sharing visuals of protests that are not carried on legacy media platforms, and initiating citizen-to-citizen discourse that provides explanations for their socio-economic and political contexts. Through such initiatives, the active digital citizens can lead to some action being taken, and to generating discourse among fellow citizens who respond to their posts and calls to action, positively or negatively. Wamunyu's term attests to Africans' agency online, showing that they are not passive users of digital media but active players using technology to transform social and political realities.

From the avatars, bios to the status updates, texts and images people post online, we are able to infer users' identities or to use Johaan Kim's (2002) term, their 'digital being'. By their discourse, performance and online behavior, digital Africans exhibit who they are and give us a glimpse of how their lives pan out offline. We can peek into the inner workings of humanity, assuming that the very act of tweeting or tiktoking is tantamount to inscribing oneself onto a digital platform. Ureke further stresses this point in his chapter, arguing that the way #zimtiktok TikTokers perform online reveals their Zimbabwean identities. Considered together, the various posts on different platforms reveal a pattern about the human beings represented by being online. It is these patterns that we refer to as digital cultures. Although the focus of this book is on how Africans interact with, perceive others and are perceived by others online, the various case studies provide a window into the cultures of those same people within their physical locations. Thus, by interacting with influential protagonists online, one is able to get a sense of, for instance, Maragoli culture in Kenya, Bulawayo female entrepreneurs in Zimbabwe, digital activists in Ethiopia, Mozambique and Kenya as well as black women in South Africa. Thus, it can be argued that the digital selves and digital lives are enmeshed with offline beings and activities. For instance, in Ndavula's chapter some of the content posted on Kenyan TikTok is about memory, where content creators explore childhood experiences. Equally, Msimanga and Kasiyamhuru's chapter by examining the YouTube videos of art activists (artivists), gives a glimpse into the continuities between Robert Mugabe and Emmerson Mnangagwa's regimes in Zimbabwe. To further exemplify the nexus between online and offline phenomena, there are many entrepreneurial activities that have emerged offline, as an extension of online activities as shown by Sihle Nyathi as well as Gifty Appiah-Adjei, Elizabeth Asiamah, Rainbow Sackey and Belinda Osei-Mensah. Their respective chapters show that Social Media Influencers (SMIs) have become the tried and tested sources of information about particular issues and products owing to their strong and intimate relationships with followers and friends. When influencers show a genuine and passionate interest in an issue, they create credibility around that issue and interest in associated products. Thus, relations that start online, expressed through commenting and liking, morph into offline business relationships expressed through trade.

REFERENCES

Archambault, J. (2013). 'Cruising through uncertainty: Cell phones and the politics of display and disguise in Inhambane, Mozambique'. *American Ethnologist 40*(1), 88–101.

Benyera, E. (2021). *The Fourth Industrial Revolution and the Recolonization of Africa: The Coloniality of Data*. London: Routledge.

Bernal, V. (2004). Eritrea goes global: Reflections on nationalism in a transnational era. *Cultural Anthropology 19*(1), 1–25.

Bernal, V. (2014). *Nation as Network: Diaspora, Cyberspace, and Citizenship*. Chicago: University of Chicago Press.

Bernal, V. (2020). African digital diasporas: Technologies, tactics, and trends. *African Diaspora*, 1–10.

Burrell, J. (2012). *Invisible users: Youth in the internet cafes of urban Ghana*. Cambridge: MIT Press.

Ferrer-Conill, R. (2018). Playbour and the gamification of work: Empowerment, exploitation and fun as labour dynamics. In P. Bilić, J. Primorac, & B. Valtýsson (Eds.), *Technologies of labour and the politics of contradiction* (pp. 193–210). Palgrave Macmillan.

Fuchs, Christian and Sevignani, S. (2013), What is digital labour? What is digital work? What's their difference? And why do these questions matter for understanding social media? tripleC: Communication, Capitalism & Critique. Open Access Journal for a Global Sustainable Information Society. 11:2, pp.237-293.

Fuchs, C. (2014). Social Media: A Critical Introduction. London: SAGE Publications

Goffman, E. (1956). *The presentation of self in everyday life*. University of Edinburg.

Hjorth, L. (2018). Digital cultures and critical studies. *The Handbook of Oxford University Press*. https://doi.org/10.1093/acrefore/9780190228613.013.648

Kim, J. (2001). Phenomenology of digital being. *Human Studies*, *24*, 87–111.

Kopf, S. (2020). "Rewarding Good Creators": Corporate Social Media Discourse on Monetization Schemes for Content Creators. Social Media + Society 6:4, pp1-12. DOI:10.1177/2056305120969877

Kraidy, M. M. (2017). Global digital culture| convergence and disjuncture in global digital culture — An introduction. *International Journal of Communication*, *11*(2017), 3808–3814.

Lee, J., & Abidin, C. (2023). Introduction to the special issue of "TikTok and social movements". *Social Media + Society*, *9*(1), 1–8.

Mare, A. (2020). Internet shutdowns in africa | state-ordered internet shutdowns and digital authoritarianism in Zimbabwe. *International Journal of Communication*, *14*, 4244–4263.

McLuhan, M. (1964). *Understanding media, the extensions of man*. McGraw Hill.

Mejias, U. A., & Couldry, N. (2023). *Data grab: The new colonialism of big tech and how to fight back*. The University of Chicago Press.

Nemmani, S., & Rodriguez, C. (2023). Between incursions and appropriations: digital technologies and pluriversal modernities in the Global South, *Communication, Culture and Critique*, *16*(4), 258–265.

Parks, L., & Kumar, S. (Eds.). (2003). *Planet TV: A global television reader*. NYU Press.

Poell, T., Duffy, B. E., Nieborg, D. B., Mutsvairo, B., Tse, T., Arriagada, A., de Kloet, J., & Sun, P. (2024). Global Perspectives on platforms and cultural production. Global perspectives on platforms and cultural production. *International Journal of Cultural Studies*. https://doi.org/10.1177/13678779241292736

Punathambekar, A., & Mohan, S. (Eds.). (2019). Global digital cultures: Perspectives from South Asia. University of Michigan Press. http://www.jstor.org/stable/j.ctvndv9rb

Pype, K. (2016). (Not) talking like a Motorola. Practices of masking and unmasking in Kinshasa's mobile phone culture. *Journal of the Royal Anthropological Institute*, *22*(3), 633–653.

Pype, K., & Bernal, V. (2023). Infopolitics and technology contracts. *Anthropological Quarterly* *96*(4), 611–624.

Striphas, T. (2015). Culture. In Peters, B (ed). Digital Keywords A Vocabulary of Information Society and Culture, Princeton and Oxford: Princeton University Press

Teschner, R. (2022). Parachute research: Analysing the unequal power relations in global health. Research African Contributions to Global Health Essay. Retrieved from https://www.globalhealthafrica.ch/wp-content/uploads/2022/08/Parachute-Research_Unequal-Power-Relations-in-Global-Health-Research.pdf 16 June 2024

Willems, W. (2020). Beyond platform-centrism and digital universalism: the relational affordances of mobile social media publics. *Information, Communication and Society*. *24*(12), 1677–1693

Yang, G. (2014) Political contestation in Chinese digital spaces: Deepening the critical inquiry. China Information. 28:2, pp.145–167

Yang, G, ed. (2015). China's Contested Internet. Copenhagen: NIAS Press.

Zuboff, S. (2019). *The age of surveillance capitalism: The fight for a human future at the new frontier of power*. New York: Public Affairs.

Notes on Contributors

Gifty Appiah-Adjei is a Lecturer and Researcher with the Department of Journalism and Media Studies at the University of Education, Winneba, in Ghana. She holds a PhD in Applied Communication from the University of Ibadan, Nigeria and an MPhil in Communication and Media Studies from the University of Education, Winneba. Her research interests include Digital Media, Digital Divide, Media and PWDs; Media and Gender; Media and Climate Change; Environmental Journalism; Ethnic Journalism; Security of Journalists; Conflict-Sensitive Reporting and on-the Job Trauma; and Journalism Education. She is affiliated with the Communication Educators Association of Ghana (CEAG), Journalism Safety Research Network (JSRN), Journalism Education Trauma Research Group (JETREG) and the International Association for Media and Communication Research (IAMCR). She is also an honorary member of Media Action Nepal.

Maud Blose is a Senior Lecturer in the Department of Communication and Media at the University of Johannesburg, South Africa. Her portfolio includes, teaching, postgraduate research supervision, being the department's Honors Level Coordinator, and Internationalization and Partnerships Lead. She is currently a Teaching Advancements at a University (TAU) Fellow. She holds a PhD in Culture and Media Studies from the University of KwaZulu-Natal. She is also a Fulbright Scholar with an MSc in Broadcast Journalism from the Medill School of Journalism at Northwestern University, Chicago, USA. She has over a decade experience as a lecturer in the higher education sector. Her research interests include media and society, representation of black women in the media, African feminism, environmental reporting, e-learning and higher education.

Constance Kasiyamhuru is a lecturer in the Department of Design Studies at the University of Johannesburg, South Africa. She teaches design theory and multimedia concepts. She holds a PhD in Communication Studies from the same university. Her research interests focus mainly on issues around digital political communication, particularly in Africa. She is interested in exploring the various political communication practices and current trends emerging within the African context and digital sphere through the use of digital communication technologies and new media platforms. She can be contacted at ckasiyamhuru@yahoo.com or constancek@uj.ac.za.

Henok Ashagrey Kremte is a project officer and doctoral candidate at the University of Pretoria's Centre for Human Rights in South Africa. He also holds the role of Academic Tutor at the same institution, where he provides academic support and guidance to students. Henok's research interests lie in the nexus between media, law and human rights issues.

Admire Mare is a Full Professor and and the Head of Department of Communication and Media Studies at the University of Johannesburg, South Africa. His research interests include analyzing the complex and messy intersections between technology and society, specifically focusing on global digital journalism studies, and global digital platform studies. He can be contacted at amare@uj.ac.za.

Nhamo Anthony Mhiripiri is an Adjunct Professor in the Department of Journalism and Mass Communication at St Augustine's University of Tanzania. He now specializes in media and communication research and consultancy. He earned his PhD from the University of KwaZulu-Natal, South Africa, and has lectured at the University of KwaZulu-Natal, Zimbabwe Open University and Midlands State University. He was the associate editor in charge of Africa and the Middle East regions for the forthcoming Oxford Encyclopedia onRace, Ethnicity and Communication.

Mbongeni Jonny Msimanga is a post-doctoral fellow at the University of Johannesburg. He holds a PhD in Communication Studies from the same university. His research interests include political satire creative performance, digital cultures and journalism practice. His work has been published in international journals such as *Journal of Communication Inquiry, Media, Culture and Society, Journal of African and Asian Studies, African Journalism Studies*, and *Journal of African Media Studies*. Mbongeni is also a part-time lecturer at the University of Johannesburg in South Africa. He can be contacted at mbongenimsimanga@gmail.com.

Job Mwaura is a Postdoctoral Research Fellow at the Wits Centre for Journalism at the University of the Witwatersrand. He completed his doctoral studies in the Department of Media Studies at the University of the Witwatersrand (Wits), South Africa. He holds an MSc in communication and journalism from Moi University, Kenya. He researches, publishes, and teaches about digital media and emerging technologies in Africa and their intersection with society, culture, and politics.

John Ndavula is a senior lecturer in mass communication at Murang'a University of Technology in Kenya. He holds a PhD in Mass Communication from Jomo Kenyatta University of Agriculture and Technology. He has published journal articles and book chapters on language, social media, political communication, and disability. His latest book is *Social Media and Political Campaigns in Kenya*. He is also the founding editor of *Kikwetu: A Journal of East African Literature*.

Sihle Nyathi is a PhD candidate in the Department of Communication and Media at the University of Johannesburg, South Africa. She researches on a broad range of media and communication issues, including the use of AI in journalism.

Chinedu Richard Ononiwu holds a PhD in Film and Multimedia Studies from Nnamdi Azikiwe University, Awka, Nigeria. His main research interests span audience reception of multimedia messages, fake news culture, and representation in animated films. His latest paper, co-authored with Chikezie E. Uzuegbunam, is titled "If it is circulating widely on social media, then it is likely to be fake news: Reception of, and motivations for sharing, COVID-19-related fake news among university-educated Nigerians", published in the *African Journal of Information and Communication*.

Belinda Osei-Mensah is a Research Fellow at the Centre for Communication Education Research and Professional Development and a PhD student in the Department of Strategic Communication, School of Communication and Media Studies (UEW) working in the areas of social media and influencer marketing, integrated marketing communication and new media from a critical perspective. She has co authored a paper titled "Mapping technology: stakeholder perspective on Ghana Post GPS." She is affiliated with the Communication Educators

Association of Ghana (CEAG), the International Association of Media and Communication Research (IAMCR).

Elizabeth Owusu-Asiamah is a Lecturer at the Department of Journalism and Media Studies and a PhD student offering Communication Studies at the University of Education, Winneba-Ghana. She holds a Masters of Philosophy in Communication and Media Studies with a major in Media Studies. Her research interests include; Social Media, Journalism Education, Popular Culture, Media and Gender and Citizen Journalism. She has co-authored papers in the areas of popular culture, Community Broadcasting, Digital Divide and Environmental and Climate Change Reporting. She is affiliated to the Communication Educators Association of Ghana (CEAG), the International Association of Media and Communication Research (IAMCR) and the International Academic Forum (IAFOR).

Rainbow Sackey is a Research Fellow at the Centre for Communication Education Research and Professional Development and a PhD Student at the Department of Journalism and Media Studies. He is interested in conducting research in areas such as Journalism Education, Newsroom Practices, Community Radio Broadcasting, Social Media Research and Gender and Journalism. Some of his previous publications have been on Gender representations in newsrooms, Newsroom convergence, Digital Divide and Environmental Journalism. He is affiliated to the Communication Educators Association of Ghana (CEAG), International Association of Media and Communication Research (IAMCR).

Dércio Tsandzana holds a PhD in Political Science at Sciences Po (France). Since 2013, he has been working on youth, internet, social media and political participation in Mozambique, including online activism for Global Voices International. Alongside his PhD, Tsandzana undertook research work focusing on digital rights and data privacy with Freedom House, Meta/Facebook, Internews/USAID, and the Centre for Human Rights Faculty of Law at University of Pretoria. He is a member of the African Digital Rights Network (ADRN) and the African Declaration on Internet Rights and Freedoms Initiative (AfDeC). His most recent book (2023) is entitled *Digital Citizenship*.

Johannes Tukondjeni is a Communication graduate currently serving as an admission and information officer at The Namibia University of Science and Technology. With a strong background in communication theory and practice, he excels in effectively disseminating information to various audiences. His role requires him to engage with prospective students, provide guidance on admission procedures, and offer detailed information on academic programs and campus resources. Johannes is skilled in utilizing various communication channels, including social media and email, to reach and engage with a diverse range of individuals. Through his work, he strives to uphold the values of transparency, accuracy, and professionalism in all interactions. He is committed to facilitating a seamless and informative experience for all individuals seeking information about his institution.

Oswelled Ureke is an Associate Professor in the Department of Communication and Media at the University of Johannesburg, South Africa. His research interests lie in screen media, cultural studies and political economy of the media. He holds a PhD in Cultural and Media Studies from University of KwaZulu Natal, South Africa. Oswelled has previously lectured at the Midlands State University in Zimbabwe, where he also worked as a journalist and video producer. He can be contacted on oswelledu@uj.ac.za or ozzieureke@yahoo.com.

Chikezie Emmanuel Uzuegbunamis a Senior Lecturer, Master's Programme Coordinator, Chair of Research Forum, and Deputy Head of the School of Journalism and Media Studies for Teaching and Research, at Rhodes University in South Africa. He is a rated research scholar by the National Research Foundation of South Africa and holds a PhD in media studies from the University of Cape Town and multiple degrees in mass communication from Nnamdi Azikiwe University in Nigeria. Dr. Uzuegbunam was a 2024/2025 Global Fellow at Northwestern University in Qatar and has held various other fellowships including in Oxford University, University of Cape Town, University of Groningen, University of Bergen, University of Xiamen, as well as fellowships awarded by Carnegie Corporation of New York. He has published dozens of peer-reviewed works on topics such as digital culture, children and youth, media and cultural studies, generative AI, and misinformation. His first book, Children and Young People's Digital Lifeworlds: Domestication, Mediation and Agency, was published in 2024 by Palgrave Macmillan.

Allan Job Wafwafwa is a PhD candidate and Sessional Lecturer at University of the Witwatersrand, South Africa. He holds a Master of Arts Degree in Communication studies from University of Nairobi and a bachelor's degree in Mass Communication from Makerere. University, Uganda. He lectures in the Department. of Journalism & Media Studies, Technical University of Kenya. He has authored several publications in communication.

Wambui Wamunyu is a Kenyan-based university lecturer and researcher who received her doctorate in Media Studies from Daystar University in Nairobi. She has conducted qualitative and mixed methods research studies in areas including disinformation, gender and media, and Internet governance. A former journalist, she also engages in scholarship focused on legacy media's use of digital technologies in journalism practice.

Index

www.ingramcontent.com/pod-product-compliance
Ingram Content Group UK Ltd.
Pitfield, Milton Keynes, MK11 3LW, UK
UKHW020201290926
15471UKWH00005B/997

9 781636 678733